D1105950

WHICH SIDE WERE YOU ON?

Maurice Isserman

WHICH SIDE WERE YOU ON?

The American Communist Party During the Second World War

 WESLEYAN UNIVERSITY PRESS
MIDDLETOWN, CONNECTICUT

Excerpt on p. 31 from "September 1, 1939" in *The English Auden: Poems, Essays & Dramatic Writings, 1927–1939*, by W. H. Auden, edited by Edward Mendelson. Copyright © 1977 by Random House, Inc. Reprinted by permission of Random House, Inc.

Passage on p. 38 from an unpublished letter by W. H. Auden copyright © 1982 by the Estate of W. H. Auden; not to be reprinted without written permission.

Excerpt on p. 18 from "America Was Promises" by Archibald MacLeish in *New and Collected Poems 1917–1976* by Archibald MacLeish. Reprinted by permission of Houghton Mifflin Company.

Excerpt on p. 127 from "Miss Pavilichenko," words and music by Woody Guthrie. TRO copyright © 1963 Ludlow Music, Inc., New York, N.Y. Used by permission.

Excerpt on p. 60 from "Why Do You Stand There in the Rain," words and music by Woody Guthrie. TRO copyright © 1975 Ludlow Music, Inc., New York, N.Y. Used by permission.

Excerpt on p. 55 from "Ballad of October 16th" copyright © 1940 by Woody Guthrie Publications. Used by permission of Sanga Music.

Excerpt on p. 83 from "Talking Union" by Lee Hays, Millard Lampell, and Pete Seeger. Copyright © 1947 by Stormking Music, Inc. Used by permission of Sanga Music.

Library of Congress Cataloging in Publication Data

Isserman, Maurice.
    Which side were you on?

    Includes bibliographical references.
    1. Communist Party of the United States.
2. World War, 1939–1945—United States. I. Title.
JK2391.C5183   324.273'75   81–16350
                                          AACR2

ISBN 0-8195-5059-0

Manufactured in the United States of America

FIRST EDITION

Designed by Sidney Feinberg

For my parents

PREFACE

The history of communism in America is bitterly contested terrain. The passions aroused by the debate over differing interpretations of that history are seldom far removed from contemporary concerns. There is, of course, no such thing as wholly objective history: whether the subject at hand is the lineage of Capetian kings or the line of Communist parties, those who write history are influenced, both in the questions they ask and the answers they seek, by the times they live in. Particularly when the subject is communism, one seldom has to dig far to uncover the writer's underlying political assumptions.

In 1957 the Fund for the Republic published the first volume of its "Communism in American Life" series, Theodore Draper's *The Roots of American Communism*. This and subsequent works in the series, under the general editorship of Clinton Rossiter, codified an academic interpretation of the history of American communism that remains influential. Lines between the "Communist bloc" and the "free world" were sharply drawn in the 1950s. The theme espoused by all the authors in Rossiter's series—many of them veterans of the ideological wars on the left of earlier decades—was the subordination of the American Communist movement to the leadership of the Soviet Communists and the attendant disastrous consequences for American radicalism. *The Roots of American Communism* set the pattern. At the conclusion of his book, discussing a 1922 directive from the Communist International ordering American Communists to end their self-imposed underground existence, Draper said:

> A rhythmic rotation from Communist sectarianism to Americanized opportunism was set in motion at the outset and has been going on ever since. The periodic rediscovery of "Americanization" by the American Communists has only superficially represented a more independent policy; it has been in reality merely another type of American response to a Russian stimulus. A Russian initiative has always effectively begun and ended it.

> For this reason, "Americanized" American Communism has been spo-
> radic, superficial, and short-lived. It has corresponded to the fluctuations
> of Russian policy; it has not obeyed a compelling need within the American
> Communists themselves.[1]

Draper made a strong case for the decisive effect Russian influence
had in shaping American communism in the 1920s. In a decade of
general radical disarray in the United States, Communists devoted
most of their energy to internal power struggles fought over phantas-
magorical issues, the real content of the struggles deriving from the
effort by all factions to sound the most like whatever was the current
definition of Bolshevik purity promoted in Moscow.

But Draper's generalization cannot stand as the whole story of
American communism in the decades that followed the 1920s, years
in which tens of thousands of Americans joined the party and hundreds
of thousands came under its influence. Draper believes that "Americanization"—the attempt by Communists to restructure their movement along lines more appropriate to American political conditions—
never had any real content, never arose from "a compelling need within
the American Communists themselves." In his view the "Americanization" of 1935–1939 and that of 1941–1945 was equivalent to the
"Americanization" of 1923, simply an "American response to a Russian stimulus."

This book takes a different view. The men and women of the Communist party, engaging in active political struggles for many years,
joining in such mass movements as the organizing of the Congress of
Industrial Organizations (CIO), could not remain unaffected by new
events and the accumulated weight of their own history. The principal
outlines of the party's political activity at any particular moment must,
of course, be examined within the general context of the Soviet Union's
foreign policy and domestic situation. However, the Fund for the Republic historians' focus on the writings and actions of the party's top
leaders and their efforts to keep in the good graces of Moscow—though
it demonstrated the bad faith, illogic, intellectual cowardice, and plain
stupidity all too often accompanying those efforts—left out, it seems
to me, an important dimension of the story of communism in America.
The Fund for the Republic's interpretation makes it hard to understand
why anyone with intelligence and integrity would have remained in
such a movement for more than the few days or weeks required to

discover its gross inadequacies. Yet many serious, intelligent, committed men and women did join the party in the 1930s and 1940s, remained in it for years, and worked their way into positions of responsibility, apparently convinced that they were contributing to the success of the causes of anti-fascism and socialism.[2]

Earl Browder was the leader of the Communist party during its years of greatest influence, until his fall from power in 1945. A decade after his expulsion from the CP, when he was a consultant for the Fund for the Republic, Browder wrote to Rossiter about *The Roots of American Communism*:

> What I miss in Draper is the understanding that he is writing about an organic part of *American* history, and not merely a study of the American section of the *Communist International*. The two phases are intertwined and interacting, in real life, and are more and more contradictory—but in reading Draper one becomes conscious of the contradiction not in the form of the Living Struggle between American reality and the Leninist dogmas, but as a great gap, an abyss, across which there was never any real contact and therefore never any real struggle.[3]

Browder was not always the most reliable interpreter of the Communist movement's history. But in this instance his criticism represented an insight of some value. The "Living Struggle" he described seldom appeared in the histories published by the Fund for the Republic.

In recent years many veterans of the radical movements of the 1960s have begun to reexamine the history of the American Communist party. Most New Leftists—including many children of former Communists—had initially ignored the CP's bitter and complicated history, though only a few years separated the collapse of the CP as the hegemonic force on the left from the founding of Students for a Democratic Society (SDS). But the collapse of the apocalyptic expectations of the late 1960s created a hunger among this new generation of left-wing activists for a tradition that could serve as both a source of political reference and an inspiration in what now was clearly to be a prolonged struggle. The publication of memoirs by such former Communists as George Charney, Al Richmond, Peggy Dennis, Harry Haywood, and Hosea Hudson (as well as broader historical treatments written by Joseph Starobin and Max Gordon) provided a link to a heretofore little-known past. A new generation of historians, with roots in the student movement of the 1960s, has depicted the party as, at certain times and places, flexible, imaginative, principled, rooted in neighborhoods and workplaces, and enjoying genuine popular support.[4]

I share a common political and intellectual background with this post–New Left generation of historians as well as family ties to the older Left. As a generation on the left we were spared the disillusionment that the Moscow show trials or the invasions of Finland, Hungary, and Czechoslovakia brought to our predecessors: Soviet communism was, for us, never even a minor deity, let alone The God That Failed. Some of our elders charge that that has made us too willing to forgive or ignore the crimes of Stalinism. I do not want those crimes forgotten, but I believe that the recent scholarship on American communism has provided a necessary counterweight to the earlier preoccupation with anti-Soviet themes.[5]

There is, however, one curious convergence in the approach that historians writing in the 1950s and those who began writing in the 1970s have taken to the history of American communism. Both the 1950s and 1970s interpretations assume that those who joined the CP were passive agents of a politics imposed on them from without rather than human beings who held and discarded illusions, learned some lessons from their mistakes and failed to learn others, interpreted events as either substantiation or refutation of passionately held beliefs—in short, people involved in, shaping, and shaped by a historical process. Behaviorist interpretations that portray the Communist party as a single-celled organism responding blindly to external stimuli (orders from Moscow in the 1950s version, the party leaders' devotion or lack of devotion to revolutionary principle in the 1970s version) are unable to account for change and development within the movement.

The 1950s historians insisted that the Communist movement was incapable of genuine political evolution. The CP's "totalitarian" character and its subordination to Soviet directives allowed individual party members only a single meaningful political choice: to stay in the movement or to break with it completely. Stalinism, Irving Howe and Lewis Coser argued in their influential history of the CP, turned the party's cadres into "malleable objects": the true Stalinist was an individual reduced to "little more than a series of predictable and rigidly stereotyped responses: his personality became a function of his 'belonging.'"[6]

Though rejecting the totalitarian model, and sympathetic to the Communists' professed goals, many 1970s historians started from abstract and often equally static models of CP conduct in the 1930s and

1940s. They focused on those brief moments when actual party practice conformed to what they believed was proper revolutionary behavior, then dismissed the rest of the movement's history as either a sectarian or an opportunistic falling away from the true path. Some celebrated the party's ultra-militant phase of the early 1930s, others the coalitionist politics of the latter part of the decade, still others the brief transitional period of 1934–1935. Yet to select one or another phase of Communist policy as a standard by which to measure the shortcomings of other phases obscures the fact that, by and large, the same group of people shared responsibility for carrying out not only the policies these historians approved but also those they scorned. By default this approach leaves the explanation for the willingness of CP members to go along with such dramatic shifts in the party line to Howe and Coser's "malleable objects" theory.[7]

The Communist party was, undeniably, an authoritarian organization that valued its members' discipline as the most potent weapon in its political arsenal. Like Bertolt Brecht's faceless young comrade in *The Measures Taken*, American Communists in the 1930s accepted the myth that the collective wisdom of the party was necessarily greater than their own individual wisdom. They proved themselves all too willing to suspend their own judgment when it conflicted with official pronouncements, believing that their willingness to advocate publicly policies they felt privately were misguided or even repugnant constituted the true test of their commitment as revolutionaries.

As enthusiastically as they participated in perpetuating the myth of the iron-willed and selfless Bolshevik agitator, however, the Communists were unable to step outside their own history. Their character and outlook were certainly shaped by involvement in the Communist movement, as Howe and Coser argued; at the same time, although in more subtle ways, they shaped the party to fit their own needs and expectations. George Charney, in his autobiography *A Long Journey*, recounted how as a young Communist in 1934 he began to feel a vague sense of dissatisfaction with the extravagant leftism of the CP's "Third Period" line. He ventured to drop the then-current slogan "For a Soviet America" from a leaflet meant to be handed out to railroad yard workers, although when called on the carpet by party superiors for this heresy he promptly recanted. Ironically, a year later the party begain carrying out the Popular Front policies decided on by the Communist International's Seventh World Congress, and the slogan "For a Soviet America'' disappeared, never to resurface. Charney concluded:

> The very speed with which we adapted ourselves to the new line and
> discarded the old shibboleths . . . was an indication not so much of our
> mercurial temper as the fact that it reflected what many of us really believed
> but could not articulate. We were prepared to live, even sluggishly, with
> the old policies, if that was the will of the party. But we were so much
> happier to live with a policy that was natural, that heeded reality, and that
> could unleash our creative talents and energies.[8]

In the 1930s Charney and other young Communists thought of themselves as soldiers of the Comintern; they would have been horrified
at any suggestion that in their day-to-day political activities they were
reshaping the intent and effect of policies decided upon by their superiors. Nevertheless, they managed to find enough ambiguity in slogans like "United Front from Below" to allow them to begin working
in effective coalition with young Socialists several years before the
Daily Worker ceased referring to Norman Thomas, the Socialist party
leader, as a "social fascist."[9]

I have found it useful to think of the history of the party from about
1930 to 1956 as a continuum, and as the history of a single generation.
A generational approach to the CP's history permits an assessment of
the long-term constraints under which the Communists operated, as
well as the shortcomings of their policies at any given moment; it allows
us to note the Communists' achievements in political, cultural, and
labor organizing without sentimentality or apology. We need to see not
only what the Communists *were*—in 1932, in 1939, in 1951—but what
they were in the process of *becoming*. The generational approach represents the wedding of social with political and intellectual history. As
Ortega y Gasset suggested:

> The changes in vital sensibility which are decisive in history appear under
> the form of the generation. A generation is not a handful of outstanding
> men, nor simply a mass of men; it resembles a new integration of the social
> body, with its select minority, and its gross multitude, launched upon the
> orbit of existence with a pre-established vital trajectory. The generation
> is a dynamic compromise between mass and individual. . . . It is, so to
> speak, the pivot responsible for the movement of historical evolution.[10]

The generation of Communists who joined the CP in the early years
of the Depression and remained in it until 1956 will be the pivot on
which the following account turns.

In 1917, two years before the American Communist movement was organized, federal agents raided the national and regional offices of the radical Industrial Workers of the World (IWW). They confiscated tons of files—membership lists, correspondence, minutes of meetings—to aid government prosecutors in putting IWW leaders behind bars for opposing the American war effort. The Communists learned a lesson from their predecessors' misfortune, keeping internal paperwork to a minimum and periodically destroying their own files. Whatever benefits in security this provided the Communists, it did nothing to make the task of historians of American communism any easier.

Until the 1970s historians had to rely primarily on official CP publications, like the *Daily Worker*, the testimony of disenchanted former Communists before congressional investigating committees, and private interviews with the limited number of former Communists who chose to make themselves available for such research. I was fortunate enough to begin my research at a time when the first major archival source in American Communist history—the Earl Browder Papers—had just recently been made available to public scrutiny at Syracuse University (and on microfilm in a number of other libraries). During the years of Browder's leadership in the Communist movement, he had filed away an enormous collection of letters, photographs, pamphlets, reports, and internal party documents of all kinds—and he saw no reason to return them to the CP's hands after his expulsion in 1946. Browder also passed on a number of other documents—including the minutes of selected meetings of the CP's top leaders between 1939 and 1945—to his close friend Philip Jaffe. Jaffe, who described these documents in his 1975 book *The Rise and Fall of American Communism*, was kind enough to make them available to me when I began research on my own book.

Other unpublished materials useful in my research include the Oleta O'Connor Yates Papers and the League of American Writers Papers at the Bancroft Library, University of California at Berkeley; the Betty Gannett Papers, deposited at the State Historical Society of Wisconsin (which I read on microfilm at the Tamiment Institute at New York University); the Peter V. Cacchione Papers and Alexander Bittelman's unpublished reminiscences, also at the Tamiment Institute; Earl Browder's oral history, and the Henry Wallace and Robert Minor Papers at Butler Library, Columbia University; and the Franklin Delano Roosevelt and Eleanor Roosevelt Papers at the Presidential Library in Hyde

Park, New York. (A research grant from the Eleanor Roosevelt Institute funded my stay in Hyde Park.)

The Tamiment Institute has a large collection of published materials pertaining to the CP; it was there that I read through the *Daily Worker,* the *Communist*, the *Young Communist Review*, and dozens of books, pamphlets, and minor publications that appeared during the war years.

The most valuable resource for any historian of communism in the United States is the memories of those who participated in the movement. This book could not have been written without the generous aid of Joseph Clark, Samuel Adams Darcy, Peggy Dennis, John Gates, David Goldway, Max Gordon, Gil Green, Carl Marzani, Steve Nelson, Al Richmond, Morris Schappes, George Watt, and several other people who were in the Communist party during the war, and who shared their memories and insights with me.

My uncle, Abraham Isserman, served as a lawyer for the Communist leaders on trial in the 1949 Smith Act case. He was an important source of information and inspiration.

This book began as a doctoral dissertation in history at the University of Rochester. My dissertation advisor, Eugene Genovese, provided warm encouragement and "hard blows" in proper measure along the way. Joseph Clark, John Diggins, Theodore Draper, Mark Erlich, Michael Kazin, Christopher Lasch, Mark Naison, Jim O'Brien, and Kenneth Waltzer read part or all of the book. I adopted many of their suggestions, and ignored others to my peril. My editor at Wesleyan University Press, Jeannette Hopkins, patiently instructed me in the mysteries of book publishing. Sonia Anna Erlich, born the day the manuscript was completed, offered no useful suggestions, did not help with research chores, and did not give unstintingly of her time and energy in proofreading and typing. Nevertheless, she was an important part of the inspiration for the work that follows.

CONTENTS

ILLUSTRATIONS

Gilbert Green, president of the Young Communist League in the 1930s.

Elizabeth Gurley Flynn, sole woman in the Communist Party's ruling Political Committee.

Alexander Bittleman, former Communist Party leader, before testifying before House Un-American Activities Committee, November 21, 1961.

Eugene Dennis after his 1949 conviction for violating the Smith Act was upheld by the Supreme Court, July 2, 1951.

WHICH SIDE WERE YOU ON?

1 PRELUDE TO WAR, AMERICAN COMMUNISTS IN THE 1930s

What was the Commune? . . . The child has the right to know the reason of the paternal defeats, the Socialist Party the campaign of its flag in all countries. He who tells the people revolutionary legends, he who amuses them with sensational stories, is as criminal as the geographer who would draw up false charts for navigators.

—PROSPER O. LISSARGAY, *The History of the Commune of 1871*[1]

ON THE MORNING OF MAY 20, 1944, Earl Browder, general secretary of the American Communist party, addressed an audience of four hundred delegates to a party convention in New York City's Riverside Plaza Hotel. He stood before a large blown-up photograph of Stalin, Roosevelt, and Churchill, taken the previous November as the Big Three sat together in their first wartime meeting, in the Iranian capital of Teheran. Browder had faced many audiences in a decade and a half as leader of the Communist movement in the United States, and had delivered many and conflicting messages over the years—in opposition to and in support of Roosevelt's New Deal, in favor of an anti-fascist Popular Front, in opposition to the "second imperialist war," and, since the Nazi invasion of Russia in June 1941, in support of the Grand Alliance of the United States, Great Britain, and the Soviet Union. Now he took what was, without question, the most startling political position of his long career. "I hereby move," he declared, "that the Communist Party of America be and hereby is dissolved." The assembled delegates held aloft blue credential cards in unanimous support, and the Communist Party USA officially passed out of existence. The delegates sang the old labor song "We Shall Not Be Moved," immediately reconvened as the founding convention of the Communist Political Association (described in the preamble of its constitution as a "non-party organization of Americans which, basing itself upon the working class, carries forward the traditions of Washington, Jefferson,

Paine, Jackson, and Lincoln, under the changed conditions of modern industrial society''), and elected Browder as the new organization's president.

One year later the *Daily Worker* reprinted an article from the French Communist party's theoretical journal *Cahiers du Communisme*, in which the French CP's second-in-command, Jacques Duclos, found Browder guilty of a ''notorious revision of Marxism'' for having advocated and presided over the dissolution of the American CP. Few doubted that Duclos's article had its genesis in Moscow. Before summer's end Browder had been stripped of office, and the Communist Party USA reborn under the chairmanship of William Z. Foster, Browder's long-time antagonist in the party leadership. Browder's expulsion from the party as ''an enemy of the working class'' followed soon after.

Browder's wartime ideological and organizational experiments have found few defenders in the years since 1945. Those historians close to the Communist party have echoed Duclos's charges of revisionism against Browder (while usually omitting Duclos's and Moscow's role in his downfall from their accounts). Anti-Communist historians regard the episode as simply one more in a long series of cynical maneuvers undertaken in the service of the shifting requirements of Soviet foreign policy. Historians of the non-Communist left have portrayed the dissolution of the party as the climax of an ideological capitulation to liberal capitalism that began during the Popular Front.[2] Joseph Starobin, in his study *American Communism in Crisis, 1943–1957,* offered one of the few sympathetic accounts of Browder's motives in establishing the Communist Political Association. But even he regarded the experiment as a futile gesture, at best a way station to the complete (and in his view necessary) acceptance of liberal reformism. In Starobin's ironic words, the Communists, under Browder and throughout their tortured history, were a ''movement of genuine Americans engaged in trying to square a circle.''[3]

A final word remains to be said before Browder's Teheran policies, as they came to be called, are consigned to the already overcrowded dustbin of history. These policies represented, if in imperfect fashion, the political lessons that thousands of Communist militants had drawn from their experiences during the Depression and the war. The repudiation of these policies in 1945 destroyed what might have been the last, best chance the Communists would have to sustain a socialist movement in the United States, and it led shortly to a political vacuum on the left which has not been filled in the more than three decades since.

Communist Fortunes in the Great Depression

In the first years of what would later be stigmatized as the "Red Decade," it was not at all apparent that the Communists would become the dominant force on the American left. A decade of factional struggle had reduced the party to a tiny, isolated sect. Although the economic crash opened up new political opportunities, between 1930 and 1932 the Communists enjoyed only modest growth, from an all-time low membership of 7,500 in 1930 to a figure roughly double that two years later. In the same years the CP's chief rival, the Socialist party, grew to about 25,000 members. The difference between the two parties' vote-getting potential was even more dramatic: Norman Thomas received nearly 900,000 votes in the 1932 presidential election on the Socialist party line, compared to William Z. Foster's 103,000. Yet by the time of the next presidential election the Communist party had established itself as the largest and most vital force on the left.

The Communists owed their relative strength in the late 1930s to a number of factors. First, the Soviet Union enjoyed a growing prestige in the West, both for the apparent ability of its planned economy to avoid the vicissitudes of the Depression, and for its advocacy of collective security against fascism, expressed most concretely in the aid it provided to the Loyalist government during the Spanish Civil War. Not everyone could pour cement for the Dnepropetrovsk Dam or stand guard with a rifle in Madrid's trenches; Communist party membership offered a vicarious sense of participation in both.

Second, by a happy coincidence for the Communists, the 1935 Congress of the Communist International made it legitimate for the American CP to moderate its political position at about the same time that Franklin Roosevelt was moving to the left to build popular support for the New Deal. The Communists began to identify themselves as part of the political coalition that supported the New Deal's domestic programs, while enthusiastically welcoming every move by the Roosevelt Administration that could be interpreted as favoring collective international security. The Communists argued that their own political program corresponded to Roosevelt's true intentions, which, they said, were frustrated by a reactionary Supreme Court, Congress, and press.

Supporting both the Soviet Union and the New Deal, the Communists could continue to think of themselves as revolutionaries even as they immersed themselves in reform-oriented day-to-day politics. Their rivals in the Socialist party were unable to straddle the chasm between reform and revolution: Norman Thomas presided over the virtual dissolution of the Socialist party in the later 1930s, as its younger half flirted with Trotskyism and its older half voted the American Labor party ticket for Roosevelt.

Third, the Communists out-organized their left-wing rivals. When the Socialists agreed to unite with the Communists in joint ventures, as in the American Student Union, the Communists quickly gained effective organizational control, recruiting some of the most talented Socialist cadres into their own ranks, without disturbing the surface appearance of friendly coalition. The American Youth Congress, the League of American Writers, the American League Against War and Fascism, and other Communist-organized or -influenced groups attracted enough adherents to keep several generations of congressional investigating committees in business.

The Communists made their most striking gains in influence in the organizational drives of the new Congress of Industrial Organizations (CIO). CIO president John L. Lewis had no sympathy for the Communists' political goals, but respected the experience and dedication of Communist union organizers. Lewis allowed Communists to remain in control of half a dozen important CIO unions and to hold powerful positions in regional and national offices in exchange for the contributions they made to the CIO's success. Socialist unionists, like the Reuther brothers in the United Auto Workers, also made important contributions to the CIO's organizing drives, but were unsuccessful (and increasingly uninterested) in translating union position into political influence for the Socialist party. Indeed, most influential Socialist unionists had withdrawn from the SP by the time America entered the Second World War. The Communists, even under the extremely awkward political conditions of the Nazi-Soviet pact period, managed to retain the loyalty of most of their union "influentials."

Browder Takes Power

Earl Browder's leadership was the final important asset the Communists had in their favor in the 1930s. Browder might have seemed an unlikely candidate to lead the CP in the unorthodox directions it took in the later 1930s. Born in Kansas in 1891, the son of a schoolteacher with Populist sympathies, he had made his living as a bookkeeper, while devoting most of his energies to the revolutionary movement. He joined the Socialist party at sixteen, shifting his allegiance in 1912 to William Z. Foster's Syndicalist League of North America, which sought to "bore from within" the American Federation of Labor (AFL) unions and win their members to the revolutionary cause. Browder seems to have been an effective, if obscure, organizer; he won election to the Kansas City (Missouri) Central Labor Council, and the presidency of the local AFL Bookkeepers, Stenographers and Accountants Union. Browder carried the stamp of his Midwestern upbringing in his Kansas twang and in his general demeanor, described by one unfriendly observer in the 1930s as that of a "harassed small-town lawyer."

Browder made his entry into national radical circles in the aftermath of the First World War. A vocal opponent of American participation in the war, he was convicted in 1917 for failing to register for the draft and for urging noncompliance with the Selective Service Act, serving two prison sentences, one for eleven months and one for sixteen months. In a brief interval between jailings he rejoined the Socialist party, supporting those in its left wing who sought to align it with Lenin's new Communist International. Following his release from prison late in 1920 he joined the newly formed Communist party and moved to New York. He was only a minor figure in the CP in the early 1920s, serving as Foster's lieutenant in the Communist-organized Trade Union Educational League (which, like the Syndicalist League before it, sought to "bore from within" mainstream unions).

Recruiting the much better known Foster into the Communist movement was Browder's one major achievement during these years. According to Max Shachtman, an early Communist leader who later became a founder of the American Trotskyist movement, Browder was regarded in the 1920s as a "very quiet, modest unassuming man. . . . No one considered that he played a decisive role in the factional struggles." In the later 1920s Browder found the opportunity to step outside of Foster's shadow when, like many future Communist leaders, he was seasoned by a term of duty overseas. Late in 1926 he went to China as a representative of the Profintern, the Soviet-organized trade-union international. He remained there for two years, working closely with the Chinese CP's leadership.[4]

Meanwhile, factional struggles within both the Soviet and American Communist parties were reaching a climax. In 1929 Jay Lovestone, the American CP's general secretary, was expelled from the party—in part for his sympathy for Nicolai Bukharin, the last major obstacle to Stalin's consolidation of power within the Soviet Communist leadership. In the aftermath of Lovestone's expulsion, Browder found himself catapulted over the head of his former mentor Foster, who was too closely identified with the recent factional bloodletting to be awarded party leadership. Browder's absence from the country during the worst of the power struggle probably constituted his chief qualification for the job in the eyes of the Comintern. Many years later Shachtman would curtly dismiss Browder as "a manufactured person. . . . As soon as the Russians decided that for this, that and the other reasons they didn't want Browder, they just snapped their fingers and Browder disappeared. . . . All the great power and prestige that he enjoyed, or seemed to enjoy was not his in the first place, because he did not exist. He was simply their invention."[5]

Shachtman may have been more formidable as a polemicist than as a political analyst. Browder entered and departed the leadership of the party at Moscow's direction, but he lacked neither native political ability nor the capacity for independent thinking. Alexander Bittelman, a major figure in the CP's internal struggles in the 1920s, a long-time Foster ally and frequent opponent of Browder during the 1930s, concluded in an unpublished memoir written in the 1960s that the Communists "discovered in Browder a very good and gifted exponent of the Party's new orientation. . . . There was no one else in our party [during the Popular Front years] that could have done better or even as well as Browder."[6]

Ruling at first as the leader of a three-man secretariat that included Foster and William Weinstone, another veteran Communist leader, Browder steadily increased his own power. In 1934 he was elected as the CP's general secretary. He proved himself an adept student of American politics and, once given the green light by the Comintern's shift to its Popular Front policy, worked hard to reverse the sectarian policies the party had adopted in the 1920s and early 1930s.

During the first decade and a half of its existence the American Communist movement experimented with a variety of strategies: "boring from within" the AFL, organizing rival revolutionary unions, running candidates on the party's own line, and organizing a farmer-labor party. But the Communists' underlying assumptions about how a revolution would come to America were never altered or questioned. Workers, they believed, in the struggle for bread-and-butter demands, came into conflict with the capitalist class in the person of their employer, and with the capitalist state in the form of police and troops sent in to break strikes. The elemental confrontation at the point of production could be lifted to a higher political level by Communist leadership (whether that leadership was to be exercised within or in opposition to the AFL varied according to the prevailing political winds in Moscow). Once having turned to Communists for militant union leadership—as supplemented by whatever forces the Communists could mobilize in the electoral arena—workers could be offered the vision of a workers' state, embodied in the Soviet Union, and a dedicated vanguard recruited into the party. Eventually and inevitably a breakdown in the capitalist system—a social and economic catastrophe comparable to the one that gripped Russia in 1917—would provide the opportunity for the party to lead the workers to the conquest of state power.

The Communists often deluded themselves about their political prospects. In the later 1920s, however, they briefly arrived at a more realistic assessment. Under Jay Lovestone's leadership a Communist writer ventured to complain in the *New Masses*, the party's literary magazine, that "factory girls in America wear silk stockings but have no class consciousness—capitalism is in blacker and more complete control than anywhere else on earth." American workers had been bribed by radios and Model-T Fords and "are, at present, ideologically a part of the bourgeois class."[7]

But Lovestone and his followers did not go on to develop any coherent alternative to the catastrophic model of revolution. Rather than directly challenging the view that the breakdown of capitalism would automatically turn workers toward revolution, they simply argued for an "American exceptionalism," which held that such a breakdown was unlikely in the near future. American capitalism had not yet reached the "apex" of its development, and until it had, the prospects for socialist revolution remained bleak. The onset of the Great Depression in 1929 dealt the economic doctrines of American exceptionalism a death blow and seemed to resolve the problem of the ideological domination of capitalism, at least as measured by its ability to bribe the working class with Model T's and silk stockings.[8]

Somewhere along the line Browder began to shed his belief in this determinist and catastrophic model of revolution. He never openly differed with official Comintern policy, and in the early 1930s rigidly implemented the ultra-left tactics mandated in Moscow. His own political leanings were only revealed by his actions during the Popular Front period, when he embraced the newly legitimized coalitionist tactics with an enthusiasm that horrified older, more orthodox leaders like Foster.

By the later 1930s, under Browder's prodding, the Communists were closing down their shop- and factory-based units, abolishing trade-union "fractions" (at least officially), and abandoning their shop newspapers. The Communists' strength in the leadership of many of the new CIO unions made such relics of the 1920s and early 1930s unnecessary. Besides, Browder did not view the shop floor as the most important locus of Communist activity. In 1937 he had the party restructured along county and assembly-district lines so it more closely resembled traditional American political organizations. George Charney, who served as an organizer for the CP's Harlem section in the late 1930s, recalled that in those years:

> Everyone became an expert on election strategy, and predicting results became the favorite indoor pastime of all functionaries. [Assembly district] maps sprang up in the headquarters; election districts were studied for every manifestation of class, ethnic, or political peculiarity. . . . The Party which hitherto had been oriented to the naked forms of class struggle, such as picket lines and relief struggles, now acquired an astonishing flair for election politics as well as a capacity for expert organization and mobility.[9]

The CP did not owe the relative political success it enjoyed in these years to Browder's theoretical acuity; he used the writings of Marx and Lenin much the same way as he did those of Jefferson and Lincoln, as ideological window dressing for successful policies. Browder's strength as a leader lay in his skill as a tactician, as shaped by a driving personal ambition. Some veteran leaders of the earliest years of the Communist movement were almost indifferent to the party's actual political influence within the United States. They derived their sense of importance and mission from belonging to a world movement that already held power in the Soviet Union and that seemed to be on the verge of a serious contest for power throughout Europe and Asia. Browder paid lip service to "proletarian internationalism," and with his training in the hard school of Comintern politics knew better than to oppose Soviet-imposed policies, however inappropriate they might be to American conditions.

But Browder wanted to be a leader of a national movement with power and influence of its own, like Maurice Thorez of the French Communist Party. Since political innovation paid off in the United States, Browder became an innovator; he did not hesitate to clear out the deadwood, ideological and individual, that cluttered up the party's policymaking. He also knew a good slogan when he heard one: the difference between his "Communism Is Twentieth Century Americanism" and Foster's "Towards Soviet America" speaks for itself. And, most important, he opened up secondary leadership positions throughout the party and its auxiliaries to the generation of politically talented young people who began entering the movement in the early 1930s through the Young Communist League, the Unemployed Councils, and various left-wing student organizations.

The "Americanization" of 1936–1939

"Communism Is Twentieth Century Americanism" has not fared well in most accounts of the CP's history. The slogan, and the policies it represented, have been dismissed as an unprincipled, and unsuccessful, bid for respectability. Irving Howe and Lewis Coser characterized the Popular Front's patriotic motif as a "kind of Machiavellian inspiration—the inventiveness that sometimes comes from total cynicism," while more recently James Weinstein argued that the CP's decision to downplay its socialist ideology after 1935 made it "an unwitting but useful ally of liberal politicians and corporation leaders in adjusting the social system to the changed needs of the corporations."[10]

There were, of course, real problems with the Popular Front as a radical strategy. The Communists did blunt their criticism of capitalism, substituting such fuzzy, Rooseveltian categories as "economic royalism" for the more explicit and starker dichotomies of Marxist class analysis. As an expedient the Popular Front did not, in the long run, protect the Communists from isolation within American unions and political life; nor did it, even in the short run, succeed in blocking the spread of fascism in Europe. The party increasingly came to rely on the goodwill, or at least the tolerance, of New Deal political leaders and mainstream union leaders. Not all Communists were oblivious to the dangers of this course. Martin Young, a Communist organizer in Minnesota, wrote to the party's central committee in late 1936 criticizing the CP's backdoor alliance with the Minnesota Farmer-Labor party in recent elections:

> Our relations with them were not political nor normal. It was not a relationship between an independent political group, following an independent political program, with a mass movement like the Farmer–Labor movement. . . . It was more or less a relationship with them [at the] top, very secretive not only to the masses at large, but even to our membership and sympathizers. . . . Here we must be enough of practical politicians to understand that they will deal with us, listen to us, and work with us only if we command mass influence, only when we have the masses backing up our policy in an independent political way.[11]

The committee's response, if any, has gone unrecorded, but the party's reliance on the kind of behind-the-scenes maneuvering Young criticized unquestionably cost it dearly when the political climate changed, and carefully wrought "understandings" with political leaders like California's governor Culbert Olson and union leaders like CIO president Philip Murray fell by the wayside.

Despite such shortcomings, to dismiss "Communism Is Twentieth Century Americanism" as a cynical or politically short-sighted maneuver as some scholars do is to miss the genuine enthusiasm with which the young Communist cadres greeted the slogan and made it their own. Until the mid-1930s, foreign-born veterans of the previous decade held most of the secondary leadership positions within the party and the organizations it influenced. After 1935, and for the next twenty years, these positions were filled by those who had entered the CP in the first years of the Depression. A significant portion of those who joined then and stuck with the movement were the children of Jewish immigrants (the percentage of Jewish membership in the CP, about 15 percent in the mid-1920s, grew to around half the party's strength in the 1930s and 1940s).[12]

Like every second generation in the history of American immigration, they hungered for the full assimilation that had eluded their parents' grasp. Had they come of age in less unsettled times they might have chosen another route, but in the early 1930s it seemed for a moment as if an American version of the October Revolution offered the quickest and surest path from marginality to influence and inte-

gration. Family ties to Russian socialist and Bundist traditions sometimes influenced their decision. But rather than join the Socialists, who
seemed unable to break out of a needle-trades constituency, they preferred the Communists, who claimed, and sometimes could demonstrate, support in the American industrial heartland. As Communists,
they were part of an organization in which (in numbers admittedly
unrepresentative of the country as a whole) they could meet and work
with Connecticut Yankees, Georgia and Harlem blacks, Northwestern
Finns, and Midwestern Poles. For these second-generation Jewish-
Americans the party served as a bridge between the Russian origins
and socialist beliefs of their parents and the "progressive" borderlands
of New Deal America. It was not by chance that in choosing their
party names (a conspiratorial touch left over from Russian revolutionary tradition) so many young Jewish Communists chose the most common Anglo-Saxon names they could think of: thus Saul Regenstreif
became Johnny Gates, Joseph Cohen became Joe Clark, and Abraham
Richman became Al Richmond.

Browder and this new generation of Communists found themselves
in alliance against older, more orthodox Communists. Young Communists repeatedly pushed outward at the boundaries of the politically
permissible. They did not do so with a conscious sense of mission or
strategy to reform party policies—indeed, they were initially attracted
to the CP rather than one of the other leftist groups because of its
public aura of resolute self-confidence, reinforced as it was by ties with
the original and only victorious socialist revolution. But immersed from
the beginning in mass movements like the Unemployed Councils, the
campus anti-war movement, and the new industrial unions, they instinctively "Americanized" their message and, like Charney, abandoned or downplayed the more sectarian aspects of the party line when
they could. Younger Communists, scrambling for position and influence in the American Youth Congress or the United Auto Workers,
developed different priorities from those of their elders, who often
seemed more concerned with how a leaflet or pamphlet would sound
when read by a supervisory committee of the Communist International
in Moscow than how it would go over with its intended American
readers. Browder allowed the new secondary leaders considerable latitude in day-to-day conduct of the party's affairs; whatever successes
they achieved, after all, were his as well.[13]

Al Richmond and other veterans of the 1930s have argued that much of the criticism leveled in recent years against the Popular Front has had a brittle and abstract quality. The Communists faced stark choices in the mid-1930s. They could submerge their political identities and participate in the organization of the CIO on the terms John L. Lewis offered, or they could remain on the outside as principled and unheeded critics. They could accept the fact that, by the mid-1930s, most American workers believed that New Deal social programs were the only thing standing between them and destitution, or they could continue to denounce Roosevelt as a capitalist tool and lose all political credibility outside their own ranks. They could make anti-fascist unity their top political priority, or they could refuse to compromise, and risk sharing the fate of their German comrades who kept insisting in 1932 and 1933, "After Hitler, our turn." These were how the choices presented themselves to American Communists in the mid-1930s. In retrospect it is easy to say that the Communists erred by making too many compromises; we should not, however, ignore their perception of the consequences of making too few compromises.[14]

At a CP-organized writers' congress in New York in 1937, Joseph Freeman, a well-known Communist journalist and poet, responded to a Trotskyist critic who argued that capitalism, not fascism, was still the principal enemy for the left to confront: "We are living in a period when our basic job is to preserve those conditions under which a congress such as this can be held at all. We could not hold a congress like ours in Germany or Italy. You who are so profoundly theoretical about the People's Front could not even discuss the question in those countries. We would all be in concentration camps."[15]

Freeman's defense of the Communist position in 1937 was ambiguous. Narrowly interpreted, it left the Popular Front's defense of democratic institutions as a temporary, necessary evil to be endured by the Communists until fascism was defeated, when they could get back to their real job of making a Soviet-style revolution in America. But the subsequent histories of the Communist parties in the United States and Western Europe suggest that a more positive appraisal of the Popular Front era may be in order. The international Communist movement emerged from the wave of revolutionary enthusiasm that swept outward from St. Petersburg after 1917. It took many years of painful experience before Western Communists learned that revolutionary enthusiasm did not require strict imitation of the Soviet model, longer still until they learned that part of their duty as revolutionaries would be to understand and criticize the limitations of the first triumphant socialist revolution.

The Popular Front, whatever the intentions of its founders, turned out to be a step in that learning process. Western communism in 1936–1939 was a strange hybrid of democratic and authoritarian beliefs. Modern socialism had its origins as a critique of the limitations of democracy under capitalism, not as a repudiation of that democracy. The distinction had been lost in the years since the transformation of the "dictatorship of the proletariat" from an awkward choice of words by Marx to a harsh and tangible reality in the Soviet Union. The Popular Front, with its emphasis on the defense of existing democratic rights under capitalism, restored some of the democratic content to Communist ideology even as Western Communists continued to celebrate the supposed "higher form of democracy" prevailing in the Soviet Union under Stalin. This contradiction led political opponents to label Communists "Red Fascists," for hypocritically mouthing democratic slogans they did not believe in.

Unlike fascism, however, Communism began from democratic premises, though some Communists grew enamored of the authoritarian aspects of Soviet-style socialism, while the rest chose to ignore or apologize for them. There was an unresolved tension within the Communist movement around questions of democracy—a tension that did not exist within any fascist movements, founded as they were on frankly undemocratic premises. This tension led to a constant stream of individual departures from the movement (like Joseph Freeman, who parted company with his former comrades in 1939), building over the years of the Nazi-Soviet pact, World War Two, and the Cold War, and finally culminating in the "de-Stalinization" crisis of 1956.[16]

The Popular Front permitted many Communists to begin to take seriously their own arguments about the absolute value of democracy. It also gave American Communists an opportunity to develop an alternative to the catastrophic model of revolution. Although, theoretically, the Popular Front only postponed the day of the final reckoning when the working class would overthrow its exploiters and establish Soviet power, it raised implicit questions about the role Communists should play in democratic societies. In 1937 Browder published some comments on one such question:

> Certainly we are not indifferent to the problem of "transition" from a
> victory over fascism to victory over the whole capitalist system, "tran-
> sition" to socialism. But the transition does not come from empty slogans,
> disconnected from everyday life. This transition arises upon the basis of
> the growing strength, organization, discipline, fighting power, and under-
> standing of the working class. . . . It is not a discouraged, defeated, and
> demoralized working class that will take up and realize the great program
> of socialism; it is the enthusiastic, victorious, and organized workers who
> will move forward from victories in the defensive struggle to the offensive
> and finally to socialism. Every strong defense passes insensibly to the
> offensive.[17]

Browder's formulation avoided as many questions as it answered;
the nature and timing of that "insensible" passage to the offensive is
precisely what has remained at issue over the years. And yet, as a
description of the process through which the working class might come
to socialist consciousness, it represented a sharp break with the party's
earlier assumptions. In the past the Communists had seen their revolutionary army gathering on the margins of society, as workers discovered the absolute antagonism that existed between themselves and
their employers and the state. Browder saw his army gathering, instead,
in the heart of that society, developing a sense of its own power and
interests as it used the unions, the government, and other institutions
to better its conditions and protect its gains. Earlier, Communists had
believed that the working class, because of its economic position within
capitalist society, was one short step away from enbracing a socialist
perspective: all the pieces could fall into place, given Communist leadership in a strike. By the end of the 1930s, however, Browder saw
nothing inherently revolutionary in working-class experience; he believed that class consciousness would grow slowly and in long-term
struggle fought on many terrains.

Browder versus Foster

Browder's personal ambition contributed to making him a more creative leader in such respects, but his ambition had a darker side. As
the party's membership and influence expanded, his self-regard grew
proportionately. The constant praise of his colleagues and the party
press, and the adulation in which the membership held him (among his

papers Browder saved a letter from a Seattle Communist addressed to the "Greatest of Living Americans, Earl Browder"), transformed the once unassuming *apparatchik* of the 1920s into an arrogant and uncompromising party dictator. Having been described as "the foremost Marxist in the English-speaking world" by no less an authority than Georgi Dimitrov, the Comintern's general secretary, Browder brooked no competition. Alexander Bittelman, in a polite understatement, would later recall that "Browder was somewhat too sensitive to his prerogatives and prestige of leadership even in the leading party committee. . . . For anybody else in the leading committee to come forward with a new and good idea before Browder did was generally to him a source of deep embarrassment and even pain. He would begin acting angrily and resentfully for no apparent reason."[18]

Browder's increasingly imperial view of his own role was in conflict with his sense of insecurity about his lack of experience as a popular leader. In 1963 he was still brooding over the other party leaders' "prejudice" in favor of Foster "as an old-time militant. . . . That was always his great advantage over me. I hadn't directly led mass movements, as he was supposed to have done."[19]

Browder's early career did indeed appear colorless compared to Foster's. Growing up in the Philadelphia slums at the end of the century, Foster soon abandoned his father's Irish nationalism and his mother's devout Catholicism for other causes. He quit school at ten, found employment in the years that followed in foundries, factories, lumber camps, and mines, on farms, on trains, trolley cars, and merchant ships, passing through the Socialist party and the Industrial Workers of the World, before founding his Syndicalist League. He achieved national prominence during the First World War, leading a brilliant organizing campaign among Chicago packinghouse workers that brought a tenfold increase in union membership and won the eight-hour day. After the war he headed up the AFL's steel organizing drive, an ambitious if futile attempt to subdue the bastion of the "open shop." The steel corporations, aided by the postwar Red Scare, withstood a strike by 365,000 steelworkers in the fall of 1919, and it would be another two decades before the CIO finally cracked the corporate resistance.

Foster, adrift once again after the collapse of the steel strike, moved on to the Communist party. Caught up in the party's factional struggles in the 1920s, and in poor health for much of the next decade after a serious heart attack in 1932, he would never again find himself in the leadership of a genuine mass movement. But the legend of Foster's heroic early years, kept alive by the two autobiographical books he published in the later 1930s, rankled Browder, as did his active opposition within the CP's ruling political committee. Browder retaliated by doing everything possible to undercut Foster's chairmanship of the party, turning it, in Bittelman's phrase, into "a kind of glorified dog house." At a meeting of CP leaders in March 1939 Foster exclaimed bitterly: "I think that Earl has to take this padlock from my hands. . . . I don't think he has to watch me at all."[20] The older and ailing Foster smarted under constant humiliations at the hands of his one-time protégé; he searched relentlessly for the issue and opportunity that would allow him to strike back at his tormentor. As long as Foster was around, Browder was unable to feel secure within his domain. Browder felt constantly reminded that he himself was an interloper—that what had so easily been given to him could just as easily be taken away.

The Second World War offered both men the opportunity to realize long-cherished goals. Browder saw his chance to establish once and for all the legitimacy of his claim to leadership through bold innovations. Foster, because Browder's ambition had at last overstepped itself, found the weapon he needed to bring his hated rival down.

And what of the ordinary members of the Communist party during the war? Lenin liked to remind his followers that the locomotive of history was prone to making hairpin turns, and that the faint-hearted or ill-prepared passenger might well find himself dumped unceremoniously. Both Communists and their opponents frequently cited this maxim in the years between 1939 and 1945, as the member parties of the Comintern struggled to keep their political programs in accord with the shifting exigencies of Soviet foreign policy. In the twenty-two months between the signing of the Nazi-Soviet pact and the German invasion of Russia, Communists loyally defended political positions that stood in bleak contrast to the beliefs they had fought for in the preceding decade. "Fascism," Soviet Foreign Commissar Molotov offhandedly commented late in 1939, "is a matter of taste." The "so-called democracies" in the West, American Communists now insisted, deserved no support in their war against Hitler. Some Communists handled the required transition with equanimity; others endured a private anguish. Many later looked back on this period with repugnance, feeling that even their own and the party's exemplary war service after

June 22, 1941, could not absolve them for having once argued, against their own better judgment, that it made no difference whether the Allies or the Axis powers won the "second imperialist war."

The story of American Communists in the Second World War is not the stuff of which revolutionary legends are made. It is not a "usable past," in the sense of providing models to emulate or political blueprints to follow. The Second World War was an episode midway through a longer historical process in which a generation of Communists would finally break with the illusions that had both sustained them and led them into a political blind alley. The war years themselves are worth focusing on because, for a brief moment, the Communists seemed to be moving toward a more realistic appraisal of their position in American life. Their failure to do so had an immense impact on the future of American radicalism and much can be learned from their experience. Every generation faces the challenge of transcending the limitations of its own vision. As William Appleman Williams argued in the introduction to *The Contours of American History*: "Only by grasping what we were is it possible to see how we changed, to understand the process and the nature of the modifications, and to gain some perspective on what we are. The historical experience is not one of staying in the present and looking back. Rather it is one of going back into the past and returning to the present with a wider and more intense consciousness of the restraints of our former outlook."[21]

2 THE LAST DAYS OF PEACE
January 1938 to August 21, 1939

> The power of the Marxist-Leninist theory lies in the fact that it enables the Party to find the right orientation in any situation, to understand the inner connection of current events, to foresee their course and to perceive not only how and in what direction they are developing in the present, but how and in what direction they are bound to develop in the future.
>
> —*History of the Communist Party of the Soviet Union (Bolsheviks), Short Course,* 1939

> There is as much chance of Russo-German agreement as of Earl Browder being elected President of the Chamber of Commerce.
>
> —EARL BROWDER, July 5, 1939[1]

ARCHIBALD MACLEISH DECLARED in a poem published in 1939 that "America is promises to take!" His poem was one of those hortatory celebrations of democracy so cherished by American liberals in the New Deal years. MacLeish, like many liberal writers in the 1930s, belonged to the Communist-organized League of American Writers and was a vocal advocate of liberal-Communist cooperation against the threatening spread of fascism in Europe, and in support of social reform at home.[2] American Communists in 1938 and the early months of 1939 had reason to agree with MacLeish's optimistic assessment, for America had seemingly fulfilled many promises to them in recent years. The Communists had made many gains during the years of the Popular Front, and they were convinced they were riding the crest of the wave of the future.

Communist Strength

With somewhere between 50,000 to 75,000 party members, and another 20,000 or so members of the Young Communist League (YCL), the Communist movement was approaching the level of strength attained by Eugene Debs's Socialist party in the decade before the First World War, the high-water mark of American radicalism.[3] The CP's political influence was considerable, its supporters a well-entrenched minority within the California and Washington Democratic parties, the Minnesota Farmer-Labor party, and the New York–based American Labor party.

Though the Communists were unable to claim a single elected official of their own, some of their candidates rolled up impressive vote totals. Anita Whitney in the 1936 California race for state comptroller, and Israel Amter in the 1938 New York election for congressman-at-large, each attracted more than 100,000 votes. In New York City, the party's strongest political base, Peter Cacchione, Communist candidate for city council from Brooklyn in 1937, received more than 30,000 first-choice votes under the city's proportional representation electoral system, raising Communist hopes for a victory in the autumn 1939 city council elections.[4]

Rank-and-file Communists were proud of the increasing votes their candidates attracted, but party leaders were convinced that their real strength lay in the support they could mobilize on behalf of non-Communist candidates. Browder told a radio interviewer after the 1938 congressional elections: "We Communists helped to build the united progressive and democratic front everywhere, and collaborated with Republicans as well as Democrats and third party and labor groupings. . . . We are learning how to take our place within the traditional American two-party system."[5]

The Communists had also made substantial gains within the union movement. In 1939 they controlled or strongly influenced such important CIO unions as the United Electrical, Radio and Machine Workers Union (UE), the International Longshoremen's and Warehousemen's Union (ILWU), the National Maritime Union (NMU), the Transport Workers Union (TWU), the American Newspaper Guild, the International Woodworkers of America (IWA), the Mine, Mill and Smelter Workers Union, the Fur and Leather Workers Union, and a number of smaller unions. Communists played an important role in organizing the United Auto Workers (UAW), the largest of the new CIO unions, and were a power to be reckoned with in its internal affairs. The party also retained a toehold in the American Federation of Labor through its influence in the American Federation of Teachers (AFT), some studio labor organizations in Hollywood, and New York

City locals of the Painters Union and the Hotel and Restaurant Employees Union.[6]

Communist strength in the union movement lay in control of office rather than in mass constituencies, though they had some rank-and-file support on the New York and San Francisco waterfronts, among auto workers in some UAW locals, among electrical workers in some UE locals, and in such traditional bastions of left-wing strength as New York City's fur industry. As Barrington Moore noted in a 1945 article assessing Communist strength, party members had "won their position in the CIO largely through their willingness to take on the more unpleasant and in some instances routine tasks of trade union organization and maintenance. . . . In this fashion they came in at the beginning of the growth of mass unionism, and won strategic positions as union officers."[7]

The party's efforts to get its members into union office had met with considerable success. According to Peggy Dennis, out of a statewide party membership of six hundred in Wisconsin in 1935, more than one hundred held office in AFL and CIO unions.[8] The party abandoned its system of shop "fractions" in the late 1930s, in part because its control of union offices had made them a redundant, and unnecessarily divisive, hold-over from earlier struggles. The *Party Builder*, the CP's internal organizational bulletin, explained in the spring of 1939 that the Communists had no need to maintain an independent network of shop newspapers when so many official union newspapers were run by "progressives."[9]

The various front organizations that the party controlled had achieved unprecedented levels of stability and influence by 1939. The term "Communist front" (used more often for abuse than analysis to discredit any group in which Communists participated or which took positions Communists favored) here refers simply to nominally independent groups, organized around single-issue or special-interest concerns, in which the Communists exercised effective organizational control.

In the classic pattern, front organizations had a well-known but relatively inactive non-Communist president and an obscure but extremely hard-working Communist executive secretary. However, front organizations were seldom the smoothly functioning cogs in an elaborately designed conspiracy that newspaper columnists and congressional investigators liked to believe. The "innocents" who filled out their membership rolls had their own purposes for joining, and proved quite resistant to Communist efforts to change organizational priorities in midstream.

As long as the Communists continued to respect the original purpose for which the various front organizations had been established, they found them to be a medium through which they could reach out and influence far broader political circles than had ever been touched by the left before. The front groups sometimes wildly overstated their membership: the American League for Peace and Democracy (successor to the League Against War and Fascism) had about twenty thousand dues-paying members in 1939 while claiming an affiliated membership of over seven million.[10] But the appearance of representativeness, carefully handled, could carry more political weight than a genuinely large membership. For example, when Eleanor Roosevelt sought a group that would allow her to express her interest in American youth, she did not turn to the YMCA, the Pilgrim Fellowship, or the Junior Hadassah, all of which, notwithstanding substantial memberships, represented only portions of the younger generation. Instead she turned to the umbrella organization with which they were all affiliated, the American Youth Congress (AYC), quietly and securely controlled by the Communists since shortly after its founding in 1934.[11]

Some front organizations were more truly representative than others. The National Negro Congress had active local chapters in more than seventy cities, played an important role in recruiting black workers into the new CIO industrial unions, and in some areas had displaced the NAACP as the leading black community organization by the late 1930s.[12] The League of American Writers, organized by the Communists in 1935, had 750 members in the summer of 1939, including such notables as MacLeish, Ernest Hemingway, John Steinbeck, and Thornton Wilder. Mike Gold, a veteran party journalist who remembered the grubbier days of the early 1930s when the Communists despised all but "proletarian literature," boasted in June 1939 that "Red-baiting this League is now like Red-baiting the reading taste of the American mind."[13]

Even at the height of their strength, there were sharp limits on the actual political clout the Communists could wield, but their cultural influence was pervasive within the left wing of the New Deal and the CIO. They provided symbols, rallying cries, and language—one part revolutionary internationalist and one part patriotic populist—in which many issues were framed. The resulting ideological synthesis could be found in such popular works as Steinbeck's *Grapes of Wrath*, which sold a hundred thousand copies within two months of publication, or in Paul Robeson's rendition of Earl Robinson's choral "Ballad for Americans," which reached millions of listeners in a radio broadcast in the fall of 1939.

Popular Front culture offered a sentimental, egalitarian, and schematic world view, and provided a bridge by which the children of immigrants could adapt themselves to the culture of the New World without renouncing the ideals that had sustained their parents in the move from the Old. Midway through the "Ballad for Americans" a questioner from the chorus asks Robeson if he is an American. "Am I an American?" Robeson replied with patient amusement in his rich bass-baritone voice. "I'm just an Irish, Negro, Jewish, Italian, French and English, Spanish, Russian, Chinese, Polish, Scotch, Hungarian, Litvak, Swedish, Finnish, Canadian, Greek and Turk and Czech and double-check American." These were comforting words for non-Communist as well as Communist homes in such immigrant neighborhoods as Red Hook, Brownsville, and East Harlem.[14] And they struck a responsive chord among native-born middle-class liberals who felt threatened by economic disaster and the spread of fascism in Europe, and who wanted to identify themselves with the great insurgent movements of the decade. It was a measure of the strength of the CP's cultural influence that one of Eleanor Roosevelt's favorite records was "Six Songs for Democracy," recorded in Barcelona by International Brigade volunteers, just as it was a measure of the real limits of the CP's political strength that it was unable to get the President to lift the embargo blocking aid to Republican Spain.[15]

Party Decision-making

These were Browder's glory days. He ruled the party securely in 1939, buttressed by the gains of recent years and the approval of Moscow. In theory, power in the Communist party was delegated upward from the base. The members of the party elected delegates to a biannual national convention, and these delegates, in turn, elected a thirty-five-member national committee, a party chairman, and a general secretary. The CP's national committee, which usually met three times a year, elected from its membership a seven-member political committee, based in New York City, which guided the party's affairs on a day-to-day basis. The national committee also appointed secretaries for specific functions: coordinating legislative activity, trade-union work, party internal organization, and so on. In practice, however, power flowed from the top down. With Moscow's general approval Browder could and did shape the composition of the political committee to suit his own purposes. The political committee, in turn, determined the composition of the national committee, and the national committee oversaw the election of delegates to the national convention.[16]

At least once every year after assuming the post of general secretary, Browder traveled to Moscow for consultation with Comintern leaders. Beginning in 1935 Foster began to actively oppose Browder's policies at these meetings. In 1936 Foster and his close political ally Sam Darcy (CP district organizer in California in the early 1930s, and in eastern Pennsylvania at the end of the decade) had argued in Moscow for a direct Communist endorsement of Roosevelt's reelection effort. Browder, who had gone to Moscow favoring the launching of a farmer-labor third-party effort, countered Foster and Darcy by convincing Comintern leaders that Roosevelt would lose more votes than he would gain from a Communist endorsement. In the strategy that was finally accepted, Browder ran as the CP's own candidate for President while directing the party's principal attack against the Republicans.[17]

Foster and Browder's conflict continued when they returned to Moscow in January 1938. This time Foster argued for launching a farmer-labor party, while Browder favored strengthening existing ties with New Deal political forces. Once again Browder's position won the support of Comintern leaders. As a token of this support *Pravda* carried an article by Comintern spokesman Otto Kuusinen praising American Communists for the role they were playing within "the broad movement of democratic and progressive forces." The Communist party, Kuusinen declared, "has become a not unimportant factor in the political life of the United States."[18]

Another result of this 1938 meeting was Eugene Dennis's appointment to the CP's ruling political committee. Dennis, a Communist organizer since the mid-1920s, with wide and varied experience on the West Coast, in Wisconsin, and in the Comintern's international apparatus, was being groomed for leadership in the party.[19] He tended to side with Browder in intraleadership battles, though he displayed more independence—or, as his detractors charged, indecision—than other political committee members. With the exception of old-timer Alexander Bittelman, who headed up the party's Jewish bureau, Browder could count on support from the rest of the party's leaders in his continuing struggle with Foster.

A meeting of the political committee on March 23, 1939—one of the few such events for which a documentary record is available—was devoted exclusively to this conflict. Foster voiced his unhappiness with Browder's continued denigration of his political abilities, and with the recent demotion of Sam Darcy from the party's national committee. Foster admitted that he had been warned by Dimitrov in 1938 of "certain sectarian remnants" in his approach to the party's role within the Popular Front. But he complained that Browder had unjustifiably used such criticism in recent years virtually to shut him out of an active political role. The party, he insisted, was "not making the best use of my services."[20]

Browder remained silent while his allies took turns in savaging Foster. Dennis led off, accusing Foster of habitual ultra-leftism and warning that "if there isn't a certain change, or better understanding on the part of Foster, in particular regarding Browder, who is the leader of our Party, it will create serious difficulties for our Party and for Foster." Robert Minor, a veteran Communist leader of the 1920s who had once been an ardent backer of Jay Lovestone until, at an opportune moment, he switched his support to Lovestone's opponents, insinuated that Foster was not in full control of his mental faculties. Foster, he declared, "has been subjective, perhaps much more subjective than he would have been [had he] been in the best of health."

Jack Stachel, the CP's national organizational secretary; Charles Krumbein, New York state party leader; James Ford, the CP's foremost black leader and perennial vice-presidential candidate; Clarence Hathaway, editor of the *Daily Worker*; and Roy Hudson, the national trade-union secretary, all contributed disparaging assessments of Foster's political outlook and personal capacities. Gil Green, president of the Young Communist League and the member of the political committee who most strongly shared Browder's preoccupation with Americanizing the party's structure and outlook, summed up the discussion by suggesting that "in Foster we have an attempt always to think of the individual role of the Party without sufficient worrying about the relationship of the Party to this broader mass movement; when in Browder's thinking I feel constantly the main emphasis being put on the question of the Party and long-time alliances with the broad democratic front movement."[21]

No one spoke on Foster's behalf. His occasional ally, Bittelman, either did not attend the meeting or decided to remain silent.

In reply, Foster again insisted that he and Darcy had been treated unfairly, but added, "As far as me being a leader of the Party, I have no such ambitions." Browder reserved the last word for himself. Good Communists, he declared, knew how "to criticize in such a way that it cements the unity instead of endangering it," a consideration that "seems to carry very little weight in Foster's opinions."[22]

International Danger Signals

Foster could never successfully challenge Browder's coalitionist policies as long as they enjoyed Moscow's favor and continued to deliver political gains in the United States. And as long as the Soviet Union appeared to be Hitler's sole determined adversary in Europe, the Popular Front thrived. The Moscow trials of 1936–1938 made many supporters of the Soviet Union (including some Communists) uneasy, but had led to only a few defections from the League of American Writers and other front organizations. Literary critic Malcolm Cowley declared in the *New Republic* that liberal supporters of the Popular Front like himself regarded "the personal character of Stalin [as] relatively unimportant. Many of the policies for which he is praised or execrated may be regarded as the inevitable result of any effort to unify and strengthen the Soviet Union in the face of an international fascist alliance."[23]

During his second term in office Roosevelt grew increasingly concerned with the threat of German and Japanese expansionism. The Communists highly praised his October 1937 "Quarantine the Aggressor" speech, and for the next two years they hoped Roosevelt would commit the United States to an anti-fascist collective security agreement with the Western democracies and the Soviet Union. The Munich pact of September 1938 added a desperate edge to the Communists' already insistent calls for collective security. Browder declared that after this "blackest and most open treason . . . in modern history," committed by the British and French governments in their willingness to appease Hitler with the gift of Czechoslovakian territory, the American government had to assume international leadership in the defense against fascism. Several weeks after Munich he told a party rally in Madison Square Garden: "The United States and the Soviet Union . . . have it in their power, by acting together, to organize the peace-loving peoples of the world to smash once and for all the threat of the Rome-Berlin-Tokyo axis." A Soviet-American alliance might inspire the French and British peoples to turn their present leaders out of office in favor of leaders who would repudiate the appeasement policies.[24]

With Britain and France clearly unprepared to go to war to stop Hitler, American Communists began to consider for the first time the question of whether the United States actually had the military capacity to confront Nazi aggression. Although the Communists had long since abandoned general denunciations of war, they had continued their traditional opposition to armaments spending. In March 1938 Browder denounced legislation calling for increased naval spending then being considered by Congress, arguing that "to the degree that all progressives can swing the country to a practical policy of concerted action for peace, to that extent we also organize the masses to cut naval and military expenditures by making them obviously unnecessary."[25] The logic of that argument was less than compelling: the military defeats suffered by the Republican army in Spain had already shown that democratic ideology and popular enthusiasm were, in themselves, a poor match for artillery and dive-bombers.

Browder returned to Moscow for consultations after the Munich pact was signed. Presumably he discussed revising the party's line on military expenditures, because soon after his trip he coined a new slogan: "For Social and National Security." No longer would the Communists argue that military spending drained funds that should have gone to improve living conditions at home. In the post-Munich world, Browder declared at a meeting of the CP's national committee in December 1938, the old Communist position on armaments was outdated: "We cannot deny the possibility, even the probability, that only American arms can preserve the Americans from conquest by the Rome-Berlin-Tokyo alliance." The party needed to "clear away all remnants of the pacifist rubbish of opposing war by surrender to the war-makers."[26]

In January the Communists began publishing a new monthly journal entitled *National Issues*, edited by Eugene Dennis. Copying the format of liberal journals like the *New Republic* and *The Nation*, it sought to mobilize the Popular Front's supporters as an effective legislative lobby. Though devoting some attention to domestic issues—seeking to block further cuts in New Deal social progams and to curb the House Un-American Activities Committee—*National Issues* placed its chief emphasis on the necessity for preparing for war. The first issue stated the case bluntly: "There can be no social security for our people, if we neglect national security against aggression."[27] In March the magazine accused Republican congressmen of blocking appropriations for combat aircraft: "In these days when our national defense must be strengthened immediately, Republican advocacy of easing up the vital programs necessary for national security is nothing less than sabotage in the interests of Hitler, Mussolini and the Mikado."[28]

In the mid-1930s, continuing disillusionment with the fruits of American involvement in the First World War and growing fears of entanglement in a new European war had prompted Congress to pass neutrality legislation making it difficult for the government to come to the aid of belligerents in future wars. In the spring of 1939 congressional advocates of collective security made a futile attempt to revise the Neutrality Act to exempt victims of aggression from its provisions. In August, *National Issues* disconsolately noted the defeat of these efforts and concluded: "Congress tilted the precarious balance of international affairs toward war. . . . We know whom to blame and where to place the responsibility should another world war break out between the first and second sessions of the 76th Congress."[29]

The Communists' public enthusiasm for collective security masked some private doubts about the likelihood of such arrangements. England's and France's acquiescence in the dismemberment of Czechoslovakia came as a shock to many Communists, soon followed by the greater shock of the fall of Madrid and the final collapse of the Spanish Republic in the late winter of 1939. The Spanish Loyalist cause had been the great unifying symbol of the Popular Front, and the Communists continued to hope in the last months of 1938 that the American arms embargo would be lifted and the Republic would finally gain the military means necessary to its survival. More than three thousand Americans, many of them Communists, had gone to Spain to fight as volunteers in the International Brigades. Half had been killed, and of the survivors more than half bore wounds from the fighting. The American CP, small as it was, paid a proportionately higher price in blood to save the Spanish Republic than many of its more eminent sister parties in Europe. As one American CP leader subsequently noted, "There was hardly a Communist family that did not have a relative or a friend on the casualty lists."[30] After the final Republican offensive of the war, resulting in the bloody defeat on the Ebro in the summer of 1938, the International Brigades were withdrawn from combat.

Early in 1939 the last large contingents of Americans left Spain and returned to the United States. Communist veterans of the Abraham Lincoln Brigade took over many of the secondary leadership positions in the party and the YCL, or became officers of left-led unions like the United Electrical Workers and the International Longshoremen's and Warehousemen's Union. The veterans combined a passionate anti-fascism with a bitter sense of betrayal at the hands of English and French politicians who had taken shelter behind the hollow noninter-vention agreement while German and Italian supplies and troops poured into Spain to aid Franco. The American veterans of the war would not soon forget who had been responsible for their lack of planes, tanks, and artillery at Jarama and other battlefields. During the spring and summer of 1939, when CP leaders condemned the French and English governments as betrayers of democracy, their words only con-firmed what a large portion of the party's most trusted cadres already knew all too well from firsthand experience.[31]

Stalin's Warning

Other events that spring suggested to some Communists that the days of the Popular Front were indeed numbered. In March, Stalin delivered the keynote report to the 18th Congress of the Soviet Communist Party meeting in Moscow. He offered a lengthy and ambiguous analysis of the international situation. According to Stalin, a new imperialist war was already in its second year, a "war waged over a large territory stretching from Shanghai to Gibraltar," one fought for "an open re-division of the world and spheres of influence." On one side was a "bloc of three aggressor states" arrayed against "the non-aggressive democratic states," particularly England and France. Thus far the nonaggressive states had backed down consistently in the face of Axis demands, and Stalin asked if "the districts of Czechoslovakia were yielded to Germany as the price of an undertaking to launch war on the Soviet Union." If so, Stalin warned, the Western powers' "dan-gerous political game . . . may end in a serious fiasco for them."[32]

American Communists had a hard time deciphering the meaning of Stalin's speech. If the war Stalin described was an imperialist war to divide markets and spheres of influence, then, following Lenin's example in 1914, the Communists knew they should not take sides. If, however, the war was to be regarded as one of fascist aggression against peaceful democracies, then, according to the guidelines established at the 1935 Comintern congress, Communists should take the side of the nonaggressors. But if the Western powers were indeed conspiring to unleash Germany on the Soviet Union, the first duty of Communists would be to defend the USSR, regardless of other considerations. In retrospect, Stalin's remark that the Soviet party would not "allow our country to be drawn into conflict by warmongers who are accustomed to have others pull the chestnuts out of the fire for them" seems to stand out as a clear signal to the Western governments and to foreign Communists of the impending Nazi-Soviet rapprochement. But at the time its meaning was harder to discern. George Charney recalled that, after the 18th Congress, American Communists "were vaguely troubled, but even as we tried to read between the lines of [Stalin's] report, we refused to believe that differences with Chamberlain could possibly affect the anti-fascist policy of the Soviet Union." As for the "chestnuts," Charney asked, "What was so clearly indicated in this cryptic phrase used by Stalin as against the years of bloody conflict in Spain and a thousand flaming manifestoes?"[33]

In March the CP published the first American edition of the *History of the Communist Party of the Soviet Union (Bolsheviks)*. Browder called its publication "the greatest event in the ideological life of the Party." The book, prepared under Stalin's personal supervision, labeled recent conflicts in Asia and Europe "the second imperialist war," and took the "so-called democracies" to task for failing to stand up against the fascist powers.[34] While the message was ostensibly pro-collective security, the very term "second imperialist war" invited comparison with the "first imperialist war" of 1914–1918—an event not highly esteemed in Communist memory. The Communists had generally refrained from using the term "imperialist" in reference to the Western democracies in recent years, but *Daily Worker* editor Clarence Hathaway reminded a meeting of New York state party leaders at the end of March that they should keep "basic economic factors" always in view: "Capitalist contradictions, conflicts and crises are at the root of the general war now beginning. We as Communists cannot lose sight of that fact."[35]

And yet American Communists in the spring of 1939 could not be sure that the designation "capitalist" necessarily implied disapproval. At the 18th Congress in March, Comintern leader D. Z. Manuilsky praised the United States for defending its economic interests in Latin America and the Far East against fascist aggression, and contrasted its behavior with the appeasement policies of Britain and France. "Thus," he concluded, "the United States is strengthening resistance to Fascist aggression in other parts of the world, including Europe."[36] Even the French imperialists, low on the Communists' scale of approval in the spring of 1939, were reproved not for their imperialism but for their lack of ardor in defending those imperialist interests. In March the *Worker* (the Sunday edition of the *Daily Worker*) predicted that France's "200 Families" were plotting a "colonial Munich" in which they would make territorial concessions to the fascist governments: "The 'friends' of the colonial peoples proposed that the French people should 'disinterest' themselves, allowing the colonies to be handed over to Hitler's racial bestiality."[37] In the midst of such conflicting signals, most party members clung to the familiar and reassuring policies of the Popular Front.

In the spring of 1939 reports began appearing in the Western press raising the possibility of a pact between Germany and the Soviet Union. Although most of these reports came from sources hostile to the USSR, some left-wing and liberal journalists like Anna Louise Strong and Vincent Sheean speculated along similar lines. In July, *The Nation* asked whether Stalin might "try to get the democracies into a fight with Hitler while he stands by until they exhaust themselves," but concluded: "This variation seems remote."[38]

Browder denounced such speculations. Writing in the *New Masses* at the end of April, he declared: "Such a turnover could only be made by fascism's infamous fifth column—such as seized Madrid for Franco, such as prevents Britain from making a stand, such as threatens to make France fascist—and in the Soviet Union all the fifth-column conspirators have been hunted out and exterminated. No, the one area of the world where the Berlin-Rome-Tokyo Axis has not a single friend is precisely the Soviet Union."[39]

Browder followed this with his soon-to-be-famous assessment of the relative possibilities of a Nazi-Soviet accord and his election to the presidency of the chamber of commerce. A more cautious leader would have hedged his statements to allow for a graceful retreat. Foster and

Bittelman were already convinced that a Soviet-Nazi understanding was inevitable, but then they felt no particular commitment to the coalitionist policies of the preceding few years. Browder, on the other hand, did not want to let the Popular Front go, so he convinced himself that a Nazi-Soviet pact was impossible. It would not be the last time he allowed a propensity for wishful thinking to cloud his assessment of international developments.[40]

Though their leaders privately differed over the shape of the impending conflict, the Communists were convinced by the early summer of 1939 that Europe would be at war in a matter of weeks, and most assumed they would take their stand with those opposing Nazi aggression. The *Daily Worker* carried favorable reports on Polish military preparations and editorially praised Poland's determination not to become another Czechoslovakia.[41] Throughout the first three weeks in August the *Daily Worker* maintained its agitation for American rearmament. On August 20 Harry Gannes, the *Daily Worker*'s chief foreign affairs commentator, asked: "Will Hitler assassinate world peace this week? . . . Only those who refuse to see can fail to observe that the Nazis have made every preparation for plunging the world into war."[42]

Until August 22, 1939, MacLeish's words "America is promises to take" seemed to many Americans—Communist and non-Communist—to sum up the lessons of a decade of struggle. The Communists, by committing themselves to the defense of democracy in America and in Spain, had made significant political gains. Many liberals who had formerly viewed the Communists with suspicion or disdain now eagerly sought their cooperation around issues of common concern. In the eyes of many Americans the Soviet Union's advocacy of collective security had ended its status as a pariah nation. Four hundred prominent American intellectuals signed a statement at the beginning of August repudiating the charge that the Soviet Union was a "totalitarian" society. Two months later W. H. Auden would provide an assessment of the 1930s very different from MacLeish's position, in a poem entitled "September 1, 1939":

> I sit in one of the dives
> on Fifty-second Street
> uncertain and afraid
> As the clear hopes expire
> of a low dishonest decade.[43]

3 WAR IN EUROPE
August 22 to December 1939

> What we have to deal with is an imperialist war in which the rulers
> of both sides are equally guilty; it is not a war waged for the
> destruction of fascism, but is carried on to extend and perpetuate
> imperialist control over the world. The character of this war in no
> principal respect can be said to differ from that of the late world
> war.
>
> —EARL BROWDER, September 13, 1939

> Unlike the first world war, the second world war against the Axis
> states from the very outset assumed the character of an anti-fascist
> war, a war of liberation.
>
> —JOSEPH STALIN, 1946[1]

ON AUGUST 21, 1939, the *New York Times* reported that the Soviet
Union and Nazi Germany had signed a seven-year trade agreement in
Berlin, providing the Russians with extensive credits to purchase German manufactured goods in exchange for Russian grain and raw materials. The agreement, the *Times* noted, stirred uneasiness in London
and Warsaw about Soviet intentions in the developing German-Polish
crisis. Closer to home, the news stirred uneasiness in the editorial
offices of the *Daily Worker* and *Freiheit*. The editors of the two New
York–based Communist dailies, unsure of how to read the meaning
of the agreement, printed articles minimizing its significance.[2]

Next morning, August 22, the Soviet news agency Tass announced
that Germany's Foreign Minister Joachim von Ribbentrop would fly
to Moscow the following day to sign a nonaggression pact with the
Soviet Union. Melech Epstein, an editor of *Freiheit*, heard the news
in the CP's national headquarters: "The party building on 12th and
13th streets was hushed. Party functionaries avoided talking to each
other. The worst sufferers were the switchboard operators. They were
swamped with telephone calls all day long by worried Communists
unable to credit their own eyes. . . . Groups of harassed people kept

coming to the two party papers, on their lips the same insistent question, 'Is it possible?'"[3]

First Reactions

Party members heard news of the pact from one another, from the radio, or from the non-Communist press. They did not learn it from the *Daily Worker,* which maintained a tight-lipped silence on the new turn in Soviet-German relations in its August 22 edition. Browder, caught totally off guard by the news, avoided reporters all day.

On August 23, as the CP's political committee assembled in emergency session, and Ribbentrop arrived in Moscow, the *Daily Worker* devoted most of its front page to an editorial by Harry Gannes on "The Soviet Union and Non-Aggression." Mustering his most authoritative tone, Gannes declared: "German fascism has suffered a serious blow in prestige in its own country as well as in the world. The author of the anti-Comintern pact, which sought to deceive the world as to the real imperialist, robber aims of German imperialism under the mask of 'saving the world from Bolshevism,' stands more clearly than ever before as an imperialist aggressor." He asserted that the pact would weaken Hitler's hold over the German people, strengthen Polish independence, and inspire anti-fascist forces around the world. Pointing out that the USSR already had nonaggression pacts with China, Poland, and Italy, he stressed that each such agreement included a clause providing that "in the event one of the parties invades or commits an act of aggression against a third nation . . . the other party (the Soviet Union) is not bound to the treaty, is free to act in defense of peace."[4]

But the actual text of the nonaggression pact, printed in the *Daily Worker* and other American newspapers the following day, contained no such clause. Even so, many Communists reasoned, in the absence of formal written commitments the Soviet Union would still act as if such a clause did exist. The September edition of the *Young Communist Review,* which went to the printer in the last week of August, expressed full confidence that "should Germany undertake aggression against Poland, the Soviet Union would denounce its pact." And as late as September 1, as German tanks rolled across the Polish border, the *Daily Worker* predicted that the USSR would sell armaments to Poland and, if requested, provide military aid.[5]

Browder finally met with impatient reporters in his office on the ninth floor of party headquarters in the late afternoon of August 23. The *New York Times* reporter noted that Browder spoke with "complete nonchalance," though those who knew him better noticed he had forgone the scholarly pipe he usually favored in public and was chain-smoking cigarettes. Browder told the gathered reporters and party functionaries who had come in to lend moral support that he had noticed "some public interest in the opinions of the Communist Party about the latest international developments." The pact, he declared, was "a wonderful contribution to peace," and he thought it would be a good idea if England, France, and the United States all signed similar pacts with the Russians. He dismissed the suggestion that the pact in any way threatened Polish security and denied it meant the end of the Popular Front. When questioned about the reaction of the party's membership to the pact, Browder replied: "I think that the reaction of the membership of our Party is one of rather complete understanding and agreement."[6]

The Party's Crisis

Browder's studied calm may have concealed his own distress over the news from Moscow, but it could not conceal the depth of the party's crisis. Opponents of the CP believed that the final collapse of American communism was at hand. The bitterly anti-Communist social-democratic newspaper the *New Leader* declared in its September 2 edition: "The Communist Party is virtually smashed, although it will take a few weeks for optimists in its ranks to understand the full extent of the damage. It is at present like a decapitated chicken running wildly around the barnyard."[7]

The Communists did indeed display a kind of frenetic, directionless activity at first. Most party leaders had not foreseen the crisis, had no way of knowing Soviet motives in signing the pact, and were at a loss whether to patch up or discard the battered remains of the Popular Front. They could hardly adjourn party activities and close down its press for a month or so until the situation became more clear. They had to keep talking, whether or not they had anything to say. Day after day in late August and early September the *Daily Worker* offered a steady diet of hastily thrown together and meaningless justifications of the latest turn in Soviet foreign policy. Browder asserted on August 30: "At one blow, the Soviet-German pact has begun to restore the

Open Door in the Far East, to dissolve the threat to the Monroe Doctrine, and has given the first ray of hope that Europe may survive."[8]

Browder and other party spokesmen abandoned these tenuous arguments almost as quickly as they dredged them up. The real battle within the party's ranks would not be won with appeals to reason, but with the far more potent appeal of the loyalty the Communists felt toward the Soviet Union and the party.

While confronting their own doubts, CP members suffered continual attack from the outside. Jewish Communists in New York City's garment districts were met with derisive greetings of "Heil Hitler." George Charney spoke before hostile crowds in Jewish neighborhoods in New York and recalled, "We . . . developed a grim sense of humor, as when one speaker in Flatbush, backed up against the wall by a heckling audience, cried out, 'All right, I'll tear up the pact.'"[9]

The initial surprise and the inability of party leaders to offer any definitive policy increased the uncertainty felt by party members, and briefly permitted a freer-than-usual internal discussion to be carried on. Melech Epstein refused to write anything in *Freiheit* in defense of the pact—a breach of discipline that in ordinary circumstances would have led to his demotion or expulsion. Instead he found that "the hostile air outside and the demoralization within prevented the party hierarchy from challenging those few who were loud in their denunciation of the pact. On the contrary, they were treated with patience and simulated understanding, the party anxious not to aggravate a threatening crisis."[10]

But this degree of tolerance did not last long. Two days after the start of the war the *Daily Worker* unleashed its most powerful weapon: "We maintain that as long as there is one Socialist state in the world surrounded by hostile capitalist powers, it is the most important and first duty of that Socialist state to prevent by all means at hand any kind of move that would threaten its destruction."[11]

Every other question paled in significance when measured against the duty of Communists to defend the survival of the USSR. Granville Hicks, literary editor of the *New Masses*, met with Browder in early September in the vain hope of resolving his own doubts about the pact. Browder brought all his powers of low-key persuasiveness to bear on Hicks, telling him (according to Hicks's later recollection): "Don't think I underestimate the seriousness of your criticisms. . . . All of them have been in my mind. In fact, what disturbs me most is that I have already faced doubts that haven't even occurred to you yet, and I wonder what will happen when they do." But for all his tone of weary reasonableness, Browder made it clear to Hicks that he either had to accept the new line or get out. "Though he could discuss matters more reasonably than most of the steadfast Communists I had talked with, he came to the same conclusion: Whatever the Soviet Union did was right."[12]

The Party Rallies

The August 22 announcement of the pact fell on a Tuesday, the regular meeting night for CP branches, and branch leaders must have been hard pressed to interpret the event to their stunned followers. New York City party leaders made desperate efforts the following week to round up enough speakers to cover branch meetings throughout the city on the evening of August 29. Traveling from meeting to meeting, top party leaders like Robert Minor and Israel Amter convinced the members to vote almost unanimous support for the pact. During the following weeks the Communists held mass meetings in Manhattan, Brooklyn, Chicago, and other strongholds to rally their followers.[13]

Communists were a tiny minority in the country as a whole, but they were a highly concentrated minority. They tended to live in the same neighborhoods, they spent most of their social life with other Communists, and their children played together. Breaking with the party over the pact would have meant accepting a status as a social pariah, and few were prepared for that step. The decisive act in restoring party unity was played out at Madison Square Garden on the evening of September 11. Despite wishful predictions by the CP's opponents that it would never again fill Madison Square Garden, twenty thousand Communists crowded in to cheer denunciations of the war. James Wechsler, who had resigned from the CP two years earlier because of his uneasiness with the Moscow trials, covered the rally for *The Nation*. He reported that there could no longer be any question that the Communist rank and file would stick with the party: "The thing that stood out in the meeting was the almost desperate huddling together of people confronted by a monumental world crisis, taking refuge in a reaffirmation of their own solidarity."[14]

The party suffered a few defections in September, including those of Hicks, Epstein, and some minor functionaries. In areas of the country where Communists were less concentrated than in New York, membership loss was more serious. But the majority of American Communists—leaders, cadres, and rank and file—remained in the party and, allowing for the CP's normally high attrition rate, would stick with it for the twenty-two-month life span of the Nazi-Soviet pact. Those who stayed may not have been happy, and may have looked back wistfully on the golden days of Popular Front respectability. But they stayed. They felt this was a testing period in which they would have to prove their mettle. As Wechsler described the Communists' state of mind in mid-September, though "perturbed by defections around them, they calmly recite Lenin's prophecy: When the locomotive of history takes a sharp turn, only the steadfast cling to the train."[15]

For liberals and independent radicals who had allied themselves with the Communists in the Popular Front, no similar satisfactions were available. Many felt a sense of personal betrayal. The *New Republic*'s editors labeled the pact "Stalin's Munich." In early September they noted with mock solemnity "unconfirmed reports from the Union Square front" that "fellow-travellers are dropping like ripe plums in a hurricane." The *New Republic* was in a position to know, for many of the ripest plums could be found on its staff and among its regular contributors. Former Soviet sympathizers like Louis Fischer, Vincent Sheean, and Ralph Bates used its columns that fall to announce their break with Stalinism.

Disillusioned fellow travelers could hardly expect Stalin to care much one way or the other about their opinions, but they had a more vulnerable target closer at hand. The *New Republic* declared in its issue of September 6: "The American Communists, who are now in such a wretched position, have only themselves to blame. For many years they prided themselves on viewing world affairs in a coldly realistic light. Their prophecies were more accurate than those of anyone else, they said. . . . If they were right about collective security, Stalin is wrong, but we take a little unholy delight in their present discomfort."[16]

Resignations began to pour into Popular Front organizations. The American League for Peace and Democracy, which had the promotion of collective security as its primary function, was especially hard hit. One former ALPD officer estimated that the group, which had about twenty thousand members in August, lost about a thousand members a month until its disbandment early the following year.[17] The League of American Writers was also ravaged. W. H. Auden was one of the first to leave, declaring in his letter of resignation:

> Whatever excellent reasons there may be for the Nazi-Soviet Pact, it has destroyed the political Popular Front in the Democratic countries. Liberals like myself were eager for a collaboration between the Soviet Union and the Democracies because we hoped that both would profit, the latter finds its reactionary elements weakened, the former feels less need for a dictatorship which, we believed, was in some measure due to the hostility of the democracies. That hope was proved vain. . . . The American League of Writers was founded, I understand, as a Popular Front body. As in most such organizations, the Liberals were lazy, while the Communists did all the work and, in consequence, won the executive power they deserved. This did not matter much so long as the Popular Front was a reality: now it does.[18]

The league declined from a peak membership of 830 just prior to the signing of the Nazi-Soviet pact to less than 700 members a year and a half later, and most of these were brought in under newly relaxed membership requirements to flesh out the ranks. Except for Theodore Dreiser and Richard Wright, few big names remained in the organization after August 1939.[19] The American Student Union lost its executive secretary, Joseph Lash, several other officers, and a large portion of its campus membership in disputes over Soviet policies. The only front organizations that survived the fall of 1939 relatively intact were those, like the National Negro Congress and the American Youth Congress, which did not have any major public functions scheduled for the fall, and could thus postpone confrontations over the war issue.

The party did its best to cast apostate fellow travelers into utter darkness. Mike Gold wrote a series of articles in the *Daily Worker* denouncing the "literary renegades" who were abandoning the League of American Writers. "Capitalism," he wrote, "so long as it lasts, must produce, as from some infernal stamping mill, generations of thieves, of fascists, of prostitutes, of mental cripples, and these social traitors and renegades."[20] The Communists never seemed to reflect on the fact that a time might come when they would again want to ally themselves with the "traitors and renegades" of the Popular Front days.

The "Second Imperialist War"

In the first weeks after the signing of the pact, in the absence of any clear guidelines from the Soviet Union, some Communist leaders groped for a way to continue to apply the Popular Front line in the new situation. For a while, the best possible solution seemed to lie with a local variation of the "two-front strategy" advocated by Harry Pollitt, general secretary of the British Communist party. Pollitt wanted Communists in Britain and France to support the war but to oppose their own governments as insufficiently anti-fascist in conviction. Although American Communists called for the United States to remain neutral from the first days of the war in September 1939, they initially left little doubt as to which side they hoped to see defeated. The September 11 *Freiheit* declared that the war was "similar to the previous ones in Manchuria, Ethiopia, Spain, and China in the sense that it is not difficult to point a finger to the aggressor." The same week the *New Masses* asked the Administration to extend economic assistance to the Polish government: "A short war—shortened with our economic aid—a war that ends with a crushing defeat for German fascism, is the best guarantee that our own fight for peace will be won."[21]

The Communists, though bitterly condemning Chamberlain and Daladier, continued to express friendly sentiments toward Roosevelt. Party leaders addressed a public letter to Roosevelt on September 11 expressing their "firm accord with the stand of the President . . . against American involvement in the war," and declaring that "the hope for firm national unity lies in rallying all Americans . . . in support of the President who has best expressed the hearts and minds of the people."[22]

Yet even in the first weeks after the pact, an alternative interpretation of the war was being formulated by some party leaders in opposition to the "two-front" line. The day after the pact was signed, Bittelman delivered a two-hour lecture to the editors of the party's newspapers, devoting most of it to a denunciation of British imperialism. The party continued to hammer away at the "Municheers" in the English and French governments, although it was no longer entirely clear whether their treachery lay in their past refusal to fight Hitler or their present willingness to do exactly that.[23]

Browder's speech to the big Madison Square Garden rally on September 11 seesawed between anti-fascist and anti-imperialist themes, but saved its harshest criticisms for the Nazis, "the immediate instigators and perpetrators of war." Browder's speech was set in type the following day to run in the September 13 *Daily Worker*. But before the issue went to press a cable arrived from Moscow with quotes from an advance copy of a *Pravda* editorial that treated the Allies and Nazi Germany as equally responsible for the war's origins. It was too late to revise the original text of Browder's speech, which, in any case, had already been heard by twenty thousand party members and supporters, and quoted in the non-Communist press. Instead Browder had to resort to the awkward device of granting an exclusive interview to Harry Gannes in which he expounded the new line—without admitting that anything had changed. The *Daily Worker* carried the interview on the front page and relegated the text of the now outdated speech to an inside page. Browder told Gannes that "the character of the war now developing is that of a struggle between two rival imperialist groups for the domination of the world," a struggle which had "nothing to offer the masses of any participating country except death and destruction."[24]

Browder soon received confirmation that he had jumped in the right direction. In England, Harry Pollitt refused to abandon his advocacy of the "two-front" line, and was removed from the post of general secretary by other British party leaders in October (though he was allowed to remain a member of the party, and would resume its leadership when the international situation went through another dramatic transformation in late June 1941).[25] Browder was probably as unhappy with the requirements of the new Soviet line as Pollitt, but he chose to retreat, fighting only rearguard actions to restrain those American CP leaders who welcomed the return of more militant policies.

The CP's political committee met in New York City on September 14. The verbatim transcript of the meeting that Browder preserved in his papers shows how, within the constraints imposed by Soviet foreign policy, Communist leaders still differed widely on policies to be followed in the United States. Bittelman, who had been playing an increasingly prominent role in the CP leadership in recent weeks, opened the meeting, and warned of the need for "mental readiness for quick, for rapid changes in the world situation"—a lesson that few in the room could have missed during the last month. Bittelman wanted the

Communists to make a sharp break with Popular Front policies. The party needed to abandon outdated slogans calling for "social and national security," for revision of the Neutrality Act, and for aid to the Polish people. More important, they needed to recognize that under the radically altered political circumstances following the outbreak of the war, socialism and revolution were once again practical questions of the day. In England and France, Communists had the responsibility of "turning the imperialist war into civil war," as Lenin had done in Russia in 1917. Bittelman admitted the American situation was a little different. Yet here too events could move rapidly, and in preparation the party needed to revive socialism as a slogan of agitation. For the last few years the *Daily Worker* had been carrying the slogan "Jobs, Security, Democracy and Peace" below its masthead; Bittelman now wanted "Socialism" substituted for "Peace." Foster supported Bittelman's call for a revived revolutionary outlook.

Bittelman and Foster found the new situation congenial since it legitimated a more intransigently leftist politics, and undermined the unity of the Browder wing of the political committee. Eugene Dennis and Gil Green, among Browder's most articulate allies in the past, chose to straddle the questions Bittelman raised in his presentation. Dennis criticized the party press for an oversimplified blurring of distinctions between England and France on the one hand, and Nazi Germany. Though these countries were all now engaged in an imperialist war, the Communists "should not draw [the] foolish conclusion that therefore a fascist regime is no different than a bourgeois democratic regime." But he went on to argue that "while not for a moment weakening our fight or exposure of Nazism in all its brutality, at the same time with equal strength . . . [we should] expose the Chamberlains and their policies." Green took partial issue with Bittelman's analysis of the European situation: "The immediate thing now is not social revolution in England but a fight for democracy." But he felt constrained to add that this was a struggle that could "develop into [a] fight for [the] revolutionary transformation of imperialist war into civil war."

Browder felt that the kind of sharp leftward swing that Bittelman was calling for could have disastrous consequences for the Communists: "It is very important that we keep [the] continuity of our line before the masses through every change. . . . We must completely disarm that angle of attack against our Party which is perhaps the most dangerous of all, the continuation of the . . . feeling that—after all the Party makes its changes disconnectedly.''

Taking up the question of reviving the slogan of socialism, Browder carefully covered his left flank, arguing that Lenin had continued to advance democratic, rather than openly socialist, demands right up until the Bolshevik Revolution. "If that was a good tactic in 1917," he argued, "it is a thousand-fold more called for . . . in Europe at the moment and especially in the United Sates. I don't think we can put the slogan of socialism as a slogan of today alongside with jobs, security and democracy.'' Browder warned against any hasty reversal of the CP's support for revising neutrality legislation, for that would only seem to be a "confirmation of all the slanders against the Soviet Union and the CP that the Non-Aggression Pact is an alliance with Hitler.'' But Foster was unimpressed: "Everybody in this country understands that the move to repeal this Neutrality bill . . . is a step to help France and Great Britain.''

Browder was clearly on the defensive in this meeting, shorn of his usual allies, obviously aware that the tone of Bittelman's and Foster's position was more in line with the new requirements of Soviet policy than his own. But he still hoped to minimize the political damage as the party moved left: if genuine continuity were not possible, then perhaps the appearance of continuity could be salvaged. Here, too, he was to be disappointed.

Unable to resolve its differences, the political committee adjourned until the sixteenth. In the interim a subcommittee consisting of Browder, Foster, Bittelman, Stachel, Green, and Dennis met to consider the questions of the socialism slogan and the Neutrality Act. Though Bittelman took issue with Browder's reading of Lenin's strategy in 1917, arguing that the slogan "All Power to the Soviets" could not be understood as anything except a call for socialism, he eventually agreed to withdraw his proposal. The group initially deadlocked over the Neutrality Act; Browder, Stachel, and Green favored continuing support for its revision, while Foster, Bittelman, and Dennis opposed such support. Browder finally agreed to a compromise formula in which the party would "favor neither revision, nor repeal or retention of the Neutrality Act" in the upcoming special session of Congress. Browder also argued, without strong opposition, that the party should withhold judgment on its future relations with the Roosevelt Administration, though even he was no longer optimistic about the long-term prospects of the "Roosevelt coalition."[26]

After three days of meetings the Communist leaders found themselves in sufficient agreement to piece together a manifesto entitled "Keep America Out of Imperialist War!", released on September 19 in the name of the CP's national committee. In addition to the by now familiar characterization of the war as one "between rival imperialisms for world domination," the statement laid the groundwork for a new united-front effort: "The previous alignment into democratic and fascist camps loses its former meaning. The democratic camp today consists, first of all, of those who fight against the imperialist war."[27]

The Fall of Poland

The Communists might have been able to effect a more graceful transition from their united front against fascism to their new united front against the war had it not been for the precipitate collapse of Polish resistance in the first weeks of September. The secret protocols of the nonaggression pact had divided Poland into German and Russian spheres of influence. On September 3, Ribbentrop instructed the German ambassador in Moscow to inform the Russians that the German high command expected to complete the defeat of the Polish army within a few weeks. He suggested that Russian armies prepare to occupy eastern Poland at the earliest possible date.[28]

The Red Army invaded on September 17. Molotov went on the radio to proclaim that the Soviet government was fulfilling a "sacred duty" in offering a "helping hand to its brother Ukrainians and Byelo-Russians who inhabit Poland." Within hours New York Communists were out on the streets with a leaflet headlined "USSR Defends Poland." The *Daily Worker* greeted the event with a front-page editorial attacking the "treacherous and semi-fascist Poiish government." National minorities in eastern Poland, "freed from the tyrannical rule of the greedy landlords and the corrupt nobility," were at last granted the "freedom, happiness and peace" enjoyed by their Soviet liberators. "Truly," the editorial declared, "the Soviet Union has scored another triumph for human freedom—destined for the brightest page of world history." The *Freiheit* used a special argument to reassure its Jewish readers. After all, it was not just Ukrainians and Byelorussians who inhabited eastern Poland. "*At least two million Jews have been lib-*

erated; at least two million Jews who were in mortal fear of Nazi oppression and degradation are to fear no more."[29]

The day after the invasion, Germany and the USSR issued a joint communiqué declaring that Soviet actions in Poland had not violated the "spirit or letter of the Non-Aggression Pact." On September 27 Ribbentrop returned to Moscow to sign a number of public and secret agreements for the further division of Eastern Europe into Nazi and Soviet spheres of influence. The two governments issued another joint communiqué, expressing their common belief that recent military operations had "created a sure foundation for a lasting peace in Eastern Europe," and their common hope that peace could now be negotiated between Germany and the Western Allies. The failure to conclude such a peace, they asserted, would "demonstrate the fact that England and France are responsible for the continuation of the war."[30]

To veteran anti-Communists, the events in Poland only confirmed what they had been arguing all along: the Soviet Union was a ruthless and aggressive dictatorship in no way preferable to Nazi Germany. The American press hammered away at this theme in the fall of 1939. *Colliers* magazine thanked Stalin and Hitler for "dropping the pretense of hating each other's gizzards" and eliminating "all doubt except in the minds of incurable dreamers that there is any real difference between Communism and Fascism."[31] Some disenchanted veterans of the Popular Front wrote similarly. Vincent Sheean, in the *New Republic,* called the history of Stalin's rule one of "a counter-revolutionary and anti-socialist regime akin to fascism."[32] Many liberals now regarded the Communists as the equivalent of Nazi Bundists, a subversive conspiracy working in the interest of a foreign power to undermine American democracy.

The epithet "Communazi," coined by a reporter in September 1939, captured the essence of the argument that the totalitarian beliefs of the radical right and left belonged to a common camp. In the fall of 1939 and throughout 1940 dozens of liberal organizations and unions adopted "Communazi" resolutions, barring members of the CP and fascist groups from joining or holding office. Even the American Civil Liberties Union, which had devoted a considerable portion of its energies since its founding to defending the civil liberties of Communists, adopted a Communazi resolution in February 1940 excluding from its own governing committees anyone belonging to organizations "supporting the totalitarian governments of the Soviet Union and of the

Fascist and Nazi countries (such as the Communist Party, the German-American Bund and others).'' The resolution was used to purge Elizabeth Gurley Flynn, a charter member of the ACLU, from the organization's board of directors on the basis of her membership in the Communist party. Only a steadily dwindling band of liberals clung to the old adage that there were no enemies on the left.[33]

Doggedly loyal to the current Soviet line, American Communists did little to restore their tarnished image in the months that followed. While still ostensibly holding both sides responsible for the war, the *Daily Worker* reserved its sternest criticisms for the Allies. The Communists never went so far as to echo the Soviet foreign office's sentiment that ''fascism is a matter of taste,'' but the party's publications consistently absolved the Nazis of any special responsibility for the war. A November editorial in the *Daily Worker* denounced ''imperialist atrocities'' committed by the Nazis in occupied Czechoslovakia, but hastened to add that these were no worse than those ''equally monstrous crimes'' that the British had carried out in India in the past.[34]

On occasion, party statements even left listeners with the impression that the Nazis were in some ways preferable to the Allies. Hitler, after all, had made his peace with the Soviet Union, while British and French intentions remained unclear and seemed to hold a more sinister potential. In October the CP's political committee blamed the war on ''the bourgeoisie of all belligerent powers'' but accused the British ruling class of plotting to ''bring to power in Germany that section of the bourgeoisie which will immediately engage in military intervention against the USSR.'' The CP leaders stressed the need to ''*prevent the British and French ruling classes . . . from transforming the present war between the two imperialist groups into a counter-revolutionary imperialist war against the Soviet Union.*''[35] The Communists were not wrong, as far as they went, in suspecting that England and France were planning to attack the Soviet Union: during the months of the ''phony war'' the Allied General Staff seriously considered various schemes to broaden the war with an invasion of Russia. But the Communists made their mistake in underestimating the greater dangers posed by a German military triumph in Western Europe.[36]

In the years after the end of the Nazi-Soviet pact many individual Communists claimed to have had misgivings in 1939–1941 over the way the party seemed to attach the lion's share of war guilt to the Allies. Such claims might be dismissed as self-serving rationalizations (which, in some instances, they no doubt were). But it is significant that in the midst of the German blitzkrieg of April 1940 the *Daily Worker* chose to explain that "the war aims of the German imperialists are just as indefensible as the war aims of London, Paris—and Washington. But the forces driving for war in this country are not seeking to involve the United States on the side of German imperialism. They are seeking to involve the United States on the side of the Allied powers. Here is the crucial danger to America's peace. Here must the people direct their utmost vigilance to prevent a repetition of the 1917 swindle."[37] Once again the myth of the iron-willed Bolshevik, coolly and incisively dissecting the meaning of current events, always taking the long view, helped Communists to justify to themselves the supression of their sympathy for France and England and their detestation of Nazi Germany.

The Break with Roosevelt

The Communists' shift in domestic political perspective lagged behind their shift in international perspective. For the first month and a half of the war, the Communists avoided all direct attacks on Roosevelt. Roosevelt was genuinely popular among the party rank and file, and many Communists were reluctant to sever the connection with the New Deal that had brought them such great political gains in the later 1930s. In an article in *The Communist* in the spring of 1940, Eugene Dennis complained that "sections of the Party" had dragged their feet when the decision was finally made to denounce Roosevelt: "In several state organizations a certain hesitancy and moments of vacillation were exhibited in helping to reorientate our comrades in the trade unions on the third term question, in New York, for example." He blamed "right opportunist tendencies" that had developed during the Popular Front for "a certain one-sided estimate of the role and policies of the Roosevelt Administration."[38] Browder was among the most reluctant to break with Roosevelt, but was left little choice if he intended to remain as the party's leader.

When Browder visited Moscow for the last time before the war, in October 1938, Dimitrov arranged with him to establish shortwave communications should the international situation require clandestine contact. Browder's radio remained silent until late in September 1939, when Dimitrov sent two separate coded messages outlining the position the Comintern expected American Communists to take on the war. For the most part Dimitrov reiterated what the *Daily Worker* was already arguing: Both sides were equally guilty for the war; the anti-fascist slogans of the Popular Front should be replaced by anti-imperialist slogans; the Soviet Union had freed the grateful peoples of eastern Poland from the "danger of foreign enslavement." But there was one significant addition. Dimitrov insisted that the American government could no longer be regarded sympathetically by Communists. His first message declared:

> USA will not be an exception. Even remaining neutral, USA with powerful financial oligarchy will inevitably take the path of intensifying reaction, if only because it knows that war raises the issue of its overthrow.

And his second message continued:

> Must stop imperialist bourgeoisie of USA from providing others, enriching itself, and later entering to save crumbling capitalist system.[39]

Browder could not expect to receive more direct instructions to pull out all the stops in the party's criticism of the American government. Yet he still hesitated to attack Roosevelt by name and kept other CP leaders from doing so. As late as October 22, when Foster criticized the Administration for shifting to an imperialist foreign policy, he resorted to the device of blaming Undersecretary of State Sumner Welles, "one of the most reactionary elements in the State Department," rather than directly attacking the President.[40]

Roosevelt's personal immunity in the Communist press would not end until late October, when federal agents arrested Browder for violating passport laws. Browder, stung by his arrest, now bitterly turned on Roosevelt, charging in early November that "the President and his Administration succumb more and more ever day to this greed for profits by American monopoly capital, and make use of its former prestige among the masses to secure their acceptance of the program of Wall Street. The economic royalists, who a short time ago hated the President . . . have rushed to his side again and are the most vociferous in protesting their undying love and devotion—and the President reciprocates their advances."[41]

Browder's indictment on charges of having made false statements in applying for a passport stemmed from his appearance before the House Un-American Activities Committee in early September. In the summer of 1939 HUAC chairman Martin Dies learned that the Department of Justice, in the course of compiling materials on past passport violations as the basis of projected anti-espionage legislation, had been reviewing old charges that Browder had traveled abroad under assumed names during the 1920s. The Justice Department had no immediate plans for taking action on these ancient charges, but Dies, seeing a chance to embarrass Roosevelt, subpoenaed Browder.

Rhea Whitley, counsel for the committee, opened the session of September 5 by asking Browder if he had ever been known by other names. Browder, unaware of the trap that was about to be sprung, replied that he had used the names Ward and Dixon as pen names. Whitley dropped this line of questioning, and for the next several hours committee members and Browder sparred inconsequentially over the CP's size, structure, and intentions. Midway through the afternoon session Whitley suddenly asked, "Mr. Browder, have you ever traveled under a false passport?" Whether lulled into carelessness from spending so many hours giving testimony, or confident that no harm could come from such outdated charges, Browder replied "I have" before the party's attorney, Joseph Brodsky, could stop him. Alerted to his blunder by Brodsky, Browder declined to answer further questions about his passport on Fifth Amendment grounds, but the damage had been done. Newspapers the next day carried front-page accounts of Browder's admission, and *The Nation* declared that "since Mr. Browder has admitted using a false passport, we do not see how the Department of Justice could avoid seeking an indictment."[42]

Justice Department officials resented the way the Dies committee had forced their hand in the Browder case, but by the time the indictment was prepared and released it seemed to them a convenient and "nonpolitical" way of satisfying the increasing popular demand that the government do something to suppress the Communist "fifth column." The menacing international situation revived the fear of conspiracy and the nativism that has always been an undercurrent and that dominated American political life in the years during and just after American participation in the First World War. In such times the Bill of Rights is treated by many as a bill of revocable privileges. Martin Dies argued that even legal and open activities by the Communists were part of a subversive conspiracy, undeserving of the normal constitutional guarantees of freedom of speech and political association: "A fifth column for propaganda must operate largely in the open even though its purposes and controls remain secret. . . . In the last analysis . . . the fifth column of propaganda may be more menacing to our national security than the fifth column of espionage."[43]

Browder's indictment in October for passport fraud was followed by similar indictments in December against William Weiner, the CP's treasurer, and Harry Gannes of the *Daily Worker.* That same month William Schneiderman, district organizer of the California CP, went to court to defend himself against a government suit seeking revocation of his citizenship for allegedly concealing membership in the Workers (Communist) party during naturalization proceedings in 1927. In late December, Secretary of the Interior Harold Ickes noted in his diary that at a recent cabinet meeting Attorney General Frank Murphy "commented with satisfaction on the indictments of Communists that have already been brought by his special grand jury in the District. Of course they are not indicted as Communists, because it is not illegal to belong to that party, but every possible effort is being made to indict any Communist who has violated the criminal laws in any respect."[44]

Roosevelt, or at least some of his subordinates, briefly considered launching a direct legal attack on the CP as "seditious." Speaking to a party meeting at Boston's Symphony Hall on November 5, Browder attributed the rising war hysteria in the United States to the fear of the American ruling class that the conflict between the Allies and Germany would prepare the way for successful Communist revolutions in Europe: "They are preparing to come to the rescue of their class brothers in Europe against the rise of the revolutionary working class." Then, perhaps remembering Dimitrov's injunction that America should not be treated as an exception in the present crisis, Browder added that "America itself, despite the political backwardness as yet of our working class, is technically, objectively, the country which is the most ripe, the most prepared, for a quick transition to socialism, for which it lacks only the understanding and the will of the masses to that goal."[45]

Browder certainly had no illusions that a society lacking "only" revolutionary consciousness among its working class was teetering on the brink of class war, however "objectively" it might be suited for socialism. But the newspapers the next day treated the speech as if it was a call to the barricades. The New York *Herald Tribune* declared: "That phrase 'a quick transition' is the important one. If words mean anything it implies that Mr. Browder is hoping for not a peaceful but a violent revolution; it sounds very much like a call to arms."[46] And on November 8 the *New York Times* carried a report datelined Hyde Park, quoting an unnamed "friend of President Roosevelt" as saying: "Whether by a 'quick transition' Mr. Browder meant to convey the idea of a socialist revolution in this country along the lines of the Bolshevik uprising . . . was a debatable question and he should have ample opportunity to explain his meaning in court with the benefit of competent counsel."[47]

Nothing ever came of the threatened indictment; in the absence of a federal anti-sedition law (soon to be remedied by the passage of the Smith Act) it is unclear on what legal grounds Browder could have been tried for this speech. The episode reflected a debate then going on within the Administration over how best to curb the Communists. In general, Roosevelt does not seem to have taken the threat of a Communist "fifth column" very seriously. He did step up FBI surveillance of both Communists and Nazi Bundists, and went along with the Justice Department's prosecutions as a means of appeasing the public's anti-Communist fervor. But he displayed little of the spirit of vengeful piety that Wilson had displayed against Socialists and other opponents of the war in 1917. When Dies wrote to him in the summer of 1940 asking whether he would support legislation outlawing the Communist party, Roosevelt replied: "There are questions of whether outlawing such organizations constitutes the most effective method in this field and whether such a step is consistent with preservation of rights of citizens of a Democracy." He did, however, express some interest in legislation requiring the registration of CP members.[48]

The Party Under Attack

The threats of federal indictment represented only a small part of the political harassment the Communists faced that fall. The Dies committee displayed an insatiable appetite for Communists and their sympathizers, badgering witnesses from the League for Peace and Democracy, the American Student Union, the American Youth Congress, the National Maritime Union, the Teachers Union, the Consumers Union, and the League of Women Shoppers.[49] State and local governments joined the attack. Sam Darcy was arrested in September on charges of perjury for having incorrectly stated his name and birthplace in registering to vote in California in 1934. State officers of the Iowa

Communist party were arrested in September and charged with violation of the state's criminal syndicalism law. In October the New York City board of elections voted to invalidate nominating petitions of four CP candidates for city council on minor technicalities. And there were mob attacks on Communist meetings in San Antonio, Detroit, and Aberdeen, Washington, that fall.[50]

By early December the *New Republic*'s "TRB," Kenneth Crawford, noted that although "a very short time ago, a Red hunt would have been unthinkable," one was now clearly taking on threatening proportions. He believed that "the price of maintaining civil liberties and public esteem for labor leaders, progressive politicians, and even for mere adherents of the Bill of Rights, is stout defense of the civil liberties of genuine Communists themselves."[51] But he spoke for a shrinking minority, even among contributors to the *New Republic*. The Communists increasingly found themselves on their own in a hostile environment.

In October selected national and state leaders of the CP began to disappear from public view, joining a list of "unavailables" assigned to lead the party from underground in case it was prevented from functioning as a legal organization. Two members of the political committee, Dennis and Stachel, went underground in October. Dennis spent the next seventeen months in backwoods cottages in upstate New York, before being sent on to the Soviet Union for safekeeping.[52] Other national officers kept as low a profile as possible. John Williamson, state secretary of the Ohio Communist party, was reassigned to New York early in 1940 to replace Stachel as the CP's national organizational secretary. According to his later account, "Before I left Ohio I was already functioning in such a way as to minimize the possibilities of arrest. . . . When it was decided that I become national organization secretary, it was thought advisable to refrain from announcing this publicly. In fact, I got a private job with a firm whose owner was friendly. My work was supposedly outside the office, so I showed up only two or three times a week, to 'make reports' and establish myself with the office staff as being attached to the firm. But most of my time was devoted to the party."[53]

The Communists also set aside an underground leadership for its state and larger city organizations; in California, for example, about twenty people in all went underground. They hid away funds, mimeograph machines, and other resources thought necessary to wage an underground political struggle. Party branches divided into small units, and held meetings in private homes instead of public halls to minimize exposure. And the Communists quietly provided shelter and support for exiled or fugitive Communists from the belligerent countries, including Tim Buck, general secretary of the outlawed Canadian Communist party.[54]

Nonetheless, John Gates, who helped set up the underground apparatus in 1939, later recalled that the preparations were nowhere near so extensive as those the party undertook in the face of the Smith Act prosecutions of the late 1940s and early 1950s. The 1939 underground effort, he felt, was "amateurish, romantic and stupid." It did seem to have its farcical moments. Isadore Begun, Communist candidate for city council from the Bronx in 1937 and 1939, was one of the New York City leaders assigned to the "unavailable" list. Gates once ran into Begun, wearing a big and obviously false mustache as a disguise, at the Stanley Theater on Broadway and 42nd Street, a movie house which specialized in showing Soviet films.[55]

Had the government undertaken a serious effort to eliminate the party, such preparations would obviously have done little to save it. All they did was reinforce the arguments of those who sought to portray the Communists as a subversive conspiracy rather than a legitimate political movement.[56]

The organization of this not-so-underground apparatus provided only the most extreme example of the air of unreality that characterized so much of the party's activities in the years of the pact. With the demands from Moscow at once so insistent and so at variance from observable reality, party members had to adopt a kind of willing suspension of disbelief to play the roles assigned to them. Communist political successes in the late 1930s had depended, to no small degree, on their shrewd assessment of the limits of their real power and influence. Sandor Voros, Browder's campaign manager in 1936, only slightly overstated his case when he later claimed that in Depression-era America "there was but one group absolutely convinced of the impossibility of a Communist revolution in America—the members of the Communist Party."[57]

Now the Communists once again dusted off the old rhetoric of "class against class"—rhetoric which a few months earlier would have marked one in party circles as an agent provocateur or latent Trotskyist. Contrary to the Hearst press and Martin Dies, the Communists were not preparing for revolution in the autumn of 1939; but they were whipping up a kind of pseudo-revolutionary élan within their ranks in order to survive in a hostile political climate. Communist publications drew repeated parallels between the domestic and foreign situations of 1917 and 1939, hoping to erase the still vivid memories and lingering habits of the years of Popular Front moderation. Any orthodox Leninist could easily understand the shortcomings displayed by the parties of the Second International in the face of the First World War: if Roosevelt was indeed the Woodrow Wilson of the present conflict and Sumner Welles his Colonel House, as the *Daily Worker* repeatedly suggested, then Communists must act as they imagined Debs, Liebknecht, or Lenin would have done in their places.[58] The analogy proved effective political psychodrama. It sustained the Communists in the face of hostility and persecution, but prevented them from making any kind of serious independent assessment of what the war meant. Instead they pounced on every scrap of evidence that could sustain their belief that the Second World War differed in no significant respect from the First, while they distorted or ignored less easily assimilable information.[59]

The Invasion of Finland

That fall Stalin dropped one more unpleasant task in the laps of the American Communists. In accordance with the secret protocols signed by Molotov and Ribbentrop in August and September, the Soviet government methodically set out to consolidate its control of the Baltic nations. On September 29 the Soviet Union forced Estonia to sign a "Pact of Mutual Assistance," allowing the Soviet military the right to maintain warships and aircraft in Estonian territory. Latvia and Lithuania signed similar treaties in early October, and all three agreements proved to be the prelude to outright annexation the following year. Stalin also had plans for Finland, demanding border adjustments on the Karelian isthmus and other territorial concessions. Following two months of inconclusive negotiations, the Soviets trumped up a border incident and on November 30 invaded Finland.[60]

The public image of the Soviet Union hit rock bottom in the West. Americans were swept up in a wave of sympathy for "shiny, self-respecting, self-supporting, debt-paying Finland" and its initially successful resistance to the Red Army. Former supporters of the Popular Front were among the most vocal of Finland's sympathizers. Freda

Kirchwey wrote in *The Nation* that "the horrors that fascism wreaked in Spain are being repeated, in the name of peace and socialism, in Finland."[61]

From the first *Daily Worker* headline of the war—"Finnish Troops Cross Soviet Border; Are Driven Back by Red Army Guards"—the Communists painted a picture of the Russo-Finnish conflict completely at odds with popular sentiment.[62] Soviet demands on Finland appeared eminently reasonable to the Communists. *New Masses* editor A. B. Magil argued that the Allied governments had spent twenty years after the First World War tying a noose around the USSR in the West: "When the Red Army moved into the Western Ukraine and Byelo-Russia . . . it made the first break in the encircling noose. The mutual assistance pacts with Estonia, Latvia, and Lithuania marked the second break. The Red Army's advance into Finland is the third."[63] Having accepted Russia's national security as sufficient justification for the Nazi-Soviet pact and the invasion of Poland, the Communists were now hardly going to balk at the Finnish adventure.

As 1939 drew to a close Russian and Finnish troops remained locked in bloody conflict in Finland; German and Russian troops shared in the occupation of defeated Poland; German and French troops kept a wary eye on each other across the fortifications of the Maginot Line. American Communists, having survived the most catastrophic three months in the history of their party since the days of the Palmer raids of 1919–1920, were preparing to regain the offensive, stepping up their campaign against the "second imperialist war." Public disfavor, the desertion of their allies, and legal and vigilante attacks had not stopped them. In mid-December nearly twenty thousand party members and sympathizers crowded into Madison Square Garden for a memorial service for *Freiheit* editor Moissaye Olgin and cheered Browder's denunciations of the war. Thousands of Communists with red-and-black mourning armbands marched down First Avenue in tribute to Olgin and in reaffirmation of their loyalty to the party in its time of danger.[64]

The moment revealed some of the Communists' most characteristic traits: their determination to carry on despite isolation and persecution, and their utter inability to admit to and act on their own doubts.

4 THE "YANKS AREN'T COMING" CAMPAIGN

January to December 1940

Oh, Franklin Roosevelt
told the people how he felt.
We damn near believed what he said.
He said, I hate war
and so does Eleanor,
but we won't be safe till everybody's dead.
—ALMANAC SINGERS, 1941[1]

THE COMMUNISTS EXPECTED A ROUGH TIME in 1940. A year earlier the CP's official songbook included a song entitled "Doing the Demonstration." One stanza went: "Now is the time to get together / This is anti-fascist weather." In 1940 it was revised to read: "Now is the time to get together / Be prepared for stormy weather."[2]

Being out in the storm was not without its own exhilarating potential. In January Browder told an enthusiastic audience at the annual Lenin memorial meeting in Madison Square Garden: "One of the outstanding characteristics of Lenin and Lenin's best co-worker is this—they never allow themselves to be carried away with the joys of victory, and in moments of sharp struggle or defeat, they never get panicky, they never get excited, they never whine. The more difficult the moment, the more steadfast and steel-like and cool they stand in the midst of the storm until, with the great rising mass movement, they not only ride the storm but control the storm."[3]

American Communists did not panic in 1940, though they had a few moments of doubt and indecision. Despite their best efforts, no "great rising mass movements" were summoned up from the deep, and by year's end they could count themselves lucky to have remained afloat.

Browder's Day in Court

Browder's trial, scheduled to open on January 17 in federal court in New York City, was the first and most pressing concern facing the

Communists in the new year. They hoped to turn it into the kind of rallying symbol that the Debs case had been two decades earlier. Browder entered as the CP's candidate in a special election to fill a vacant congressional seat for the 14th District, New York's Lower East Side. During the First World War the district had elected the Socialist candidate Meyer London to Congress. It was a Communist stronghold in the late 1930s, with nearly three thousand party members among its residents.[4]

At Browder's kick-off campaign rally on January 8, New York state CP leader Israel Amter called the congressional race a "testing ground" for 1940: "Not since Eugene V. Debs polled over one million votes while serving a prison term for opposing the last imperialist war has there been such a dramatic and vital candidacy." The Communists knew that the Nazi-Soviet pact had badly damaged their standing in this largely Jewish community. Taking no chances, they flooded the area with hundreds of thousands of campaign leaflets in Yiddish, Italian, Russian, Polish, and English. Hundreds of party members drawn from all over the city went door to door canvassing for the Browder campaign. The *Daily Worker,* never exactly restrained in its praise for the CP leader, carried its adulation to new extremes. Robert Minor contributed a series of articles on "Browder—The Man They Want to Get," which included stories under such headlines as "Littleberry Browder Was 1776 Soldier of Liberty, Ancestor of CP Leader," and "Lincoln, Brown, Browder, Names Negroes Revere."[5]

Browder's trial before Federal District Court judge Alfred Coxe was short and undramatic. The prosecution stuck carefully to the technical aspects of the case, charging that in 1934 Browder had misleadingly written the word "None" on a passport application in response to a question of whether he had previously held an American passport. In fact, they charged, Browder had obtained three separate passports under assumed names during the 1920s. Though the statute of limitations had long since expired for those violations, the government could still charge Browder with two counts of "willfully and knowingly" using the 1934 passport to return to the United States from abroad in 1937 and 1938. Since he had not mentioned his earlier passports at the time of his 1934 application, the prosecution contended Browder was guilty of using a passport obtained through giving false information.

Acting as his own lawyer, Browder contested the government's interpretation. In a one-and-a-half-hour summation to the jury he argued that when he had written the word "None" in 1934, he meant only to deny that he had any old passports in his possession to surrender at the time of application. Since the government had known of these other passports long before 1934, he argued, it could not have been deceived by his response at the time.[6]

The outcome of the case hinged on the jury's estimate of what Browder had in his mind in 1934, that is, whether or not he intended any deliberate deception by writing the word "None" on his application. Given the public sentiment about communism in January 1940, there was little chance that it would choose the less damning interpretation. After forty-five minutes of deliberation the jury returned a unanimous verdict of guilty. Coxe then sentenced Browder to four years in jail and a $2,000 fine, though allowing him to remain free on bail pending appeal. The reporter from the *New York Times* recorded Browder's reaction to the sentence (and in doing so revealed not a little about the prevailing political climate): "There was neither smile nor frown from beneath the little Hitleresque mustache on his upper lip."[7]

Browder abandoned the stoic demeanor he had maintained in the courtroom when a few hours later he addressed a crowd of party loyalists in Madison Square Garden, denouncing what he felt was the treachery of the party's former New Deal allies. Attorney General Murphy, he declared, had often met with Communists during his tenure as governor of Michigan, welcoming their support in election campaigns, as had New York's governor Herbert Lehman, who "occupies his position, instead of Thomas E. Dewey, on account of the votes of the Communist Party." Browder's comments on the collapse of the "democratic front" carried a ring of unrestrained petulance: "So long as the camp of reaction found any obstacle in the New Deal camp, we supported it. But when peace was made with the economic royalists, they could not carry us along with them. The progressive Democratic bloc was broken up. We Communists were part of that bloc. We were never officially recognized of course. We were the poor relations."[8]

Browder spent the next two weeks campaigning on the Lower East Side, while party lawyers successfully defeated a move to remove him from the ballot. The Communists would have been spared some embarrassment if their lawyers had been less successful. Despite the financial and physical resources they poured into the campaign, Browder received just over three thousand votes (about the number of CP members living in the district), less than 14 percent of the total cast in the three-way race. The *New Masses* nonetheless declared that Browder's meager vote had "national significance. It may well prove an important milestone on the road toward a new political alignment of all who stand for peace and democracy."[9]

Confrontation with Roosevelt

For the first time since the 1936 election the Communists were actively working to encourage the emergence of a third party. "The issue among the masses," Browder told the CP's national committee in late February, "is no longer third term, it is third party."[10] For the next few months the Communists devoted most of their efforts to the attempt to launch "an anti-imperialist party of peace," while holding a Browder-Ford candidacy on the CP ticket in reserve.

The third-party campaign began in earnest on a rainy day in February on the White House lawn. Back in the summer of 1939 the American Youth Congress had begun talking about holding a "Youth Institute" in Washington, D.C., the following spring. The institute was originally envisioned as a small conference of AYC activists and New Deal administrators to cement the AYC's already close ties to the Administration. That was, of course, before the signing of the Nazi-Soviet pact. The AYC survived the months immediately following the pact with less difficulty than other Popular Front groups because it had no major public functions scheduled. But by late December Communists and their allies in the AYC leadership decided to reshape the character of the upcoming meeting in Washington. The small workshops were replaced with large public meetings and a demonstration, and the tone shifted from cooperation to confrontation (though the organization as a whole had not taken a stand on the international crisis, the large Communist-controlled AYC local in New York City voted overwhelmingly in December for a resolution opposing proposed American loans to Finland).

Despite evidence that the AYC was committed to the new Communist line, the group continued to receive sympathetic patronage from people in Roosevelt's administration. Some of Roosevelt's more idealistic lieutenants were disturbed by the defeat of many of the New Deal's programs at the hands of an increasingly conservative Congress, and even more disturbed by the fear that, with the onset of war, Roosevelt himself might step back from the more ambitious goals of the mid-1930s. The day after the Germans invaded Poland, Harold Ickes confided to his diary: "We are in danger of repeating the terrible mistake that President Wilson committed at the time of the First World War. He had started out to give a really liberal Administration, but when war came everything was thrown to the big financial and other interests." Joseph Lash, who had broken with the Communists in the Youth Congress and the American Student Union in the fall of 1939, described the plight of the Administration's liberals in 1940 as that of "men groping in the dark for landmarks that were no longer there."[11]

So some New Deal leaders looked to the AYC's upcoming Youth Institute as a chance to revive the New Deal's flagging sense of social mission. Attorney General Robert Jackson agreed to deliver the keynote speech, while Mrs. Roosevelt and a committee of congressional wives took responsibility for finding lodging for the delegates. She also prevailed upon her husband to speak to the delegates on February 10, the second day of the three-day institute, following a march by participants to the White House.

AYC organizers must have been surprised by Roosevelt's willingness to address them; even in the years when the Communists had been the most fervent supporters of the New Deal, Roosevelt had never agreed to address any of the meetings held by the various Popular Front organizations. Roosevelt did not share his wife's faith in the liberal credentials of the AYC gathering. He may have agreed to speak simply to placate his wife, who had long had a proprietary interest in the success of the AYC. He may have been trying to strengthen the liberal caucus within the group. He may have intended his speech as a gesture of reassurance to the troubled liberal wing of his own Administration. Or it may have been a warning and rebuke to the left itself. Whatever the motives, his speech transformed the Youth Institute into a major national event.

The AYC's march down Constitution Avenue on February 10 to the White House was an impressive affair, despite the day's steady rain. Joseph Lash noted that the group had learned to stage "as colorful a parade as the Shriners and the American Legion. . . . Even I, knowledgeable as I was about the mechanics of these affairs, wondered whether I was not being paranoid and overemphasizing the Communist influence."[12] The marchers shouted slogans and carried banners opposing the war. Nearly forty-five hundred of them passed through the White House gates and stood waiting on the lawn to hear Roosevelt speak from the south portico.

Roosevelt welcomed them to the White House and swung into a long recitation of statistics to prove that his Administration was pulling the country out of the Depression. It was the kind of speech, filled with denunciations of the "money changers," that would have moved Popular Front audiences to hearty applause, but the AYC marchers listened in silence. Roosevelt warned his listeners not to "seek or expect Utopia overnight" and asked them instead to support his efforts to eliminate unemployment "as fast as the people of this country as a whole will let us." He then devoted the last third of his speech to a "final word of warning." Noting the resolution of the AYC's New York local opposing American aid to Finland, he advised the young marchers against taking stands "on subjects which you have not thought through and on which you cannot possibly have complete knowledge." Suggestions that aid to Finland would lead the United States into war with the Soviet Union were "unadulterated twaddle."

Some of the AYCers began booing the President's remarks, but others in the crowd quickly hushed up their outburst. Roosevelt made clear his disapproval of the Soviet Union, "a dictatorship as absolute as any other dictatorship in the world." As for those of his listeners who were Communists, he allowed that they had the right to "peacefully and openly" advocate their views, but concluded: "You have no American right, by act or deed of any kind, to subvert the Government and the Constitution of this Nation." It was a curious afternoon, as the last sentimental ties of the New Deal and the Popular Front were washed away. Woody Guthrie composed a song memorializing the event, with the chorus:

> These are strange carryings on
> on the White House Capitol lawn.
> Tell me, why do you stand there in the rain? ©[13]

The bedraggled marchers, in a sullen mood, returned to the Labor Department auditorium where they had met earlier. The evening's main speaker, CIO president John L. Lewis, skillfully played on their anger. Since 1937, when Roosevelt wished a plague on the houses of both labor and capital in the midst of the bloody Little Steel strike, Lewis had grown increasingly disenchanted with the New Deal. He was also adamantly opposed to American involvement in the European war. The Communists in the CIO could not have been happier with Lewis's opposition to the Administration. Lewis, in turn, sheltered the Communists against those who sought to use the changed international situation as justification for driving them out of the union movement. "If the Communists are good enough to work for General Motors," he had told reporters at the November 1939 CIO convention, "we have little choice but to accept their dues in the United Auto Workers."[14]

Standing before the assembled AYC delegates that evening, Lewis ridiculed the President's speech. The President seemed to think that the marchers should be grateful for enjoying "the opportunity of standing on the lawn in the rain to ask for jobs." Roosevelt might consider the AYC's opposition to foreign loans to be "twaddle," but he should remember that the United Mine Workers had recently passed a very similar resolution (Lewis did not mention that the UMW's resolution opposing loans to Finland was coupled with one denouncing the Soviet invasion). Who, he demanded, had a greater right to question American foreign policy than the young men who "in the event of war will become cannon fodder?" Finally, and to the enormous gratification of the YCL organizers in the audience, Lewis invited the Youth Congress to "come to a working agreement with Labor's Non-Partisan League."[15]

The implication of Lewis's speech was clear to the Communists: he wanted to start a third party to challenge Roosevelt in the upcoming election, and he wanted the Communists to help build it. The outcome of the Youth Institute pleased many of its participants. Lewis was encouraged by the response he received from the AYC audience, and went on that spring to repeat the performance before meetings of the National Negro Congress, the NAACP, and the Townsend Old Age Convention. And the Communists had caught a glimpse of a path that promised to lead them out of the political isolation they had been mired in since the previous August. A third-party movement headed by Lewis would lend a legitimacy to their opposition to the war and to Roosevelt that they could never hope to achieve under their own banners. The *New Masses* commented enthusiastically: "It doesn't take a prophet to predict that following the Democratic convention in July, Lewis may very likely take practical steps toward the formation of an inclusive third party of labor and all progressive organizations. . . . The new and tremendously significant political movement that is on its way has found a far-sighted leader.''[16]

Only those who had hoped to see a reconciliation between the Administration and the remnants of the Popular Front were disappointed by the way the AYC meeting had turned out.

The Yanks Aren't Coming

The old anti-fascist coalition was shattered, but the Communists hoped to replace it with a new united front against American involvement in the war, organized around the slogan "The Yanks Aren't Coming."[17] The Communist press maintained a drumbeat of criticism of the Allied war effort that spring, seeking to counter popular revulsion against Nazi Germany that might lead to a "one-sided" understanding of the war's imperialist nature. France came in for its share of criticism, but the British Empire, "The Prison House of Nations" as it was dubbed by headline writers in the *Daily Worker,* was the preferred target. The Communists championed the cause of Indian and Irish independence, revived much of the stock imagery of American Anglophobia, and piously celebrated all of America's revolutionary holidays (even adding a few, like the rarely observed anniversary of Andrew Jackson's defeat of the British at New Orleans in 1815).[18]

The Communists carried the "no lesser evil" argument to its extreme when they equated German and British anti-Semitism. The Nazis had not yet embarked on their "final solution" of the Jewish problem, but by 1940 reports from occupied Europe already offered a glimpse of the coming horror to those who were willing to look. The Communists did not completely overlook German mistreatment of the Jews, but at times they made it seem as if Britain posed a greater danger to Jewish survival. In October the *Daily Worker* carried a story on an inside page about the Nazis' registration of Jews in occupied France and the passage of anti-Jewish legislation by the Vichy government. But when a ship carrying Jewish refugees sank in Haifa harbor in November after being turned away by British authorities in Palestine, the *Daily Worker* went all out. Along with a front-page news story, the edition of November 27 featured a cartoon portraying Hitler and Churchill jointly whipping a ship labeled "Jewish refugees," and an editorial declaring that the victims were "murdered by Winston

Churchill as surely as the pitiful victims of the storm troopers were murdered by Adolph Hitler." The Jewish refugees "had found among the British ruling class the same wolfish inhumanity they had fled from in Nazi Germany."[19]

Jewish Communists may have felt discomfort over such "even-handed" treatment, but they did nothing to challenge it. As late as the spring of 1941 the *Jewish Voice*, the monthly newsletter of the National Council of Jewish Communists, could run an article describing Nazi atrocities against Jews in Poland, Holland, Rumania, France, and Austria, and then ask rhetorically: "Is it not true that the British and American imperialists are blueprinting a Hitlerite future for the Jews? What is happening to the Jews of Palestine today, under British rule, does not differ essentially from what is happening to the Jews under Nazi rule."[20]

In opposing the war, the Communists thoroughly mined the literature and imagery of the First World War. The *Daily Worker* serialized Dalton Trumbo's *Johnny Got His Gun*, a bitter and macabre novel about a maimed American veteran of 1917, and followed it with selections from Henri Barbusse's great novel of the war, *Under Fire*. Elizabeth Gurley Flynn turned out a pamphlet entitled *I Didn't Raise My Boy to Be a Soldier—For Wall Street* and portrayed in luxuriant detail the "tearful farewells" and "sleepless nights" that were to be the lot of American mothers, should their sons be sent to Europe's trenches to be "bombed from the skies, torn by sharpnel, maimed, wounded, crippled, gassed with deadly fumes, shell-shocked, or killed outright." She advised mothers to visit local veterans hospitals to see the "poor twisted wrecks of humanity" left from the last war.

The Communists also argued that mobilization for war would lead inevitably to a suppression of democratic rights equal to or surpassing that which took place during the First World War. Browder argued in May 1940: "All the irksome problems of 'disciplining' unruly labor, of dissolving all 'democratic nonsense' in the country, could be so easily cut through with the sword of belligerency, of official entrance into the war!"[21]

Though direct attacks on Hitler's Germany were now infrequent in the Communist press, comparisons between the Nazi regime and a militarized United States appeared regularly. In July the *New Masses* labeled Roosevelt's proposal for universal compulsory services a "Hitleresque plan" and concluded: "It goes beyond anything that the totalitarian British and French governments have attempted. The democratic label pasted on cannot hide the stamp beneath: made in Germany."[22] And in September Browder proclaimed: "Mr. Roosevelt has studied well the Hitlerian art, and bids fair to outdo the record of his teacher."[23]

"Paper," Stalin once noted, "will put up with anything that is written on it." Organization was a more complicated task. The American League for Peace and Democracy, fatally identified with the policies of collective security, and uncomfortably straddling the issues raised by the Nazi-Soviet pact, the Soviet occupation of eastern Poland, and the Russo-Finnish war, had been dissolved in February by mutual consent of the Communist and remaining non-Communist members of its executive committee. The same day that the ALPD was dissolved, the National Maritime Union issued a call for nationwide anti-war demonstrations to take place on April 6, the anniversary of American entry into the First World War. The Communists could not afford to waste any time. Not only did they need to prepare for whatever military developments the spring might bring, they also needed to catch up with and displace the Socialists, who were in a better organizational position than they were. Socialists were strongly entrenched in the leadership of the Keep America Out of War Congress (KAOWC), having helped found the organization in 1938. The KAOWC, the only national anti-war coalition in existence in the spring of 1940, had a secure base among traditional pacifist groups, to whom the Communists were by now anathema. The CP did make a brief bid to work through the KAOWC, but the organization's leaders required local chapters to condemn Soviet aggression, while refusing any cooperation with such CP-influenced groups as the Youth Congress.[24]

Though their April 6 demonstrations were poorly attended, the Communists plunged on alone. Over Labor Day weekend they scraped together what forces they could from across the country and assembled them in Chicago for an "Emergency Peace Mobilization," out of which came the American Peace Mobilization (APM). The new front organization never attracted significant non-Communist support, and by the following spring the Communists would be looking for alternative forums for spreading their anti-war message.[25]

The Communists, for all their hostility to the Allied cause, were unprepared for and dismayed by the swift collapse of French resistance in May 1940. They assumed, as Stalin had when he signed the nonaggression pact, that the German and French armies were relatively well matched. When and if the "phony war" ever came to an end, the Communists expected the conflict to turn into a stalemate similar to the one on the western front in the First World War. In the first months of the German offensive, the Communists held closely to the official "anti-imperialist" line. After Norway fell to the Nazis, the *People's World* announced that the British imperialists, "intent on spreading the war," remained "the greatest danger to Europe and all mankind." After Belgium and Holland were conquered, the *Daily Worker* insisted "this is not our war," and blamed "imperialist bandits" on both sides for "turning the world into a madhouse of murder." And after that symbol of Munich, Neville Chamberlain, was turned out of office as Prime Minister in Britain, the Sunday *Worker* declared that it was a "toss-up" as to whether Winston Churchill or Hitler would "win the laurels of mass slaughter."[26]

The fall of France eventually provoked some anxious second thoughts among the Communists. Party leaders had, from the beginning, been divided in their assessment of the war. Although Foster and Bittelman were both convinced that the Nazi-Soviet pact represented a long-term rapprochement between the two countries, Browder felt otherwise. When John Gates wrote an article in the February 1940 *Young Communist Review* speculating that the USSR might, justifiably, seek a full military alliance with Germany in the face of Allied machinations, Browder, according to Gates, was furious, called him on the carpet, and told him never to write anything like that again.[27]

But questions about the direction the war was taking did not spill over into public party pronouncements until after the collapse of French resistance. Communists who might have excused the Nazi-Soviet pact the previous year as a necessary and shrewd act of *Realpolitik,* one permitting the Soviet Union to strengthen its own defenses while England and France kept Hitler occupied in the west, now had to face up to the possibility that Hitler got the better bargain. There was, of course, no official criticism of Soviet policies. In May the *New Masses* commented complacently: "Consider this curious fact: though it is next door to one of the belligerents, the Soviet Union is actually in less danger of involvement in the war than is the United States thousands of miles away. A paradox? The relations of capitalism and socialism abound in such seeming paradoxes."[28] And when a reader sent in a highly sensible question to the *Daily Worker* in early June,

"Will not Hitler, in the event of a crushing victory over Great Britain and France, turn his armies against the USSR?", Foster replied that the Germans would not dare to launch an attack: "Such a situation could well provoke a general European revolutionary war, one which would put the life of the capitalist system in jeopardy."[29]

But not all Communists found such heady fantasies persuasive. Reporters at the New York State Communist party convention in May noted the reappearance of uncomplimentary references to the Nazi government. At times Communist spokesmen veered close to advocating a "people's war" against the Nazi invaders. In early June Browder blamed German military victories on a fifth column at work in the French army's high command, and suggested that the time was rapidly approaching when "the French people are going to begin to take charge of their own defense."[30] And at the July convention of the American Youth Congress, the YCL's new president, Max Weiss, surprised both opponents and supporters by conceding that Hitler's conquest of Europe did constitute a grave threat to the United States. He urged close collaboration between the United States and the Soviet Union to offset the danger. The *New Republic* took note of Weiss's speech and suggested: "For once the party-liners seemed somewhat confused and uncertain, which suggests that the line itself may be changing as Stalin entertains increasing doubts regarding the wisdom of his tacit alliance with Hitler."[31]

Stalin had good reason to entertain doubts about Hitler's intentions. By midsummer, Hitler, whose generals had just barely talked him out of going through with plans for an autumn 1940 invasion of Russia, informed his military planners that all efforts were to be made to launch an invasion by May 1941.[32]

But Stalin wanted to delay a confrontation with the Germans as long as possible. On August 1 Molotov addressed the Supreme Soviet and reviewed Germany's victories in the west. He stressed the role that the nonaggression pact had played in giving Germany "a calm feeling of assurance in the East" and observed: "Our relations with Germany, which underwent a turn nearly a year ago, remain entirely as laid down in the Soviet-German Agreement. . . . The good neighborly and friendly relations that have been established between the Soviet Union and Germany are not based on fortuitous considerations of a transient nature, but on the fundamental interests of both the USSR and Germany."[33]

So American Communists put aside their doubts and returned to the anti-war campaign with full vigor. The issue had been decided: the ''imperialist war'' had not changed its character.

Red Scare

By early summer Lewis had abandoned the chimera of a third-party campaign. The Communists had been hedging their bets, and in late spring set in motion the organizational machinery necessary to gain a place on the ballot for Browder and Ford in the fall elections. The CP's campaign platform, published in August, still called for the establishment of an independent farmer-labor party, but insisted that a good-sized Communist vote in November would be a step toward building that party.[34] Even this rather modest hope would be gutted by the most ferocious and concerted anti-radical campaign since the Palmer raids of 1920. The Communists called it ''the Conspiracy Against Free Elections''—a misleading label since the campaign lacked a single directing center. But by intention and effect the Red Scare of 1940 worked toward a single end: forcing the Communist party off the ballot in as many states as possible.[35]

The Roosevelt Administration played a limited but critical role in creating the 1940 Red Scare. During Roosevelt's first two terms the newspapers and various congressmen had been in a state of continuous uproar over the danger of Communist subversion, but for most of that period Roosevelt had carefully refrained from doing anything which would lend legitimacy to their charges: Hearst and Dies, after all, were hardly friends of the New Deal. But in the fall of 1939 Roosevelt gave a free hand to his Attorney General, Frank Murphy, in launching a wide-ranging series of investigations. Browder and other CP leaders were indicted for passport violations; a federal grand jury sitting in Washington probed the operations of the *Daily Worker* and other party publications; FBI agents arrested a dozen people in pre-dawn raids in Detroit and Milwaukee in February, and charged them with illegal recruitment of volunteers for service in the Spanish Civil War; and Murphy publicly charged that Robert Minor and other prominent Communists were unregistered foreign agents, and hinted at future indictments.[36] Murphy left the Justice Department to take a seat on the Supreme Court that spring, and his successor, Robert Jackson, behaved in more restrained fashion. But the damage had been done. If flaming New Deal liberals like Frank Murphy were concerned with the threat posed by the Communists, then the Republic truly had to be in grave danger.

Congress, in an election year, needed little persuasion to solve the nation's security problems in a time of international menace at the expense of the traditional scapegoats, aliens and radicals. The Alien Registration Act, better known as the Smith Act, passed both the House and Senate in mid-June by overwhelming margins. The act required registration and fingerprinting of all resident noncitizens, and authorized the deportation of aliens belonging to revolutionary groups. It also established the first peacetime federal sedition law passed since the Alien and Sedition Acts of 1798, making conspiracy to advocate or teach the necessity or desirability of overthrowing the government a crime. With its passage, prosecutors had no need to prove that a defendant, whether citizen or alien, had taken any overt steps toward overthrowing the government. Nor was it necessary to prove that an individual had personally taught or advocated the need for such actions. Prosecutors need only show that the accused had joined an organization that favored such advocacy—three steps from any physical act such as storing dynamite in the basement in preparation for the Final Struggle on the barricades. Little attention was paid to the constitutional implications of the legislation; Marcantonio was the only congressman to speak out against its passage.[37]

The Smith Act's sponsor, Representative Howard Smith of Virginia, was one of the most conservative representatives then serving in Congress, while Jerry Voorhis of California was one of the most liberal. It is a measure of the anti-Communist consensus prevailing in 1940 that he attached his name to the second major piece of Red Scare legislation to pass Congress that year. The Voorhis Registration Act grew out of proposals made in the spring of 1940 to the Dies committee by Morris Ernst, a prominent New York attorney and the fiercely anti-Communist co-counsel of the American Civil Liberties Union. The act required all organizations "subject to foreign control" to register with the Justice Department. In early July, after the bill had already won House approval, Browder appeared before the Senate Judiciary Subcommittee to testify against it. He quoted Lincoln in defense of working-class internationalism, and warned that fascism had always come to power under the banner of suppressing communism. Browder's opinions, however, did not carry much weight with the Senate, which passed the bill in late September. Roosevelt had not been a strong supporter of either the Smith or Voorhis act, but he signed both without apparent qualms.[38]

The House Un-American Activities Committee thrived under these conditions, and Dies conducted himself with his usual contempt for civil liberties. Throughout the spring he subpoenaed Communist officials, found them in contempt for refusing to hand over membership lists, and tossed them in jail. In April two Dies committee investigators, along with a platoon of Philadelphia detectives and motorcycle police, broke into the local headquarters of the Communist party and made off with a truckload of literature and files. Federal District Court judge George Welsh ordered the arrest of Dies's agents and of a Philadelphia detective, charging them all with "conspiracy to violate the Bill of Rights." Dies piously returned his illegally obtained evidence, having first taken care to make secret copies.[39]

So-called Little Dies Committees were established by state legislatures in California, Oklahoma, and Texas. Suspected Communist sympathizers were purged from the California State Relief Administration, while in New York the legislature's Rapp-Coudert committee conducted an investigation of the City College system that eventually led to thirty-five dismissals and eleven resignations of faculty and staff accused of Communist party membership. Specific acts of wrongdoing were rarely revealed in these investigations, but this had no effect on their outcome. The Rapp-Coudert committee argued in a report to the legislature: "The Communist Party is not a political party as that term has historically been understood in this country. It is a political conspiracy aimed both at the social structure and the political framework of this nation. Since it is a conspiracy, the persons actively engaged in it are conspirators." The committee thus felt no need to prove any tangible misconduct in the classroom or outside of it on the part of the accused teachers: "The very acceptance of Communist Party membership is, in and of itself, an overt act incompatible with the public service."[40]

The fall of France, popularly attributed to subversion behind the lines by sinister if vaguely defined "fifth columnists," boosted public apprehension about the possible effects that similar disloyalty might have on American defense efforts. In this volatile situation Communist canvassers began appearing in cities and small towns across the country in the late spring of 1940, gathering signatures to put the Communist party on state ballots in November. The CP hoped to get on the ballot in forty-two states; in more than half they faced mob and vigilante violence, arrests, and legislative attempts to drive them off the ballot.[41]

In April twelve Communist canvassers were arrested in Kalamazoo, Michigan, and charged with robbery, assault, housebreaking, and disturbing the peace. The Michigan secretary of state announced that state employees who signed the Communist petitions would be dismissed. When Communist canvassers drove to Peoria, Illinois, in April they were attacked by a mob that burned three of their cars and beat the occupants. One canvasser lost an eye in the assault. There were also physical assaults on Communists in Freeport, Rockford, Albany Park, and Chicago. In Lewiston five canvassers were charged under Illinois' criminal syndicalism law and held in jail for a month on $80,000 bail. Nine Communist canvassers were arrested in Maine, three in Arizona, two in Indiana, six in Maryland, eleven in Ohio, nineteen in California, three in New Hampshire. In Oklahoma City police, armed with liquor search warrants, raided the CP-run Progressive Book Store and several private homes, seizing seven thousand books as evidence and arresting thirteen men and five women on charges of criminal syndicalism. Four of the arrested were later convicted and sentenced to ten years in prison and $5,000 fines.[42]

The Communists faced particularly fierce campaigns to keep them off the ballot in West Virginia, New York, and Pennsylvania. In each state the pattern was similar. When the Communists filed their ballot petitions, the newspapers and the American Legion published lists of the signers. Legionnaires and local officials (sometimes police officers and detectives) would then go door to door seeking to "persuade" petition signers to repudiate their signatures. Where such relatively subtle intimidation failed, more coercive measures were tried. Public and WPA employees were fired from their jobs, as were factory workers in Pennsylvania and coal miners in West Virginia, if they refused to repudiate their signatures.

In West Virginia 150 people were indicted under a never-before-invoked state law that prohibited independent petition signers from voting in the state primary. When such tactics produced a sufficient number of repudiations, state authorities began arresting Communist canvassers for having obtained petition signatures under false pretenses. After Oscar Wheeler, the CP's candidate for governor in West

Virginia, had collected fourteen hundred signatures on ballot petitions, the state accused him of failing to inform signers that they were being asked to endorse a Communist petition, although the petitions had been headed by the words "Communist Party" and carried a hammer and sickle. After a speedy trial and conviction he was sentenced to from one to fifteen years in state prison. In Pennsylvania seventy-four Communist canvassers were arrested on charges of conspiracy, false swearing, and false pretense. All were convicted, and received sentences ranging between three months and two years in jail.[43]

The result, "the most peculiar election in the history of the Republic," as Browder labeled it, was to demolish the Communist party's presidential campaign. On Election Day the Browder-Ford ticket appeared on the ballot in only twenty-two states; in fifteen other states they were ruled off the ballot after initially completing all the requirements to win a place, including such centers of party strength as New York, Illinois, and Ohio.[44]

Browder's trial judge saddled the Communists' presidential campaign with one further legal handicap in early September when he issued an order prohibiting Browder from leaving the jurisdiction of the Southern District of New York's Federal District Court. As a result, Browder could not even travel to Brooklyn to campaign. Ford, Foster, and a half dozen other party leaders toured the country on his behalf, a poor substitute for a campaign tour. When the election results were tabulated in November, Browder was credited with 48,789 votes, roughly half of what he received in 1936 (a year, of course, in which he was, indirectly, calling for votes for Roosevelt). Even if the party had faced no legal restrictions, Browder's vote would undoubtedly have been very low in 1940. This total, however, can hardly be taken as the full measure of Communist support among the electorate. It included none of the write-in votes Browder received in the states in which he was not on the ballot, including New York, which ordinarily would have provided the largest single portion of his support.[45]

In a speech to the CP's national committee in February, Browder had warned against laying too much stress on "technical safeguards" of party security. He argued that "without the most intensive reaching and consolidating of mass contact, all technical safeguards will be valueless."[46] Despite his warning, the party continued to turn in on itself in the face of the onslaught of legal repression and public hysteria.

Publications begun in the flush of Popular Front prosperity were now shut down: *National Issues* disappeared after its September 1939 edition, while the *Midwest Daily Record,* the party's Chicago-based newspaper, was first reduced to a weekly and then shut down entirely by the spring of 1940.[47] The *Daily Worker,* beset by declining circulation and advertising revenue, and facing threats of legal action, formally cut its ties with the Communist party and began to be published by the nominally independent "Freedom of the Press, Inc." The CP's Harlem leader Ben Davis and managing editor Louis Budenz continued to oversee its operations, but the Communists hoped the paper's new status would give it some maneuvering room in case of any government attempt to suppress the party.[48]

The party took other "technical" measures to protect itself that year. At its nominating convention at the end of May it replaced the old sixty-five-member national committee with a stripped-down seventeen-member committee. It did not include a number of formerly prominent leaders like Dennis, Stachel, and Williamson, who were now functioning in partial or total underground status; nor did it include Alexander Bittelman, who had been demoted to leadership of the party's Jewish Bureau for having opposed Browder once too often within the political committee.[49]

The Voorhis Act, scheduled to take effect in January 1941, prompted the CP's most dramatic organizational change. In November 1940 delegates from CP districts all over the country met in an emergency convention in New York to ratify a national committee resolution formally ending the American Communist party's affiliation with the Communist International. Browder told the delegates that the party would be unable to function if the Justice Department could use its Comintern affiliation as cause for subjecting it to the regulatory statutes of the Voorhis Act. At the same time, Browder took pains to argue that passage of the act did not represent "such a definite fascization" that the party no longer had any choice except capitulation or a totally underground existence. He cited the example of England, where "after more than fourteen months of war and several months of horrible bombardments from the air, the Communist Party of Great Britain still functions as a legal party, with a member of Parliament." (Browder did not say why, since this was so, the Communist press throughout 1940 had described the British government as "totalitarian.") His comments showed a continuing commitment to maintaining the CP as a legal and open political movement, even in the face of the kind of fierce anti-Communist campaign then hemming it in on all sides.[50]

Something seems to have been going on beneath the surface appearance of party solidarity in 1940. In an off-the-record meeting of the party's leaders nearly five years later, Eugene Dennis would refer to the "unhealthy division and internal situation which existed in the Political Committee . . . between September 1939 and June 1941."[51] Neither Browder nor any other veteran of the political committee subsequently chose to reveal the nature of those disagreements, nor are minutes of political committee meetings after mid-September 1939 available. At that September meeting Browder had attempted to retain as much as possible of the moderate stance of the Popular Front years, while Foster and Bittelman called for a more overtly revolutionary line. Did Browder continue his arguments with Foster in 1940 and 1941? In a private conversation with John Gates, Browder had vigorously objected to the idea that the Nazi-Soviet pact represented a permanent state of affairs. On at least two public occasions, the national committee meeting in February and the emergency convention in November, he argued against those Communists who wanted the party to shift its operations to a fully underground status; and finally, in a curious campaign speech in October, he called for an American-Soviet alliance, a position that did not mesh at all with the party's current anti-imperialist line (and one which he would soon publicly repudiate as a "careless formulation").[52]

Perhaps too much should not be made of all this. On most occasions Browder hewed closely to the official line, denouncing Roosevelt and the war with a vehemence Foster himself must have found unexceptionable. Browder was not a rebel. He had risen to power as a loyal Stalinist and, in case he had any doubts on the matter, Harry Pollitt's recent downfall reminded him of the fate of dissenters in the Comintern. Nevertheless, his discomfort with the requirements laid down by the Nazi-Soviet pact remains clear. Unlike Foster, who delighted in the role of militant opposition, Browder had been happiest during the years of Popular Front respectability, during which he had moved to center stage in international Communist politics while Foster had slid into near oblivion. It seems probable that Browder and Foster continued to clash throughout 1940 and into the new year, at the very least on questions of style and phrasing, and perhaps on more substantive questions.

The Labor Movement and the War

As blows rained down upon them, as former allies departed, and as their efforts to gain new allies proved stillborn, the Communists found there was one terrain on which they still held on to a modicum of real power: the labor movement. Here too they suffered setbacks. Yet as they abandoned hopes for a third party, for a significant Communist vote in the presidential election, and for a mass anti-war movement under their leadership, they grew all the more hopeful that the labor movement would provide the key necessary to end the party's political isolation. Here was a constituency eager to do battle in its own interests, even if that battle led it to a head-on collision with the government's national defense program.

The labor movement as a whole, apart from the largely Jewish garment unions, displayed little enthusiasm for American aid to the Allies in the early days of the war. The Communists were not alone in saying the Yanks would not be coming; AFL president William Green declared in the October 1939 *American Federationist* that the unions wanted "policies best calculated to keep us free of European entanglements."[53] CIO president John L. Lewis was even more emphatic in denouncing the war, and what he believed was Roosevelt's calculated schemes for America's gradual involvement on the side of Great Britain. As Lewis moved into open conflict with Roosevelt, he faced increasing opposition within the CIO, particularly from Amalgamated Clothing Workers president Sidney Hillman.

As relations with Lewis cooled in the late 1930s, Roosevelt had turned to Hillman as his most dependable labor ally. In 1940 Hillman offered all-out support to Roosevelt's reelection campaign, and was emerging as the union movement's unofficial representative in Roosevelt's rearmament program. In May 1940 Roosevelt set up the National Defense Advisory Commission (NDAC) to coordinate production of war materials. Hillman sat on the seven-member commission, along with Edward Stettinius of U.S. Steel and William Knudsen of General Motors. Lewis glowered out in the cold, while the Communists denounced Hillman as "an agent of Wall Street."

Hillman was the only union leader to be attacked by name in the CP's 1940 election platform. *The Communist* explained: "Progressives in the labor movement 'concentrate' on Hillman not because he is 'worse' than [AFL leaders] Hutchinson or Woll; they are all essentially

Social-Democrats and reformists. The reason is that the Hillman re-
formist influences are today the main obstacle on the road of freeing
labor from the Roosevelt 'leadership'; hence Hillman is the main obstacle in the labor movement towards the further progress of labor's
independent power."[54]

Nor did Hillman do anything to lessen the Communists' animosity
by his attacks upon them and their allies at the local and national levels
of the CIO. The Amalgamated Clothing Workers refused to affiliate
with the newly organized and left-led Greater New York Industrial
Union Council (CIO). Hillman's supporters attempted to purge left-
wing delegates at the September 1940 New York State CIO convention—a move blocked only by Lewis's personal intervention.[55]

Lewis himself gave the Communists an occasional public rebuff to
remind them who was in charge, and to placate the CIO's anti-Communist wing. At the Mine Workers' convention in January 1940 he
forcefully spoke out in favor of continuing his own union's ban on
Communist members, declaring: "No man can serve two flags or two
masters, and if a man is a Communist and is a servant of a foreign
power, he cannot be an American or a member of the United Mine
Workers of America."[56] But Lewis was always to disappoint those
anti-Communist CIO leaders who hoped such gestures signaled a break
with the Communists. Communist-influenced unionists were, after all,
the only forces outside of the UMW machine upon whom Lewis could
rely to back his opposition to the war, to Roosevelt, and to Hillman.
And the Communists played up their tie with Lewis for all it was worth
because they knew that without him they would be lost.[57]

While the Communists casually wrote off many of the political gains
they had won during the late 1930s, they behaved with more caution
in the labor movement. Here, too, party members were expected to
swing behind the new line. But the party's union leaders, tied down
to the responsibility of holding power in organizations vitally concerned
with the day-to-day needs of thousands of workers, retained a more
realistic appraisal of their situation. CP leaders could thunder on to
their hearts' content about "proletarian internationalism" without fear-
ing for their positions; this was a luxury most Communists in the unions
did not enjoy. When Communist unionists did speak out against the
war, they soft-pedaled the more exotic elements of the new line. When
Transport Workers Union president Mike Quill was called before
HUAC in the spring of 1940, Dies attempted to pin him down on his

judgment of the Nazi-Soviet pact. Quill carefully side-stepped the issue: "I am not expressing ideas on European pacts. The more the American people keep out of Europe the better."[58]

From his underground vantage point Dennis complained that Communists underestimated the prestige of the Soviet Union among American workers: "Because of this, many Party organizations neglect or are reluctant to develop a mass campaign and movement in the trade unions . . . in support of the peace moves and aims of the Soviet Union."[59]

Despite such exhortations, party leaders refrained from forcing left-wing union leaders into a choice between breaking with the CP or committing political suicide within their unions. Roy Hudson, the CP's trade-union secretary, conceded early in 1941: "Progressive trade union leaders undoubtedly have far greater understanding of the problems facing the working class than the membership they represent. . . . To attempt to express as the viewpoint of the national organization an understanding that has as yet been achieved only by its leaders and by some locals would be wrong, and would tend to create unnecessary division."[60]

But the issues raised by the pact and by aroused anti-"Communazi" sentiment worked to the disadvantage of the Communists and their allies in the union movement. Left-wing leaders in the American Newspaper Guild and the International Woodworkers of America were deposed, and the American Federation of Teachers expelled Communist-controlled locals in New York City and Philadelphia.[61]

The Communists also came under heavy attack in the United Auto Workers Union. At the 1939 UAW convention a coalition of Communists and independent unionists of various political leanings had consolidated control of the union after defeating the factional movement led by former UAW president Homer Martin. The anti-Martin coalition had been strained from the beginning, with each group keeping a careful eye on the strength of its temporary allies. With Martin out of the way, the struggle for power began in earnest, with the most ambitious contestants being Walter Reuther and his two brothers, opposed by an uneasy coalition of two independent leaders, George Addes and Richard Frankensteen.

The Communists, who had played a major role in the union's initial organizing drive, were unable to win anything near commensurate power in the national leadership of the union because of the exigencies of national CIO politics. In the name of maintaining the "Center-Left Bloc" in the CIO, the Communists had voluntarily withdrawn their own candidate for president at the 1939 UAW convention, throwing their support to R. J. Thomas, who had the backing of Philip Murray and Sidney Hillman. Wyndham Mortimer, the most prominent Communist in the union, was eased out of his vice-presidency in 1939 and sent off to California to organize aircraft workers. Though the party had over a thousand members in the UAW in 1939 and controlled several large union locals, the Communists had to be content playing the role of spear carriers for the factional ambitions of others.

Because the 1939 UAW convention had been held in the waning months of the Popular Front, the Communists were spared the full revelation of their organizational weakness in the union. The 1940 convention, held in St. Louis in July, brought this lesson home to them in full force.[62]

The UAW was the largest and most vital of the new CIO unions, and its convention an important event in the union movement's annual calendar. Both Lewis and Hillman attended and stumped for their respective positions on Roosevelt and the war. Lewis had put his prestige on the line in standing against Roosevelt. Wyndham Mortimer, in opposing a resolution that would put the UAW on record as endorsing Roosevelt's reelection, argued: "To pass this resolution would be a direct kick in the face to the greatest labor leader that America or any other country has produced. . . . I would not give one hair of John L. Lewis' bushy eyebrows for all the politicians in both the Democratic and Republican parties."[63]

Despite a frenzied pro-Lewis floor demonstration, Hillman's appeal for support for Roosevelt won out. Reuther had aligned himself with Hillman in internal CIO politics; union president R. J. Thomas was cooperating with the Reuther forces at that point; and Addes and Frankensteen could see which way the wind was blowing. Their delegates all supported Roosevelt's reelection, and the resolution passed by a vote of 550 to 30 (a good indication of the real limits of Communist strength in the UAW). The convention also passed resolutions condemning the "brutal dictatorships" of the Soviet Union, Germany, Italy, and Japan, and barring members of subversive organizations from holding union office. Lewis was infuriated by the results of the

convention, while the Communists' only consolation came from a resolution passed in favor of stepped-up organization of workers in the
rapidly expanding aircraft industry.[64]

By the fall of 1940 most major CIO unions had endorsed Roosevelt,
and rank-and-file sentiment, even in the left-led unions, was overwhelmingly pro-Roosevelt. As a last-ditch gesture of opposition, Lewis
went on the radio to endorse Wendell Willkie, the Republican party's
candidate for President, and to announce that he would step down
from the presidency of the CIO if Roosevelt won reelection. The Communists, who had denounced the Republicans and Democrats alike as
war parties, handled Lewis's quixotic gesture gingerly. Browder
praised Lewis's "historic service" in breaking with Roosevelt, but said
he was disappointed that Lewis remained the prisoner of the "capitalist
two-party system." Left-wing union leaders reaffirmed their support
for Lewis while maintaining a tactful silence on the Willkie endorsement. But they were appalled by his threat to step down in the event
of Roosevelt's reelection. No sooner were the election results in than
left-led CIO locals, councils, and unions began to pass resolutions
urging him to remain in office.[65]

Lines were sharply drawn at the Atlantic City CIO convention in
late November. Hillman strongly endorsed Lewis's heir-apparent
Philip Murray for CIO president in order to block any "Draft Lewis"
movement which might allow Lewis to renege gracefully on his threat
to step down. The Communists raised no objection to Murray's candidacy since he had Lewis's formal endorsement, had spoken out
against American involvement in the war—and since they had no
alternative.

Hillman led the attack against the Communists in Atlantic City, the
first time they had faced open criticism at a national CIO gathering.
The delegates from the Amalgamated Clothing Workers union proposed a resolution banning Communists, fascists, and Nazis from holding office in the CIO. Hillman spoke in favor of the resolution, pointing
out that it resembled one that the Mine Workers union had been functioning under for years, and concluding innocently: "What is good
enough for the United Mine Workers is good enough for the CIO."
Lewis blocked the resolution by referring it to the convention's resolutions committee, which he had stacked in favor of the left. But
with Murray joining Hillman in insisting that some kind of anti-Communist statement be passed, the committee could not simply table the

question. With the tacit approval of the Communists they put together a compromise resolution which declared: "We firmly reject consideration of any policies emanating from totalitarianism, dictatorships, and foreign ideologies such as Nazism, Communism, and fascism. They have no place in this great modern labor movement."

Once again, in the name of "Center-Left" unity, Communist unionists found it necessary to go down the road of self-abnegation. To complete their humiliation, Lee Pressman, left-wing general counsel of the CIO and secretary of the resolutions committee, was required to move adoption of the resolution before the assembled delegates. It passed by unanimous standing vote. The Communists felt they had little choice. If they stood against the resolution, they risked their alliance with Lewis and a full-scale purge. But they did little to enhance their already besmirched political reputation within the CIO by the maneuver.[66]

Having paid the necessary price, the Communists found the remainder of the convention palatable. Lewis would permit no purge of their supporters in the national CIO office. When the Clothing Workers delegation attacked *CIO News* editor Len DeCaux for his anti-Roosevelt coverage of the presidential campaign, Lewis quickly squelched the effort by saying that DeCaux had only been carrying out his policies. The Communists picked up another position in the national CIO leadership when their ally Joseph Curran, president of the National Maritime Union, succeeded Murray as vice-president. The convention passed resolutions opposing "foreign entanglements" and "foreign wars." In its convention wrap-up, the *Daily Worker* expressed satisfaction that Hillman had been unable to swing the delegates to a pro-interventionist position, but regretted that the convention's opposition to the war "omitted concrete reference to and condemnation of the imperialist foreign policies and war measures of the government and Wall Street, including its predatory war alliance with Great Britain." As for the "Communazi" resolution, the editors felt it was "entirely out of harmony" with the rest of the convention's achievements. The *Daily Worker* did not acknowledge or comment on the role Communists had played in writing and passing the resolution.[67]

But while the Communists faced a serious challenge to their influence at the top of the CIO, they were finding new opportunities for expanding their influence at its base. In 1940 the UAW stepped up its organizing campaign among aircraft workers, hoping to get in on the ground floor of the war-inspired production boom. In the late summer the union won a National Labor Relations Board (NLRB) election at the Los Angeles Vultee aircraft plant. Wyndham Mortimer was heading up the UAW's organizing effort in California. In November he broke off negotiations with the Vultee management, charging that it was not negotiating in good faith. Vultee workers voted by a large majority to go out on strike.

The "Roosevelt recession" of 1938 had temporarily dampened the labor militancy of the mid-1930s, but as defense spending in 1940–1941 finally ended the Depression, workers once again showed themselves eager to do battle for increased wages and union recognition. Communist organizers did not create the new militancy, though they were often blamed for it. The fall of France had created widespread public apprehension about the dangers posed by the "fifth column" in America, and employers and conservative politicians were quick to use the word "sabotage" to describe any interference with maximum industrial production. Vultee was the sole manufacturer of training planes for the armed forces, and Mortimer's prominent role in the strike led to charges in the press and in Congress that the whole affair was a Communist conspiracy to cripple American defense. Mortimer, who could count on the support both of the Vultee strikers and the national UAW leadership, responded that "some persons think anyone who wants more than $20 a week is a Communist." The strike held firm and the company capitulated after twelve days, raising starting wages by 25 percent and instituting paid vacations.[68]

The Vultee strike impressed the Communists, and influenced the debate within the political committee over the party's strategy for the coming year. At a meeting of the national committee in November, Browder tried to salvage some sense of achievement out of a generally dismal year. He argued that "allegiance to the two old parties" had never been weaker, and that the CP's political influence, inadequately measured by an election vote in which they were prevented from running in the centers of their greatest strength, was "many-times multiplied . . . as compared with 1936." The formation of a national farmer-labor party, Browder suggested, was just around the corner.

As general secretary, Browder had to put the best possible face on the party's situation in his public statements. But his speech, reprinted and circulated in pamphlet and book form among the membership, was more than an exercise in left-wing boosterism. Browder was defending a political position. The party, he was arguing, could succeed in the future only if it held to the path of legality and open political campaigning. Whether or not his listeners chose to believe that in the past year the Communists had displayed "multiplied influence and deepening roots among the masses" was less important than how they chose to carry on in 1941: "We multiplied our strength because under the most extreme difficulties . . . we never allowed ourselves to drift or be drawn into sectarianism. . . . This campaign was for us, from first to last, a mass campaign." He stressed the importance of making a fight in the electoral arena even when, as in 1940, that fight had to be centered on defensive issues. The struggle for maintaining a place on the ballot, he argued, was "the front line of struggle for all the immediate demands of the working class," for without that fight all democratic liberties were threatened.[69]

But Browder could no longer decide the party's outlook by executive fiat. Foster, shunted off for so many years, was once again a formidable opponent. The rush of events seemed to be favoring Foster's quasi-syndicalism over Browder's commitment to electoral activity. Nothing else the Communists had been involved with in 1940 could match the drama of the Vultee strike. Here workers in basic industry, following Communist leaders, defied their employers, the government, and public opinion in militant defense of their immediate interests. And once workers had been set in motion around bread-and-butter issues, Foster argued, they could be swiftly led on to more advanced positions.

In a speech to YCL leaders in December, Foster declared: "The first thing we must clearly realize is that economic questions relating to the living standards of the people are of decisive importance, because, in the given American situation of so-called non-belligerency, they are the main starting point in the struggle for peace." Workers who might be reluctant to join an anti-war movement "are far more sensitive and responsive to the domestic economic side of American imperialism's war program." This did not mean abandoning efforts to build a movement against the war, since economic struggles tended "to develop into the general struggle to keep America out of the war." Foreign imperialism and domestic retrenchment were but two sides of the same coin. Foster urged Communists to "strive to politicalize the economic struggles of the workers. . . . It is our special task as Communists to make this politicalization tendency a reality by teaching the workers who are particularly receptive during immediate demand struggles, the real nature of the war, the war significance of their union leaders' 'sacrifice' policy, the imperialist and pro-war character of the 'national defense' program, the importance of friendly relations with the USSR, the need for a broad Farmer-Labor party, and the necessity for socialism in the United States."[70]

This was a pretty tall order for left-wing unionists, who were having a hard enough time conducting purely economic struggles without being driven out of the union movement. The most "politicalization" Mortimer felt he could bring to the Vultee strike was to tell the *Daily Worker*, "These workers would rather see these planes being used for peaceful purposes."[71] In practical terms, Foster's proposal meant that Communists in the unions would conduct themselves as militant unionists, trusting to the clash of the workers' immediate interests with government and employers to produce radical, if not revolutionary, consciousness. Foster did not explicitly repudiate the need for political struggle outside of the workplace. Nevertheless, the effect of his strategy would shift the party's emphasis away from the kind of broadly focused political movement Browder was always calling for.

In the first six months of 1941 the Communists would find the opportunity to test Foster's ideas.

5 THE LAST DAYS OF THE NAZI-SOVIET PACT
January to June 21, 1941

Now boys, you've come to the hardest time.
The boss will try to bust your picket line.
He'll call out the police, the national guard.
They'll tell you it's a crime to have a union card.
They'll raid your meetings, they'll hit you on the head.
They'll call everyone of you a damn red.
Unpatriotic . . . Japanese spies . . . sabotaging national defense.
>   —ALMANAC SINGERS, 1941

The imperialist stakes for which the White House and the Wilhelmstrasse are playing offer no benefit to the people. The people want none of this war. They will have to state this strongly, to stay the hand of the war crowd.
>   —Sunday *Worker*, June 22, 1941[1]

LENIN'S "LOCOMOTIVE OF HISTORY" took yet another sharp turn in the spring of 1941. American Communists, tenacious and myopic as always, were not prepared for it. Down to the last day of the Nazi-Soviet pact, they remained adamantly opposed to the "second imperialist war." Though in late June their political world would again turn upside down, American Communists would never completely rid themselves of the bitter legacy of the preceding twenty-two months.

America First

With the reelection campaign safely out of the way, Roosevelt had turned his full attention to the problem of meeting Britain's need for war materials. Neutrality legislation, which prohibited government loans to countries, like Britain, that had defaulted on their World War One debts, and which permitted sales of arms to belligerents only on a "cash and carry" basis, sharply restricted the amount of American arms the British could purchase. By late November 1940 they had almost exhausted their financial credits in the United States. Roosevelt did not want to confront directly the waning but still formidable public sentiment against American intervention. Rather than attempting to repeal the neutrality legislation, he sidestepped legal obstacles by proposing that the United States "lend" Great Britain the necessary war materials, to be returned or replaced by the British after the war. When Congress reconvened in January, Roosevelt introduced the Lend-Lease Bill, his plan for turning the United States into the "great arsenal of democracy."

Isolationist forces in and out of Congress attacked the wide discretionary powers the bill would grant Roosevelt in determining the amount and recipients of American aid.[2] Communists joined their campaign against lend-lease. In January, at the annual Lenin memorial meeting in Madison Square Garden, Browder accused Roosevelt of resorting to the "Hitlerian tactic of concentrating upon a single step at a time" in leading the country into war. And Israel Amter declared: "President Roosevelt tells us that the war is being forced upon us. But is it not a strange fact that the Soviet Union lies next door to Germany and yet it cannot be forced into the war? The reason is clear: the Soviet Union has a policy of peace while President Roosevelt pursues a policy of war."[3]

The American Peace Mobilization and the American Youth Congress sent delegates to Washington to lobby and demonstrate against the bill, but to no avail. When Congress passed the Lend-Lease Act in March, public debate shifted to Roosevelt's plans to use armed American convoys to protect merchant ships carrying supplies to Britain. The Communists now made "No Convoys!" their slogan of the hour.[4]

The Communists were forced that spring to recognize that their "united front against the imperialist war" was faltering badly. The APM claimed to have chapters in nearly two hundred communities, but even in New York City proved itself unable to attract more than a few thousand people to any of its events.[5] While the APM foundered, the conservative America First Committee, organized the previous fall, had grown into the country's leading anti-war organization. By mid-1941 it boasted 800,000 members. Enjoying financial support from wealthy contributors, and political support from the Chicago *Tribune* and the Hearst press, and able to draw on the services of such disparate speakers as Charles Lindbergh and Norman Thomas, America First rallies dwarfed the APM's activities.[6]

Although Communists publicly adopted a critical attitude toward America First, accusing its leaders of seeking "to exploit the present war to secure for the imperialists of the United States as much foreign territory [and] spheres of influence . . . as possible,"[7] privately the CP leaders recognized that they shared some common goals with America First. That spring Communists quietly began to infiltrate local chapters of the organization.[8]

Browder's Imprisonment

The Communists had other worries that spring. In February the U.S. Supreme Court declined to review Browder's conviction for passport fraud. Ordered to surrender for prison on March 25, he used his remaining weeks of freedom to set up a caretaker regime to rule in his absence, with Robert Minor assuming the post of acting general secretary. The Texas-born Minor, a talented political cartoonist who made his early reputation on the St. Louis *Post-Dispatch*, had shifted to a career as a full-time revolutionary during the First World War. Though he had proven himself an effective organizer in the Tom Mooney defense campaign of 1916, he had, since his conversion to communism in the early 1920s, turned into a political hatchet man for the CP's top leaders.[9] Lacking any independent following in the party, he had proved a useful and pliant lieutenant for Browder in the 1930s, and was a logical compromise candidate to run the party during Browder's absence. Foster, once again cut off from the top job in the party, acquiesced in Minor's appointment because Minor would not overshadow him as a younger and more vital leader like Dennis might have. It was probably no coincidence that Dennis found himself dispatched to Moscow that spring, much to the surprise of Comintern leaders, who had made no request for Dennis's presence. According to Peggy Dennis, when her husband arrived in Moscow, Comintern leader Manuilsky asked him, "Who back there always wants you out of leadership? Is it Foster or is it Browder?"[10]

On March 25, as scheduled, Browder surrendered to U.S. marshals at the Foley Square Courthouse in New York City. Two days later, shackled between two other prisoners, his face hidden behind a mask made from a ripped Pullman pillowcase to foil photographers, Browder was led into the federal penitentiary in Atlanta to begin serving his four-year sentence.[11]

Though outwardly calm in those last weeks, Browder was deeply disturbed by the prospect of his imprisonment. He felt little trust for his colleagues on the political committee, and undoubtedly felt reluctant to turn power over to them. Browder considered the party's successes in the late 1930s his personal handiwork. He had always concerned himself with minute questions of political tactics, alliances, and slogans. Now he feared the consequences of his absence. Federal prison authorities permitted him only limited correspondence. He assumed that as a matter of course all his mail would be studied by government agents, so he worked out a simple code with Minor to use in their letters, relying on literary references, chess problems, and personal anecdotes to enable him to maintain at least a limited means of receiving information and issuing instructions. Minor had excerpts from Browder's prison correspondence copied and distributed to all political committee members.[12] But this slow and clumsy system allowed Browder to make only the most general comments about the party's activities.

Political considerations aside, Browder was psychologically unprepared for jail. He had served time before when he was imprisoned for his opposition to conscription in the First World War. But it was one thing for a young man to go to prison in the first flush of revolutionary enthusiasm, and something quite different for a man of nearly fifty, with a wife and three children. What may have cut even deeper into Browder's resolution was the sense of personal betrayal he felt he had suffered at Roosevelt's hands. Gil Green, who was probably closer to Browder than any other member of the political committee in the late 1930s, recalled how Browder cherished the illusion of having personal influence over Roosevelt's actions during the Popular Front years: "He believed in this fiction that because he saw somebody who in turn would see somebody else who in turn would see Roosevelt, when something then came out of the White House that was to his liking he could take credit for it. All that built up his own estimate of himself to such an extent that he took it very hard when he had to face the fact it was Roosevelt who had him indicted. In 1918 he went to prison a young man from Kansas, but now he was going in as Earl Browder, *the* Earl Browder, and he found it very hard to take." [13]

Defense Strikes

Though the level of legal attack the Communists faced tapered off after the election, public sentiment against them continued to run high. A Gallup poll taken in the spring of 1941 showed that 71 percent of the respondents would favor passage of a law outlawing the party. [14] The role that the Communists played—or were accused of playing—in strikes in defense industries that spring kept the anti-communist sentiments alive and flourishing.

In the spring of 1940 Roosevelt had called on American industry to begin turning out fifty thousand airplanes a year; in November he urged the United States to take on the responsibility of serving as the arsenal of democracy; in the same month he instructed the War Department to be prepared to turn over half of the production of new weapons to Great Britain, at a time when American soldiers were training with wooden guns and dummy tanks. Despite pressure from Roosevelt, American industry converted to war production at an agonizingly slow pace, and the cumbersome and internally divided National Defense Advisory Commission did little to prod it. At the end of December 1940, Roosevelt issued an executive order establishing the Office of Production Management (OPM) to replace the NDAC. The OPM had greater authority and a smaller directing board than its predecessor: its four-member directing board consisted of William Knudsen, Sidney Hillman, Secretary of War Henry L. Stimson, and Secretary of the Navy Frank Knox.

Roosevelt continued to use Hillman as his chief link to organized labor. Lewis's ill-fated endorsement of Willkie and subsequent departure from CIO leadership had enhanced Hillman's prestige. The new CIO president, Philip Murray, was determined not to be cut out entirely from the power accruing to Hillman for his role in spurring war production. In December 1940, with considerable flourish, Murray released a plan for establishing "Industrial Councils" in all major war industries. Murray's councils would bring together union and management officials to share authority in coordinating production, overseeing material and manpower distribution, and guaranteeing labor peace. Other union officials clambered onto the bandwagon: Walter Reuther, for example, came out with a plan for converting idle production facilities in the auto industry to turn out "five hundred planes a day."[15]

Reuther was an easy target for the Communists. "Sounds a little funny, doesn't it," the *Young Communist Review* declared, "when a 'labor leader' undertakes to solve production problems for the manufacturers. . . . Reuther is acting as a time-study man for the bosses." But they had more trouble with Murray's Industrial Councils. The last thing they wanted to do was force a public break with Murray, who had thus far refrained from taking any administrative measures against the left in the CIO's national office and constituent unions. When the February *Communist* took up the question of Murray's plan, the criticisms it offered were distinctly muted compared to the vehement attacks leveled against Reuther: "It has to be said plainly that its principles and underlying assumptions are unsound from a working class point of view. At the same time we are fully conscious of the fact that the plan reflects in a way the profound dissatisfaction of the workers with Big Business domination of the 'national defense' machinery."[16]

For all the plans being floated for labor-capital harmony in the national emergency, 1941 was not a year of industrial harmony. One out of every twelve workers in the nation's work force went out on strike that year, and the number of strikes and man-days lost were nearly at the level of the great sit-down strike wave of 1937.[17] Both the CIO and the AFL took advantage of renewed worker militancy to expand the membership of their unions. The UAW, with the full backing of all the union's factions, launched its long-prepared offensive against the Ford Motor Company, with a massive strike in April at Ford's River Rouge plant. Murray's Steel Workers Organizing Committee led strikes for union recognition at the Bethlehem Steel Mills at Lackawanna, New York, and elsewhere. These were all strikes directed by mainstream union leaders for traditional union goals, but union opponents were quick to smear them as Communist-inspired. Harry Bennett, the strong-arm manager of Ford's "Service Department," or goon squad, called the NLRB election in May 1941 that awarded recognition to the UAW a "great victory for the Communist Party."[18]

With the capitulation of Ford and Little Steel in the spring of 1941, the CIO took a giant step toward completion of the task it had set out to accomplish in 1935: to break the back of employer resistance to unionization in the mass-production industries. But by late spring, as press and congressional outcry against "sabotage" in defense industries rose to a crescendo, CIO leaders wavered. Even before the full dimensions of the 1941 strike wave became apparent, voices were raised attributing the unrest to a Communist conspiracy. Victor Riesel, an influential labor columnist, in an article in the February *American Mercury*, cited an antique Comintern directive instructing its member parties around the world to organize unions in "munitions factories, in ports, in factories, on railroads and on ships, for the purpose of developing mass activity and carefully prepared protest strikes and economic strikes to prevent the transport of munitions and ships." Riesel could produce no recent documentary evidence of Communist intentions, but warned that the party had organizers strategically placed to "gum up the American defense program."[19]

Roosevelt held a number of discussions with his advisers in 1940 and 1941 about alleged Communist plots to disrupt national defense. J. Edgar Hoover kept the President supplied with reports from FBI agents who had infiltrated the party. On May 18, 1940, for example, Hoover wrote to Secretary of the Treasury Henry Morgenthau to report that a "confidential source" had heard the California CP district organizer William Schneiderman tell a party meeting in San Francisco that, "the CP and the CIO will combine to carry the Party program out effective immediately, concentrating their activities and delaying production in aircraft factories, chemical plants and shipyards. Orders will be given the section leaders, who will follow their own initiative in delaying production."[20]

Informers had a vested interest in providing such material, and it is not difficult to imagine how a speech calling for militant unionism could, with a little creativity, be transformed into this tabloid-style conspiracy. At the end of May 1941 Stimson and Knox sent a joint letter to Roosevelt expressing concern over Communist activities in defense plants. The President replied on June 4, agreeing that "strikes and slow-downs are in many cases instigated by Communists and other subversive elements acting in the interest of foreign enemies." He promised to recommend to the Attorney General that the FBI's "investigative responsibility . . . in the fields of subversive control of labor" be widened.[21] Earlier that spring Roosevelt had suggested at a cabinet meeting that Army military intelligence be assigned responsibility for investigation of strikes in defense plants. Secretary of Labor Frances Perkins eventually talked him out of the idea, arguing that the Army might lack the sensitivity to know the difference between a Communist and a non-Communist strike.[22] While weighing alternatives for covert surveillance of strikes, Roosevelt established the National Defense Mediation Board (NDMB) to intervene in industrial conflicts as a mediator.[23]

Communists were prominently involved in a number of strikes that spring. One of the most controversial strikes of 1941 took place at the Allis-Chalmers plant in Milwaukee, where workers in UAW Local 248 walked out three months before the scheduled end of a one-year contract. The plant had been working on a $40 million government contract to produce turbines and generators for Navy destroyers, and the long and close association of Local 248 president Harold Christoffel with the Communists inevitably led to charges of sabotage of national defense.[24]

The strike began in January, sparked by an incident in which two UAW members had been fired. The chief issue was union security. The plant had been a battleground between rival AFL and CIO forces for some time, and Christoffel wanted to nail down the UAW's bargaining position with a decisive strike victory. Allis-Chalmers president Max Babb had never extended more than the most grudging recognition to the union, and both sides settled in for a protracted battle. After three weeks of stalemate Hillman, in his role as OPM director, summoned Christoffel and Babb to Washington, where a compromise "maintenance of membership" arrangement was worked out. Hillman's diplomacy proved a little too subtle, since the antagonists apparently left Washington with radically different interpretations of the meaning of their agreement. Upon returning to Milwaukee, Christoffel announced he had secured the UAW's path to a closed shop at Allis-Chalmers; when Babb heard this he insisted he would no longer agree to the compromise unless it included a clause specifically repudiating the closed shop.

With Hillman unable to resolve the dispute, Secretary of the Navy Knox and OPM Director General Knudsen went behind his back and sent a telegram to Local 248 ordering the strikers back to work. About a quarter of the 7,800 striking workers tried to enter the plant the following day, leading to a violent clash on the picket line, the intervention of the state militia, and no progress toward a settlement. Secretary of War Stimson wanted Roosevelt to send in the army. But the strike had been authorized by the UAW national leadership soon after it started. Murray and R. J. Thomas were outraged over the peremptory Knox-Knudsen back-to-work order, and Roosevelt did not want to do battle with the mainstream of the union movement. The strike was finally resolved after seventy-six days by the newly created NDMB, which recommended a settlement similar to the original "maintenance of membership" compromise.[25]

The press charged that Communists in the leadership of Local 248 had deliberately prolonged the strike in order to delay war production. *Time*, in its article on the strike settlement, asserted: "Chief danger of Communism was the damage its agents could do—and have undoubtedly done—in fanning flames, inciting to riot, disrupting negotiations."[26] Despite the controversy it produced at the time, the relatively brief Vultee strike had not prevented the company from meeting its contract deadline with the War Department; as the *CIO News* reported in February 1941, Vultee delivered its three hundred training planes to the Army a full forty days ahead of schedule.[27] The lengthy Allis-Chalmers strike was another matter. A congressional committee investigating the naval defense program reported in January 1942 that the strike had delayed completion of some war vessels for up to six months.[28] Even allowing for partisan exaggeration, a strike of this duration clearly did not aid rearmament in the few months remaining before American entry into the war.

The Communists, as long as they viewed the war as an imperialist conflict, were not particularly upset about slowing down war preparations. As Foster's speech to the YCL in December made clear, they hoped to gain politically by standing up as militant defenders of the workers' right to strike in the face of government claims of a national emergency. Can it then be assumed that American Communists deliberately set out to provoke strikes in vital defense industries for the purpose of slowing down rearmament?

The Communists denied it. After the Vultee strike, Wyndham Mortimer turned his attention to the Ryan Aeronautical Company in San Diego. UAW organizers called off a threatened strike at the plant in January when the company granted a pay raise. The Sunday *Worker* commented: "The Ryan settlement gives the lie to the claim . . . that the workers are engaged in some kind of 'conspiracy.' The fact is, as the Ryan settlement shows, that when conditions are improved the necessity for strike action is eliminated."[29]

No one expects a conspirator to admit the existence of a conspiracy, and Communists might have been using legitimate trade-union demands to mask ulterior motives. The *New York Times* thought so, and argued editorially in June that "the remarkably strategic points at which some of the most serious strikes have been occurring must be set down to more than coincidence."[30]

The *Times* editorial was prompted by the strike at North American Aviation in Los Angeles, and strikes in the aircraft industry drew the most criticism for harming national defense. But despite the prominent role that Communists like Mortimer played in these strikes, the Communist party had not made the decision to concentrate union activity in these "strategic points." The 1940 UAW convention resolved to step up the organization drive among aircraft workers—a decision supported by Communists and anti-Communists alike. UAW leaders knew Mortimer's politics when they assigned him to head up their West Coast aircraft division. Following the controversial Vultee strike there was no attempt to remove Mortimer from the organizing drive; nor did any of the UAW's anti-Communist leaders repudiate him when he told the *CIO News* in early December: "This is only the beginning. We are going to organize the aircraft industry all over Southern California in the next two or three months."[31]

Philip Murray, concerned about the charges of Communist control of the aircraft drive, did arrange to have the CIO co-sponsor the organizing campaign, under the overall direction of UAW vice-president Richard Frankensteen. But Murray was still content to leave Mortimer and another Communist, Lew Michener, director of the UAW's West Coast region, in charge of day-to-day operations in California.[32] The *New York Times* correctly argued that the decision to concentrate on this "strategic" link in the country's defense program was more than coincidence, but it was not a decision that the Communists had made on their own.

Did the Communists deliberately prolong strikes that could have been resolved by arbitration? The party's line in general was in a militant phase, and what might have been accepted as a reasonable compromise in ordinary times was likely to be denounced as a "sell-out" by Communist unionists in the spring of 1941. The only true guarantee of the workers' living standards, a hundred editorials in the *Daily Worker* declared, lay in their willingness to go out on the picket line. After the Vultee strike Hillman complained that UAW organizers at the plant had failed to give the National Defense Advisory Commission adequate notice of the impending walkout, a charge UAW regional director Michener denied. Whatever the truth of the matter, there was no love lost between Hillman and the Communists that spring; undoubtedly the Communists would much rather have won settlements on their own than share the credit with Hillman and government mediators. If party unionists were allowing such considerations to keep them from using the government's arbitration services, they might justifiably be charged with political irresponsibility—but instances of Communist obstinacy do not seem to add up to any clear pattern of deliberate sabotage of contract negotiations.

During the Allis-Chalmers strike, for example, the press accused Christoffel of sabotaging negotiations with the company. But months after the strike was settled some of the Communists' most bitter opponents in the union movement conceded that Christoffel did not deserve the sole or even the major blame for the duration of the strike. Reuther, who sought to have Christoffel censured by the UAW convention in the summer of 1941, suggested at the same time that it was the Allis-Chalmers management who had wanted to prolong the conflict for political purposes. According to Reuther, Max Babb "was tied up with the America First Committee, and I think he was playing Hitler's game and wanted that plant tied up." Sidney Hillman, who met with both sides in the dispute, later blamed the last month of the strike on the obstinacy of the Allis-Chalmers management.[33]

In retrospect, it is surprising just how few strikes Communists led that spring in industries directly tied to defense production. Some of the strikes in which they participated, like the Transport Workers Union bus strike in New York City, had little or no relation to the state of American military preparedness (though they fed public hysteria about Communist conspiracies).[34] In outlining the "Communist grip on our defense" in the February *American Mercury*, Victor Riesel pointed in alarm to the party's strength in such unions as the United Electrical Workers, the International Longshoremen's and Warehousemen's Union, the National Maritime Union, and the American Communications Association, "a bloc . . . strategically located in relation to defense work."[35] In all these unions the Communists were much stronger than they were in the UAW; yet, with the exception of a few minor strikes by UE locals, these unions avoided strikes throughout 1940 and 1941. The West Coast longshoremen and the East Coast seamen were certainly in a strategic position to interfere with defense preparations, had that been the Communists' plan. But in November 1940 the ILWU arrived at an agreement with waterfront employers to eliminate the frequent work stoppages that had characterized labor relations on West Coast docks. And though the NMU and its more conservative AFL rival, the Seafarers International Union (SIU), were both demanding bonus pay in 1941 for sailing into war zones, only the SIU ever pushed the matter to a major work stoppage.[36]

The Communists were vulnerable to the charge that they sought to cripple rearmament whenever they led strikes, because of their outspoken opposition to the war. Conspiracy theories are always difficult to refute since, after all, the point of a conspiracy is to commit a crime without being detected. Nevertheless, the available evidence does not substantiate the charges made against the Communists, and the burden of proof remains with their accusers.[37]

However unfounded the charges of Communist-directed "sabotage," the Communists undeniably viewed the strike wave that spring with satisfaction. Following Foster's lead, Communist leaders predicted great political gains from the increasing militancy being displayed in the workplace. Gil Green, writing in the January *Communist*, declared: "It is precisely in the struggle for its demands, in the struggle to defend its living standards, that labor will emancipate itself from the Roosevelt myth, will learn who are its true friends and who its sworn foes, and will move in the direction of independent political action."[38]

At different points in its history the Communist party had attached varying degrees of importance to trade-union activity. In theory, the Communists were always trying to strike the proper balance between economic and political struggles. No party leader would ever openly disparage the value of economic struggles: that would be the "Lassallean" error so forcefully criticized by Marx in the nineteenth century. Nor would even the most union-oriented Communist ever call for abandoning political struggle for a purely economic strategy: Lenin had criticized such views in *What Is to Be Done?* and, closer to home, American Communists remembered their own disputes with the syndicalist ideology of the Industrial Workers of the World.

Nevertheless, an ideological mood resembling syndicalism took root in the party in the spring of 1941, the most tangible expression of which can be found in the discussion over whether and how to change the party's organizational structure. Under Browder in the late 1930s, the CP moved decisively toward a more politically oriented structure, with neighborhood branches replacing shop and industrial branches. In the spring of 1941 the pendulum swung back the other way. Israel Amter wrote an article in the April 5 *Daily Worker* entitled "Face to the Shops," in which he noted the "unparalleled militancy" displayed by workers in recent strikes, but complained that these same workers did not seem to "fully understand" the CP's anti-war line. The problem, he believed, was one of organization. There was no better place to carry on political agitation than "at the point of exploitation, namely the shop, and in the workers' basic organization, the trade union. . . . Here we can show them the connection between their struggle for wages and the administration's war program. . . . Here we can most readily concentrate upon individual militant workers and recruit them for our Party." Amter believed the party needed to "reorientate all of our work—turning our face to the shops, particularly of basic and key industries. . . . This will require a major reorientation of the Party's activity, a readjustment of its work and possibly also of some forms of organization."[39]

Increasingly, economic struggles carried the Communists' hopes for the future. A year and a half of anti-war agitation had not made a dent in working-class political outlook. The Communists were forced to recognize that Roosevelt's step-by-step involvement in the war had gained at least the tacit approval of American working people. "Large sections of the workers supported the 'defense program' and the 'aid-to-Britain' because they were told this was the best way to keep out of the war," the *Daily Worker* admitted in early May. "But," the editors continued, "by their determination to fight for a higher standard of living and for the maintenance of civil and labor's rights, these same workers revealed an instinctive feeling that this was not their war."[40]

The Communists may have found it consoling to believe that workers "instinctively" agreed with them, whatever misguided sentiments they might consciously espouse. But there was no demonstrable connection between the strike wave of 1941 and opposition to the war; instead, there was a growing, if reluctant, recognition among the majority of Americans that the United States would not be able to remain out of the conflict much longer. Gallup polls taken in early June showed, for the first time, that a majority of respondents supported sending convoys to Britain, a move widely interpreted as being the last step short of full military participation.[41] Confronted with the failure of their anti-war campaign, the Communists were unwilling and unable to reexamine the fundamental premises underlying their position. They could turn their face to the shops, or any direction they chose, but no amount of organizational tinkering could rescue them from this political impasse.

The mainstream CIO leadership was also drawing closer to Roosevelt. Murray was working hard to catch up with Hillman's lead in securing a place in the defense establishment. When Roosevelt appointed the eleven-member National Defense Mediation Board in March, Murray accepted a position as one of two CIO representatives. At its inception the NDMB was granted only advisory powers, but increasingly it came to regard its recommendations for settlements as binding on both parties in strikes in which it chose to intervene. Despite Murray's presence on the board, Communist unionists denounced the NDMB as "an all-out labor-busting and strike-breaking device" and defied its authority.[42]

The North American Aviation Strike

The lines were being drawn for a showdown. Roosevelt went on the radio on May 27 to issue a proclamation of unlimited national emergency. He warned against the divisive activities of "fifth columnists, who are the incendiary bombs in this country," and pledged that the government would "use all of its power to express the will of the people, and to prevent interference with the production of materials essential to the Nation's security."[43]

Out in California, Mortimer had been concentrating his organizing efforts on the North American Aviation plant in the Los Angeles suburb of Inglewood. The UAW was locked in fierce competition with the International Association of Machinists (IAM) to win representation of the plant's workers. In the late winter of 1941, despite a mud-slinging anti-communist campaign by the IAM, the UAW won an NLRB election at North American. The UAW national leadership, increasingly sensitive to charges of interfering with defense production, banished Mortimer to Seattle to keep him away from the North American contract negotiations. But the Communists remained influential at North American: local president Elmer Freitag was a party member, as were several other local officers.[44]

Frankensteen went to Los Angeles to oversee contract negotiations. As a bargaining device he allowed leadership of the local to take a strike vote, which passed by an overwhelming majority. The union's demands centered on a wage increase from the 50-cent-an-hour minimum wage the workers were then receiving to the 75-cent minimum prevailing in most plants in Los Angeles, as well as a 10-cent-an-hour general raise for all workers in the plant. When the strike vote was taken, the NDMB immediately certified the dispute, and Frankensteen, Michener, and three members of the local's nine-member negotiating committee went to Washington to present their case. Before departing, they agreed with the company to postpone any strike until three days after the NDMB had made its recommendation, in return for a promise to make all pay increases granted by the board retroactive to May 1.

The NDMB let six crucial days slip by without holding hearings. Back in Inglewood the remaining members of the negotiating committee decided that the board was stalling. The UAW's position in the plant was insecure. The IAM still retained a following among the workers; nearly four thousand new workers had come to the plant since the NLRB election; and the local leadership feared that if they did not win a contract soon, they would either lose the loyalty of the plant's workers or see their strength dissipated by a series of uncoordinated wildcat strikes. And it is possible that the Communists among the local's leadership hoped to make political capital by defying the NDMB. North American Aviation held more than $200 million in War Department contracts, turning out ten fighter planes a day, about a quarter of the country's total production of fighter aircraft at the time. A new strike in a major defense plant little more than a week after Roosevelt's emergency declaration would be a slap in the face to the Administration, as the Communists surely understood.

The local's leaders felt they could depend on the support of the workers in the plant in a strike, and expected that the national UAW would back them up once they went out. The Vultee and Allis-Chalmers strikes had both begun as unauthorized strikes, and both gained authorization once it became clear that the majority of the local membership supported them. With national UAW backing they could call Roosevelt's bluff on using force to keep defense plants open. But they had made a serious miscalculation. The national UAW leaders no longer had any intention of letting themselves be dragged into possible confrontation with the government. This time the tail would not wag the dog.

On June 5 workers leaving the night shift at North American set up picket lines around the plant. When the day-shift workers arrived they joined in, swelling the picket lines to the largest in California's history. Stimson, who had been urging a hard line against defense strikes all spring, saw the perfect opportunity for the government to crack down without facing undue political repercussions. The strike clearly affected war preparations; it had been launched while the dispute was still pending before the NDMB; and there was a heavy concentration of Communists among its leadership. Stimson wanted Roosevelt to send in the army immediately, but Roosevelt, unwilling to risk any head-on clash with the UAW, waited until the national union leadership had taken its own steps to end the strike. R. J. Thomas and Philip Murray both wired the strikers, ordering them back to work. On June 7 Frankensteen flew to Los Angeles. When UAW leaders on the scene refused to end the strike, Frankensteen lifted the local's charter, suspended its negotiating committee, suspended Michener from office, and fired Mortimer and four other UAW organizers. That evening he went on the radio and blamed the "infamous agitation and vicious underhanded maneuvering of the Communist Party" for the strike.

Frankensteen underestimated the strikers' militancy. At a mass meeting on June 8 in a bean field near the plant he was booed off the platform. On Monday, June 9, only about a third of the plant's 11,200 workers attempted to obey the back-to-work order. Despite the liberal use of tear gas by Los Angeles police, few made it into the plant through the four-deep picket line. Stimson, who now had the support of Hillman, convinced Roosevelt that it was time to send in troops to seize the plant.

Later that morning several thousand soldiers with fixed bayonets moved in to clear a path through the booing pickets. It was a dramatic, though bloodless, confrontation: for the first time since the Bonus March of 1932, federal troops had been used against American civilians; for the first time in the twentieth century, federal troops had been used to break a strike. And it proved effective. At the bean-field meeting, Freitag had defied Roosevelt with a variation of the old coal miners' taunt, "Bombers can't be built with bayonets." But by the second day of the seizure fewer than three thousand workers remained on strike, and the following day the rest went back.[45]

This was the kind of showdown battle between workers and the government the Communists had been hoping for all spring. The day after the plant seizure, the *Daily Worker* accused Roosevelt of seeking to wipe out the right to strike: "The use of troops against the strikers in California is one act in the growing militarization of the country, under the war drive of the administration. It is bringing a military dictatorship to our very doorsteps. The workers are opposed to such militarization. They do not want an AEF [American Expeditionary Force] abroad, nor do they want an AEF used against them within our own borders."[46]

The use of troops aroused protest from other quarters. Lewis bitterly denounced Roosevelt and Hillman, and called the week of the plant seizure "the blackest in American labor history." Although Murray had urged the strikers to return to work, he was not prepared to condone open strike-breaking by the government, and criticized Roosevelt's action. But outside of CIO ranks, the strikers found few supporters. *Life* magazine's coverage of the event was typical. It headlined its account of the events of June 9 "President Roosevelt Breaks a Red Strike," and accused the Communists of being "allies of Adolf Hitler and his Bundists" in seeking to "sabotage U.S. defense."[47]

The North American strike sparked widespread press speculation about an impending left-right split within the CIO. *Newsweek* predicted that "the CIO is finally ready to crack down on its radical element."[48] But Murray was not yet willing to take on John L. Lewis, who might have sided with the Communists against a purge, and left-wing unionists were doing their best to convince Murray of their loyalty: the Greater New York Industrial Union Council, Harry Bridges, Mike Quill, and Joe Curran all sent telegrams to Murray praising his condemnation of the use of troops at Inglewood. On June 12 Murray sent out a tortuously-worded letter to CIO officers denying reports of impending splits or Red hunts within the CIO. The letter even-handedly condemned the "subversive work of any group in the United States, whether corporate, communist, nazi or fascist, that may be interesting themselves in the promotion of selfish things designed to undermine the interests of the United States of America in its national defense effort."[49] Communists in the CIO could breathe a little easier after reading Murray's letter, especially if they knew it had been drafted by one of their own, *CIO News* editor Len DeCaux.[50]

The Communists had gained nothing and risked a great deal with the affair at North American. Although the strike undoubtedly created anti-Roosevelt sentiment in the plant, the party was no longer around as an organized force to take advantage of it. The strike ended the party's influence in the UAW's aviation division and greatly strengthened its factional opponents within the national union. A few more political victories like the one at North American and the Communists would have eliminated themselves as a significant force in the union movement.[51]

Operation Barbarossa

The soldiers in Inglewood were not the only troops on the march that spring. Despite Molotov's assertion the previous August that German and Soviet interests remained in firm accord, relations between the two countries had steadily deteriorated. The future of the Balkan countries proved to be the sticking point. The Russians had begun the process of partitioning Rumania in July 1940 when they occupied Bessarabia and Northern Bukovina. In the weeks that followed, Hungary and Bulgaria helped themselves to large sections of Rumanian territory. Germany finally "guaranteed" the country's remaining frontiers by pouring in its own troops, much to the dismay of the Russians. In November, Molotov met with Hitler and Ribbentrop in Berlin. Hitler offered the Soviets a free hand for expansion in Central Asia and India. But Molotov was more concerned about what was happening on the Soviet Union's northern and western borders. He demanded that Southern Bukovina be ceded to the USSR, and asked about the intentions of German troops in Finland. Hitler refused to surrender any Rumanian territory, and minimized the importance of his troops in Finland, who, he assured Molotov, were only passing through on their way to Norway.

Before Molotov returned to Moscow, Hitler presented him with a draft treaty that would have admitted Russia as an equal partner along with Germany, Italy, and Japan in the Axis Alliance. But even as Hitler and Ribbentrop were wooing the noncommittal Molotov with visions of sharing the spoils of the British Empire, Hitler issued a secret directive to his generals declaring that military preparations for the invasion of Russia were to continue regardless of the outcome of the discussions.

After consulting with Stalin, Molotov informed the Germans that the USSR would only sign the draft treaty if Germany withdrew all troops from Finland and the Soviets were granted a "mutual assistance pact" with Bulgaria, similar to the one which had served as a prelude to the annexation of Latvia, Estonia, and Lithuania into the USSR. The Germans did not bother to reply. Two weeks later Hitler issued an order, code-named Operation Barbarossa, detailing plans for the spring invasion of the Soviet Union.[52]

The spring of 1941 brought more disturbing events. Italy invaded Greece, an adventure from which the hapless Mussolini eventually had to be rescued by the Wehrmacht. Bulgaria announced on March 1 that it was joining the Axis, and German troops moved into the country. The Yugoslav Crown Council, under considerable pressure from the Germans, made a similar announcement on March 25, but two days later the council was overthrown by the Yugoslav army. The new government signed a treaty of friendship with the USSR on April 5. Hitler, enraged by the Yugoslavs' defiance, unleashed the Luftwaffe on Belgrade the following day, and within a week the country was overrun by the Germans.[53]

For the second time since the signing of the Nazi-Soviet pact, dramatic German victories provoked second thoughts among American Communists. In an article in the *New Masses* in mid-April, Starobin argued that the USSR should not be "expected to be passive" in the face of German advances. John Gates, repudiating his own earlier speculations on the long-term possibilities for Soviet-German rapprochement, now initiated a discussion in YCL leadership circles about the changing character of the war. The May *Communist* declared that "the attacked peoples" in Yugoslavia and Greece were "waging a valiant and just war of liberation." Greek and Yugoslav resistance, together with the Soviet-Yugoslav treaty, had "unleashed a powerful solidarity movement throughout the world, and, above all, gave a strong impulse to the national movement of liberation of many other peoples," including those in the occupied countries of Western Europe. But again, as in the aftermath of the fall of France, the Communists stopped short of a genuine reassessment of their anti-war position. If it was now praiseworthy in Communist eyes for Greek and Yugoslav resistance fighters to kill Germans, it was still an act of imperialist aggression for British soldiers to do the same. "People's Peace" remained the Communist slogan.[54]

As in the summer of 1940, internal doubts were not allowed to deflect the party from carrying on its anti-war campaign. In May the American Peace Mobilization launched a twenty-four-hour-a-day "perpetual peace vigil" on the sidewalk in front of the White House. Pickets carried a railroad lantern with the slogan "Keep the light of peace burning" and placards reading "No Convoys" and "No AEF." On Saturday, June 21, after forty days of continuous picketing, the APM finally called off its vigil, vowing to continue the anti-war struggle in other forms.[55]

Stalin, warned of Operation Barbarossa by the American and British governments and by his own agents in Europe and Japan, had convinced himself that Hitler was preparing only an ultimatum, not an invasion. He avoided any steps that might provoke the Germans, refusing to mobilize or even to put his army into the state of limited alert it had assumed in September 1939. The Soviet press continued through the middle of June to denounce all rumors of impending war as Allied provocations.[56]

If the Soviet press denied the possibility of an impending German-Soviet war, American Communists were not about to disagree. The June 20 *Daily Worker* complained: "Reports of a 'break' between the Soviet Union and Germany, with rumors of war, continue to flare up in the capitalist newspapers. What is immediately noticeable about this whole press campaign is the lying character of the stories being published as the gospel truth." Such fabrications, the editors were convinced, would soon be "repudiated by life." On June 21 the *Daily Worker* dismissed war rumors as "wishful thinking on the part of the monopoly publishers and the imperialist war mongers." And on the following day the Sunday *Worker* accused the British press of spreading "tales" of an impending German invasion of the Soviet Union in the hope of inciting a conflict between the two countries.[57]

By the time American Communists opened the paper that Sunday morning, the Nazi army was rolling toward Moscow.

6 THE RETURN TO ANTI-FASCISM
June 22 to December 1941

Looking back today, we believe that our policy of the past two years has been vindicated. We are proud of the part we played in helping clarify the issues. . . . In our struggle against fascism . . . there is an unbroken continuity even though the forms and tactics of this activity now require change.

—*New Masses*, July 8, 1941[1]

NEWS OF THE INVASION reached the United States in the early morning hours of June 22. Party and YCL leaders, roused from their beds in the middle of the night, went into emergency meetings. By late morning most Communists had learned of the attack. The party rank and file displayed none of the hesitation and bewilderment that had marked their reception of the news of the Nazi-Soviet pact. They had been preparing to respond to an attack on the Soviet Union for as long as they had been Communists: "Defend the Soviet Union" was the one party slogan that, through all the other changes in political line, had remained constant. Mike Gold wrote in his *Daily Worker* column shortly after the invasion, "The first hour was awful—I shall never forget it. Now it had come—the thing we feared for five, ten, twenty years."[2] In the days after June 22, the Communists dramatically reversed political direction, while attempting to convince the world and themselves of the underlying consistency of their position.

The CP's opponents had mocked it during the Nazi-Soviet pact as the "Russia First Committee." Indeed, the Communists' emotional attachment to the Soviet Union could hardly have been overstated. Ten years earlier Mike Gold had said of a trip to Russia for the *New Masses*: "It's Revolution, it's dull, it's normal, it's not a dream, it's the daily bread and cabbage soup of 150 million human beings. . . . I am in the USSR about to see a big slice of the Revolution in my own lifetime. It comes with a great stab of joy and wonder at first."[3] Now that the Russian Revolution was under military attack, the Communists responded as if German bombs were landing on their own homes.

First Reactions

Shock and dismay for many American Communists were accompanied by a sense of relief, even of exhilaration. Whatever conflicts in their viewpoint might have been apparent to outsiders, Communists felt no clash between their ties with the Soviet Union and their loyalty to the United States. The effects of the party's "Americanization" of the 1930s had not worn off during the years of the Nazi-Soviet pact. The Communists had been bewildered and angered by accusations that they were "fifth columnists." Even before the party's official line had time to catch up with new events, Communists experienced, as Al Richmond put it, "an enormous sense of release. Not just from the status of pariah in the period of the Nazi-Soviet treaty. And not only in the identification with the Soviet resistance. . . . The anti-Nazi passion had not been extinguished, it had smoldered, and now it burst forth, all the more fervently for having been restrained so long."[4] When George Watt and other YCL leaders in New York City were summoned from their beds in the early morning hours of June 22 to meet with John Gates, Max Weiss, and a few others, one sentiment was universal. "We all felt relief," Watt recalled. "We felt like we had come home again."[5]

The party's top leaders were more cautious as they drafted a statement offering the CP's official reaction. Molotov had gone on the air at midday on June 22 to denounce the Nazi invasion, but he did not indicate what Russia's attitude would be toward other opponents of Germany. Later in the day Churchill, on the BBC, pledged full cooperation with the Soviet Union: "The cause of any Russian fighting for his hearth and home is the cause of free men and free peoples in any quarter of the globe."[6]

American Communist leaders were nonetheless reluctant to break new ground without a definite signal from the Soviet Union. The CP's first public statement on the invasion, released late in the evening of June 22, warned that "the rulers of fascist Germany are dangling before the imperialists of all countries, especially in England and the United States, the vista of a new Munich, a new conspiracy to redivide the world at the expense of the peoples of all nations." The statement called for "full support and cooperation with the Soviet Union in its struggle against Hitlerism," but also renewed the call for a "People's Peace."[7]

The first official reaction from the American government came on the afternoon of June 23, when Acting Secretary of State Sumner Welles told reporters that the government welcomed "any defense against Hitlerism . . . from whatever source these forces may spring." He did not mention American aid to the Soviet war effort. Long-standing antipathy toward the USSR, combined with a widespread belief that the Red Army was incapable of standing up to the Wehrmacht, made the State and War Departments reluctant to embrace Stalin as an ally. Secretary of War Stimson told Roosevelt on June 23 that the Germans would defeat the Russians within three months at the maximum. Many people in the Administration undoubtedly shared the sentiments expressed by Missouri senator Harry Truman on June 23: "If we see that Germany is winning we ought to help Russia and if Russia is winning we ought to help Germany and that way let them kill as many as possible."[8]

Roosevelt felt differently, and at a press conference on June 24 pledged to send "all the aid we possibly can to Russia." Public opinion polls showed that a majority of Americans favored a Russian victory over Germany, but opposed extending lend-lease aid to the Soviet Union. Roosevelt, always eager to go around rather than over political obstacles, relied on a series of makeshift arrangements to get some aid to the Red Army in the summer of 1941. He did not extend full lend-lease aid to Russia until October.[9] American Communists began demanding full lend-lease aid for Russia a few days after the Nazi invasion, reversing their position of the previous winter that the lend-lease bill was an unconstitutional abuse of executive power, "FDR's coup d'état."[10] The Communists were not oblivious to the awkwardness of their position, but decided that the only thing they could do was to brazen their way through. They began waving the anti-fascist banners of the Popular Front days as if they had never dropped them. "Communists are proud of their record of consistent struggle against Fascism," Louis Budenz declared in the *Daily Worker* of June 26, retelling the story of the CP's struggle against Nazism in the 1930s, its support for the Spanish Republic, and its calls for collective security. As for the intervening twenty-two months of the pact, fast fading in memory as far as Budenz was concerned, the Communists had "joined with the majority of the American people in saying: 'This is not a war against Hitlerism. It is an imperialist war.'" Unable to support a war fought against Germany for the wrong reasons, the Communists had devoted their efforts during those months to building up "people's movements," the only sure "guarantee of the defeat of Hitlerism and of fascism in any form."[11]

Six days after the start of the invasion, the CP assembled its national committee in New York City to bury the remains of the "Yanks Aren't Coming" period. On the eve of the meeting Minor wrote to Browder to assure him that all members of the political committee understood the need for a return to Popular Front–style policies:

> During this weekend some of my best friends and I are going to discuss the nature of the world in general. . . . There is not the slightest doubt that a harmony of view exists now. . . . Not that I and my friends had anything wrong or outworn to worry about. All are in good health; incidentally I have a high appreciation of Bill [Foster] at this time particularly. Last Sunday three or four of us had a little gathering to talk over things, and although not everything could be brought to final detail—and such could hardly be expected—I was much pleased with the outcome. . . . I am still more pleased with the ripening of our thoughts since then.[12]

Gil Green provided the best formulation of these "ripened" conclusions in his report to the national committee members, writing that "every blow against Hitler today is a blow in the interests of the Soviet people. . . . We must support these blows completely, for no matter who delivers them or for what reasons, they help to defeat and annihilate the main enemy of mankind." This required a dramatic shift in political orientation: "The Roosevelt Administration represents those groups of the American bourgeoisie which aim to bring about the military defeat of Hitler," and was thus entitled to the Communists' full support, Green declared.[13]

Minor explained why the slogan "People's Peace," included in the party's initial statement on the invasion, was "not in keeping with the changed situation. . . . The military destruction of the Hitler government is the precondition for any peace." And Foster urged Communists to break sharply with tactics "adapted to the past period" and "to proceed boldly to develop the broadest united front and People's Front activities. . . . Our greatest enemy is sectarianism." But he warned, "While supporting the Roosevelt Administration in all blows that it may deliver against Hitler, we do not forget the imperialist character of the government nor its imperialist aims in this war."[14]

Foster's reservations did not appear in the resolution adopted by the national committee on June 28. This "People's Program of Struggle for the Defeat of Hitler and Hitlerism" announced that the involvement of the Soviet Union in the war had changed its character decisively. Up until June 22, "the war was not really a war against fascism but a struggle between rivals for imperialist aims." But the German attack on Russia imparted "a new and sinister aspect to the menace of Hitlerism for the American people, the British people and the people of the world." The invasion proved "conclusively" that Nazi Germany was bent on world conquest. The statement made no mention of any continuing American and British imperialist aims in the war; it warned only against those circles within the American ruling class who might seek "to come to terms with Hitler at the expense of the most vital national interests of the American people." The "People's Program" called for full and unlimited collaboration of the Western Allies and the Soviet Union against Germany. The imperialist war had at last become the people's war.[15]

Though the Communists' new line on the war stood in implicit repudiation of almost everything they had been saying for nearly two years, they would never publicly acknowledge having been mistaken in their earlier "anti-imperialist" stance. The fervor with which they returned to an anti-fascist politics suggests that many felt at least a private distaste for their earlier "no lesser evil" characterization of the war. The party's internal structure included no effective institutional channels for reevaluation. Public dissent was regarded as a breach of discipline punishable by expulsion; private dissent could brand a member as unreliable, or bring charges of factionalism, also punishable by expulsion. The CP's periodic exercises in "self-criticism"—like the campaigns against white chauvinism in the early 1930s—had been authorized from the top and had a controlled, ritualistic tone. There was one other deterrent to any kind of honest reevaluation of recent policies: any criticism of the party's political line during the pact would logically extend to criticism of the Comintern and the Soviet leadership, a step that remained unthinkable for most Communists, especially when the Soviet Union was engaged in a struggle for its survival.

Max Gordon, a party organizer in upstate New York, wrote to the *Daily Worker* in early July to complain about press treatment of the

Communists' new position: "To accuse us of 'flip-flop' . . . is really ludicrous. Even a bourgeois newspaper editor should be able to grasp the simple fact that there is a difference between a socialist country fighting for existence against a fascist aggressor, and an imperialist power fighting to retain domination over a quarter of the world's population."[16] Gordon's formulation was forthright: British war aims were imperialist, Russian war aims were not.

After the Anglo-Soviet agreement of July 12, in which the two countries exchanged pledges of mutual aid, the CP would no longer permit such distinctions to be made between the war aims of the Allied powers. "The war," the *New Masses* declared on July 22, "has now become indivisible."[17] The Communists did not withdraw their characterization of the earlier part of the war as "imperialist." When a reader wrote to the YCL's *Weekly Review* in December to ask, "Wasn't the bourgeois democracy of the British during the imperialist war better than Hitler's fascism? Why didn't we support the British then?" YCL leader Claudia Jones offered the standard litany in reply: until June 22 the war had been a struggle for the imperialist redivision of the world, but "Hitler's attack upon the Soviet Union as a bid for world conquest endangered the continued independence and existence of all nations and peoples."[18] In the rush of events after June 22, most Communists were willing to accept the less than compelling logic of this argument. But if the party's rank and file remained convinced of their leaders' infallibility, it was only at the price of accepting a magical view of the world in which imperialist aggressors could be transformed into embattled democrats in a matter of a few days.[19]

The CP's new line stirred up painful memories of earlier political reversals. The July 8 *New Masses* resurrected the image of "that famous locomotive of history," which, the editors noted, "has taken another sudden turn. And as in 1939, there may be a few who find themselves flung off and sprawling by the roadside because they lost their grip in rounding the bend."[20]

Browder, isolated in his prison cell and remembering the last "sudden turn," was more apprehensive. On June 23 he wrote to his wife asking her to tell Minor to try to get permission to visit him in Atlanta. He wrote again on July 6, emphasizing the importance of his request, saying, "I asked for a visit to discuss policy in view of the radically transformed international situation. There is good reason to believe that this request today is not in contrast with sound public policy as understood by the administration.''

Browder clearly doubted that his comrades on the political committee were up to meeting the demands of the hour. ''I am burdened to the point of sleeplessness by the fear that not everything possible may be done to reorient all those friends who had learned to trust my judgment on large issues—particularly I have in mind our friends throughout Latin America, and among U.S. youth organizations.'' The Communists had already required its supporters in the American Youth Congress to follow it through one major political reversal. Browder wanted to be sure they followed the CP through the return to anti-fascism. ''Any hasty or slipshod handling of those contacts runs the danger of merely breaking them off and throwing them into the arms of the Lindberghs. . . . It is possible to lose contact and influence much quicker than it was gained, if there is a single false note struck in carrying out even a generally correct policy.''[21]

The New Popular Front

The party shifted its line in the front organizations with about as much grace and as few casualties as the situation allowed. The American Youth Congress's annual convention, scheduled for the July 4 weekend in Philadelphia, had been given advance billing in CP publications as ''American Youth's answer to the President's drive to get the United States into war.''[22] The AYC convention was the first public meeting of a front organization since June 22, and the Communists brought in their most attractive and articulate spokesmen to explain the new line. The eleven hundred delegates, said to represent five and a half million affiliated members, cheered Milton Wolff, national commander of the Veterans of the Abraham Lincoln Brigade, when he pledged: ''If need be, we veterans are prepared to march again.'' They adopted a resolution calling for the government to extend material aid to the British and Soviet peoples.

But in spite of intense lobbying by young Communists, the delegates also approved a resolution putting the AYC on record in opposition to sending American soldiers to fight in Europe. ''The Yanks Aren't Coming'' was still a popular slogan with the AYC rank and file. Jack McMichael, the AYC chairman, who went along with the Communists on almost all issues had warned that defeat of the resolution would provoke a "crisis in the American Youth movement." The Communists decided not to risk a split. The official YCL delegation abstained on the vote, along with about one-quarter of the delegates. Joseph Clark, editor of the YCL's *Weekly Review*, concluded that, all in all, the delegates had risen to the challenges presented by "this titanic struggle for freedom," even if "the tremendous changes wrought in the world could not be fully understood and completely clarified at the sessions of the congress."[23]

The AYC's display of independence underlines the oversimplification of anti-Communist analyses that treat all front organizations as puppets. The more bogus CP-organized "people's organizations," however, did swing smoothly from anti- to pro-war positions. When the American Peace Mobilization wound up its "perpetual peace vigil" on the White House sidewalks on June 21, its leaders announced they would be back in Washington at the end of July with a new anti-war campaign. The news from Russia the next day led to an abrupt change in plans. The APM's national board, on June 30, adopted a resolution declaring: "The essential prerequisite for achieving a people's peace has now become the military defeat of Germany." On July 23 the APM announced that it had changed its name to the American People's Mobilization and adopted a new slogan, "For Victory Over Fascism." The reborn APM laid plans for a "Smash Hitler" campaign for early August. The *Daily Worker* reported that "100 lovely young women all dressed in white" would circulate the APM's new pro-war petition in midtown Manhattan, and that APM activists would dump inflated balloons bearing the slogan "Stop Hitler, Fight Appeasement, Maintain Democracy, Join APM" into the water near New York City's public beaches.[24]

The Communists' former allies from the Popular Front were not eager to help them inflate more balloons. Shortly after the Nazi invasion of the Soviet Union, the *New Republic* commented acidly that "the Communists will no doubt make another attempt now to set up a United Front; we doubt whether they will succeed with anybody whose memory is good enough to go back a couple of years."[25]

At the June 28 national committee meeting, Gil Green urged that every effort be made to reorient party allies in the existing front organizations. But he warned that the "antagonisms and suspicions of yesterday" could not be expected to disappear overnight: "This means that where masses or organizations agree with the common fight against Hitler but do not wish to enter any of the aforementioned organizations, this cannot be placed as an obstacle to unity and struggle. The interests of the struggle require the most flexible and most varied approach to organizational forms."[26]

Green's speech amounted to a death warrant for most of the organizational relics of the Popular Front, too shopworn and discredited by now to attract new supporters or win back former allies. Although the American Youth Congress, the American Student Union, and the League of American Writers continued to exist as letterhead organizations, they sponsored no more rallies, picket lines, or congresses, and were all quietly buried in the next few years.[27]

In a remarkably short period of time the Communists pulled together a network of new pro-war front organizations, which in the course of the war would attract considerable public support.

In the fall of 1941 the Communists set up Russian War Relief, to raise funds for food, clothing, and medical supplies for the Soviet Union. But they carefully concealed their role in its organization, and Russian War Relief was soon granted a clean bill of political health from the *New York Times*: "The bitterest enemy of the Communist doctrine may contribute to this fund."[28]

In the spring of 1942 they organized the American Slav Congress, an umbrella organization that sought to unite Americans of Slavic descent as a lobby to influence American government policy toward resistance movements and governments in Eastern Europe. Its strength varied among national groups, depending on the previous level of Communist influence and the politics of the leaders of the resistance in their home countries (the congress was far stronger among South Slavs, for example, than among Poles). The congress made its greatest show of strength in the summer of 1942 when fifty thousand people gathered in Soldiers Field for a victory demonstration called by its Chicago branch. The congress's actual influence over State Department policy in Eastern Europe was probably negligible, but Roosevelt had sufficient respect for its domestic political strength to send Attorney General Francis Biddle and other prominent members of his administration to address its meetings.[29] And in the fall of 1942 Corliss Lamont, the apostate son of the chairman of the board of J. P. Morgan, oversaw the organization of the National Council of American-Soviet Friendship, which sought to mobilize American public sentiment in favor of full and continuing cooperation with the Soviet Union. The Communists had set up similar groups in the past, but never under such favorable circumstances. Joseph E. Davies, former American ambassador to the Soviet Union, announced plans for the new organization at a reception in his Washington home in September 1942, an event attended by Soviet ambassador Maxim Litvinov, Vice President Henry A. Wallace, and the chairmen of the Senate and House Foreign Relations committees. By the summer of 1943 the council had active branches in twenty-eight cities across the country.[30] All of this was a far cry from the thread-bare days of the Nazi-Soviet pact when the Communists had to draw repeatedly on the same small circle of trade union "influentials" and left-leaning Protestant ministers to fill out the vice-presidencies of its front organizations.

Shifting Ground in the CIO

Setting up a group like Russian War Relief was a simple task for the Communists. They were skilled at behind-the-scenes organization, they had a popular cause to work with, and they faced no serious organizational or ideological competition. They faced a far more difficult task, however, in changing their line in two areas of special concern for them, the labor movement and the black community. Here they had to reverse direction in the full glare of hostile publicity, while staving off attacks from powerful and politically sophisticated opponents.

Roy Hudson delivered a report on the labor movement at the June 28 national committee meeting. Though Roosevelt had sent in the army to break the North American Aviation strike only two and a half weeks before, all that now seemed part of a different world. Hudson argued that the biggest danger Communists faced in their work in the unions was "sectarianism, a narrow approach that would create barriers between us and large sections of workers who, while sharing our anti-fascist feelings, nevertheless in the past disagreed with us." He pledged that Communist unionists would continue to organize the unorganized and defend the workers' living standards. He did not, however, offer any ringing reaffirmation of the sanctity of the right to strike, of the type so frequent earlier in the Communist press. Instead, in a clear reference to the North American strike, he said: "Some of the lessons of recent struggles show that certain sections of the labor movement must still learn that labor has need, not only for militant resistance to attacks on its living standards and rights . . . but that it is also necessary to understand how to maneuver, how to adopt the most flexible tactics. . . . In general, they must not follow a policy which would result in a single group of workers being thrown into battle against great odds.''[31]

Hudson also criticized left-wing unionists who had responded with ''No comment'' when asked by reporters after June 22 if they had changed their position on the war. The initial reluctance of the CP's union allies to adopt a more outspoken stance in favor of aid to the Soviet war effort embarrassed the Communists. A front-page headline in the *Daily Worker* of June 25 proclaimed, ''U.S. Aid to USSR Urged by CIO, AFL Leaders Here.'' The leaders referred to turned out to be the manager of Local 76-B of the CIO United Furniture Workers Union and the president of Local 89 of the AFL Hotel and Restaurant Employees Union.[32] As in the months after the signing of the Nazi-Soviet pact, Communist unionists were unable or unwilling to reverse direction quickly. When Harry Bridges appeared as a guest speaker at the National Maritime Union's annual convention in July, asking NMU delegates to endorse a resolution calling for American material aid to Britain and the USSR, he announced his continued opposition to sending an American Expeditionary Force to fight in Europe. Roy Hudson, without mentioning his name, immediately slapped Bridge's wrist in the *Daily Worker*: ''Unconditional support for every measure and force and country that seeks to defeat Hitler is the only policy that will guarantee Hitler's defeat. . . . No honest American, and certainly no Communist, will say that a limit should be set to the measures we should take to defend our country.''[33]

Left-wing CIO leaders were reluctant to embrace policies which would force them to sever ties with John L. Lewis. Lewis's prestige and United Mine Workers' money had helped many of their unions organize, and he had sheltered them from enemies during the last two difficult years. Sentiment aside, they did not want to sever connections with their one powerful protector only to be left to their own devices in the CIO's fierce internal struggles, where Murray was an unreliable friend and Hillman still openly antagonistic.

Lewis soon made it clear he was not going to follow the Communists into the interventionist camp. On August 5 he joined Herbert Hoover,

Alf Landon, and thirteen other Republican leaders in condemning Roosevelt's "step-by-step projection of the United States into undeclared war."[34]

The *Daily Worker* had maintained a cautious silence on Lewis all summer, and even after the August 5 statement declared that it "remains to be seen" if Lewis's signature really represented "a final considered judgment." Left-wing CIO insiders may have been using the intervening time to attempt to persuade Lewis to change his stand, but by September the CP's leaders decided it was time to end the uneasy truce.[35] *The Communist* declared that it was "absolutely impossible for the Left and progressive forces to collaborate with Lewis." The *Daily Worker* denounced him as an "appeaser" who was giving "comfort to the foes of the United States." In the weeks that followed the party's union "influentials," some with private misgivings, severed relations with Lewis.[36]

During the pact, Communists in the United Auto Workers had been at the center of the controversy over strikes in defense industries. The Vultee, Allis-Chalmers, and North American Aviation strikes set the stage for a showdown between the Communists and their opponents in the UAW. Walter Reuther, in particular, hoped to use the August UAW convention as the occasion to break the CP's remaining strength in the union. He made his first move by blocking the seating of Harold Christoffel and the other delegates from Allis-Chalmers on a voting technicality, but since the Allis-Chalmers strike had been authorized by the international union, Christoffel was relatively immune from attack. When new elections were held in the Allis-Chalmers local, Christoffel and the other left-wing delegates were reelected by a three-to-one margin.

The leaders of the North American strike did not fare as well. The strike itself, unauthorized by the union, became the central issue. Wyndham Mortimer took the floor to defend his actions at North American, arguing that Richard Frankensteen had whipped up strike sentiment only to betray the workers when they actually did walk out. The convention accepted Frankensteen's version of the dispute, that "the wildcat strike was engineered by Communists, inside and outside the union, who were interested in demonstrating their effectiveness in obstructing national defense."[37]

The UAW committee that investigated the North American strike submitted three separate reports to the convention, the chief disagreement among them concerning the punishment of West Coast regional director Lew Michener. The majority report proposed barring him from union office for a year; a minority report called for expulsion from the union, and the "super-minority" report for barring him from membership on the UAW's executive board for a year (implicitly allowing him to be reappointed as an international representative). The convention unexpectedly voted for the mildest of the three recommendations. Frankensteen had gone to the convention in tacit alliance with Reuther, intending to squeeze UAW secretary-treasurer George Addes, a third major factional contender, out of his post. Michener escaped harsher punishment because Frankensteen, under prodding from Murray's representative at the convention, CIO organizational director Allen Haywood, had begun to have second thoughts about his alliance with Reuther. Murray, jealous of the attention that Reuther and his "five hundred planes a day" proposal was receiving from the press and the Administration, wanted to keep Reuther as only one of several contenders for power in the UAW. It dawned on Frankensteen that once he had cooperated with Reuther in eliminating Addes, he would find himself alone and at Reuther's mercy, so he returned to his former alliance with Addes and the anti-Reuther faction.

The Communists, who could expect only the worst from a Reuther victory, swung their own remaining forces behind Addes and Frankensteen. Addes was reelected as secretary-treasurer, Frankensteen and Reuther as vice-presidents, and R. J. Thomas, who carefully maintained his distance from this round of factional struggle, as president. The Communists avoided rougher treatment by their timely reconciliation with Frankensteen, but suffered one final humiliation when the convention passed a resolution barring from union office members of Communist, fascist, or Nazi organizations.[38]

On balance they had done better than they might have expected. The Reuther forces had not enjoyed the clear field they had hoped for in their anti-Communist drive. The party had remained entrenched in a number of important UAW locals and had forged a new alliance, albeit as a weak junior partner, with the Addes-Frankensteen forces. The UAW, at Thomas's urging, had endorsed a resolution calling for aid to the Soviet Union, though it continued to oppose American military intervention. Roy Hudson, in his post-convention summary in the *Daily Worker*, criticized the "Communazi" resolution and complained that too many delegates still clung to "old factional ties, old line-ups, old groupings, old prejudices . . . without regard to the new situation." Considering the vehemence with which Communists on the convention floor had denounced Reuther—Michener had called him the "red-headed stooge" of Hillman—Hudson struck a surprisingly conciliatory note, blaming both the Reuther and "progressive" camps for a lack of understanding of the meaning of June 22, and criticizing the left, in particular, for having descended to "unprincipledness in the personal attack on Walter Reuther." Hudson's article suggests that party leaders, as distinct from UAW Communists, now sought to leave a door open for reconciliation with the Reuther forces.[39]

In the American Newspaper Guild and the Woodworkers union, anti-Communist factions turned down Communist offers of reconciliation, and swept left-wing administrations out of power.[40] But events at the September convention of the United Electrical Workers took some of the sting out of defeats elsewhere in the CIO. Ever since the signing of the Nazi-Soviet pact, UE president James Carey had been gradually moving away from his alliance with left-wingers James Matles and Julius Emspak, who filled the other top leadership positions in the union. Carey endorsed Roosevelt in 1940 and took an interventionist stand on the war. He seemed nevertheless reluctant to break with his Communist associates (he agreed, for example, to address the summer 1940 convention of the American Youth Congress), and did not openly challenge the Communists' role in the union until the late winter of 1941. He moved into open conflict with them when he supported the right of UE locals to ban Communists from election to union office. When the question was placed before the union's general executive board, Carey's position was defeated by a vote of nine to two.

After June 22 the CP instructed its supporters in the UE to oppose efforts to remove Carey as president, in the name of anti-fascist unity— much to the dismay of UE Communists.[41] But Carey turned down offers of reconciliation from Emspak and Matles. He wrote in the *UE News* that "a back flip with a full twist and presto—Great Britain is purged of all her sins. Hitler is to be hated even more than Roosevelt. The 'imperialist blood bath' becomes a people's war for freedom. . . .Political acrobats in pink tights posing as labor leaders are a disgrace to the union and insult the intelligence of the membership."[42]

Bread-and-butter issues swung the convention vote against Carey in September. The UE, under the effective leadership of its left-wing leaders, signed up more than one hundred thousand new members in 1941 and won written contracts from a number of important and, heretofore, recalcitrant employers. Even if UE Communists were still willing to work with Carey, many non-Communist delegates to the September convention, long resentful of his inattention to union business, were not.[43] The convention voted down Carey's recommendation that union locals be allowed to bar Communists from office, and elected Albert Fitzgerald, a union officer from the Lynn, Massachusetts, UE local, to succeed him as president. Had Carey made his bid to defeat the Communists a year earlier, when they were saddled with defending the pact, he might have succeeded. By the fall of 1941, with the union rapidly expanding and the Communists urging the widest possible unity behind Roosevelt and the war effort, Carey appeared to most delegates to be playing a spoiler's role. The UE, which grew to be the third largest CIO union during the war, was now the centerpiece of Communist influence in the union movement.[44]

In the aftermath of this reshuffling of alliances, the Communists remained a powerful force in the CIO, by one estimate controlling eighteen unions with about 17 percent of the CIO's total membership.[45] They controlled or strongly influenced a number of state and city CIO councils, and important locals in unions like the UAW. Lee Pressman, a close ally, remained CIO general counsel and Len DeCaux remained editor of the *CIO News*. The Communists no longer found themselves a target at national CIO gatherings. Their most formidable opponent from the days of the Nazi-Soviet pact, Sidney Hillman, had yet to display any sign of interest in Communist offers of reconciliation, but the Communists could hardly complain about the stand he was taking on international affairs: At the November CIO convention he called on American workers to step up productivity because "tanks delivered now to the Russian Armies . . . are bulwarks against Nazi invasion of American soil."[46]

Problems in the Black Community

For many years the Communists had prided themselves on being "the Party of Negro and White." They had built their political strength in black communities like Harlem, Chicago's South Side, and Birmingham, Alabama, on the militant defense of the rights of blacks to equal protection under the law, and equal access to jobs, to housing, and to relief.[47] The CP's shifting stands on international questions had only marginally affected its political fortunes within the black community in the past. But the Communists' embrace of pro-war policies after June 1941 threw them into conflict with the most powerful nationally organized black protest movement to appear since the decline of the Garvey movement. A. Philip Randolph, the black Socialist founder of the Brotherhood of Sleeping Car Porters, had worked closely with the Communists in the late 1930s. He had served as president of the CP-organized National Negro Congress from 1936 until 1940, when he broke with the Communists over the issue of opposing Roosevelt and the war. The Communists denounced him viciously at the time as the representative of "the frightened Negro petty bourgeoisie, chattering with fear, pleading for mercy before the white master."[48] After his split with the Communists, Randolph organized the March on Washington Movement (MOWM), an all-black organization which threatened to bring tens of thousands of black Americans to Washington to demand an end to racial discrimination in defense industries and in the army. More than one hundred thousand blacks committed themselves to march on July 1, 1941. To head off the event Roosevelt issued an executive order establishing the Fair Employment Practices Committee (FEPC) to supervise efforts to end discrimination in hiring in defense industries. The order represented a partial victory for the MOWM (it did nothing to end segregation in the armed forces), and on June 24 Randolph agreed to call off the march.[49]

The Nazi invasion of the Soviet Union caught black Communists at an awkward moment. The National Negro Congress had been atrophying since Randolph's departure. Communists had infiltrated local chapters of the MOWM (which officially opposed any collaboration with the CP), and denounced Randolph for insufficient militancy. At the first meeting of the CP's national committee after the invasion, on June 28, black CP leader James Ford was still trying to outflank Randolph on the left, criticizing Roosevelt's FEPC order for failing to take any steps to disband the Jim Crow system within the armed forces.[50] But the Communists soon abandoned this position. Randolph's MOWM held large public protest meetings against discrimination in New York, Chicago, St. Louis, and elsewhere in 1942, while black newspapers promoted a "Double V" campaign that raised the slogan "Victory over discrimination at home" to equal status with "Victory over the Axis abroad."

By the fall of 1941 the Communists were arguing that a too militant defense of black rights at home would interfere with the war effort. In an article in the October *Communist*, James Ford declared that while demands for equal voting rights, the elimination of the poll tax, and the end of discrimination in the armed forces and elsewhere should not be abandoned for the duration, "it would be equally wrong to press these demands without regard to the main task of the destruction of Hitler, without which no serious fight for Negro rights is possible." The satisfaction of demands for an end to discrimination could not be made a prerequisite for black support for the war.[51] Some black leaders at the time denounced this position as a smokescreen behind which the Communists opposed any efforts to win more civil rights and better living conditions for black Americans, but few black Communists broke from the party in 1941.[52]

Political Gains

The Communists began to collect the political dividends from their new position on the war in the fall elections. They had maintained their influence within the American Labor party in New York, despite the fierce opposition of the ALP's state leaders, Alex Rose of the milliners union and David Dubinsky of the ILGWU, who controlled the ALP's state organization and most of the county committees outside of Manhattan. The Communists held on in the Manhattan county organization, bolstered by close ties with the ALP's sole, and invincible, congressman, Vito Marcantonio.[53] Before June 22, the Communists had planned to run an anti-war candidate on the ALP ticket in the New York City mayoral election; by midsummer they had swung their support to incumbent mayor Fiorello LaGuardia, a close Roosevelt ally. The CP's expert on New York City politics, Si Gerson, wrote in the *Daily Worker* in early August that LaGuardia (whom the Communists had bitterly reviled during the Nazi-Soviet pact) was showing "the beginning of recognition that a fight against Hitler fascism demands a progressive anti-fascist municipal program." For Gerson and the Communists, the "issue of aid to those people fighting fascist aggression will supersede . . . local political issues in the fall campaign."[54] In October, "in the interests of anti-Hitler unity," the Communists withdrew all candidates for city and county office, except for one candidate for city council from each borough.[55]

By the late 1930s the Communists had learned how to make skillful use of the city's proportional representation voting system.[56] Their candidate for city council from Brooklyn, Peter Cacchione, had won more than 30,000 first-choice votes in the 1937 election, and been barely edged out of victory by a questionable vote count. In 1939, when the New York City board of elections threw all the Communist candidates off the ballot, Cacchione still managed to attract more than 24,000 first-choice write-in votes. Jewish neighborhoods in Brooklyn were the strongest center of Communist popular support in the United States. Coney Island, Brighton Beach, Flatbush, Brownsville, East New York, Williamsburgh, as well as some Italian neighborhoods in Williamsburgh, Red Hook, Bay Ridge, and the Brooklyn waterfront, and pockets of strength in black and Irish areas formed a kind of Red belt that turned out, election after election, to back Cacchione.

The Brooklyn CP county committee was under the sway of younger Communists who had come up from the unemployed and student movements of the early 1930s. They were often at odds with the national party leadership—and sometimes with the foreign-born members of their own sections—over their constant efforts to Americanize the party's political activities. They became experts in the art of urban politics, and learned from the lesson of their 1937 defeat. One former Brooklyn CP leader later described the 1941 election count in the Brooklyn Armory: "By this time we were very knowledgeable. When the vote was in, we stayed in the Armory and watched it all. When they started counting, if the other parties had one guy watching at the table, we had three. We bought lunch every day for the counters, so nobody would say 'Fuck this Communist bastard' and throw ten votes in the wrong pile. We only put people in there who wouldn't be quarrelsome. We did all the right things."[57]

Because of poor health Cacchione was unable to campaign actively that fall, but the efforts of his campaign committee still paid off. In other boroughs the Communists had not yet recovered from the impact of the pact; their vote was 11 percent below that of 1937 in the Bronx, and more than 20 percent below that of 1937 in Manhattan. But in Brooklyn, Cacchione received nearly 35,000 first-choice votes, 15 percent more than he had received in 1937. An additional 14,000 second-choice votes put him over the top to win one of the nine council seats from Brooklyn.[58]

Cacchione's victory was the most important electoral office American Communists had ever won. A Brooklyn CP leader recalled the "wild exuberance" of Brooklyn's Communists the night they learned they had won: "The feeling was that we had achieved citizenship. Even the foreign born workers felt we had now crossed the line. We had used the system to get our guy in—not under a disguise, but as a Communist."[59]

The Communists had other political victories to celebrate that fall. They hailed the election of Adam Clayton Powell on the ALP ticket, the first black elected to the New York city council. Their political alliance with Powell in Harlem, broken by the Nazi-Soviet pact (during which they denounced Powell as one of "the little errand boys of Roosevelt"), was back in force.[60] In the September primary elections the Communists won control of ALP county committees in Richmond (Staten Island), Brooklyn, and Queens, which, added to their control of the Manhattan county committee, made them a formidable power within the ALP. (And the ALP itself had proven that it controlled the swing vote in New York politics. The more than 400,000 votes La-Guardia attracted on the ALP line was three times his margin of victory over his Democratic opponent.)[61]

Political Trials

The party was coming alive again, reaching out beyond the narrow circles to which it had been confined during the period of the Nazi-Soviet pact, but it still had to contend with one nagging reminder of its recent past. As long as Browder remained in Atlanta federal prison, the political respectability the Communists aspired to would remain elusive. If he had to serve his full sentence, even with time off for good behavior he would not be released until April 1944. Browder became eligible for parole in July 1942, but a release on parole would saddle him with continuing legal restrictions and would take another year to effect in any case.[62]

The Communists mounted an effort to win executive clemency, organizing the "Citizens Committee to Free Earl Browder" in August. With Tom Mooney as honorary chairman and Elizabeth Gurley Flynn as executive secretary, the committee launched an elaborate campaign on Browder's behalf. Ninety thousand copies of Flynn's pamphlet *Earl Browder, The Man from Kansas* rolled off the presses in November, spreading the message that "Earl Browder, as an American Communist, is as home-grown in the radical atmosphere of Kansas as the rolling prairies or the waving corn.''[63] The Communists organized special committees for trade unionists, blacks, youth, and professionals to support the Browder campaign. There was even a group for descendants of 1776, who held a meeting at Cooper Union in early December, ''in the Spirit of the Old Town Meetings of New England,'' to petition Roosevelt for executive clemency.[64] On December 18 Congressman Marcantonio presented to Attorney General Biddle petitions asking for clemency for Browder signed by two hundred thousand people, along with resolutions from various trade-union and fraternal groups, supposedly representing the support of a million and a half others.[65]

The prominent roles played in the Citizens Committee by Mooney and Flynn were clearly intended to stir up memories of the great labor and civil liberties battles of earlier decades. Yet Browder's case attracted little of the kind of public interest and sympathy that had attended the Mooney, Debs, and Sacco-Vanzetti cases. Browder's four-year sentence, though unduly harsh for the offense, was not severe enough to shock liberal opinion. The Communists were still regarded with resentment and suspicion by many of their former Popular Front supporters. And despite Flynn's best efforts, Browder's personality could not evoke the same kind of instinctive sympathy that a Sacco or a Vanzetti could summon up. No one ever mistook him for a ''good shoemaker'' or a ''poor fish peddler.'' Even the Communists, for all the resources they poured into the campaign, seemed unable to work up much indignation over Browder's plight. Unable to attack Roosevelt directly, they lacked a villain to rally against. The whole ''Free Browder'' campaign took on a rather plaintive tone. Flynn ended her pamphlet on the Browder case by expressing confidence that if ''our President Franklin D. Roosevelt . . . knows the facts we feel sure he will act on our appeals, in a spirit of justice and fair play, as befits Americans.''[66]

The activity on Browder's behalf had little immediate effect on Roosevelt. Molly Dewson, vice-chairman of the Democratic National Committee, wrote to Eleanor Roosevelt in late November, commenting, ''My *social* friends Grace Hutchins and Anna Rochester—leading Communists—want me to sign a petition that the President release Earl Browder by Christmas.'' She did not sign the petition, but forwarded to the White House a copy of *The Browder Case*, a pamphlet published by the Citizens' Committee. Mrs. Roosevelt passed the pamphlet on to her husband with the notation, "For your amusement." Roosevelt's penciled response was, "I think I will send Browder as Ambassador to Berlin. The place is vacant."[67]

The Communists invoked the "spirit of justice and fair play" on Browder's behalf, but they displayed little of that spirit when their opponents on the left, the Socialist Workers party, came under attack by the government in the summer of 1941. Between 1939 and 1941 the Communists accused the Trotskyists of covertly supporting the war. In May 1941 Foster declared that "the degenerate Trotskyites, in their May Day manifesto, single out Hitler as the enemy to fight, let British and American imperialism escape condemnation, and virtually accept the war."[68] A month later the Communists would adopt the stance that Foster, unjustifiably, had attributed to the Trotskyists. The *Daily Worker* began to carry analyses of "the disguised Nazism of the Trotskyites."[69] The spirit of the Moscow trials never strayed too far from Union Square.

The Trotskyists had to contend with more serious problems than unfriendly editorials in the *Daily Worker*. During the 1930s they had built a strong base in Local 554 of the Teamsters Union in Minneapolis. Trotskyists in the International Brotherhood of Teamsters had long been at odds with union president Dan Tobin, who on several occasions had sought their expulsion. When Tobin launched a new offensive in the spring of 1941, Local 554 seceded from the Teamsters and joined the CIO's Motor Transport and Allied Workers Industrial Union, a Lewis fiefdom. Tobin appealed to the White House for aid, citing his support of Roosevelt's reelection the previous year. Two weeks later U.S. marshals raided the Minneapolis headquarters of the Socialist Workers party, confiscating literature, red flags, and pictures of Trotsky. Twenty-nine SWP members were indicted shortly afterward for violation of the Smith Act, and most of them were brought to trial in late October. Though the prosecution could not prove any overt acts on the part of the defendants to overthrow the government, the Smith Act, by making advocacy a crime, led to guilty verdicts against eighteen of them.[70]

The Communists displayed some ambivalence about these proceedings at first. They had spent the better part of a decade arguing that Trotskyists were no better than, and were in fact in the service of, the Nazis. They applauded the purge trials in the Soviet Union for supposedly cleaning out a fascist-Trotskyist conspiracy against the government. Since they supported the execution of those they denounced as "Trotskyites" in the USSR as a stern but necessary measure of self-defense, they were not going to have many qualms about the far milder punishment meted out to American Trotskyists. But they were not completely unaware of the dangerous precedent being set. The *Daily Worker* carried its first report on the Minneapolis indictments in mid-August. While labeling the Trotskyists "agents of fascism," the article warned that "the Smith Act may in time be used as the medium for attacking genuine labor organizations, including the Communist Party."[71] But when the defendants were convicted and sentenced the Communists raised no objection, and in the next year the party openly began to advocate government suppression of anti-war groups. As Robert Minor explained to a national committee meeting in April 1942: "We defend the Bill of Rights for those people who use the Bill of Rights to help in the triumph of the American Army in this struggle of life or death."[72]

The Communists would themselves fall victim to this selective approach to civil liberties before the end of the decade, when their enemies would not fail to remind them of their own position on the question during the war.

The Russian Front

In the fall and early winter of 1941 the Communists always kept one eye anxiously focused on the military situation in Russia. Every morning newspaper maps showed the Wehrmacht penetrating deeper into the heart of the Soviet Union. In the first months after June 22, the Communists minimized the significance of Soviet military defeats. They sought to present Russia as an able and desirable ally in the war against Nazism, and to demonstrate that American material aid to the Red Army would not be thrown away. The editors of the *New Masses*, in their first issue after the Nazi invasion, fairly glowed with confidence in an editorial that said, "You get a special kick writing when every word is, in effect, a shovelful of earth over the grave which Hitler and his crowd dug for themselves last weekend."[73]

Within a few weeks of the Nazi invasion, the Communists had begun to call for American military intervention. John Gates, the highest-ranking American officer in the International Brigades at the end of the Spanish Civil War, became the party's unofficial spokesman on military affairs. At a conference of the YCL's national council in mid-July, Gates declared: "Every YCLer must be ready to give his life to the great cause of defeating Hitlerism. . . . We must wipe out of our ranks all vestiges of petty-bourgeois pacifism . . . and devote ourselves with all youth for the military annihilation of Hitler."[74]

The YCL came out in favor of extending the service of men already drafted and for drafting women.[75] And by mid-July the Communists had made their first demand for a "second front" in Western Europe to draw pressure off the beleaguered Red Army.[76]

Russian losses in troops and territory in the first months of the war were devastating. On the last day of September the Wehrmacht launched an offensive which Hitler announced was the "final drive" on Moscow. In less than two weeks the vanguard of the Nazi army reached positions forty miles from Moscow. The Red Army newspaper *Red Star* warned that "the very existence of the Soviet state is in danger." In November German soldiers were close enough to the city to glimpse the spires of the Kremlin through their field glasses. But Russian resistance, bolstered by the arrival of fresh troops from Siberia, and Stalin's appointment of new and more effective generals, broke the back of the German advance. The Russians launched a counteroffensive in early December and, for the first time in the war, the Germans suffered a major military setback.[77]

As the German army continued to roll toward Moscow in October, the *Daily Worker* began to sound panicky. Editorial headlines on the front page that month tell the story: October 9, "Hitler's Western Front Is Weak—Strike Now!"; October 12, "All Out Drive to Destroy Hitler!"; October 16, "Moscow Is in Danger!"; October 19, "America Must Act Now!"[78] On October 30 Foster declared that "the Communist Party is fully in favor of the United States' full participation in the war, for a declaration of war against Nazi Germany."[79] Two days later, in response to the news of the torpedoing of the U.S. Navy destroyer *Reuben James* with the loss of 115 crewmen, the *Daily Worker* called for "full war measures, barring none" to avenge the sinking.[80] The Communists would not have long to wait.

When the CP's national committee met in New York City on the weekend of December 6–7, they reviewed a year in which their movement had undergone astonishing changes. An embattled and isolated minority the previous December, the Communists had scrambled back into the mainstream of public opinion, now being among the most outspoken supporters of Roosevelt and national defense. Their support for the Soviet Union no longer branded them as part of a subversive fifth column. The *Daily Worker* ran a front-page story when a Scranton radio station refunded the money paid to it by Frank Cesare, a Pennsylvania YCL leader. Cesare had paid for and made a broadcast calling for aid to the Red Army. His broadcast, the radio station owner told him, had been "in the interests of national defense."[81]

If most Americans still regarded the Communists with suspicion, at least the party no longer had to face the concerted legal attacks of the year before. Despite setbacks in several unions, the Communists' position in the CIO remained strong and was more secure than it had been any time since 1939. In their most important political stronghold, New York City, the party had strengthened its position within the American Labor party and elected an avowed Communist to the city council. The Communists had not gained respectability, but they had at least gained a new and welcome degree of toleration.

On the early afternoon of December 7, the second day of the national committee meeting, the news arrived that Japanese planes were bombing Pearl Harbor. Minor, quoting Marx, told the committee members that the moment had come when "the weapon of criticism is replaced by the criticism of weapons."[82] Browder wrote to Minor that afternoon, saying, "I have asked Warden Sanford to transmit to the proper authorities my offer of my services in any way they could be useful in the emergency. I am taking it for granted that all my friends have the same attitude."[83]

Browder need not have worried. On December 9 the *Daily Worker* ran a new slogan under its masthead: "National Unity for Victory over Nazi Enslavement." In the next months hundreds of CP and YCL members, many of them veterans of the Spanish Civil War, enlisted in the army. John Gates was among the first. At a meeting of some two thousand Communists at New York City's Royal Windsor Hotel a week after Pearl Harbor, he announced that he had been sworn into the army that morning, and led the audience in reciting the Pledge of Allegiance. Three decades later George Charney would write of the occasion: "I will never forget the meeting at which Johnny Gates announced that he had volunteered for the Army and saluted the flag. It released a tremendous emotional feeling, as though by this exhibition we were atoning for the sins of the past."[84]

7 THE GRAND ALLIANCE
January to December 1942

Miss Pavilichenko's well known to fame;
Russia's your country, fighting is your game;
The whole world will love her for a long time to come,
For more than three hundred Nazis fell by your gun.©[1]
—WOODY GUTHRIE, 1942

Communists, being human beings, make mistakes like anyone else.
—EARL BROWDER, 1942

NINETEEN FORTY-TWO was an exhilarating year for American Communists. They had praised and defended the Soviet Union through the good years and the bad, and now, in the year of Stalingrad, they eagerly grasped at each new symbol of Russia's unprecedented popularity with the American public. Most party members were happy to put the nightmare years of the Nazi-Soviet pact behind them. But a few were moved to draw some hard conclusions from their own recent history. They were disturbed by the American CP's inability to shape its own political fortunes: Communist influence in the United States rose and fell depending on the current state of Soviet prestige. As long as this remained the case, they feared, Communist political gains would prove illusory.

"Mission to Moscow"

After the Battle of Moscow had demonstrated that the Nazis were not invincible, the popularity of the Soviet Union skyrocketed. Americans of all classes and political persuasions united in praising its resistance. In the spring of 1942 CIO president Philip Murray hailed "the heroism of the Russian army and people in repelling Nazi barbarism," while William P. Witherew, president of the National Association of Manufacturers, responded to a reporter's question about the USSR with the comment, "I frankly do not know where we would be without her.

Nothing in supplies should be stinted in support of her great valor in arms."[2]

During the war American publishers released a flood of pro-Soviet books. Among the first and best known was Joseph E. Davies's *Mission to Moscow*. Davies, a wealthy and socially prominent corporate lawyer, had served as American ambassador to the Soviet Union in 1936–1938. *Mission to Moscow* was a mixture of his reports to the State Department, correspondence, and journal entries from those years, along with a commentary written after the German invasion. Davies dignified some of the worst features of Stalin's rule in the 1930s by using them as the explanation for the Red Army's unexpected military prowess: "There were no Fifth columnists in Russia in 1941— they had shot them. The purges had cleansed the country and rid it of treason." While praising Stalin's achievements, Davies assured his readers that the "impractical" idea of communism was already disappearing in the Soviet Union and posed no threat to America.[3]

Mission to Moscow, published in December 1941, came out at just the moment when Americans wanted to believe in the virtue of their new Russian ally. Davies, who for all his pro-Soviet sympathies was untainted by radical ideology, was the right man to do the convincing. *Mission to Moscow* quickly became a best-seller, and the *New York Times* called it "the one book above all to read on Russia." The Communists were delighted with the book's reception. Joseph Starobin politely disagreed with Davies's observations about the impracticality of communism, but declared in the *New Masses* that "we must be grateful for a book that confirms irrefutably the truth that many Americans had been fighting for all during the Thirties."[4]

The Russians, for their part, skillfully wooed American public opinion. The new Soviet ambassador, Maxim Litvinov, widely known and respected in the West for his advocacy of collective security before the signing of the Nazi-Soviet pact, proved to be a gracious and sophisticated spokesman for Soviet interests.[5] Exemplary Red Army soldiers toured the United States on goodwill missions, the most popular of them being Lieutenant Luidmila Pavilichenko, a twenty-six-year-old "girl sniper" who was credited with killing 309 German soldiers in the Odessa and Sevastapol campaigns. She spoke at Russian War Relief meetings across the country, asking for a second front to aid her compatriots in the Red Army, and endured questions by women's-page reporters as to whether she was allowed to wear makeup while out sniping. "Yes," she responded dutifully, "but when you are fighting, you do not think of that."[6]

Americans eagerly contributed money, clothing, wristwatches, and other needed items to the Russian War Relief campaign. By the summer of 1942 RWR chapters in fifty-six cities sponsored luncheons, dinners, cocktail parties, dance festivals, recitals, art exhibits, and auctions to raise funds for the Soviet war effort. The organization distributed hundreds of thousands of collection cans that spring, and the *Reader's Digest*—no friend of the USSR in years past—devoted three pages to promoting the campaign in its May 1942 issue, telling how one "proud mother" attached her collection can to a baby carriage and asked donations from all strangers who stopped to admire her twins: "John Doe doesn't pinch his pennies when it comes to such matters," the *Reader's Digest* said. "John Doe's pennies, dimes and quarters are helping to fight Hitler right now along the Russian front."[7]

Unlike the period of Western fascination with the USSR in the 1930s, the wartime era of good feeling did not spring from or promote any widespread interest in revolutionary socialism. Stalin was widely admired as the man who saved Russia from the ideologues who had founded the Soviet state. Undersecretary of State Sumner Welles offered a typical view of the history of the Russian Revolution in his book *The Time for Decision*, published in 1944. In the years after 1917 the Soviet Union "gradually swung back from the early and fantastic extremes of the Trotskyist school of violence." The factional battles of the 1920s had seen the defeat of those Bolshevik leaders who pursued the chimera of world revolution by new, sober, and pragmatic leaders "who followed Stalin in desiring to set the course back toward the establishment of a workable form of state socialism." Since the expulsion of Trotsky, "each year that passed marked an advance from the earlier stages of impractical and unproductive Communism toward state socialism."[8]

Liberals continued to look to the Soviet Union as a model, but what they now sought to emulate was not its ideology, but rather its ability to transcend the narrow limits of ideology. They believed that if Americans could only abandon their sectarian anti-communism to the same extent that the Soviets had abandoned their sectarian commitment to Communist ideals, then practical men of affairs in both countries could join to guarantee international cooperation in the postwar world.

American goodwill toward Russia did not necessarily entail any change in attitude toward domestic Communists. Kenneth Crawford suggested in the *New Republic* that the Russians could substantially aid the cause of anti-fascist unity by cutting all connections with the "irritating connivers who run the Communist Party of the United States and who continue to bask in reflected Russian glory." Vice-President Henry Wallace, among the strongest proponents in the Administration of close ties with the Soviet Union, confided to his diary that "a typical American Communist is the contentious sort of individual that would probably be shot in Russia without a ceremony." His wistful tone suggested some regret that American policymakers were unable to resort to such straightforward measures.[9]

But some of the spillover of goodwill toward Russia inevitably aided the CP. American soldiers were not killing Germans, and lend-lease supplies to Russia were still more of a promise than a reality. Symbolic gestures counted heavily in 1941 and 1942 in the American government's efforts to solidify its alliance with the Soviet government, and American Communists provided a handy symbol.

At the end of December 1941 the House passed a bill transferring supervision of foreign agents from the State Department to the Justice Department. HUAC's indefatigable Martin Dies got an amendment attached to the bill requiring Communist party leaders and members to register as foreign agents with the Justice Department. When the bill went to the Senate for consideration, Hatton Sumners, chairman of the House conferees, asked Supreme Court Justice James Byrnes for the Administration's position on the bill. Byrnes told Sumners that he could "rest assured" Roosevelt favored elimination of the Dies amendment. In January Roosevelt instructed a legislative aide to telephone Sumners and tell him "I agree absolutely with Jimmy Byrnes on this." Sumners went back to the House at the end of the month with the Senate version of the bill, deleting Dies's amendment, and asked his colleagues, "What motive would Soviet Russia have for refusing a separate peace with Germany if Congress took a position like [the Dies amendment]? Thousands of Russians are out in the field fighting Nazi Germany and doing a better job of it than anybody on our side right now." The House approved the Senate bill (and in effect repudiated Dies) by a vote of 228 to 4.[10]

The most important symbol of all was still languishing in the Atlanta penitentiary. Browder was now allowed visits from Robert Minor on a regular basis, and thus could stay in closer touch with party strategy, but he did not take his continued imprisonment well. Browder's brother William told CP leaders in April that Browder had been looking forward to imminent release for months, and that the frustration of waiting was wearing him down. He was neither reading nor exercising regularly, and was showing signs of "extreme nervous tension."[11]

The Communists' "Free Browder" campaign never really got off the ground, and probably would have had little effect on Browder's fortunes even if it had successfully tapped liberal sympathy. Josephine Truslow Adams, one of the "Descendants of 1776" who had rallied for Browder in December, wrote frequently to Eleanor Roosevelt that winter and spring asking her to intervene with her husband on Browder's behalf. In mid-April she asked Mrs. Roosevelt to meet with Elizabeth Gurley Flynn to discuss the case. Mrs. Roosevelt replied: "I have your letter but I do not feel I should ask the President about Mr. Browder. As I understand it, Miss Flynn is a proven Communist and therefore she would carry no weight in his behalf."[12]

But early in 1942 the case began to attract the attention of some influential figures who cared little about Browder's plight, but a great deal about its impact on American-Soviet relations. Utah senator Elbert Thomas, chairman of the Senate Foreign Relations Committee, wrote to Roosevelt in February urging a pardon for Browder. Browder he argued, had received too stiff a sentence for his crime: "That has happened before and it can be brushed aside. But should it be? I say that much because I know the importance of Russia in our international relations and the importance of Labor's unity and best effort in our National endeavour."[13]

Roosevelt had more urgent problems on his mind in the spring of 1942, and did not rush to resolve the Browder matter. But on May 16, shortly before Soviet Foreign Minister Molotov was due to arrive in Washington, Roosevelt commuted Browder's sentence to time served. The White House issued a statement declaring that Browder's release would "have a tendency to promote national unity and allay any feeling . . . that the unusually long sentence in Browder's case was by way of penalty upon him because of his political views."

At the prison gate Browder passed out a typewritten statement to reporters expressing gratitude and pledging to "intensify every effort to weld unbreakable national unity under the Commander-in-Chief."[14]

The Communists had been planning a "Free Browder" rally in

Madison Square Garden for May 20, Browder's fifty-first birthday. When the organizers learned of Browder's release they initially hoped to turn the event into a victory celebration. But Browder, apparently acting at the Administration's request, wired them from Atlanta to call the whole thing off. Veterans' groups were already raising a protest about his release, and Browder obliged Roosevelt by keeping his homecoming low-key. He got off the train that was bringing him home from Atlanta in Newark to avoid the crowds waiting for him in New York City's Pennsylvania Station.[15]

Second Front

When Browder returned, the party was in the midst of a campaign demanding a second front in Europe. The Communists were eager for the United States to get into the fight—in part, of course, because that was the line, but also to give meaning to past sacrifices. The CP was a small group, a community with a few tens of thousands of members scattered across the country. Communists were linked together, not only by a common set of ideological beliefs and organizational discipline, but also by a densely interwoven set of personal relationships. One thousand Communists had died in Spain in 1937 and 1938 fighting fascism. In the first year after Pearl Harbor a hundred more Communists in the National Maritime Union died when their ships were torpedoed by German U-boats, many of them losing their lives because they volunteered for the dangerous run through the North Atlantic to carry supplies to Murmansk.[16] Thousands of other Communists were entering the armed forces that year, often astonishing fellow GIs by doing everything they could to get overseas and into combat units.[17] Even after American casualties began to mount in the later years of the war, Communists were more likely than other Americans to have lost close friends or associates in battle. Communists were also more likely to know, or at least to know of, men and women fighting in the European resistance or dying in German concentration camps.

The Communists took the war with deadly seriousness and sometimes seemed at a loss to understand the lack of martial fervor displayed by many other Americans. The Second World War evoked relatively little of the kind of "Over There" enthusiasm that had characterized the early days of American involvement in the First World War.[18] Remembering the government-promoted atrocity tales of the earlier war, Americans tended to be skeptical or even apparently indifferent to reports of the horrors being committed by the Nazis in the conquered nations of Europe. But Communist publications printed detailed accounts of Nazi atrocities, and grew increasingly fierce in their denunciation of the German people. Soviet journalist Ilya Ehrenberg's reports from the Russian front, reprinted in the *Daily Worker*, insisted that the Germans themselves (and not just Hitler, or the German ruling class, or the military high command) should be held responsible for war crimes. Claudia Jones told readers of the YCL's *Weekly Review*: "Hard as it sounds, the truth must be faced: the most corrupt elements in Germany today are the youth." To hate the enemy, Jones declared, "is to love one's country."[19]

So the Communists had little regard for those who expressed reservations about a full-scale American military commitment to fighting the Nazis on the European continent, or who favored a reliance on air power in place of ground combat forces, or who favored a "Pacific first" strategy to win the war. An Anglo-American invasion of Western Europe could bring victory in 1942; a delay could allow Hitler to consolidate his victories in the east and the west. The decision on whether or not to launch a second front, the *Daily Worker* declared in April, "may spell the difference between victory in 1942, or a terribly prolonged and agonizing struggle in which we might even face defeat."[20]

Communists in the CIO persuaded their unions and city CIO councils to pass resolutions calling for a second front. In July sixty thousand people answered the Greater New York Industrial Union Council's call to rally in Madison Square Park to hear U.S. Senators Claude Pepper and James Mead endorse the call for an Anglo-American offensive.[21] Roosevelt was known to be leaning toward the idea of launching a second front in 1942, as were many of America's military leaders. After Molotov's visit to the White House in May 1942 the American and Soviet governments released a joint communiqué declaring that "full understanding was reached with regard to the urgent task of creating a Second Front in Europe in 1942."[22]

But Churchill vetoed the project. Haunted by memories of the bloodletting on the western front in 1914–1918 and of Britain's humiliating defeat in 1940, he opposed any major offensive on the European continent until an overwhelming invasion force could be built up. Since any invasion in 1942 would, by necessity, have to be composed mainly of British and Commonwealth soldiers, Roosevelt was not in a strong position to argue with Churchill. Popular sentiment in favor of a second front began to fade by late summer, particularly after the bloody failure of the Dieppe raid raised the specter of the disastrous consequences of a too hasty invasion effort.[23]

Meanwhile events in Russia made a second front in Europe seem more urgent than ever to American Communists. The Germans renewed their stalled offensive at the end of June, and in rapid succession captured Sevastapol, Voronezh, and Rostov. In late summer the German Sixth Army crossed the Don and fought steadily toward the strategic and symbolically important city of Stalingrad on the Volga River, entering the city on September 13. The Red Army resisted with artillery fire from the eastern bank of the Volga and from an ever-shrinking bridgehead within the city on the Volga's western bank, in savage house-to-house and even room-to-room battles.[24]

The Communists believed, correctly, that this would be the decisive battle of the war, but they feared that the Red Army would not be able to win on its own. The *Daily Worker* warned that the "only way Stalingrad can be saved and the tide turned against Hitler this year is by the opening of a Second Front now. . . . We must not permit Stalingrad to fall. We must not permit our great and perhaps final chance for victory to slip through our fingers."[25]

By the time the Germans reached Stalingrad, Stalin already had been told by Churchill not to expect a second front until mid-1943 at the earliest. Stalin responded by publicly chiding his allies for failure to "fulfill their obligations promptly and on time." There was some sentiment among American Communists to come out in open criticism of Roosevelt and Churchill for the delay in aiding the Russians. But the Allied invasion of North Africa in November, warmly praised by Stalin, cut such discussions short. Browder announced that the landings in North Africa, "while not yet the realization of the Second Front in Europe," represented a "military commitment to the war which is the essence of the Second Front and brings the full realization of the Second Front close."[26]

Against "Unionism as Usual"

As Browder shelved the second-front campaign, he instructed Communists to concentrate "on the problems of a centralized war economy and production for the war. The solution of these problems . . . has become unquestionably the key link now for the mobilization of the full striking power of our country in the Anglo-Soviet-American coalition."[27]

The role the labor movement would play in the war was a major concern not only of the Communists, but also of the Roosevelt Administration. During the First World War, Samuel Gompers and the AFL had endorsed the war effort; they had committed the unions to a no-strike policy, and supported government mediation efforts—and American workers had nevertheless taken advantage of wartime labor shortages to strike for improved wages and working conditions.[28] The Second World War promised to bring more of the same. The succession of government agencies Roosevelt established to oversee war production and labor relations lacked the authority and the ability to push the country toward full economic mobilization. American corporations were reluctant to retool for war production until they were guaranteed high profits and generous government financing. And Roosevelt's proclamation of national emergency in the spring of 1941 had not tamed John L. Lewis, who had waged and won a war of nerves against the Administration over the issue of gaining a union shop for miners in the "captive mines"—those mines owned by and producing coal for the steel corporations.

In September and October Lewis took his miners out on short strikes, each time returning to work upon a promise of settlement by the National Defense Mediation Board. Roosevelt realized it was one thing to send in the army to back up the NDMB's authority against one Communist-led UAW local, and quite another thing to take on the power of the whole United Mine Workers. When the NDMB finally rejected Lewis's demands in November, he called their bluff, refused to accept the recommended settlement, and took his miners out a third time. Roosevelt quickly capitulated, appointing a Labor Department mediator known to be sympathetic to the UMW's position in exchange for the miners' return to work.[29]

The NDMB collapsed as a result of the captive-mine controversy. Ten days after Pearl Harbor, two dozen industry and labor representatives met in Washington, summoned by Hillman and Secretary of Labor Perkins. Green, Woll, and Frey represented the AFL; Murray and Lewis represented the CIO, along with Julius Emspak of the UE (a curious choice, unless he was deliberately included in unofficial recognition of the support that left-wing unionists were now offering the war effort). The conferees agreed on a no-strike, no-lockout pledge for the duration, but deadlocked on the question of the closed shop, and never even got around to discussing the question of a wartime wage policy. Roosevelt decided to call the conference off before the proceedings could get too acrimonious. In January he established the twelve-member War Labor Board (WLB) to take over the work of the now-defunct NDMB, leaving it up to the new board to settle the potentially explosive questions of union security and wages.[30]

Having voluntarily relinquished the right to strike, the unions lacked bargaining power in negotiations. Management would have no reason to offer concessions if the government did not establish compulsory wage standards. And workers would have little incentive to join or to continue to pay dues to unions that could win them only limited and predetermined gains.

The War Labor Board devised two formulas to solve these problems. In the "Little Steel" decision on wage increases in smaller steel companies handed down in July 1942, the board tied wage increases for all workers to the roughly 15 percent rise in living costs between January 1, 1941, and May 1, 1942. In future wage disputes brought before the board, increases would be granted to bring real wages up to the earlier level. And in a series of decisions that spring the board devised a "maintenance of membership" formula that required all workers within a union's contract jurisdiction to remain members of the union unless they resigned during the first fifteen days after their hiring or the signing of a new contract. The WLB bolstered this decision by awarding dues checkoff to the unions: union dues were to be automatically deducted from workers' paychecks by the companies and handed over to the unions. Although these decisions did not add up to a closed or union shop in which all workers had to belong to a union to get a job, they did place significant bureaucratic obstacles in the way of workers who might otherwise let their membership lapse.[31]

The Communists strongly favored these measures. Months before Pearl Harbor unionists who were close to the CP, like Harry Bridges, had already committed their unions to no-strike policies.[32] In November 1941, when the fate of Moscow was still in doubt, Foster argued in the *Daily Worker* that "the strike should be used only in defense of the workers' most basic economic interests or to protect the life of the trade unions, and then only as a last resort. . . ."[33]

CIO counsel Lee Pressman played a major role in convincing the

WLB to grant the maintenance of membership formula. He told the board that the unions wanted to transform themselves from agents of collective bargaining to tools for increasing production. But for the labor movement to do that, "it has to have union security today so that it doesn't have to worry about how to maintain its membership, how it can continue to collect its dues from its members." The WLB agreed with Pressman that this was the only way to dispense with "trade unionism as usual."[34]

The Communists believed that the no-strike pledge and the War Labor Board measures would both guarantee uninterrupted production of war material, and allow the new (and still shaky) industrial union movement to consolidate its strength in steel, auto, rubber, electrical manufacturing, and other major industries. And they believed this could be achieved without sacrificing union members' basic interests. In *Victory and After*, a book Browder wrote right after his release from prison, he urged union officials to become "Philadelphia lawyers"— that is, to learn to use the board's guidelines to wring out every possible benefit for their members.[35] And within these narrow, self-imposed tactical limits, CP-influenced unions did gain many benefits for their members. The United Electrical Workers, for example, had brought nearly two thousand cases before the War Labor Board by 1945, winning substantial improvements in wages, holidays, bonuses, and job classifications. The union movement as a whole expanded its membership by about 40 percent during the war, but UE expanded at a phenomenal rate, almost quadrupling its membership between 1940 and 1945.[36] In the years after 1945 the Communists criticized many of the positions they had taken during the war, but they never repudiated the no-strike policy.

In recent years the no-strike pledge has not fared well in most historians' accounts. Many younger labor historians see the Second World War as the period in which the turbulent, independent, democratic rank-and-file sentiment that characterized some of the new CIO unions in the late 1930s was brought under control by union bureaucrats whose interests were closely tied to those of Democratic party politicians.[37] And, in retrospect, it is clear that voluntarily relinquishing the right to strike, limiting the nature of demands that could be made during a national emergency, and coming to rely on the goodwill of the Administration and its official mediation services could not help strengthening conservative trends within the labor movement. Major corporations, who had a few "Philadelphia lawyers" in their own employ, discovered that they had something to gain by making concessions on hours and wages to stable union bureaucracies, as long as the unions took on the responsibility for curtailing any unpredictable and disruptive behavior on the part of their members.

What is clear in retrospect, however, was not so easy for the Communists to see in 1942. The war preoccupied them. Hitler was master of Europe, from the English Channel to deep into Russia, from Norway to the Mediterranean. If the Soviet resistance collapsed, Hitler's control of his new empire would become virtually unassailable. Even had the Communists been gifted with perfect foresight, they undoubtedly would have felt it was more important to deliver a thousand extra tanks to the Red Army in 1943 than to reinforce the cause of rank-and-file democracy in the American labor movement by repudiating the no-strike pledge.

As it was, based on their own experience, the Communists had no reason to believe there was any conflict between close government/union cooperation and the long-term prospects for "progressive" unionism. They remembered the vulnerability of the labor movement in the face of the "American Plan" open-shop drives of the 1920s, a time when the unions lacked close ties with the government. They understood that the popular perception that Roosevelt sympathized with the labor movement had proved an invaluable asset to CIO organizers in the 1930s. Their own fortunes within the union movement had risen and fallen, depending on whether the party line favored or opposed Roosevelt. Each congressional election since 1938 had seen a more vociferously anti-labor Congress returned to office, and without Roosevelt's goodwill the unions might have been swamped by a wave of punitive legislation. All the lessons the Communists had learned since the early 1930s seemed to argue that the best interests of the labor movement (and of Communist influence within the unions) would be served by establishing the closest possible institutional ties with the government during the war, whatever short-term disaffection that might create on the shop floor.[38]

So Communist unionists became the most enthusiastic enforcers of the no-strike pledge, and of labor-management cooperation for increased production. In March 1942, Donald Nelson, chairman of the newly organized War Production Board (WPB), called on unions and employers to organize "labor-management committees" in defense plants. Nelson made it clear to worried businessmen that these committees were not harbingers of the cooperative commonwealth, and were intended to offer labor the symbol, not the substance, of administrative power. The committees would not "put management in labor or labor in management. . . . It is a perfectly simple, straight-forward attempt to increase production." CIO leaders chose to interpret the plan as a partial endorsement of Murray's old "industrial councils" proposal, and by the end of the year had helped establish hundreds of committees in defense plants.

The Communist-led United Electrical Workers eagerly responded to Nelson's call, and organized more labor-management committees than any other union except Murray's own Steel Workers. The results were not inspiring. By November 1942 Julius Emspak complained that the labor-management committees were "stagnant." By his estimate only three out of several hundred committees the UE had set up thus far were "functioning at all the way they should." Management, he complained, was interested only in using the committees as a public and labor relations gimmick: "They try to keep the council alive by using the stuff the War Production Board sends out: slogans and stickers and things like that. . . . They leave out the most important thing, which is joint, cooperative work. Managements don't give the information that is needed—and no council can do a good job on production without the necessary information."[39]

Despite Emspak's gloomy assessment of the marginal role of the labor-management committees, the CP and the unions it influenced continued to promote them. By the end of the war nearly five thousand such committees were operating in war plants, running blood and bond and scrap drives, while permitting the workers a sham participation in production decisions.[40]

Communist unionists urged workers to step up the pace of production of war materials, abandoning for the duration of the war the informal but pervasive systems of restriction of output they used to protect their jobs and pay scales. James MacLeish, president of UE District 4, admitted at a 1942 "Production for Victory" conference sponsored by the UE that "many workers are still fearful of relinquishing, even temporarily, any of the gains for which they have worked for so many years."[41] Max Gordon, CP organizer in upstate New York, worked closely with the leaders of UE Local 301 in the General Electric plant in Schenectady. The party had a comparatively strong base among the rank and file in the local, and even there the union could drum up no great enthusiasm for all-out production. As Gordon recalled: "Skilled workers in a shop like General Electric had gotten their work down to a point where they were producing a day's work in a couple of hours. The guys in the shop said to me, 'For Christ's sake, Max, if we go all out and quadruple our production, what happens after the war?' They wouldn't do it."[42]

The Communists had to pay a political price on the shop floor for the gains they felt they were making in hearings before the War Labor Board and in the inner councils of the CIO leadership. They compounded their losses by attributing all rank-and-file restiveness to the influence of "defeatist groups," and by continually drawing inept analogies between soldiers on the front line and workers in defense plants. In March 1942 Roy Hudson exhorted workers to make heavier sacrifices for the war effort: "We are soldiers in overalls. . . . Do your duty like the Wake Island Marines!"[43] Instead of offering a reasoned explanation of their support for the no-strike pledge, the Communists made the dubious political choice of following what they assumed would be the line of least resistance, relying on the kind of militarist appeals they remembered from the Liberty Bond drives of the First World War. Such appeals wore thin very quickly. Soldiers at the front line at least had the consolation of knowing that the army was not making cost-plus-10-percent profits off of their sacrifices.

There were some more positive aspects to the CP's wartime tradeunion strategy, for which the Communists seldom receive credit. They fought to open up employment opportunities for women, to win them equal pay on the job and equal citizenship within the union movement. By January 1942, UE District 4 had set up a program to train hundreds of New York City women in wiring, welding, drill-press work, and other skills they would need in order to find industrial jobs. The UE brought a series of cases before the War Labor Board that sought to eliminate pay differentials for women workers, and by the end of the war had won equal-pay guarantees in the majority of its contracts. In 1945 the UE counted more than 250,000 women among its 600,000 members, the highest percentage of any major American union.[44]

Women Communists pushed the party to take a strong stand against the prejudices of male union leaders, including some of the CP's own union "influentials." Elizabeth Gurley Flynn complained in a memo to Browder about the lagging recruitment of women workers by some left-led unions: "They don't want women organizers. They claim they can't find any trained women to do the work [and] assert that women will only be in industry for the duration, 'then we'll be rid of them, so why bother?'"[45] And she complained publicly in a *Daily Worker* article about the continued exclusion of women from union leadership, concluding, "It is high time that outstanding male leaders, those of the left especially, take a stand on these issues and begin to practice what we all preach."[46]

Male Communists often responded to discussions of the "woman question" with derision or condescension, but there were few other organizations in the country at the time in which women would even consider it their right to challenge such attitudes.[47] (Flynn's comments also show that, far from a single-minded, disciplined conspiracy, Communist party policies were sometimes determined by the outcome of a behind-the-scenes struggle of groups with conflicting interests.)

The CP and Blacks in World War Two

It has become a truism of writing on the CP in World War Two that the Communists "abandoned" all efforts on behalf of blacks after June 22, 1941. Irving Howe and Lewis Coser state flatly that "the CP believed the struggle for Negro rights should be suspended entirely during the war."[48] Sumner Rosen, in an essay on blacks and the CIO, charged the CP with "abandoning its commitment to Negro equality" during the war. "The CIO, in contrast, continued its pressure to improve the economic status of Negro workers. . . . When the Communists downgraded the issue of Negro rights, the first meaningful differences between the two groups [CP and CIO] began to become clear."[49]

In fact, the Communists were the most outspoken group pushing the CIO to fight for equal employment rights for blacks. In the unions they controlled they consistently promoted blacks to leadership positions, and they fought hard in unions they did not control, like the UAW, to open up union offices to blacks (in the face of opposition from such anti-Communist stalwarts as Walter Reuther). The Communists did not abandon the struggle for black rights during the war, but rather forced that struggle into narrow channels.

At the December 1941 meeting of the CP's national committee, Robert Minor outlined what the Communist position on the black struggle would be for the remainder of the war. Back in the Civil War,

Minor argued, slaves had received their freedom "not as a humanitarian gift . . . but as a war measure to weaken the enemy and to strengthen the military position of the United States." The war against fascism could bring a second emancipation for blacks, so long as they learned to direct their struggle "in the first place against those measures of brutality, of the Jim Crow system, that prevent their participation in the war effort."[50]

The Communists' opponents in the black community dismissed this as empty rhetoric. But an examination of the record of CP-influenced unions during the war shows it to have been something more. Employers in the maritime industry, for example, had a long tradition of allowing blacks to serve in only the most menial positions aboard ship. During the war the National Maritime Union (NMU) conducted an extensive educational campaign within its own ranks opposing racism, and pressured the government and employers to end Jim Crow hiring practices. In January 1942, when a New York shipping firm refused to accept twenty-five black NMU sailors among a crew of 140 sent from the union dispatching hall, NMU president Joe Curran wired Roosevelt to protest and warned the company that the ship would not sail without the black crew members. NMU vice-president Frederick Myers, a Communist party member, told the *Daily Worker*: "This is not only a white man's war. . . . Every man regardless of the color of his skin will have a right to do his share to win this war."[51] The ship owners backed down, and black and white NMU members shipped out together. By 1944 NMU contracts with 125 shipping companies stipulated that there would be no discrimination in hiring black union members. By the following year a tenth of the NMU's membership was black.[52]

The NMU also led the fight to commission black ship captains in the American merchant marine. With union backing, Hugh Mulzac, a black NMU member who had earned his master's license in 1918 but who had had to serve as a steward for over two decades, was given command of the Liberty ship *Booker T. Washington*. His victory opened the way for other blacks to become ships' officers. The NMU's racial policies stood in marked contrast to those of the AFL's Seafarers International Union (a union celebrated in some recent accounts as a model of class-conscious militant unionism), which attempted to win white sailors away from the NMU by advertising its own racially discriminatory policies.[53]

Communist union leaders defending the right of black workers to equal employment opportunities sometimes had to contend with the violent opposition of their own union members. At the East Pittsburgh Westinghouse plant and the Point Breeze Western Electric Company near Baltimore, white workers disrupted production when blacks joined them on the assembly line. But UE officials would not back down on their support for the black workers, and at Point Breeze actually called on the government to send in the army to take over the plant and end the walkout. Later in the war the Transport Workers Union won a representational election among Philadelphia transit workers. When eight blacks were hired in 1944 as driver-trainees, white workers went on a rampage that did not stop until the government sent in five thousand troops to patrol the streets. The TWU stuck with the black workers, and they kept their jobs.[54]

The CP limited its struggle for black rights to those areas that it believed benefited the war effort. The policy proved an inadequate response to the black community's demands for redress of long-standing grievances, but it was not the "abandonment" so often alleged.

Plight of the Nisei

There was one racial minority in the country whose rights the Communists did regard as expendable. Well before Browder's release from prison, the Communists proved that they would go to almost any length to avoid criticism of the Roosevelt Administration's conduct of domestic affairs, so long as they were satisfied with its behavior in international affairs. Roosevelt has generally been credited with conducting the American war effort with far greater respect for domestic civil liberties than Woodrow Wilson brought to the First World War. But he bears responsibility for going along with one act of wartime intolerance that outweighed the entire dismal record established by Wilson: the forced evacuation and incarceration of 120,000 Americans of Japanese ancestry. Racial hysteria, the desire to punish a scapegoat for Pearl Harbor, and the self-interest of groups like the Western Growers Protective Association who cast covetous eyes on the well-tended fields of Japanese-American farmers, all led to the demand that the government take Japanese-Americans into custody. Though advertised at the time as a stern but necessary measure for national security, there was probably less organized pro-Axis sentiment among Japanese-

Americans than among Americans of Italian or German ancestry—whom no one seriously proposed rounding up.[55]

A month after Pearl Harbor, Mike Gold warned in the *Daily Worker* against any "blind, undisciplined, individualistic" attacks against people of German, Italian, or Japanese descent living in America. "There is one thing I dread and that I would blush with shame for America should it happen. It is any possibility of the stupid, cruel and un-American persecutions and mob actions against aliens" that had accompanied the last world war.[56]

But when this "stupid, cruel and un-American" persecution was undertaken by the federal government—not only against aliens, but against naturalized and native-born American citizens of Japanese ancestry—Gold and the CP remained silent. Only late in the war would the Communists begin showing evidence of bad conscience on the question. In August 1944 the *New Masses* printed an article by the independent journalist Carey McWilliams on the "Plight of the Nisei," detailing their harsh treatment in the relocation camps and calling for their release. The *New Masses* felt obliged to print an editorial disclaimer calling the evacuation "a necessary war measure," and declaring that "the question of the time of their release is a matter for the federal authorities to decide." But it was an unusual step for the *New Masses* to print any article so at variance with the official line. McWilliams had obviously touched a raw nerve when he submitted the piece. A week later Abner Green, a leader of the CP's Committee for the Protection of the Foreign Born, wrote in to complain about the editorial stance. Although he agreed that the initial evacuation was necessary, he could see no justification for the continued incarceration of loyal Japanese-Americans.[57]

Japanese-American Communists, shipped out to detention camps with the rest of their countrymen, faced the unpleasant task of having to justify their own incarceration as a contribution to the anti-fascist cause. In May 1942 the *CIO News* published a letter from Karl Yoneda, a longshoreman and veteran Communist union organizer, describing how he and others interned at the Manzanar, California, relocation camp were conducting drives to buy war bonds and to save tin for the war effort. Without apparent irony he wrote, "The workings of democracy are clearly demonstrated before our eyes. . . . Those of us who are American citizens of Japanese ancestry are grateful to our government for the way this grave question of evacuation is being handled. What a difference from fascist-controlled countries."[58] Yoneda, like a number of other Japanese-American Communists, would eventually be released from detention after volunteering for military service.[59]

"Victory and After"

By the time Browder returned to active party leadership following his release from prison in May 1942, the main elements of the Communists' wartime policy were already in place: support for a second front, opposition to all strikes, opposition to discriminatory hiring practices, and uncritical support for virtually any domestic policies Roosevelt chose to pursue. Communist leaders had made no systematic effort to justify these policies: they were presented, on the whole, as expedient measures required by the wartime emergency. But in his book *Victory and After*, published that fall, Browder sought to tie together all the loose ends of policies adopted since June 22, 1941, and present them as a coherent political platform. *Victory and After* was a frank justification of the case for class collaboration during the war—and, as the title suggested, in the postwar era as well. "We must find a way to finance, organize and fight this war through to victory," Browder argued, "a way which is acceptable to the owning class. . . . If these persons should become disaffected and sabotage the war, they could do enormous damage."[60]

Most Communists could accept this outlook as a domestic equivalent of the Grand Alliance, imposed on them by stark wartime necessity. They knew that neither the CP nor the labor movement nor even the whole "win-the-war camp" had the power necessary to step in and commandeer capital in the name of the war effort. Even if they succeeded in pushing through partial measures along those lines, they would only antagonize business owners and run the risk of provoking the kind of "sit-down strike of capital" that had proven so damaging to the French Popular Front, and led indirectly to the collapse of French resistance in 1940.

But Browder took that argument a step further. He was now predicting that cooperation between the capitalist powers and the Soviet Union would extend into the postwar period, and would shape domestic relations between labor and capital. Victory for the "United Nations" would "make possible the solution of reconstruction problems with a minimum of social disorder and civil violence in the various countries most concerned."[61]

Contrary to his normal practice, Browder did not submit *Victory and After* to his colleagues on the political committee before its publication, and some were surprised to see him make such an argument.[62] Until that point Communist leaders had refrained from public discussion of the postwar world. They were privately convinced that wartime international and domestic alliances would break down soon after the Nazis had been defeated. Minor told the CP national committee in an unpublished speech in April 1942: "The bourgeoisie has not lost its teeth. The bourgeoisie is still the bourgeoisie and the relationships of the labor movement to the bourgeoisie in this war are war relationships and the alliance for the war does not extend to any postwar problems."[63]

But now Browder was insisting that the party place the question of the postwar world at the center of its political activity. "To the degree that we conduct and win this war as a war of the United Nations, to that same degree we are preparing the United Nations as the instrument for ordering the post-war world."[64] No Communist was about to encourage speculation about impending American-Soviet conflict at a time when the USSR was in desperate need of every scrap of aid it could get from the United States. Browder, however, took what had been simply a tactic and made it the centerpiece of the CP's political outlook.

Browder viewed Roosevelt as the guarantor of Soviet-American cooperation. "Support for President Roosevelt," he argued in *Victory and After*, was the "essential guiding slogan for our country in finding its way through this war."[65]

After the war, conservative newspaper columnists and Republican congressmen repeatedly charged that Browder and Roosevelt had maintained close personal and political ties following Browder's release from prison. Browder himself, or an intermediary (sometimes described as a mysterious "Madame X"), was supposed to have met with Roosevelt at the White House on numerous occasions. The truth turns out to be somewhat less melodramatic. There was a "Madame X," but she never met Roosevelt. Josephine Truslow Adams, a former Swarthmore art instructor who had been active in Communist causes since the late 1930s (valued by the Communists for her impeccable DAR credentials), kept up a steady, though largely one-sided correspondence with Eleanor Roosevelt all through the war. Beginning in

1943 Browder began to feed her information and suggestions to pass along through Mrs. Roosevelt to her husband. Some of Adams's letters did find their way to Roosevelt's desk (with occasional disparaging comments attached by Mrs. Roosevelt: "I know nothing about her reliability," she scribbled on a letter from Adams in January 1944). But there is no evidence that Roosevelt paid any serious attention to the missives from Adams.[66]

Browder found one other, more substantial contact with the Administration. In a column in the October 4, 1942, issue of the *Worker*, Browder charged that "powerful appeasement forces in the State Department" were conspiring with Chiang Kai-shek, encouraging him to use his troops to contain the Communist armies rather than fight the Japanese. Sumner Welles wrote to Browder two days later, taking issue with the charge and inviting him to come down to Washington to discuss the State Department's China policy. Browder responded eagerly, and on October 12 he and Minor met for about an hour with Welles and Lauchlin Currie, administrative assistant to Roosevelt who had just returned from a diplomatic mission to China. In their short but cordial meeting Welles assured Browder that the State Department favored full cooperation between the Kuomintang and the Chinese Communists.[67]

Four days later Browder issued a front-page retraction in the *Daily Worker* of his earlier charges: "I believe it established that no responsible official of the State Department is contributing to disunity in China." He was obviously delighted with the welcome he had received at the State Department, declaring, "What I had thought of as a heavy door that needed pushing open proved to be but a curtain of lack of information."[68]

During the next half-year Browder corresponded with Welles on a number of occasions and met with him twice, discussing the plight of French Communist prisoners in North Africa, the political situation in Puerto Rico, and Browder's unsuccessful request for permission to visit Mexico to meet with Latin-American Communists. Welles's motive for initially contacting Browder and making himself available on subsequent occasions remains obscure, but it seems unlikely that Welles would have gone ahead without Roosevelt's foreknowledge and approval. Perhaps this represented Roosevelt's token payment for the CP's support for Administration foreign policy, as the appointment of Emspak to the Labor Victory Board had been a reward for Communist help in the "Battle for Production." The publicity that the Communists gave Browder's contact with Welles shows they valued it more as a symbol of political respectability than as a means to actually influence State Department policy.

In any event, Browder's link to the corridors of power proved short-lived. Secretary of State Cordell Hull forced Welles out of the State Department the following year, and his successor made no efforts to reestablish contact with Browder.[69]

Organizational Problems

The war affected the party's organizational structure as well as its political outlook. By the fall of 1942 John Williamson, the CP's organizational secretary, reported that 7 percent of the party's members were already in the armed forces.[70] The actual impact on the CP's operations was much heavier than that figure suggests. A large proportion of the CP's most trusted and experienced leaders, its district and section organizers and officers, as well as trade-union and front-organization leaders, had joined the YCL or the CP in the early 1930s. They had then been in their teens or early twenties; now they were in their late twenties or early thirties, of prime military eligibility. In October Williamson announced that in New York State 20 percent of state committee members, 22 percent of section organizers, and 30 percent of section organization secretaries were already in the service. In the next six months, he warned, "We must be prepared to replace a majority of our functionaries in all state organizations."[71]

The party began to promote women to fill the gaps in the secondary leadership. When Joseph Clark, editor of the YCL's *Weekly Review*, left for the army in the spring of 1942, Claudia Jones succeeded him; in California, Oleta O'Connor Yates succeeded Steve Nelson as chairman of the San Francisco party organization. By mid-1943 more than half of all YCL members were women, and by 1944 nearly half of all party members were women (compared to less than 10 percent in 1930, and just over 25 percent in 1936). Women still remained a distinct minority among the party's top leaders, most of whom were well past military age. The twenty-eight-member national committee elected in December 1942 included seven women, and Flynn was the only woman on the nine-member political committee.[72]

One other, less desirable, consequence of the CP's wartime shortage of experienced cadres was the ease with which government informers now found it possible to move up in the party hierarchy. The Justice Department had dramatically stepped up its surveillance and infiltration of the Communist party during the period of the Nazi-Soviet pact, and saw no need to reverse the policy after America and Russia joined together in the Grand Alliance. In May 1942, CP waterfront leader Al Lannon wrote: "We must follow a bold policy of promotion of comrades from the ranks, even without any previous experience, who show possibilities for development." That same spring FBI agents recruited Angela Calomiris, a young New York City photographer, as an informer. She joined the CP, soon found herself swamped with organizational responsibilities (passing on to the FBI copies of hundreds of photographs she casually snapped of her new party friends and associates), and in 1949, when she was financial secretary of the West Midtown Branch of the CP, took the witness stand as a government witness in the first Smith Act trial.[73]

The Communists' return to the anti-fascist camp at first brought them only modest gains in membership. At the April national committee meeting, delegates learned that CP membership stood at just under 44,000, representing a growth of less than 4 percent over the previous year (this was, however, the first time since 1938 that the CP had shown any gain in membership). More people were now joining, but turnover remained high. With 10,000 new recruits in 1941, the party ended the year with a net gain of just over 1,500 members.

John Williamson blamed the dismal internal life of many branches, the basic unit and "weakest link" of the party's political activity, for the problem of high turnover. The branches were clinging to "methods of work . . . forced upon us during days of repressive measures." Communists had to come up from underground, "appear publicly in their neighborhood as political clubs setting an example of patriotic activity," and operate more "in accord with the established organizational forms of all parties." When Connecticut Communists openly took part in a community scrap drive in Hartford, Williamson pointed to them as a model for the CP's wartime role. The Hartford City Salvage Committee, Williamson proudly related, "chose the Communist Party branch to organize salvage collection in one ward just as it chose the American Legion or the Kiwanis, or a church, for others."[74]

The organizational pendulum, which had swung so sharply toward tight-knit, Leninist forms during the Nazi-Soviet pact, was now swinging back to more loosely structured, neighborhood-based groups. Williamson announced that the party would no longer make attendance at branch meetings a requirement for its members. He painted a grim picture of what life in the party had been like up until that point. "The demands we sometimes put on members," he said, "places them almost in the category of abnormal people, with no regard for health, family or contact with the masses."[75] In the name of national unity the CP sought to reduce the differences between the lives of its own members and those of other Americans. "Too often," Williamson declared at the December 1942 meeting of the national committee, "we want to set as standards for all party members the yardstick of the professional revolutionist."[76]

And yet, if becoming a Communist meant nothing more than joining a Democratic party reform organization or an American Labor party club, the CP ran the risk of losing any special reason for existence. In the midst of a world war in which the very existence of the Soviet Union was at stake, Communists could not easily shed the Bolshevik heritage of discipline and self-sacrifice. In the fall of 1942 a woman wrote to Elizabeth Gurley Flynn to complain that she and other women Communists were being pressured to take on additional organizational responsibilities or to seek work in defense plants, even if they wanted to move near army bases where their husbands were stationed. Flynn replied unsympathetically: "If you want to help morale, don't be a camp follower." She summoned up the image of the sacrifices that Soviet women were making, noting that Lieutenant Pavilichenko had never even mentioned during her tour of the United States that her own husband had been killed during the siege of Sevastapol the previous February. "Women stay at their posts today," Flynn declared. "Our feelings—neither yours nor your husbands', nor any of our personal feelings—are important today."

Flynn's reply sparked a debate which continued through several weeks' issues of the *Worker*, with the general response summed up in one letter appearing in early January: "You're right—but not kind."[77] The conflict between Williamson's and Flynn's messages was not the product of personal differences between the two Communist leaders (if anything, Flynn tended to be the member of the political committee most concerned with having the party present a nonsectarian public image).[78] Rather, it reflected the fact that the party was pursuing two very different goals: seeking to reduce the requirements for general membership, while at the same time pushing its militants to redoubled sacrifices. The conflict only widened the already existing split between the world of the CP's cadres and its rank and file. Some Communists would be encouraged to think of the party as a kind of left-wing Kiwanis Club, while others would continue to be judged and judge themselves by that "yardstick of the professional revolutionist."[79]

Williamson's criticisms of organizational problems provided the most visible sign of reevaluation going on among Communists during the early war years. But they represented only a limited change in political perspective. Top leaders like Williamson sought to push the party in a new political direction without coming to an understanding of the causes of past failures. Williamson never offered an explanation of why branch life had atrophied so severely in past years—what, for example, such problems might have had to do with the party's undemocratic internal structure. In *Victory and After* Browder admitted that Communists could make mistakes, but in a brief survey of the party's history since 1939 he found no such mistake to criticize. He noted that "an unfortunate chain of events" had thrown the CP into opposition to Roosevelt between 1939 and 1941, but he defended the party's "principled disagreement" with the Administration in those years and concluded, "Enough of this ancient history!"[80]

CP leaders maintained tight control over this process of reevaluation, at least as reflected in the party press, which only printed rank-and-file criticisms in connection with such limited questions as the debate over "camp-following." And by rigidly separating all questions of current CP policies and structure from the question of how to conduct the long-term struggle for socialism—an event postponed to the ever more distant future—leaders evaded the most fundamental questions. What would happen when the question of socialism was once again on the party's agenda? Would the CP then revert to the traditional Bolshevik outlook and organization? How would socialism be achieved in the United States, and what would it look like? These may have seemed like remote and abstract concerns in the midst of world war. Yet, if Browder's and Williamson's reforms were to become more than temporary expedients to fit the wartime emergency, these were questions that needed to be openly discussed.

Rethinking the Past

During the Nazi-Soviet pact, outside attacks made it mandatory for Communists to close ranks. If individual Communists felt uncomfortable with their abandonment of Popular Front policies during 1939–1941, they kept silent. But in the course of the war after June 22, 1941, a few Communists did begin to reflect on their own "ancient history." For some, service in the armed forces had a dramatic impact on the way they looked at the world, lifting them out of parochial party circles, throwing them into direct, intimate contact with the "masses" whom they had so often discussed in abstract or romantic terms. George Charney, who entered the army in 1942, said of the experience:

> I had lost the native, familiar touch and the intuitive readiness to judge individual and group actions in broad human and social terms. The Army and these ordinary GIs helped me to recover them, as I discovered to my chagrin and amusement that I had no special authority or spoke from no dais in a pyramidal tent to summarize the discussion in customary party style. What I had to say I had to get in edgewise, like the others, and sometimes shout to be heard. . . . After years of Communist separateness, in part self-imposed, the war reunited me with my fellow Americans.[81]

For most Communists in the military, such political insights as they gained during the war remained intuitive and half-formed. Isolated from one another, they had no means of discussing and developing their conclusions. Communists who remained at home may have had parallel experiences as they threw themselves into the coalition politics of the Grand Alliance. But here the ceaseless round of party activities, the desire to get one more signature on a second-front petition or sell one more subscription to the *Daily Worker*, also checked critical self-judgments.

Such subterranean shifts in political sensibility are difficult to measure until they spill out into the open during crises, as they would in 1945 and again—with far more profound consequences—in 1956. But Browder received two letters in the year after the publication of *Victory and After* that illustrate the more radical rethinking that at least a few Communists had undertaken.

The first letter, from an unidentified party member, was written in late 1942 or early 1943. It argued that Communists had no reason to be optimistic about the recent upturn in their political fortunes: "The CP appears to be no stronger numerically than it was in 1936. Actually

. . . it is weaker. Its prestige is far lower, and it is isolated from a large part of the liberal movement." Liberals had not forgiven the Communists for their behavior during the Nazi-Soviet pact, and if the CP genuinely sought to mend its fences with them it needed to do so on an entirely new basis. "Far too often in the days of the people's front," continued the writer, "what we called cooperation with progressives was actually cooperation with ourselves under different guises." Since June 22 the Communists had attempted to "recreate the people's front through an automatic repetition of the slogans of 1935." Results had proven meager. The CP itself was a barrier to American-Soviet cooperation in the war, since most Americans believed that Communists were "working for the dictatorship of the proletariat in America. We have not yet made it clear that America's social revolution must develop according to American conditions."

The writer concluded that the party needed to undertake a "reevaluation of the basic aims of the CP" representing "as great an advance over present conceptions as the 7th World Congress" had represented over the Third Period: "It requires also a fundamental reevaluation of the methods adopted by the CP, in its actions with the progressive movement, and its attitude towards progressive leaders. It requires more self-criticism, which has been sadly lacking. It requires the rejection of crude forms of personal attacks and intriguing for power that characterized 1939–1941. This re-evaluation must come sooner or later. The sooner it comes, the better."[82]

The second letter came from Frank Meyer, who had been a YCL and then party functionary in Illinois in the Popular Front years. He wrote Browder in November 1943, following a medical discharge from the army, and confessed to feeling a little "trepidation" in writing, since his army service and subsequent convalescence had removed him from "the hard facts of day-to-day Party life" for several years: "But it is exactly the rather rude immersion among the American people in the most undifferentiated sense, which my Army career represented," he said, "which made me think very hard about problems of our Party . . . which personally, at least, I feel I had faced rather abstractly before."

Meyer did not feel that "we are drastically and radically . . . and self critically enough overhauling our theory and our practice." In the past the Communists had amply proven their ability to make tactical shifts in new situations, but had let theoretical development lag far behind. Meyer felt it was time to remedy this situation. First, he questioned whether a "modification of imperialism" might now mean that American capital could aid economic development in Latin America, China, India, and the Middle East without resorting to undue exploitation. Such foreign investments could serve as "one foundation of an expanding economy and a decent standard of living at home." Second, he asked whether it was useful to continue to regard the state in traditional Leninist terms as "simply the executive committee of the bourgeoisie." He noted the "danger of placing the state above the class struggle, as the Social Democrats did," but still wondered if "in a period of transition, such as the whole world is going through today, the state is not something to be wrestled over by the contending classes."

Meyer believed that the present international anti-fascist coalition could carry over into the postwar period, laying the basis for a "peaceful transition to socialism." This transition would consist of expanded democratic control of the economy and society coexisting with private capital ownership in a mixed economy for an extended period. "I don't mean class peace, which is of course impossible in a class society. But a very different form of class struggle—one which might repeat—in a higher level and in very different circumstances, the people's liberation movement of Marx's time, with the same passing over into socialism which he saw possible then." After the "frightful catastrophes" of recent years, this vision of gradual socialist transformation could, he believed, attract much wider popular support than an apocalyptic revolutionary strategy.

Finally, Meyer turned to the question of party organization. If the Communists were to adopt a democratic, gradualist political approach, they had to abandon the Bolshevik model of organization. Instead Meyer advocated "a party something like that described in the Communist Manifesto—and incidentally, something like that which Jefferson and Jackson led. Isn't the Leninist Party designed for an immediate, sharp and final struggle? Is it possible to build a mass Marxist party to meet the challenge that lies in front of us today on such a basis?"

The average American worker simply could not spare the amount of time required to be a Communist, even under the relaxed wartime requirements. As for the party's "actives," Meyer said, they wasted most of their time and energy in an endless "inner round" of party functions. "The kind of party I would like to see is one in which its members attended bi-monthly or quarterly meetings, received general guidance and education there, read the press of the party; in which those who are interested carry out specific activities of the party on committees for that purpose; but in which the one main task of every party member is to think and act where he lives, works, plays, participates in the life of his community, as a Communist."

The Communists had to reevaluate the concept of democratic centralism in the light of "traditional American concepts of democracy" and pay more than lip service to the idea of basing political activity on American conditions. "A people's America and a socialist America must be presented all the time—not simply in an occasional article or on the Fourth of July—as a natural, integral outgrowth of our whole past history, and presented in terms of our tradition. And this will only come about when our leaders from top to bottom are as familiar with the struggles of Jefferson and Jackson and Lincoln, and what we have inherited from those struggles, as they are with 1848, 1902, 1917."[83]

Together, these two letters sketched out a far-reaching critique of theory, organization, and political practice. And they paralleled the reevaluation going on within at least one other major Communist party. In discussing the question of the transition to socialism, Meyer referred to a pamphlet by the Italian Communist "Ercoli" (PCI general secretary Palmiro Togliatti), written during the Spanish Civil War. Though he did not name the pamphlet, Meyer probably meant Togliatti's *The Spanish Revolution*, published in translation by the American CP in 1936. Togliatti had argued in this pamphlet that events in Spain should not be compared to the Russian revolutions of 1905 and 1917 since "big events and moments in history do not repeat themselves with photographic exactness either in time or space." In particular, "the democratic republic which is being established in Spain is unlike the usual type of bourgeois-democratic republic." Emerging out of a war against fascism, in an international situation transformed by the existence of the Soviet Union, a victorious Spanish Republic would "be alien to all conservatism; for it possesses all the conditions necessary for its own further development, it provides the guarantees for further economic and political achievements by the working people of Spain."[84]

The way Meyer chose to interpret Togliatti's comments—plausibly, in view of the subsequent political history of Italian communism—was that a "bourgeois-democratic republic," given the proper balance of political forces, could be an instrument for achieving socialism rather than simply an obstacle to be smashed by Communists in preparation for the dictatorship of the proletariat.

Meyer's letter, and that of his unknown comrade, foreshadowed the kind of rethinking that would characterize "Eurocommunism" three decades later. Only two important subjects remained taboo: the letters contained no explicit criticism of the USSR, nor any examination of the American CP's relations to the international Communist movement. Either the writers were not yet prepared to take that step, or else they decided that to retain any credibility with Browder they could not offer such criticisms.

Some of the positions Browder adopted over the next year and a half roughly approximated those that Meyer advocated, including the weakest of Meyer's suppositions: that American capital could play a benevolent role in developing what would later be called the Third World. But Browder never seriously addressed the larger questions—on the role of the state, the transition to socialism, or the Communists' relations to other political movements—that the two letters raised. Meyer had asked that the entire party—and not simply the top leaders—be involved in any discussion of the future direction of the Communist movement. And, perhaps anticipating that Browder would be reluctant to unleash the floodwaters of genuine reexamination, Meyer had warned: "If these things are correct, they are burning, immediate problems that must be solved, not tomorrow but yesterday. They are overdue. They are the main tasks of the Party because they are the one thing that the Party can do which nobody else can do."[85]

More than a decade would pass before American Communists finally took up the task Meyer assigned them in 1943.

8 HOLD THE HOME FRONT
January to December 1943

Well, a Union Sun was shining
And November it was ending
And the year was Nineteen Hundred Forty Three.
They shook hands across the table
In the city of Teheran.
Joe Stalin! Churchill! and Franklin D.!

[Chorus] Joe Stalin! Churchill! and Franklin D.!
Joe Stalin! Churchill! and Franklin D.!
And our new union world was born on that spot.
—WOODY GUTHRIE, 1944

If J. P. Morgan supports this coalition and goes down the line for
it, I as a Communist am prepared to clasp his hand.
—EARL BROWDER, December 12, 1943[1]

NINETEEN FORTY-THREE, a year that began with the Soviet victory at
Stalingrad and ended with the first wartime meeting of Stalin, Churchill,
and Roosevelt, marked the beginning of the end for Nazi Germany.
As America entered its second year of war the Communists were
convinced that if Roosevelt had his way he would fulfill his promise
to bring the combined force of the country's military and industrial
capacities to bear against Hitler. But the sense of national mission and
unity prevailing in the months immediately following Pearl Harbor was
now beset by political, racial, and class antagonisms. The CP attributed
the growing domestic discord—revealed in the Erlich-Alter controversy, the Detroit and Harlem race riots, and the wave of wildcat
strikes—to the machinations of pro-Nazi fifth columnists. The Communists argued that, if allowed to go unchecked, a lack of national
unity in the United States could yet win the war for Hitler. "To hold
the home front line," Browder declared in mid-1943, "is now of equal
importance to holding the battle line."[2]

Reactions to Stalingrad

The months during and just after the Battle of Stalingrad saw Soviet prestige in the United States reach its highest level. In November 1942 the Red Army launched an attack in support of Stalingrad's embattled defenders. Five days later they had completely encircled the German Sixth Army. For the next three months Russian artillery and the Russian winter tore holes in the once-proud Sixth Army, which had conquered Belgium, marched triumphantly into Paris, and invaded Yugoslavia and Greece. "Hitler has lost the war," the *New Republic* declared in February 1943, shortly after the surrender of the Sixth Army, "and for this the Russians deserve the major share of the credit."[3] Shortly afterward *Life* magazine, in a special issue devoted to the Soviet Union, paid the Russians the supreme compliment of being "one hell of a people," who "look like Americans, dress like Americans, and think like Americans."[4]

As the Russians battled toward victory at Stalingrad, American Communists expressed high hopes for the future of the Grand Alliance. On November 8, 1942, 22,000 people gathered in Madison Square Garden for a "Salute to Our Russian Ally," organized by the Council of American-Soviet Friendship. Mayor LaGuardia declared "Stalingrad Day" in New York City, and the gathering was addressed by Vice-President Wallace, Governor Herbert Lehman of New York, and other dignitaries. Alvah Bessie described the event for the *New Masses* in almost beatific tones: "It was a dream come true. . . . The international unity we have shouted for so long is being achieved; the international solidarity of all who toil is being cemented."[5]

The years of the Grand Alliance, paradoxically, made it possible for American Communists to begin to shed old domestic political orthodoxies, while binding them all the more closely to defending the Soviet Union against any criticism. It would have seemed unthinkable to even the most reform-minded Communist to justify criticism of Soviet actions at a time when the Russian people were being called on to make immeasurably greater sacrifices than their American or British allies, and when Stalin's political and military leadership was leading to Hitler's defeat. When confronted with criticism of the USSR, the Communists reacted as vehemently as they would have in the most sectarian days of the Third Period.

The Erlich-Alter Case

The revelation of the Soviet execution of two Polish-Jewish Socialists, Victor Alter and Henryk Erlich, provoked the first significant public criticism in the United States against the Soviet Union since the end of the Nazi-Soviet pact.

Erlich and Alter, leaders of the Socialist Jewish Bund in prewar Poland, had long histories in the Polish and Russian revolutionary movements. Erlich, who had suffered imprisonment and exile under the tsar, was a member of the executive committee of the St. Petersburg soviet in 1917 before the Bolsheviks gained control of it. Though opponents of Lenin, Erlich and Alter stood to the left of most of the other leaders of the Socialist International in the 1930s, calling on the Western powers to join with the Soviet Union in an anti-fascist alliance. When the Germans invaded Poland, Erlich and Alter first attempted to rally Polish resistance, then fled to eastern Poland, where they were quickly arrested by Soviet occupation forces. Several months after the German invasion of the Soviet Union, Stalin had them released from prison. Upon their release they took part in the organization of the Moscow-based Jewish Anti-Fascist Committee.

But Stalin was already worrying about the political complexion of postwar Poland. Once the immediate survival of the USSR was no longer in question, he decided to eliminate the Bundists. In December 1941 Soviet police rearrested Erlich and Alter. Despite repeated inquiries from Socialist and labor leaders in the United States, the Soviet government would release no information on their fate. But in February 1943 Ambassador Litvinov finally responded to a cable from AFL president Green, CIO president Murray, and others, revealing that Erlich and Alter had been executed the previous December for allegedly urging Red Army soldiers to "stop bloodshed and immediately . . . conclude peace with Germany."[6]

The utter implausibility of the charges against the two men, and the brutal and offhand announcement of their deaths, shocked many ordinarily pro-Soviet commentators. The *New Republic, The Nation*, and the liberal New York newspaper *PM* all condemned the executions. The *New Republic* declared that it was "time that we learned to know our ally . . . and not allow our admiration for his fighting abilities to blind us to the problems his participation in the war creates. The announcement of the deaths of Erlich and Alter should take the scales from our eyes.''[7] An Erlich-Alter memorial meeting in New York City in March, organized by ILGWU president Dubinsky, attracted several thousand unionists to hear speeches by AFL president Green, CIO secretary James Carey, and messages of support from New York Senator James Mead and Mayor LaGuardia.[8]

The Communists chose to regard the controversy as part of a Nazi-inspired anti-Soviet conspiracy. Joseph Starobin, who had privately questioned the legitimacy of the Moscow trials in the late 1930s, revealed no qualms over the Erlich-Alter case in a lengthy analysis in the *Daily Worker*: ''Among the spies and wreckers eliminated by the Moscow Trials in 1936–1937 there were many non-Jews, and Jews also, like Leon Trotsky.'' As for Erlich's and Alter's three decades of revolutionary activity, ''Jewish workers will tell you that Alter and Erlich specialized in denouncing to the Polish police members of [the Bund] who left its ranks because they could no longer tolerate its leadership or policies.'' And in words that take on special meaning in the light of Starobin's own buried doubts about the legitimacy of Soviet judicial procedures, he concluded: ''Anyone who remembers what happened during the Moscow trials, anyone who has the humility to realize what damage was done to the whole world by the anti-Soviet campaign of that period, who has the honesty to admit . . . that they were wrong about the Moscow trials, ought to be careful not to burn themselves twice.''[9]

The CP worked hard to limit the scope of the protest over the executions. The New York CIO Council overwhelmingly defeated a motion to support the Erlich-Alter memorial meeting, and then denounced the event as a ''deliberate effort of disruption'' of the war effort. The National Maritime Union sent pickets to the meeting. Even without these efforts, the Erlich-Alter controversy would soon have played itself out. Though the Michigan state CIO, controlled by Reuther and his allies in the UAW, passed a resolution in April condemning the executions, few people outside of New York City labor and liberal circles cared very much about the fate of two obscure Jewish Socialists. Important arbiters of liberal opinion—Roosevelt, Hillman, and Murray—maintained silence on the case. Even those liberals most disturbed by the deaths were not prepared to allow their protest to disturb Soviet-American relations. The *New Republic*'s editors cautioned that the Erlich-Alter case should not be allowed to interfere in any way with American aid to the Russian war effort, nor should it cast a shadow over postwar cooperation between the allies. Citing the Sacco-Vanzetti executions, the *New Republic* declared: "All the chief United Nations have sins on their conscience like the Erlich-Alter case."[10]

Wartime Strikes

The Communists regarded the labor movement as their most important battlefield on the "home front." Though most union leaders continued to support the no-strike pledge, by 1943 many rank-and-file members had come to view it as a bad bargain. The War Labor Board's loose enforcement of the "Little Steel" pay formula was tightened up in April 1943 by Roosevelt's "Hold the Line" order, which rescinded the board's power to grant wage increases in order to eliminate pay inequalities in a given industry or plant. The Office of Price Administration was nowhere near as diligent or as successful in holding down price increases as the War Labor Board was in enforcing wage limits. Soaring corporate profits and Congressional opposition to Roosevelt's plan for a $25,000-a-year income limit turned the liberal slogan "Equality of Sacrifice" into a hollow joke. Thousands of workers responded by launching unauthorized—or in the case of the United Mine Workers, tacitly authorized—wildcat strikes. The number of man-days lost in strikes tripled in 1943 over the previous year.[11]

Communists in the unions continued to defend the no-strike pledge. They saw no alternative. Unlike their Trotskyist rivals (who opposed the no-strike pledge and baited the Communists as sell-outs), they no longer viewed World War Two as an imperialist conflict. The Communists knew that the Allied armies—particularly the Russians—desperately needed every tank, plane, and gun that American factories could provide. They had learned through firsthand experience in Spain that political virtue armed with obsolete weaponry could not stand up to German artillery and dive-bombers. The Republicans in Spain could not have permitted strikes in their armaments factories during the Civil War, the Soviets certainly were not permitting strikes in their own industry, and American workers, whose standard of living was much higher than than that of their Spanish or Russian counterparts, would have to make some sacrifices as well. There was no such thing as a partial or conditional no-strike pledge. Once the strike weapon was made legitimate in certain industries or under certain circumstances, the unions would face an impossible task convincing workers in non-exempted categories to refrain from its use. Given their commitment to supporting the war, the Communists' continued defense of the no-strike pledge was a difficult but principled political stand. However, the Communists' response to those who did challenge the no-strike pledge was something less than principled.[12]

The Communists complicated the task of defending the no-strike pledge by linking it with a proposal to make pay increases dependent on improved worker productivity. In a speech to the December 1942 meeting of the CP's national committee (reprinted in a pamphlet entitled *Production for Victory*), Browder warned that moral exhortations alone were not going to keep workers on the job. He proposed that unions introduce the principle of "incentive pay" in future contracts. Increases would go to workers in proportion to the total increase in productivity in a given workplace, and management would have to agree for the duration of the war not to use increased productivity as cause for slashing pay rates.[13]

Browder's incentive-pay proposal became the Communists' panacea for almost all problems in war production and labor relations in 1943. He told a meeting of party trade unionists in February that incentive pay "corresponds to the interests of the workers; it corresponds to the *true* interests of the capitalists; it corresponds to the interests of the government; it corresponds to the interests of winning the war as quickly and cheaply as possible."[14]

Browder's proposal did represent a way to get around the rigid ceiling on wages imposed by the "Little Steel" formula, since both the War Production Board and the War Labor Board had gone on record as favoring incentive pay. Although the CIO had not officially endorsed the idea, it was not hostile to it. After Roosevelt's "Hold the Line" order was issued, Lee Pressman sent a letter over Murray's signature to all CIO officers saying that incentive wage plans promised "to be of extreme importance to labor and should be examined carefully."[15]

Unfortunately for the Communists, neither employers nor rank-and-file workers wanted anything to do with it. Browder argued that unions could sell the scheme to management by talking "cold turkey" to them: "It is more in the interests of the boss and his profits than his own illiterate point of view. It is strange but true that the working class of this country has the task to force better profits on unwilling employers."[16] Browder cherished the notion that he knew the capitalists' interests better than they did themselves. He was wrong. With the government handing out cost-plus contracts with minimal if any review of expenditures, employers had little interest in holding down the cost of production. In fact, by being less labor-efficient they could use the war to expand and upgrade their existing capital plant.

Workers had even less reason to embrace incentive pay. The plan pitted workers against one another, making them agents of their own speed-up. Faster workers would pressure slower workers to increase their productivity. Even if existing piece rates were guaranteed for the duration of the war, the higher productivity norms established would almost certainly be used by managers to justify slashing rates and laying off workers when peace came and demand slackened.[17] Yet Browder kept pushing his pet idea until it had ballooned into a major issue—and liability—for the Communist-backed anti-Reuther faction within the UAW.

In March, Paul Ste. Marie, president of the huge Ford Local 600 in Detroit, circulated leaflets with quotations from *Production for Victory*, arguing that a victory for the CP-backed opposition slate in upcoming local elections would mean the return of the speed-up and the management time-study man. In a public letter to Ste. Marie, Browder insisted that "old prejudices" against increasing the speed of production should be laid aside for the good of the war effort. Ste. Marie was in political trouble within the UAW for having backed the Republican candidate in the last Michigan gubernatorial election, while the opposition slate, which included a black UAW leader allied with Communists, Sheldon Tappes, could count on support from the sizable black membership of the local. Nevertheless, the left slate had to repudiate the incentive-pay proposal to ensure their victory.[18]

That same month UAW vice-president Richard Frankensteen introduced the controversy into the top leadership of the union. Frankensteen, who had been overseeing the UAW's floundering aircraft organization drive since 1941, saw the higher wages as a means to attract new members in West Coast aircraft factories. Secretary-treasurer George Addes and the Communists backed Frankensteen's proposal.

For the Communists it was a fateful error. Walter Reuther succeeded brilliantly with the stratagem that Ste. Marie had unsuccessfully tried in Local 600. Reuther grabbed hold of the incentive-pay issue, tying Frankensteen and Addes to the Communists as exponents of the speed-up, and building a coalition that ranged from the anti-Communist Association of Catholic Trade Unionists to the Trotskyists. Reuther had backed the no-strike pledge during the first year after Pearl Harbor, and was not prepared to repudiate it openly—but the incentive-pay issue offered him a middle ground from which he could defend workers' interests without moving into opposition to national CIO leadership. His emergence as spokesman for rank-and-file unrest would lead him to control of the UAW in 1947, an event marking the final defeat of Communist influence in the auto industry, and serving as the prelude and catalyst for the purge of the remaining Communist-influenced CIO unions in 1949 and 1950.[19]

The UAW executive board voted down the incentive-pay proposal when Frankensteen and Addes brought it up at the board's March meeting, and again when they reintroduced it in April. The debate quickly spread into the lower ranks of UAW leadership at regional conferences in Detroit and New York City in May, where incentive-pay proposals were overwhelmingly repudiated. At the national UAW convention meeting in Buffalo in October, the Reuther faction skewered their opponents with an inspired piece of malicious doggerel:

> Who are the boys who take their orders
> Straight from the office of Joe Sta-leen?
> No one else but the gruesome twosome,
> George F. Addes and Frankensteen.
> Who are the boys that fight for piecework,
> To make the worker a machine?
> No one else but the gruesome twosome,
> George F. Addes and Frankensteen.[20]

John L. Lewis was taking a more direct approach to the problem of lagging wages. Between May and October UMW miners walked out on strike four times, defying public and press condemnation, government seizure of the mines, hostile congressional legislation, and threats of prosecution. Lewis had staged a similar war of nerves against the Roosevelt Administration's labor policies in the 1941 "captive mines" dispute, winning most of his demands and undercutting the authority of the National Defense Mediation Board in the process. He hoped to gain an even greater victory over the War Labor Board and its Little Steel formula this time around.[21]

The CIO's national leaders, from ex–Mine Worker Murray on down, were aghast at this challenge to the no-strike pledge, well aware of the sentiment in their own ranks for following Lewis's lead. They feared that Lewis, who had pulled the UMW out of the CIO the year before, was hoping to regain leadership of the labor movement by challenging the government's freeze on wage increases. The Communists saw an even more sinister motive behind the UMW campaign. According to the *Daily Worker*: "John L. Lewis is seeking to shift the battlefront from Tunisia, Guadalcanal, and the soon expected European theatre to the hills of West Virginia, Pennsylvania, Ohio and the rest of the Appalachian region. . . . He is playing the so-called 'labor part' of the long planned effort of his America First associates to shift the fire away from Hitler." [22] And in a speech in May entitled "The Strike Wave Conspiracy" Browder accused all of the CP's major opponents in the labor movement of participating in a plot to undermine the war effort.

It was no accident, Browder asserted, that David Dubinsky, James Carey, and Walter Reuther were the most important union leaders supporting the Erlich-Alter protest. All three, despite their professed loyalty to Roosevelt, were out to subvert the Administration's labor policies. Dubinsky had allowed dressmakers in New York City to go out on strike; Carey had made speeches critical of some Administration decisions; and Reuther opposed incentive pay because, like Lewis, he wanted dissatisfied workers to go out on strike. All of this, in Browder's eyes, added up to a "well-developed, organized conspiracy against the war, to prevent the solution of the grievances of labor and then to manipulate those grievances in order to whip up strike sentiment." The mine strike was the conspirators' greatest success to date. Browder cited a headline in the Trotskyist newspaper *The Militant* labeling him a strikebreaker, and proclaimed, "As regards the fomenting of the strike movement that threatens America at this present time, I consider it the greatest honor to be a breaker of this movement." [23]

The violence of Browder's verbal assault could not make up for the party's actual impotence in the mine conflict. The Greater New York Industrial Union Council assembled a crowd of fifty thousand in Yankee Stadium on May 2 for a "Labor for Victory" rally which booed every mention of Lewis's name—but New York City was not a center of the mining industry. In the 1920s and 1930s the CP had held pockets of strength in mine districts, chiefly among foreign-born miners in western Pennsylvania, eastern Ohio, and Illinois. If the Lewis machine kept Communists out of positions of power within the UMW, Communist miners at least carried the moral authority of a history of doomed but heroic strikes, including the legendary confrontation in Harlan County in 1931. In 1939 the party counted almost thirteen hundred miners among its members. But by the spring of 1942, after the CP's break with Lewis, only about three hundred remained, a tiny group that could hardly hope to influence the half-million miners Lewis took out on strike.[24] The Communists squandered their few remaining resources in the coalfields by having Communist miners continue to report for work throughout the strikes in 1943. In an article analyzing the CP's recruiting campaign for the spring of 1943, John Williamson dolefully noted that "the number of coal miners in our party is at the lowest point in party history."[25]

In the end, Lewis won wage increases substantially above those permitted under the Little Steel formula and, by arriving at a settlement with Secretary of Interior Ickes in the midst of the fourth and final walkout, effectively demolished the War Labor Board's policy of refusing to negotiate with unions while their members were on strike. The lesson was not lost on thousands of workers in other industries.

The Communists' unyielding defense of the no-strike pledge did not, however, lead to any general flight of working-class members out of the party. In fact, Williamson announced in June 1943 that 62 percent of the 15,000 members joining the CP in its spring recruiting drive held working-class occupations, and more than half of these were "basic industrial workers" (mining, steel, metal, auto, and transport workers). This compared quite favorably to the 23 percent basic industrial workers listed in the January 1943 party registration. And since these figures represented new recruits, this was not simply a case of Communist office workers or teachers getting readily available wartime factory jobs and changing their designation on the party rolls. Williamson did not break down the figures any further to show what industries were supplying the bulk of new recruits, but they most probably came out of the rapidly expanding ranks of those CIO unions in which the party already held power, such as the UE, ILWU, and NMU.[26]

Communists and Race Riots

The figures from the 1943 recruiting drive also showed an increase in the number of blacks joining the party. Nearly one-third of new CP members that spring were black, compared to their one-tenth representation in the January registration. The Communists' break with A. Philip Randolph had damaged but not destroyed their strength in the black community. Although in the first year of the war Randolph's March on Washington Movement attracted capacity crowds to its rallies in Madison Square Garden and in halls in Chicago and St. Louis, the MOWM had floundered because of internal difficulties and its reluctance to undertake its long-promised civil disobedience campaign. The NAACP was the major beneficiary of heightened expectations of change among blacks, increasing its membership nearly ninefold in the course of the war. But the Communists also benefited from the decline of the MOWM. In 1943 the CP-organized Negro Labor Victory Committee filled Madison Square Garden for a "Negro Freedom Rally." By this time much of the indifference that blacks felt toward American participation in the war had been replaced by a cautious hope that a world-wide conflict waged in the name of Roosevelt's "four freedoms" would finally give substance to the long-deferred promise of equality at home. Mayor LaGuardia told a 1944 rally sponsored by the Negro Labor Victory Committee that "there definitely is a new world a-coming," and many blacks were now eager to believe him. The Communists, second to none in portraying World War Two as a people's war of national liberation, gained influence from these hopes.[27]

The Communists enjoyed a tight political alliance with the Reverend Adam Clayton Powell, Jr., in Harlem. They had supported his successful campaign for election to the city council in 1941, providing him with much-needed organizational machinery in areas of Manhattan outside Harlem. When he declined to run for reelection in 1943 in order to prepare for a congressional race the following year, the CP decided to run Ben Davis, Jr., leader of the Harlem section of the party. The Communists mounted a polished campaign on his behalf. With Powell's endorsement and the backing of the New York City CIO, Davis won handily, attracting more than 33,000 first-choice votes in Manhattan, the third largest vote total for the borough. (In Brooklyn, Cacchione was swept back into office with more than 53,000 first-choice votes— the highest vote total in the borough, and an increase of more than 50 percent over his 1941 total.)[28]

Davis was the first black Communist ever elected to public office in the United States, and only the second black to be elected to New York's city council. Harlem spokesmen treated his election as a triumph of the entire black community. The *Amsterdam News* praised him as "a close student of social problems, courageous, honest and highly dedicated. . . . He should be a real asset to the entire citizenry of New York." [29]

Whatever hope they invested in the promise of the Four Freedoms, American blacks could have few illusions about the prevailing state of race relations in the United States in 1943. That spring mobs of white shipyard workers attacked newly hired black workers in Alabama and Texas, while white auto workers in Michigan walked off the job to protest the hiring of black workers. On June 20 Detroit exploded in one of the worst race riots of the century. A racial brawl in a city park set off a wave of looting in black neighborhoods, while gangs of whites, seldom hindered and sometimes aided by Detroit police, attacked isolated blacks in white neighborhoods. When federal troops restored order three days later, thirty-four people had been killed, most of them black. Hundreds more were injured or arrested, and property damage amounted to $2 million. The underlying causes of the riot were easy enough to discern: 350,000 whites, mainly from the South, and 50,000 blacks had poured into an already crowded city in the months after Pearl Harbor to take jobs in war industries, swamping the city's housing, transportation, and recreation facilities. The Ku Klux Klan and other racist demagogues found the city a fertile ground for their activities. "Detroit," *Life* magazine had observed nearly a year earlier, "is Dynamite." [30] The Communists denounced the rioting as the product of a pro-Nazi conspiracy. "The Enemy Attacks in Detroit!" the *Daily Worker* declared in a front-page editorial. [31]

Two weeks after the Detroit riot, YCL leaders in New York City publicly urged Mayor LaGuardia to call a conference of labor, civic, and religious groups to discuss ways to avoid a similar disaster. Continued discrimination in jobs, housing, and the military, the YCL warned, had created dangerous resentment among younger blacks. [32] Three weeks later rioting broke out in Harlem, after a false rumor swept the community that a white policeman had killed a black soldier.

When the riot started, LaGuardia, accompanied by Max Yergan, president of the National Negro Congress, and by Ferdinand Smith, a black Communist vice-president of the National Maritime Union, spent the night touring the streets, urging the crowds to return to their homes. The Harlem CP sent out a sound truck calling for calm, and hundreds of Communists walked the streets, trying to dispel the rumor about the death of the black soldier. After a single night, at the cost of six lives, the rioting came to an end. [33]

The next morning the *Daily Worker* carried a front-page editorial headlined "Negro and White, Close Ranks! New York Wants No Detroit." The *Daily Worker* this time did not blame the outbreak on pro-Nazi fifth columnists, but instead called attention to "shocking problems of housing, lack of jobs, discrimination in every field of social life facing the Negro people." At the same time, the editorial insisted that "reestablishment of order" was the "central question of the moment."[34] Later that day Max Yergan and Ben Davis took part in a meeting organized by Adam Clayton Powell in the Abyssinian Baptist Church, and signed a joint statement calling for economic relief for Harlemites to prevent future riots.[35]

The Communists' response to the Harlem riot, and Ben Davis's electoral victory three months later, raise further questions about the conventional interpretation that the Communists "abandoned" the struggle for black rights during World War Two. Ironically, the Communists themselves played an important role in creating this interpretation when, in the aftermath of Browder's downfall in 1945, they searched their wartime record for evidence of the negative effects of "revisionism." In the summer of 1945 Doxey Wilkerson, a black CP leader, found "a striking gap between ideological profession and actual performance" by Communists in the "fight for Negro rights." Wilkerson noted that the CP had made "tremendous gains" in membership and influence among blacks during the war, but argued "these achievements are minor, indeed, when measured by what could have been achieved by a correct policy."[36] Still, the Communists reached the high-water mark of their political influence in Harlem during the very years when, if the conventional account was true, they logically ought to have been losing strength.

European Communists in America

The Communists set up a number of groups like the Negro Labor Victory Committee, hoping to channel nationalist sentiments among black and white Americans into support for the anti-fascist cause in Europe. By 1943 the Communists had established such groups as the United Americans of Italian Descent for United Nations Victory, the Greek-American Labor Committee, the National Council of Hungarian-American Trade Unionists, and the American Polish Trade Union Committee.[37] One of the most influential of these new front organizations was the United Committee of South Slavic-Americans, headed by the popular writer Louis Adamic. Adamic's committee helped swing American public sentiment in favor of Marshal Tito's Partisans in Yugoslavia, and away from the rival chetnik resistance movement.[38]

American Communists gained in political prestige in some ethnic communities because of their ties with leaders of the European resistance movements. This connection with Europe was a two-way street, as many European Communists sought wartime refuge in the United States. Some Communist exiles, like the German playwright Bertolt Brecht, carefully refrained from political activity while living in the United States, but others put themselves at the service of the American CP.[39] Among the latter group was another German exile, named Gerhardt Eisler.

After the war, Louis Budenz (editor of the *Daily Worker* from 1940 until his well-publicized defection from the CP in 1945) charged that Eisler, operating under the pseudonym "Hans Berger," had secretly directed the CP's policies since 1941. "This man never shows his face," Budenz charged in a 1946 radio address. "Communist leaders never see him, but they follow his orders or suggestions implicitly."[40] Eisler had, in fact, been a Comintern operative since the late 1920s— his experiences in China had inspired Brecht to write *The Measures Taken*—and came to the United States for the first time in 1934 to raise funds for the exiled German Communist party (KPD). He stayed through 1936 and may have functioned as un-official Comintern "rep" in the United States during that time. But by the mid-1930s that post retained less of the aura of mystery and authority that earlier Comintern representatives had wielded with such disastrous consequences for the American Communists. (Al Richmond, a cub reporter on the *Daily Worker* in 1936, did consult with Eisler on one question of political orthodoxy that year: whether the Sunday *Worker* should run a feature article on Shirley Temple. Eisler assured him it was all right.)[41]

Later that year the Comintern reassigned Eisler to more pressing duties in Spain, where he remained until the Loyalist defeat. Fleeing to France, he was imprisoned with other Spanish refugees in a French concentration camp. In 1941 he received a transit visa from the American consul in Marseilles permitting him to travel through the United States to Mexico. But when he arrived in New York, U.S. immigration officials prevented him from continuing on. Making the best of his enforced residence, he took on whatever tasks were assigned him by the American CP, going so far as to become an air-raid warden in

"COMMUNISM'S 20TH CENTURY AMERICANISM":
Communist Party slogan, Popular Front period

Earl Browder, center, general secretary, American Communist party, surrounded
by phalanx of red flags and American flags, 1937. (*From The Earl Browder Papers,
Courtesy of The George Arents Research Library, Syracuse University*)

Lincoln, Washington, and Jefferson join Marx, Lenin, and Stalin on a Communist float in a Chicago parade, 1938. (*Courtesy, Syracuse University*)

Browder with members of the Abraham Lincoln Battalion in Spain. A number of American veterans of the brigades later filled leadership posts in the Party. (*Courtesy, Syracuse University*)

"THE YANKS AREN'T COMING":
Party slogan during Nazi-Soviet pact period

Browder at New York City press conference called to explain the Party's defense of the Nazi-Soviet pact, August 23, 1939. (*Wide World Photos*)

by Ellis

Editorial page cartoon, *The Daily Worker*, August 30, 1939. British Prime Minister Neville Chamberlain deterred from offering Poland to Hitler; the Communist Party leadership was struggling to justify new "anti-imperialist" line of Nazi-Soviet pact.

In early 1940 CIO president John L. Lewis and the Communists united to oppose Roosevelt. Detractors unfurled the Soviet hammer and sickle flag as Lewis began to speak, United Mine Workers convention, January 26, 1940. (*Wide World Photos*)

"Why do you stand there in the rain?" (Woody Guthrie). President Roosevelt addresses unsympathetic American Youth Congress delegates, February 10, 1940. (*Wide World Photos*)

Founding of American Peace Mobilization, Chicago, August 31, 1940. (*Wide World Photos*)

Confrontation between L.A. police and United Auto Worker strikers at North American Aviation, Ingle-

"FREE EARL BROWDER": *Party rallying slogan*

Browder with October 24, 1939 *Daily Worker* story on his indictment for passport fraud. (*Courtesy, Syracuse University*)

Browder, slit handkerchief hiding his face, arrives in Atlanta, March 27, 1941, to begin four-year sentence in federal penitentiary. (*Wide World Photos*)

Browder on his way home after his sentence was commuted after 14 months, May 16, 1942. (*Wide World Photos*)

"SOVIET-AMERICAN FRIENDSHIP":
Party slogan after Hitler's invasion of the USSR

Joseph Curran, president, National Maritime Union; Vito Marcantonio, American Labor Party's only Congressman; and Mayor Fiorello LaGuardia, "Defend America" labor rally, Madison Square Garden, December 15, 1941. (*Wide World Photos*)

Vice President Henry Wallace (right) with Soviet Ambassador Maxim Litvinov and former US Ambassador to the Soviet Union Joseph E. Davies (left), at "Salute to Our Russian Ally" celebration, sponsored by the Congress of American-Soviet Friendship, Madison Square Garden, November 8, 1942. (*Wide World Photos*)

Browder at Communist rally in New York City's Union Square, demanding a second front in Europe, September 24, 1942. (*Wide World Photos*)

John Williamson, British-born organizational secretary of the American Communist party during World War Two, at a deportation hearing of the US Immigration and Naturalization Board, February 13, 1948. He was deported to England. (*Wide World Photos*)

Browder, James Ford, and William Z. Foster, chairman. Ford ran for vice-president as Foster's running mate in 1932, and as Browder's running mate in 1936 and 1940. (*Courtesy, Syracuse University*)

Gilbert Green, president of the Young Communist League in the 1930s. Green sympathized with Browder's attempts to "Americanize" the movement, and helped train a generation of young Communist leaders. (*Courtesy, Syracuse University*)

Elizabeth Gurley Flynn, signed "To Earl and Irene [Browder]—with comradely greetings and love—Elizabeth." Flynn, the only woman in the Communist party's ruling Political Committee, led the "Free Browder" campaign of 1941–1942. (*Courtesy, Syracuse University*)

Alexander Bittleman, former CP leader, before testifying before House Un-American Activities committee, Washington, D.C., November 21, 1961. He was a member of the Party's Political Committee in 1939–1940 and headed the Party's Jewish section during the war, expelled in 1960 for unorthodox views. (*Wide World Photos*)

Eugene Dennis, July 2, 1951, enroute to the Federal House of Detention in New York after his 1949 conviction for violating the Smith Act was upheld by the US Supreme Court. Dennis was a rising star in the Party in the 30s and 40s; after Browder's expulsion he became general secretary. (*Wide World Photos*)

Queens in line with the CP's emphasis on wartime service. He also worked with the CP-organized Joint Anti-Fascist Refugee Committee, established in 1942, which helped Spanish Republican and other left-wing political refugees escape from Europe. The FBI closely monitored the committee's activities; according to a confidential FBI report, Eisler was an indispensable asset to its work because "he was sort of a dictionary as he knew the people and the conditions in the concentration camps in Europe."[42]

Interestingly enough, FBI reports, which state that Eisler was a Comintern agent during his first visit to the United States, do not label him as such for the years 1941–1945, saying only that he was "closely connected with CPUSA affairs."[43] It seems very unlikely that Eisler played anything like the commanding role later assigned him by Budenz, and alleged by various congressional investigators. Browder, by that time, was not about to take instructions from stray German exiles, and Eisler was known to be privately critical of some of Browder's wartime ideological initiatives.[44] Eisler did write a series of articles in collaboration with Starobin under the pseudonym "Hans Berger," but they dealt with inconsequential matters. One "Berger" article in *The Communist* was entitled "Our Nation Discovers the Soviet Union" and listed favorable comments about the USSR from prominent Americans—hardly the kind of material that the "underground boss" of all Communist activities in the United States would spend his time turning out. After the war Eisler found his return to Germany blocked by the House Un-American Activities Committee, who wanted to keep him on display.[45]

Not all European exiles were willing to work as closely with the American CP as Eisler had been. For some time American Communist leaders had been annoyed by the truculently independent behavior of Italian Communist exiles. In 1938 an internal party document complained that the party's Italian bureau (which oversaw the work of Italian-American Communists and the Italian exiles) was maintaining "a double allegiance—to the American Party and the Italian Party."[46] Over the next year PCI leaders in Europe and American Communist leaders quarreled quite unfraternally over the role Italian Communists should be playing in the United States: the PCI viewed America as a convenient base for its work in Europe, while the American CP wanted Italian exiles to subordinate themselves to its discipline and priorities.[47]

In the spring of 1939 the PCI sent Ambrogio Donini, who had

previously lived in the United States for several years, to New York to edit the Italian-language newspaper *L'Unita Del Popolo*. Meanwhile Giuseppe Berti, a member of the PCI's executive committee, was editing the party's theoretical journal *Stato Operaio* in Paris. The signing of the Nazi-Soviet pact made France an inhospitable asylum for foreign Communists, and Berti left for the United States, hoping to continue on a round-about route back to a haven in Switzerland. Finding his return to Europe blocked, he began to publish *Stato Operaio* in New York, receiving a small subsidy from the American Communists. The CP also aided Berti in smuggling the journal back to Europe and in communicating with Togliatti and other PCI leaders in Moscow.[48]

Eisler had no reason to remain aloof from the American CP, since his home party, the KPD, had virtually ceased to function outside of Moscow. But the PCI was vitally connected with the anti-fascist resistance movement within Italy. As soon as Allied troops landed in Italy in 1943, Berti and Donini went to the State Department seeking permission to return to their homeland. The State Department official they spoke with told them frankly that American authorities "did not want elements to return to Italy who might work against the formation of the right kind of Italian government," and so, like Eisler, they remained unwilling guests of the United States.[49] But they continued to guard their own autonomous political positions. A member of the CP's Italian bureau complained in a private memorandum to Browder in 1945 that Berti and Donini had worked "to build a separate apparatus in America. . . . With their attitude of passing themselves off as representatives of the Communist Party of Italy they have created among some of the comrades a split in allegiance that is very detrimental. Their whole behavior is due to their wrong conception of not being subject and part of the Communist movement of the country in which they find themselves."[50]

Berti and Donini cast a jaundiced eye on Browder's wartime reforms and, shortly before their departure for Italy in 1945, would play a role in hastening his disgrace.

The CP and American Jews

Among all the nationality groups to whom they hoped to appeal, the Communists found their greatest opportunities, as well as their most bitter opponents, in the Jewish community. Though the prestige of the

Soviet Union had been gravely damaged during the Nazi-Soviet pact, every advance by the Red Army gave Hitler a little less time in which to complete the destruction of European Jewry. The Erlich-Alter affair only briefly checked Jewish enthusiasm for the Grand Alliance. When the Yiddish actor Solomon Mikhoels and the poet Itzik Feffer visited the United States in 1943 under the auspices of the Soviet-organized Jewish Anti-Fascist Committee, they received a tumultuous welcome from American Jews. Nearly fifty thousand New Yorkers turned out to cheer them at an open-air rally sponsored by the Jewish Council of Russian War Relief. Stephen S. Wise, president of the American Jewish Congress, told the gathering that the Soviet Union was the nation that was doing the most to save Europe's Jews. Only Socialist organizations like the Jewish Labor Committee, the Workmen's Circle, and the Labor Zionists—all longtime opponents of the Communists—actively boycotted the rally.[51]

The Communists worked hard to gain respectability in the Jewish community. The *Morning Freiheit* began to suspend publication on Jewish religious holidays for the first time in its twenty-year history, and audiences sang "Hatikvah" (the Zionist anthem) along with the "Star-Spangled Banner" and the "Internationale" at rallies of the Jewish Council for Russian War Relief. Alexander Bittelman, who oversaw the CP's Jewish work, held out an olive branch to the CP's longtime antagonists among the Zionist groups, suggesting cautiously that "there are the possibilities that, with time, there will emerge a new form of Jewish national existence for the Jews living in Palestine."[52]

Despite such overtures, the Communists did not find ready acceptance among the established Jewish organizations. In the summer of 1943 the Jewish section of the International Workers Order (a CP-organized fraternal group that offered sickness and death benefits, and a range of cultural activities, summer camps, and schools to its members) attempted to get delegates accredited to the founding meeting of the American Jewish Conference—an umbrella organization seeking to mobilize Jewish resources to aid European refugees. The IWO's bid for affiliation was blocked by delegates from the Jewish Labor Committee, who accused the group of being a Communist front, rather than an independent Jewish organization. To counter this accusation, the IWO adopted a new constitution at its 1944 convention, granting each of its fifteen national divisions the appearance of organizational autonomy. The IWO's Jewish section (which accounted for about a third of its 140,000 members in 1944) changed its name to the Jewish People's Fraternal Order (JPFO) and reapplied for admission to the American Jewish Conference. This time they were successful, despite the Jewish Labor Committee's threat to withdraw its own affiliation if the Communists were taken in. But Rabbi Stephen S. Wise convinced the committee debating the JPFO's affiliation that it would be "unwise for American Jewry to exclude a Jewish group on the grounds of its Communist views, when an attempt is being made to bring all the Jews of the world, including those of Soviet Russia, into the great circle of Jewish fellowship."[53]

The End of the Comintern

The Communists' ties with the Soviet Union proved to be a two-edged sword. In some instances, as with the American Jewish Conference, concern for future Soviet-American relations provided the Communists with the tool they needed to dislodge old barriers. When the Supreme Court decided by a five-to-three ruling in the spring of 1943 that William Schneiderman's membership in the CP in 1927 was insufficient cause for revoking the American citizenship granted him that year, the Communists were elated. The Schneiderman decision was a major victory, the closest the Communists had yet come to being granted full legal acceptance. Though the court denied the decision had anything to do with current American foreign policy, the *New York Times* noted that after June 1941, "it was an open secret that the government wished to have the issue delayed because of possible friction with Russia."[54]

But the American Communists' continuing ties with the Soviet Union also cut the other way. At the end of April 1943, the *New York Times* called on the Russians to instruct the American CP to disband. The editors looked forward to welcoming the Soviet Union into the "family of nations" at war's end, but warned: "If Russia uses Communist Trojan horses either as agents of world revolution or as shock troops of a Bolshevist imperialism, neither peace nor the Four Freedoms will remain secure anywhere."[55]

As if in answer, on May 15 the executive committee of the Communist International moved to dissolve itself. The Comintern's leaders declared that "deep differences of the historic paths of development of various countries" had made centralized leadership of the world Communist movement obsolescent—"a drag on the further strengthening of the national working class parties." Two weeks later, in an interview with a Western correspondent, Stalin said that the decision would expose the "calumny" that foreign Communists acted as Moscow's agents within their own countries, and would aid "patriots of all countries" in "uniting the progressive forces of their respective countries, regardless of party or religious faith, into a single camp of national liberation."[56] On June 10, twenty-four years after its founding, the Third International officially passed out of existence.

The reaction in the West was all that Stalin could have hoped for. The *New York Times* rated the dissolution of the Comintern as a contribution to the war effort "second only to the heroic struggle of the Russian armies and the Russian people themselves." Even Martin Dies was temporarily swept up in the enthusiasm, declaring that the House Un-American Activities Committee could now close up shop.[57]

But the *Times* remained skeptical as to the loyalty of American Communists. Browder entered into a lengthy printed exchange with the editors over the role that Communists were playing in the war effort. Browder's side of the debate, he later explained to the CP's national committee, was an effort "directed to all Americans, including the responsible governmental leaders of our country." In a letter to the *Times* that appeared on May 29, Browder declared that the CP had subordinated all other considerations to the cause of winning the war, and would be willing to consider dissolving itself if that would aid the anti-fascist struggle. But he argued that the *Times*'s hostility to the Communist party had no rational basis, based as it was on the "fable" that Communists favored the violent overthrow of the government.

The *Times* editors sniffed at Browder's assertion that the CP could make a useful contribution to the national war effort: "Like its dissolved parent organization, the Third International, it has become 'obsolete' and the best service it can render to America and to Russo-American relations is to follow the example set in Moscow and disappear."[58]

The sparring continued the following week. Browder argued that "if American democracy cannot tolerate even the physical existence of Communists without suffering from the jitters, it is going to have a hard time winning the war in coalition with Communists in many other nations." The *Times* countered that the CP had proven itself an untrustworthy ally of democracy in the past: "The abrupt conversion of the Communist Party to support of the war against Hitler dates from the morning that Hitler attacked Russia. It will be as abruptly converted to anything else which it believes will aid the cause of 'proletarian internationalism.' "

The exchange ended inconclusively, though Browder later professed to have detected a "defensive tone" in the *Times*' second response, encouraging him in the belief that prospects were favorable for "further broad discussions which . . . will finally place the problem of the Communists in America in a new light entirely."[59]

As part of this "broad discussion," the *New Masses* took the unprecedented step in the summer of 1943 of opening its pages to liberal opponents. In an exchange with Max Lerner, a columnist for *PM* and a caustic critic of the CP since the Nazi-Soviet pact, *New Masses* editor A. B. Magil went so far as to admit that prior to June 1941 the Communists had erred in treating the war "too statically," overlooking its progressive aspects and failing to foresee the possibility of Soviet involvement. Lerner was unimpressed. Regarding the Communists' professed desire to work with liberals in common cause, he declared, "I don't see how the old bureaucracy, the old and tired doctrinal spokesmen, can make the movement at once progressive and democratic." Another critic, the educator and civil libertarian Alexander Meiklejohn, told the *New Masses* that the CP could not hope to become a "useful American party" until it abandoned "the procedures of the military mind, both in its internal discipline and its relations with other groups." Liberals were not going to cooperate again with Communists as long as the Communists treated them as "potentially or actually an enemy rather than a friend," who could "be used and then dropped."[60]

The Communists, casting around for a way to become accepted as a legitimate political force in the United States, continually bumped up against the heritage of mistrust left over from their abrupt shift of line in September 1939. They would need to make some kind of dramatic gesture if they hoped to purge those suspicions. George West, in an article in the *New Republic* in the spring of 1943, called on the CP to "issue an official statement admitting its policy of conspiracy and secrecy, justifying that policy as well as it can, and then condemning it and repudiating it for the future." Only after such an open reappraisal of past mistakes by the Communists, West suggested, could there be a sound political basis for their cooperation with liberals.[61]

Some Communists privately called for this same kind of reevaluation. But even if Browder and other CP leaders had been willing to undertake such an onerous task—which, as Lerner implied, would have involved calling their own right to leadership into question—a thorough reexamination of the party's history would necessarily lead to criticisms of past Soviet policies. Since this was out of the question, some other kind of gesture had to be found, one that was dramatic enough to prove to all the doubters that the Communists were indeed committed to democratic politics. At the June meeting of the national committee, several speakers toyed with the idea of altering the CP's structure to end its political isolation. Referring to the Comintern's dissolution, Williamson suggested it would now be possible to build "a broader American working class party—a Marxist party, not only in our own way as we have known it, but in any way the development of history makes possible."[62] But the CP leaders did not go beyond such vague speculations in public or, apparently, in private. If Browder already had plans for doing away with the old party structure, he was keeping his own counsel.[63]

The Communists did a lot of organizational tinkering that year, hoping that a series of minor adjustments might dissipate public hostility. To counter the stereotype of the conspiratorial Communist cell, the CP combined many of its smaller units into large community branches, with New York City branches often having as many as three hundred members. It tried to make branch activities more visible, with public meeting halls and open, advertised evening events. While this was relatively easy to arrange in New York, it proved much harder in other parts of the country. Williamson complained in the October 1943 *Communist* that in New England "in the twenty-five cities and towns where there are party organizations there are still only five in which the Party appears publicly, with its own open address and publicly-announced officials."[64]

Browder renewed his campaign to shift party trade unionists out of shop and industrial branches and into community-based branches. He told the national committee in June that it was "more necessary than ever now that we clean up in the odd corners of our party whatever remnants may be hanging around of old methods of work, carryovers from the days when we were a persecuted minority," including the "special organizational forms" and "special discipline" that had characterized the CP's presence within the trade unions. The CP had formally abandoned "fractions" in 1938, but the continued organization of Communists in units based on employment in a single shop, factory, or industry amounted to much the same thing. Whether Browder's proposed reorganization would have or even was intended to have any practical effect is debatable: the Communists had fought long, bitter battles to win power in the unions; they faced determined opponents; and they knew that to drop the tactics that had served them so well in the past would be tantamount to political suicide.

Williamson noted in the autumn of 1943 that "members in the shop and industrial branches have expressed hesitation, and, in some cases, even resistance, to the transfer recommendation." It was a resistance he attributed to their fears that the reorganization would weaken them in "the struggle for correct policy in the inner union fight." As it turned out, Communists in any union could, and in many instances did, still function as a closed caucus if that was considered necessary to maintain or gain power. But the reorganization was good public relations, and released Communist trade-union "influentials" from the requirement of meeting with rank-and-file Communists in their union to develop or justify policies they followed (a tradition which, by this time, was rarely observed in any case).[65]

The Young Communist League underwent an even more dramatic transformation. Since its founding in 1922 the YCL had served as a training ground for the CP's secondary leadership. Unlike its parent organization, the YCL was always largely English-speaking and native-born, and in the 1930s its cadres had been entrusted with important organizing assignments in the party's unemployed and trade-union work, as well as within the student and youth movements. But by mid-1943 the YCL was no longer the organization it once had been. Its most experienced leaders, and much of its male rank and file, had enlisted or been drafted into the armed forces. In an article in the April *Communist* YCL president Max Weiss noted that "the considerable turnover in leadership, as well as the continuous lower average age level of the YCL membership, makes it impossible for the party organization to 'take things for granted,' as there was a tendency to do when a more experienced, older leadership functioned."[66]

In May the YCL attempted to get some of its members accepted as delegates to the founding convention of a new college student group, the United States Student Assembly. Eleanor Roosevelt was on hand and, describing her experience with the American Youth Congress, told the delegates: "You can work with anyone who has the courage to stand up and say what he believes, but you can never work with anyone who says one thing and does another or who stays silent and does not state his objectives." The delegates voted to ban all Communists and suspected Communists from membership.[67]

The experience at the Student Assembly convention and the dissolution of the Comintern that same month convinced party leaders it was time to transform the YCL. The following month Weiss announced plans for an autumn convention to found a new anti-fascist youth group. On October 16 several hundred, mostly teen-aged, delegates met in New York City and voted unanimously to disband the YCL. The next day they reassembled in the same hall and founded the American Youth for Democracy (AYD). The AYD's statement of principles called for American-Soviet-British cooperation in the war and postwar era, the launching of a second front in Europe, and universal military training for young Americans. It made no mention of socialism or of any continuing organizational ties with the Communist party. Naomi Ellison, a veteran of the American Youth Congress, was elected chairman along with ex-YCL leader Robert Thompson, just returned from military service in the South Pacific. Carl Ross, former New York state chairman of the YCL, assumed the position of the AYD's executive secretary.

The Communists had hoped that the AYD would serve as a kind of all-purpose substitute for the YCL and the decrepit American Student Union and American Youth Congress. However, it had a difficult time shaking the stigma of its rather obvious line of descent from the YCL. The AYD survived for the remainder of the war and into the early postwar years as a temporary organizational home for the teen-aged children of Communist families, but, outside of a few strongholds like Brooklyn, achieved little else.[68]

The YCL's dissolution set an important precedent. Over the preceding decades the Communists had created, revamped, and discarded dozens of front organizations, while the YCL and the CP itself had remained untouched. With the Comintern's dissolution, the old rules no longer seemed to apply.

Communists in the Armed Forces

The Communists viewed all their activities on the "home front" as working toward a single end: creating the material and political conditions necessary for launching a second front. The CP hailed the Allied invasions of Sicily and Italy in 1943, but continued to call for a full-scale invasion of Western Europe. The renewed campaign put the Communists in the untenable position of arguing that they were Roosevelt's firmest backers while they continued to criticize the actual course of the American war effort. At first they sought to sidestep the dilemma by blaming the delay of the invasion on anti-Soviet appeasers in the State Department. After Churchill declared in September that "no political considerations of any kind" would determine when the Allies launched their invasion, Browder eagerly lay all responsibility for the delay at his feet: "The evidence inescapably indicates that Winston Churchill made the decision not to open the second front, and that Franklin D. Roosevelt submitted to that decision because he was unwilling to have a public disagreement with Churchill. I feel sure that any time Churchill's ready to open the second front he will find no obstacles from the side of Roosevelt."[69]

Browder was only half right. In 1942 American military planners had been more enthusiastic about the prospects for an early invasion than their British counterparts. But at Casablanca in January 1943, Roosevelt and Churchill agreed it would be unfeasible to launch a major invasion until 1944. Browder, with his fervent identification with Roosevelt, may well have believed that the President was still champing at the bit to get on with the second front. But he was treading on dangerous political ground in attacking Churchill. British CP leader Harry Pollitt wrote to Browder shortly afterward to complain about Browder's speech. According to Pollitt, it was "the American Administration that has been the chief obstacle as far as the opening of the Second Front is concerned." British Communists had never attacked Roosevelt—why then did Browder attack Churchill? "The way you put the question only leads to one political conclusion, namely we should be demanding the removal of Churchill. That is an impossible demand at this moment, yet inevitably there are certain hostile forces who will use your speech against us in this direction."[70] Browder got the message, and for the remainder of the war the *Daily Worker* awarded Churchill a status as above reproof as Roosevelt's.

When the second front finally became a reality, many American Communists hoped to be there. By January 1943 nearly one-fifth of all male Communists, including hundreds of veterans of the Abraham Lincoln Brigade, were serving in the armed forces. Fifteen thousand Communists would serve in the military before the end of the war.

They went, for the most part, enthusiastically, but met a mixed reception once in uniform.

The army, by design or accident, allowed unit commanders some flexibility in the treatment of Communists. Some, like Robert Thompson, were in combat by the end of 1942. But official army policy, adopted in 1940, called for assigning "potentially subversive personnel"—Communists, fascists, and enemy aliens—to military units "in which there is a minimum opportunity for damage." In 1942 the War Department instructed commanders of units scheduled for overseas duty to notify Military Intelligence of all soldiers under their command whom they judged to fit the category "potentially subversive," who would then be transferred to specially organized service and labor battalions slated to remain in the United States.[71]

Hundreds of Communists ran afoul of these regulations. Military Intelligence agents rifled their lockers, read their mail, and questioned their barracks-mates to uncover evidence of disloyal utterances or behavior. Their confidential files carried the notation "S.D." (suspected of disloyalty). They were stigmatized by one army officer as "premature anti-fascists." They were usually allowed to complete training with their outfits, and many were even accepted into officer candidate school (OCS). But when their outfits were being shipped to England, Africa, or the Pacific, they suddenly found themselves reassigned to supply or service or medical units in places like Fort Shenango, Pennsylvania, and Camp Ripley, Minnesota.

Jerry Cook, for example, had been a company commander in the Lincoln Battalion, a twice-wounded and decorated veteran of the Brunete and Ebro campaigns. In February 1943 he was in OCS at Fort Benning, Georgia, ranked at the top of his class, when he was suddenly yanked out of the school and without explanation reassigned to a medical unit. His repeated requests to be transferred to an infantry or paratroop unit were turned down. In a letter to his mother he complained bitterly about the way Military Intelligence read all his mail: "Apparently they disapprove of clippings concerning the progress of the only member of the United Nations who is doing any fighting in this war. And then, a man who saw fit to fight the Nazis and fascists six years ago while they (those who run our army) were sitting blindly on their fat backsides—just might prove dangerous to them. Such a man might even rise to a comparatively important command. No—that would never do!"[72]

The CP maintained public silence on the discrimination its members faced in the military until Browder complained about it at the annual Lenin memorial meeting in January 1943. The liberal press then began investigating the fate of Communists in the army. *PM* and Drew Pearson devoted columns to the fate of another Lincoln veteran, John Gates, who as a private in the U.S. Army had been conducting a lonely struggle since enlisting in December 1941 to get assigned to overseas combat duty. Several liberal congressmen wrote to the War Department in April asking for an investigation of the treatment of Lincoln veterans.[73]

The unfavorable publicity—and the army's growing need for manpower as it prepared for the invasion of Europe—finally led it to drop most such discriminatory measures. In February 1944 the War Department instructed commanders to make individual actions and attitudes, rather than membership in any organization, the test for loyalty. That order did not mention the Communist party by name, but a subsequent order, issued in December 1944, prohibited discriminatory actions against soldiers "predicated on membership in or adherence to the doctrines of the Communist Party unless there is a specific finding that the individual involved has a loyalty to the Communist Party as an organization which overrides his loyalty to the United States."[74]

Even before these orders were issued, Communists who had long been blocked from overseas duty suddenly found themselves on troopships heading toward Europe or the South Pacific. Jerry Cook landed as a combat engineer with the first attack wave on Utah Beach in Normandy, and soon won a field commission as a lieutenant and a Bronze Star. John Gates, sent to do garrison duty in the Aleutians after the publicity about his case had died down, finally won reassignment to a combat unit and parachuted into Germany in time for the last battles of the war. Hundreds of other Communists and Lincoln veterans saw combat in the last year and a half of the war.[75]

The army may have been nonplused by the Communists it found in its ranks, but there was at least one place in the American war machine where Communists were not only tolerated but actively recruited. Shortly after the invasion of the Soviet Union, General William Donovan, director of the newly created Office of the Coordinator of Information—better known by its later name, the Office of Strategic Services (OSS)—contacted Eugene Dennis. Donovan needed recruits for the new American intelligence service who were fluent in foreign languages, familiar with partisan warfare, and able to work effectively with foreign resistance movements, many of which were led by Communists. Not many Americans in 1941 fit that description, so Donovan went straight to the most likely source. The party quietly did what it could to aid Donovan, preparing dossiers on likely recruits among its own members and passing them on to the OSS.[76]

Donovan acted with great circumspection in his contacts with the CP, more concerned about the hostile snooping of the FBI than with Axis intelligence agencies. J. Edgar Hoover, who regarded the OSS as a group of arrogant amateurs encroaching on his own terrain, had not let the small matter of the American-Soviet alliance interfere with his own hatred of radicals. FBI agents harassed left-wing OSS recruits. Carl Marzani, former CP section leader for the Lower East Side, joined the OSS in the spring of 1942 and served in the research and analysis branch of its economic division throughout the war. He was twice brought up before the Civil Service Commission by the FBI in attempts to get him fired for his past affiliation with the CP, and both times Donovan sent his personal lawyer to sit in on the hearings as a gesture of support for Marzani.[77] A number of other leftists, Communist and non-Communist, also served in the research and analysis branch, and Communists were well represented in OSS clandestine operations. At one point during the war the FBI provided to Donovan dossiers on three Lincoln veterans engaged in covert operations in Europe, insisting that they be fired as Communists. Donovan is reported to have replied: "I know they're Communists; that's why I hired them."[78]

Spanish Civil War veterans were valuable recruits. They had combat experience, and their political credentials gave them a special authority in the eyes of many of the partisans they would be working with. Irving Goff and Vincent Lossowski, both veterans of the Lincoln Battalion, recruited and trained agents for clandestine OSS operations in Spain from among Spanish Republican sailors interned by the French in North Africa. Later, with two other Lincoln veterans, Milton Wolff and Irving Fajans, they ran an OSS intelligence center in Italy, training and coordinating the activities of agents operating behind German lines in northern Italy. George Wucinich, another Lincoln veteran, was smuggled into Yugoslavia by the OSS and served for nine months as a liaison officer with Tito's Partisans. In 1945 he was sent on a mission behind Japanese lines in China, where he established contact with

Chinese Communist forces.[79] Donovan never publicly admitted employing Communists in the OSS (denying it even in sworn testimony before a congressional investigating committee).[80] But ironically the Communists found their best opportunities for wartime service in the predecessor to the Central Intelligence Agency.

The Teheran Meeting

In the last week of November 1943, Roosevelt, Churchill, and Stalin met together for the first time. At their conference in Teheran they agreed to set the date for the Anglo-American invasion of Western Europe for the spring of 1944. Churchill offered Stalin a large piece of eastern Poland in postwar border adjustments, while Roosevelt explained to a sympathetic Stalin his problems with Polish-American voters. The two Western leaders left Stalin with the clear impression that he could have a free hand in shaping the postwar regime in Poland, provided he showed due respect for Western public sensibilities. Stalin, in turn, promised to be lenient in his treatment of Finland and to participate in a postwar international organization. The three leaders then signed a joint communiqué that became known as the Teheran Declaration, a brief statement of just over three hundred words. Except for stating that "complete agreement as to the scope and timing of operations" for the defeat of Hitler had been agreed upon, it gave few hints about the content of the discussions. Roosevelt, Churchill, and Stalin pledged that their nations would "work together in the war and the peace that will follow" and would seek to make a peace which would "banish the scourge and terror of war for many generations."

The important decisions made at Teheran about the future of Eastern Europe were not made public. After reading the text of the Teheran Declaration, columnist Dorothy Thompson joked that "never before in history had so few kept so much information from so many." But at least one American did pay careful attention to the declaration. "To me," Browder told an audience in Bridgeport, Connecticut, on December 12, a week and a half after the end of the Teheran Conference, "this is no ordinary and routine announcement. I understand this as the greatest, most important turning point in history." For Browder there was no ambiguity in the accord achieved at Teheran: "As a matter of fact, there is only one way to understand this agreement, and that is to take it at its face value—that it means what it says."[81]

This was the moment that Browder had been waiting for since returning to the leadership of the Communist party in the spring of 1942. In the course of that year he went from being a prisoner in a federal penitentiary to an invited guest of the second-ranking official of the Department of State. A quarter of a century after his release from prison, he still glowed at the memory: "After I had gone to prison President Roosevelt commuted the sentence *in wartime* as a contribution 'to national unity.' Apparently my prosecution had weakened America in the war."[82]

In the past Browder had enjoyed a reputation in the Communist movement as an innovator—but he had been a cautious innovator, never straying too far from formulas approved in Moscow. His actions in the year and a half after the Teheran Conference seem reckless by comparison. Browder was an intensely private person, and we can only speculate as to the nature of the motives that shaped his policies in 1944–1945. One possible explanation is that Browder's wish to win acceptance as part of the "Roosevelt coalition" had, by this time, acquired as much personal as political meaning for him. Roosevelt was the symbol of everything Browder himself wanted to be—a consummate leader, exuding self-confidence, with an aristocrat's grace and the common touch. Above all, Roosevelt was someone who felt at home with and spoke for Americans. Browder was none of these things and, after almost a quarter-century in the party, he longed for something better than the petty, grubby style of day-to-day Communist politics. In a speech he delivered in Chicago in September 1943, Browder reminisced about how "every one of us, especially the old timers whose experience goes back into the early twenties and before, can remember the interminable and dreary meetings we had to get through, year after year, before we began to get a Party which, on the whole, was capable of effective organization."[83]

Teheran finally gave Browder the confidence he needed to undertake that dramatic historical leap which, he hoped, would bring him and the party all the way to the public acceptance and influence he wanted so badly. The Teheran Declaration, Browder told the audience that night in Bridgeport, meant that the launching of the second front was no longer at issue. America and Britain would soon join the Soviet Union as full military partners in the anti-Hitler struggle. The declaration meant that the capitalist democracies had finally agreed to accept the Soviet Union "as a permanent member of the family of nations," abandoning once and for all their hopes for its destruction. And it meant that there would be no class war in Europe following the war. Browder predicted that "Europe west of the Soviet Union probably will be reconstructed on a bourgeois-democratic, non-fascist capitalist basis, not upon a Soviet basis." This would be a reformed capitalism, "setting up no obstacles to the development of democracy and social progress in accordance with the urgent desires of the peoples."

Finally, the Teheran accords meant a complete and lasting peace after the war, presided over by the "united moral forces of Britain, America and the Soviet Union." But the promise of Teheran would not be realized without a struggle. Affirming or opposing the Teheran agreements, Browder declared, "is the great dividing line within our country today, and it will divide us in the election of 1944; everything else is incidental to that."

According to Browder, the success of the agreements hinged on actions of the CP in the coming months. Communists "must help to remove from the American ruling class the fear of a socialist revolution in the United States in the post-war period."

The Communists had devoted their energies in 1943 to defensive measures, countering what they interpreted as a pro-Nazi conspiracy against national unity. They found themselves hampered in that effort by a legacy of distrust left over from past political battles. Browder had known for many years that he would never lead his party to revolution; now he believed he could accomplish something of equal historical importance by leading his party *away* from revolution. "Old formulas and old prejudices," he argued, "are going to be of no use whatever to us as guides to find our way in this new world." And so Browder offered to shake hands with J. P. Morgan, if that would aid the cause of American-Soviet cooperation in building the new world to follow the war. He had made his decision. Nineteen forty-four was to be the year of the Spirit of Teheran.[84]

9 REDESIGNING THE COMMUNIST MOVEMENT

January to December 1944

I hereby move that the Communist Party of America be and hereby is dissolved.
—EARL BROWDER, May 20, 1944[1]

NINETEEN FORTY-FOUR WITNESSED the self-dissolution of the American Communist party and its replacement by the Communist Political Association (CPA). Browder turned aside a challenge to his plans and authority from Foster. But just how he intended his new association to differ from its parent organization remained unclear and subject to differing interpretations by his followers. Though Browder's organizational reforms won easy acceptance within the Communist movement, they established very shallow roots. Browder, at the height of his glory, was near the end of his career.

The Meaning of Teheran

Browder's Bridgeport speech took many Communists by surprise. In his 1942 book *Victory and After* Browder had predicted that postwar "reconstruction problems" could be solved "with a minimum of social disorder and civil violence." But *Victory and After* contained no image as jarring to Communist sensibilities as the Bridgeport speech's pledge to shake hands with J. P. Morgan. In mid-1942, moreover, the very survival of the Soviet Union had still been in doubt, while by late 1943 victory was certain and the possibility of a Soviet Europe now seemed within reach. Browder's speech made it clear that, as far as he was concerned, no revolutionary uprising like 1848 or 1919 would follow in the wake of the Second World War. He admitted in his opening report to the CP's national committee meeting on January 7, 1944, that his offer to shake hands with Morgan had raised "very sharp objection" among some Communists. But he had no intention of withdrawing the offer: "In order that we waste no time quibbling, I now make explicit what is inherent in the thought expressed. . . . I was rejecting the political slogan of 'class against class' as our guide to political alignment in the next period. . . . We will choose our associates first and above all according to whether they are for or against the Teheran policy.''[2]

National committee members attending the January 7 session had expected to hear a report on the party's plans for the 1944 elections—a subject that Browder would treat only tangentially that evening. They knew something unusual was afoot when they arrived at the meeting hall: the twenty-eight-member committee usually held closed sessions, but this time they found themselves meeting in a room with some two hundred specially invited guests. At the start of his report Browder reviewed the importance of the Teheran meeting, summing it up with the pronouncement: "Capitalism and socialism have begun to find their way to peaceful coexistence and collaboration in the same world." Although such collaboration was—objectively—in the interests of all classes in the United States, Browder saw no guarantees that America would remain committed to its wartime rapprochement with the Soviet Union.

"The weakest point in our wartime national unity," he said, "is the widespread belief that it will inevitably, at the moment of Victory over Hitler, explode in a simultaneous release of all the inner conflicts that have been held in abeyance by the war." Worries over domestic stability, if allowed to go unchecked, might convince American capitalists to embrace a go-it-alone policy in postwar international relations. That danger gave Communists a special responsibility because "the American people are so ill-prepared subjectively for any deep-going change in the direction of socialism that post-war plans with such an aim would not unite the nation but would further divide it." This would allow "anti-Teheran forces" to come to power and reverse Roosevelt's policy of cooperation with the Soviet Union. Defense of the Teheran accords made it the duty of Communists to reaffirm "our war-time policy that we will not raise the issue of socialism in such a form and manner as to endanger or weaken that national unity"—even after the war ended.

Browder not only believed that the struggle for socialism should be shelved for the foreseeable future, he also wanted to abandon any ideological challenge to the prevailing capitalist consensus on domestic issues. In *Victory and After* he had called on American capitalists to admit that Adam Smith's ideas about the free market could not direct a modern economy, particularly one engaged in a total war effort. A year and a half later he had decided that this position was too provocative. Noting that the "most reactionary and pro-fascist circles" in the United States were using the slogan "Free Enterprise" to oppose Roosevelt's economic policies, Browder now insisted that "Marxists will not help the reactionaries by opposing the slogan of 'Free Enterprise' with any form of counter slogan. If anyone wishes to describe the existing system of capitalism in the United States as 'free enterprise' that's all right with us, and we frankly declare that we are ready to cooperate in making this capitalism work effectively in the post-war period."

He felt Communists could safely advocate a government-sponsored program of expanding foreign markets for American manufactured goods. Here was one area, at least, where almost all capitalists had proven themselves willing to lay down their prejudices against state intervention in the economy, and one that Browder thought depended on continued cooperation between the wartime Allies: "The Teheran Conference," he declared, "for the first time, gave a realistic perspective of the quick organization of such huge foreign markets. [These markets] are unthinkable except under stable conditions, without international or civil wars of major proportions."

Browder saved his biggest bombshell for last. He recalled that in his exchange of letters with the *New York Times* the previous spring he had mentioned the possibility of dissolving the CP in the interests of national unity, and "received no response from anyone to discuss this or any other proposals for changes in the form of activities of the Communist movement in this country." By no means discouraged by the lack of response, he decided that it was time for the Communists "unilaterally, and without discussion with anyone else" to take such organizational steps as they deemed necessary to cement national unity. He continued to believe that an organized Communist presence was vital to the labor movement and the war effort, but that a Communist "party" as such was not. The two major American political parties, he argued, were not parties at all in the European sense of "representing well-defined alternative policies," but rather represented "coalitions of local and regional interests, diverse tendencies of political thought, and institutional politics." They were, in effect, umbrella groups sheltering many separate parties. The Communists had long recognized this situation in practice, making their influence felt through support of New Deal candidates running on the Democratic or ALP tickets. In coming years the CP would find itself "in a long term alliance with forces much larger than itself. It follows from this fact that in the peculiar American sense of the word, the Communists will not be operating as a 'party'—that is, with their own separate candidates in elections."

Consequently, Browder concluded, "Communist organization in the United States should adjust its name to correspond more exactly to the American political tradition and its own practical political role." The Communists could accomplish this by changing their name to "something like 'American Communist Political Association,'" which, he believed, would make it "much easier to explain our true relationship with all other democratic and progressive groupings which operate through . . . the two party system, and take our place in true collaboration at their side."[3]

Browder's report should have provoked serious questions from his audience. It repudiated much of the party's traditional outlook without solving any of the problems the Communists had long faced. The shift from "party" to "association" hardly penetrated to the underlying causes of the Communists' political isolation within the United States. And assuming the Communists remained committed to socialism as their ultimate goal—and Browder said nothing to indicate that they would not—it was unclear how the American people would ever shed their "subjective unpreparedness" for socialism without some public discussion of that economic system's advantages over "free enterprise." But none of the national committee members challenged Browder's proposals.

Political committee members had met to discuss Browder's plan before the January 7 meeting, and they tailored their reports to support his position. Gil Green introduced a torrent of statistics to illustrate American capitalism's need for foreign markets, arguing that only international stability could reverse the decline in foreign investments that had characterized capitalist economies since the 1930s. Roy Hudson hinted at the idea of continuing the labor movement's no-strike pledge into the postwar period. Robert Minor, with characteristic theoretical subtlety, labeled the idea that social change depended on class struggle a distortion of Marxism fostered by "a very despicable character who met his deserved fate in the Moscow trials not long ago, a gentleman by the name of Bukharin." John Williamson, as organizational secretary, bore the special responsibility of explaining how a "political association" differed from a "party." The change, he announced, meant a sharp break with "old formulas and practices," but he was unable to get more specific than his prediction that "even more than now—but with better political equipment—we will react to and develop mass activity around all vital issues . . . whether in a neighborhood, a shop, an industry, or in the nation." He did call for a more democratic organizational structure in the new association, but insisted that Leninist norms of centralized authority would continue to be observed. Internal democracy "shall not be allowed to degenerate into a sloppy liberal approach of a Section or County Committee deciding for itself whether it will carry out a decision or a policy of a State or National Committee."[4]

In summarizing the discussion on the final day of the plenum, Browder admitted that there seemed to be a lack of "complete" understanding among the delegates as to just what the change to a political association would mean. He himself seemed hard pressed for definitions, and chose to focus instead on what the change did *not* mean: "The Communists are not joining the Democratic Party; the Communists are not joining the Republican Party. We are not endorsing either of the major parties, and we are not condemning either of the major parties. We are taking the line of issues and not of parties and of choosing men as they stand for or against issues without regard to party labels." But he framed the question so that his own strategic incoherence appeared to be a triumph of nondogmatic Marxism. He urged the delegates to think of Marxism as a "theory of deeds, not of don'ts," and observed that "history never yet has been known to follow anyone's private blueprint. The great turning points of history are in this sense always unexpected; there is always something new, something fresh in them that has to be fundamentally evaluated. We are in such a period today."[5]

At the plenum's final session the national committee voted unanimous approval for Browder's proposals and established subcommittees to draft a new constitution, to prepare for a May convention to ratify the constitutional changes, to oversee the party's activities in the 1944 elections, and to prepare the celebration of the party's upcoming twenty-fifth anniversary. Rank-and-file Communists learned of the proposed sweeping changes for the first time in the next morning's *Daily Worker*.[6]

That evening, January 10, between fifteen and twenty thousand Communists in various states of uncertainty and bewilderment came to Madison Square Garden for the annual Lenin memorial meeting. Browder once again reviewed the possibilities that the Teheran accords had opened up for the peaceful coexistence of capitalism and socialism, and the need for Communists to adjust program and organization to fit new political realities.

The *Daily Worker* reported that Browder's speech was greeted "enthusiastically" by the crowd, but the *New York Times* reporter on the scene got a different impression: "About the middle of his address, after he told them that socialism and class struggle were being post-poned, a few began to leave singly and in pairs. From then until the end there was a steady trickle moving through the exits. The speech itself was not greeted with the volume of applause that had marked previous talks by Mr. Browder at Communist rallies in the Garden. Throughout there was only polite handclapping, never enough to halt the speaker."[7]

Browder, apparently, was prepared for this reaction. The following evening he dispatched national committee members to address party branch meetings all over the city to defend his proposals, and he set in motion plans for a massive "educational" effort that spring to win the membership over to the Teheran perspective.[8]

Browder had called for a fundamental reevaluation of party policies, but soon made it clear that only one conclusion would be allowed. The seeming unanimity with which party leaders hailed Browder's political-association proposal at the national committee meeting was illusory. Foster had voted against the plan at a closed meeting of the political committee held sometime prior to January 7. Sam Darcy, the district organizer for eastern Pennsylvania, and a close friend and political ally of Foster, also had misgivings, but neither Foster nor Darcy spoke out in opposition to Browder's position at the national committee meeting. Darcy had to leave the meeting early, so he did not actually vote for Browder's proposal, but he did express "hearty" support for it in his own report to the audience.[9] The presence of several hundred onlook-ers at the meeting inhibited dissent (as Browder probably counted on). Open criticism would have meant a breach of party discipline, since

Communist leaders were expected to present a picture of monolithic unity to the rank and file and outside observers.

Foster's Letter

Foster and Darcy were convinced that Browder had finally overstepped himself, and that a private appeal to Communist leaders might force him to back down. They met repeatedly during the week following the national committee meeting to draft a letter explaining their opposition to the Teheran line. The final draft of the letter, which carried Foster's signature, did not take explicit issue with Browder's decision to replace the party with a political association, nor did it criticize any of the Communists' current stands in support of the war, the no-strike pledge, and the Roosevelt Administration. Foster directed his fire solely at Browder's predictions about the postwar world. He saw two basic problems in "Comrade Browder's rather rosy outlook for capitalism." First, Browder was underestimating "the deepening of the crisis of world capitalism caused by the war," a general crisis from which the United States would not be exempt. Second, Foster could not accept "the idea that the main body of American finance capital is now or can be incorporated into the national unity necessary to carry out the decision of the Teheran Conference." Teheran had "by no means liquidated American imperialism." The dominant sections of the American ruling class remained "strong, greedy and aggressive." This meant that instead of relying on the goodwill of capitalists, the Communists need to "tell the people precisely who the enemy is that they are fighting—organized big capital—and mobilize our every resource to help make their fight succeed." In the postwar period Foster looked forward to renewed class conflict in which Communists would continue to advocate socialism as the "only final solution for our nation's troubles."

Foster's letter posed a sharp alternative to Browder's assessment of the pacific intentions of the American bourgeoisie, yet it hardly amounted to the defense of orthodox Marxism-Leninism that he subsequently claimed. The primary practical lesson he drew from these theoretical disagreements with Browder was that the Communists needed to fight all the harder for Roosevelt's reelection in 1944. Foster accused Browder of describing the Democratic and Republican parties "almost in a tweedle-dee, tweedle-dum manner" in his report to the national committee meeting. Since Browder believed that the decisive sectors of American capitalism were united behind the Teheran accords, the logic of his argument suggested that it made no difference who won the election. To the contrary, Foster argued, finance capital hated the Roosevelt Administration, around which "the great democratic people, the real backbone of national unity" were now arrayed, and it was the primary duty of Communists to "go all out for a continuation of the Roosevelt policies" in this "most crucial election since 1864." Browder could not fairly be accused of underestimating the importance of Roosevelt's reelection, but Foster apparently chose to out-Browder Browder on this issue in the hope of winning support for his other criticisms of the Teheran line.

Foster offered a variation of another familiar Browder theme by suggesting that capitalists, because of ideological blinders, did not know where their true interests lay. Most big-business spokesmen placed "complete reliance upon privately owned industry along the accustomed paths of the past" to solve the country's economic problems. But the slogan "Free Enterprise," which Browder did not want to challenge, would prove an inadequate guide to peacetime reconversion problems: "The far-reaching economic programs, involving government intervention in industry on an unprecedented scale that will be necessary to guide our country from an economic collapse worse than that of 1929, will originate in a truly progressive camp, consisting of the masses of workers, farmers, middle class and liberal sectors of capitalists."[10] Foster was countering 1944-style Browderism with something very closely resembling 1938 Browderism.

Foster had intended his letter to go out to all national committee members, but Browder kept it within the innermost circle of the leadership.[11] The political committee, along with a few national committee members and trade-union "influentials" carefully chosen by Browder, met on February 8 to discuss Foster's and Darcy's objections to the Teheran line.[12]

Foster and Darcy opened the meeting. Foster stuck closely to the position he had outlined in his January 20 letter, but Darcy went much further in his criticisms. Like Foster, he believed that a major economic crisis would follow once the "bottomless market which is the battlefield" was removed. However, he argued against a position (shared by both Browder and Foster) of having the Communists participate in "solving the economic contradictions of the post-war period or try achieving an economic stability." He warned that "we will not determine the conditions of the imperialist activities of our ruling class but we will share responsibility for the spread of imperialism." He did add a conciliatory note near the end of his speech, saying that he did not want to make Browder's leadership the issue. He only hoped to see the discussion of the Teheran policy extended throughout the party's ranks. "I have raised some questions which Comrade Browder may differ with," he said, "and I would like to know that Comrade Browder can say I am wrong without any aftermath."

Darcy's apprehensions about the consequences of his dissent were well founded. He and Foster found no defenders among the assembled leaders. Minor called Darcy the author of "the most unprincipled speech that has been made in a number of years." Dennis accused Foster of being "consciously or unconsciously the victim of factional considerations and a factional approach." This raised the ante in the dispute considerably. Under party rules Foster and Darcy were entitled to disagree with policy proposals as long as they kept their disagreement within appropriate circles and agreed to support the new line once it had been officially adopted. Organizing a faction, however, was cause for expulsion. (The line between permissible dissent and factionalism was deliberately kept hazy, allowing dissent to be equated with forbidden behavior whenever the need arose.) Dennis ended with a pointed warning: "If Comrade Foster insists on raising his viewpoint in the pre-convention discussion . . . he may provide ammunition to the Trotskyites, the *New Leader*, the *New Republic* and the *New York Times*. And there is also the danger that Comrade Foster by such an action may destroy his own prestige and usefulness in and to the Party."

Browder was not going to let an opportunity like this pass by without totally humiliating his opponents, especially Foster. Darcy's political opinions were of the sort, he declared, "that have to be decisively combatted, defeated and eliminated from the thinking of our Party," while Foster was "terribly confused, tragically confused; I think he has lost his way. The world has become too complex for him." Browder expressed confidence that if Foster were allowed to make his arguments known in the pre-convention discussions, the rank and file would overwhelmingly repudiate them, but the Communists could not take the chance that their enemies would use Foster's views to confuse the "broad circles" that were influenced by the party. "We are not a friendly debating society nor a friendly club," Browder declared. "We are a political army engaged in the struggle for the world. . . . And if we are faced with the necessity of dealing with this question after tonight, that will be merely one more unfortunate casualty of a war that has had many casualties."[13]

Browder was not subtle, but he was effective. When he called for a vote on a resolution to reject Foster's letter, only Foster and Darcy voted in opposition. Foster, who did not intend to have his name added to Browder's list of "unfortunate casualties," vowed to confine his dissent to the political committee.[14]

There were other, uninvited, listeners at the February 8 meeting. Sometime earlier in the war the FBI had bugged the party's headquarters. On March 9 the New York *World-Telegram,* probably tipped off by the FBI, ran a brief and accurate account of Foster's and Darcy's opposition to the Teheran line. Foster issued a statement, which appeared in the next day's *Daily Worker,* expressing his amazement "at the florid imagination" of newspaper reporters who specialized in "conjuring up imaginary struggles within the leadership of the Communist Party."[15]

The *Daily Worker* did not bother to solicit a denial from Darcy. After the February 8 meeting Darcy stepped down from his office as district organizer, although he was kept on the party's payroll with the suggestion he "devote his immediate efforts to a full study of the line and policy of the National Committee plenum." According to Darcy's later account, John Williamson approached him sometime after the February meeting and offered him six months in Florida at the party's expense to think things over. He declined.[16]

With the failure of the carrot, the stick emerged. The April 1 *Daily Worker* carried a statement from the new eastern Pennsylvania district organizer describing how Darcy had spoken in approval of Browder's report to the January national committee meeting, only to have subsequently "proceeded to engage in factional activity and to mobilize in a concerted and underhanded fashion against the policy that he himself had professed to support."[17] Later that spring the CP expelled Darcy for factionalism. The decision against him was brought by a special commission chaired by Foster—a test of Foster's discipline and willingness to back the new line. (In his 1952 book *History of the*

Communist Party of the United States Foster described his own opposition to the Teheran line in some detail, but never mentioned
Darcy's name.)[18]

Foster's capitulation was assured when Browder, at his request,
cabled Dimitrov a summary of Foster's letter to the political committee.
Browder, by other channels, sent the complete text of the letter to
Moscow, along with the minutes of the January national committee
and February political committee meetings. Dimitrov responded with
a message to Foster advising him to withdraw his objections.[19]

The Party's Reaction

There was some resistance among rank-and-file members to Browder's
new policy. Foster received several letters from members offering to
support him in a battle against the Teheran line, but he dutifully turned
the letters over to Browder.[20] Mike Gold, whose "Change the World"
column in the *Daily Worker* proved a fairly reliable mirror of rank-and-
file sentiment, offered an extremely reluctant endorsement of Browder's proposals a few days after the Lenin memorial meeting. Of all
the points Browder had made that evening, Gold felt that the suggestion
they "give up the old minority dream of socialism . . . was perhaps
the biggest and most bitter of new pills. . . . As for pledging to aid
capitalism to stabilize itself, this is a pill fit only for a horse. Where
is the human who can swallow it?" Still, he concluded, if the CP's
dissolution contributed "only a feather's weight" to victory over fascism, it was worth the sacrifice.[21]

Without leaders, this limited mood of resistance quickly dissipated. The party discussions and educational programs on the Teheran policy proceeded according to plan. Most rank-and-file Communists were soon swept up into the year's election campaigning. Since
the CP's dissolution did little to change the content of the Communists'
day-to-day political activity, they had little cause or time to continue
to worry about what it all might mean. Besides, this was the spring
that finally saw the launching of the long-awaited second front. The
drama of the invasion of Normandy overshadowed all questions of
political orthodoxy. Starobin wrote in the *Daily Worker* a month before
D-Day: "We have been fighting everything which the word 'Hitler'
stands for so long, so many years and years now, that perhaps we

ourselves do not realize what a tremendous event is about to take place: the utter destruction of Hitler the individual, and the system which bears his name."[22]

With such a monstrous evil about to be destroyed, at a terrible cost, it is perhaps not surprising that many Communists began to find Browder's vision of a harmonious postwar world more appealing than the prospect of further disorder and bloodshed.

The party's secondary leaders had weathered many previous shifts in its political line. They had greeted some changes with enthusiasm, others only by going through the motions. By and large they were sympathetic toward Browder's new policy. Steve Nelson, chairman of the Oakland, California, party organization in 1944, recalled no surprise at hearing Browder's proposals:

> I saw no sense for the Party to run candidates in its own name. I had been a candidate myself in 1936 when I was active in the unemployed movement in the Pennsylvania anthracite fields. We had twenty thousand people organized in the unemployed movement, I was the vice-chairman of the organization plus a known Communist organizer in the area, yet when I ran for Congress I got two hundred votes. . . . By 1944 I had already gone through the Party's electoral efforts of 1928, 1932, 1936 and 1940, and I thought we weren't really doing anything effective in those elections. It was a formality, a hell of a lot of work gathering signatures, and no results. The guys we called the *actives*, the second layer leaders in the areas and districts, had all faced this business and to them Teheran was an attempt to remedy the situation.[23]

George Watt, a Lincoln veteran and former YCL leader, was in England in the Army Air Corps when he heard of Browder's Teheran proposals. He recalled that he did not find it "shocking to dissolve the Party. We had already seemed to be logically moving in this direction from our experience in the mass movements. We had never really thought that we could make it as a party in the electoral field. We always thought we had to do it through coalitions. We had already done away with the concept of fractions in unions and mass organizations as being divisive. So when Browder came out with these ideas, they didn't seem to be far-fetched."[24]

The very vagueness of Browder's political-association proposal made it easier to support, since members could read into it whatever they wanted. But the expectations created by the Teheran policy were not always what Browder had intended. His private comments at the

February 8 political committee meeting made it clear that the new policies were intended to have little effect on the way the Communist organization actually functioned. In Williamson's phrase, no "sloppy liberalism" would be allowed to creep in. Yet the constant rhetorical emphasis on using Marxism creatively, instead of treating it as dogma, led some Communists to hope that truly fundamental changes were in the offing. Steve Nelson wrote to Elizabeth Gurley Flynn in October 1944, mentioning some questions that he had intended but failed to discuss with Minor in California earlier in the month. He decided that he would not "get very far with Bob." He felt less constrained with Flynn:

> Some of the points I have in mind are our organizational problems. We keep talking about the changed character of our association, but we continue to function very much in the old way. Some of the recent national directives from Williamson are particularly distressing since I don't note enough of a change that would indicate our changed role—It's still the same old stuff, and the same old "inner party" way of writing.[25]

Other Reactions

Browder's ambitions for the Teheran line extended well beyond the United States. At the behest of the Comintern, the American CP had long played a supervisory role over Communist movements in Latin America, supplying them with funds, technical assistance, and ideological direction. Since assuming the post of general secretary, Browder had kept careful watch over the internal affairs of the Latin-American parties, and had on occasion personally intervened in their leadership disputes. In one of the first messages that Browder sent to his wife from prison after the invasion of Russia, he expressed worry that not enough would be done by the American CP's leaders to "reorient all those friends who had learned to trust my judgement on large issues," particularly "our friends throughout Latin America."[26]

Browder devoted the months after the January 1944 national committee meeting to writing a book-length elaboration of his report, published at the end of April under the title *Teheran, Our Path in War and Peace*. It spelled out in some detail the policies he thought the American government should undertake to develop those new foreign markets essential to postwar prosperity. One chapter was devoted to a vision of a mutually beneficial trade relationship between the United

States, Britain, and Latin America, in which Anglo-American capitalists would gain a "huge and sure market" and the Latin-American countries would in turn receive the financial and technical assistance necessary to develop industrial economies, all done in the spirit of "Good Neighbors."[27]

Browder wanted to make sure that Latin-American Communists did nothing to mar this vision with any atavistic mistrust of Yankee imperialism. He relied on Cuban Communists to do much of the missionary work of spreading his Teheran doctrine throughout the rest of Latin America. In February the Partido Union Revolucionario Communista of Cuba changed its name to the less strident Partido Socialista Popular. Blas Roca, the Cuban Communist leader, wrote to Browder in January 1945 to report that Cuban Communists had already sold more than twenty thousand copies of a Spanish translation of *Teheran.* He apparently took its message to heart, telling Browder: "We have maintained until now, that only through nationalizing foreign investments and properties, in violent opposition to British and North American interests, would we be able to reach a higher degree of economic development. . . . [Teheran] opened up the perspective of achieving these progressive results through collaboration in a program . . . which would yield a reasonable interest to the British and North American investment properties and commercial enterprises in our countries."[28]

Browder's vision of international cooperation also depended on maintaining class peace within Britain and its empire. But most British and Commonwealth Communists had little use for his ideological innovations. Browder got his most sympathetic hearing in Canada, where many Communists regularly read American Communist publications. Browder met with Canadian CP leader Tim Buck and tried to win his support for the new line. Buck did not openly challenge Browder's position, but worked quietly to limit its influence within his own party.[29] L. L. Sharkey, general secretary of the Australian communist party, was far enough away from American shores so that he felt no need to humor Browder. He published an article in the Australian CP's newspaper in June 1944 entitled "Why Communist Programs Vary." Contrasting the political programs of the British Communist party and the newly formed Communist Political Association in the United States, Sharkey observed that "different historical developments and present political conditions" accounted for the fact that the Americans chose to dissolve their party while the British had not. But he made it clear that Australian Communists would follow the British example: "The enemies of Communism misrepresent Browder's statements and, making little or no mention of the policies of the British Party, endeavour to create the impression that Communists everywhere are 're-nouncing socialism.'"[30] The implied rebuke did not escape Browder's notice.

British Communists ignored all suggestions from Browder that they emulate the American example. By late 1944 Browder decided he had to go to England if he hoped to make his British comrades understand the logic and necessity of adopting his policies. This was no simple matter in wartime, with transatlantic traffic strictly controlled by the government. Since Sumner Welles had left the State Department, Browder used his only other channel to Roosevelt to press his cause. Josephine Truslow Adams wrote to Eleanor Roosevelt in November, complaining that in England "the groups which should unite to uphold Churchill's hand are weak and divided in leadership." It was her understanding that British Communists saw "the policy of unity upheld by the American Party as good in theory but impossible in practice." But Browder's presence in England might give British Communists a much needed push in the right direction: "If E.B. were in a position to talk British Party leaders into the same self-sacrificing and intelligent position that he took . . . Churchill would be better off."[31]

Mrs. Roosevelt passed the letter on to her husband, who apparently was unimpressed by the argument, for Browder did not get to make his trip. He eventually sent an emissary to speak on his behalf. Joseph North, editor of the *New Masses,* went to London in the late winter of 1945 to cover the founding convention of the World Federation of Trade Unions. Later that spring he met with British CP leaders, urging them to continue their support for Churchill even after the Nazi regime was crushed. They laughed at the suggestion, having a much better understanding than Browder of the mood of British working-class voters on the eve of Labour's greatest parliamentary victory.[32]

Australian and British Communists were not the only groups skeptical of the spirit of Teheran as revealed to Browder. Closer to home, most of the organs of American liberal opinion showed as little appreciation for Browder's innovations, though for very different reasons. A *New York Times* editorial derided "Communism, 1944 Model" and declared, "We would feel more certain that a genuinely American, law-abiding left-wing movement were being born if the Party would retire the outstanding leaders who have wriggled and wobbled all over the political map. The men who sneered at Britain's agonies in 1940 and called strikes in 1941 can hardly inspire confidence now."[33] Max Lerner, writing in *PM*, dismissed the Teheran line as "pipsqueak Machiavellianism."[34] Granville Hicks, reviewing *Teheran* for the *New Republic*, came the closest to a positive assessment: "Quite apart from the resolute official optimism, there is, I think, a new kind of confidence in this book, as if Browder believed that the line might stay fixed for some time to come."[35]

Browder's utter lack of candor in discussing the party's past with liberal journalists did little to build confidence in the CP's new policies. In February, Peter Kihss of the New York *Herald Tribune* asked Browder, perhaps as a tongue-in-cheek comment on the CP's strenuous political moderation, "if there has ever been a Communist movement in the United States that ever advocated violence to overthrow the government." Browder responded flatly that there had not. When Kihss then quoted several inflammatory passages from Foster's 1932 book *For a Soviet America,* Browder admitted that the CP had had a "very sectarian past," which often made it hard for Communists to make their true political position understood. But he insisted that

> even in the period in which there were these abstract statements [like Foster's book] which were susceptible of distortion or misrepresentation . . . the practical work of the Communist Party, and its programmatic declarations and proposals made to the country, were always directed towards merely improving the conditions of the masses of the people, and there was never even an indirect proposal that the Communists in the United States asked anyone to join in any effort directed towards the weakening or overthrow of the government.[36]

Browder needed to consider the fragile legal situation when responding to such questions. Less than a year before, William Schneiderman had won his case before the Supreme Court on the grounds that there were conflicting interpretations of the party's attitudes toward the overthrow of the government. It would have been unseemly for the general secretary of the Communist party to turn around and endorse the more damning interpretation, even if he was repudiating it as representative of the Communists' present outlook. But if Browder's less than accurate response protected the party's recent legal gains, it did little for its political reputation. If the Communists could not be honest about their own past, why should anyone whose memory extended back ten or more years be willing to accept their word on their present outlook or future intentions?

Founding the Association

During the 1930s the Communist party had grown adept at the mechanics of staging public rallies. The meetings at Madison Square Garden had drawn from a considerable pool of talent—left-wing scenery designers, songwriters, and choreographers—and Browder paid personal attention to the staging of these polished mass spectacles. The convention of May 20–22, which ushered in the Communist Political Association, was Browder's masterpiece. It displayed an almost obsessive attention to symbolic detail designed to express both the magnitude of changes being made and the continuity with the Communist movement's past.[37]

The delegates to what was meant to be the final convention of the American Communist party assembled on Saturday morning, May 20, in a hotel ballroom in New York City. Standing in front of a poster of Stalin, Roosevelt, and Churchill, Foster called the meeting to order. The front of the podium from which he addressed the audience was covered by a red-bordered service flag with a gold star (displayed by families with a son killed in action), a blue star (signifying a son in the service), and the number 9,250, the number of American Communists then on leave for service in the military.

Browder had sent Gil Green to talk to Foster before the convention, to remind him of the consequences of any challenge to the Teheran line he might be considering. But Foster behaved impeccably. He made a brief address, noting that in its twenty-five-year history the party had made many changes in organizational structure, but had always remained "in the front ranks of every fight for freedom." In his capacity as chairman of the national committee, Foster then recommended that the delegates endorse the proposed constitutional changes that would turn the Communist party into the Communist Political Association.

Browder, following Foster to the podium, offered the official resolution that the Communist party of the United States be dissolved and that its assets be turned over by party leaders to "any organization . . . that in their opinion [is] devoted to our country's winning of the war . . . and in the achieving of a durable peace." One half hour after

Foster called the meeting to order the delegates voted unanimously in support of Browder's resolution. They sang "Happy Birthday" in tribute to the general secretary of the now deceased Communist party— Browder's birthday, not coincidentally, falling on the opening day of the convention—and finished with a chorus of "We Shall Not Be Moved." And indeed they did not move. Taking their seats, they constituted themselves the founding convention of the Communist Political Association and continued with their well-choreographed deliberations.

There were few surprises in the sessions that met over the next two days. The convention stood in tribute to the honored dead, and adopted greetings to Stalin, Tito, and General Eisenhower. Twenty-five "old-timers" (as they were described in the convention proceedings), headed up by the redoubtable "Mother" Ella Reeve Bloor, sat on stage to symbolize twenty-five years of Communist history. Minor praised Earl Browder as "tribune of the people." Browder, addressing the delegates as "Ladies and Gentlemen" instead of the customary salutation "Comrades," read aloud the proposed preamble to the CPA's constitution. The new constitution made adherence to any group that "conspires or acts to subvert, undermine, weaken or overthrow any or all institutions of American democracy" an offense punishable by immediate expulsion from the CPA.

At the convention's closing session on May 22 the delegates unanimously elected Browder as the CPA's first president. The new constitution, by eliminating the position of chairman, in effect demoted Foster, now only one of eleven vice-presidents elected by the delegates. The delegates also elected an organizational secretary (John Williamson) and a treasurer (Charles Krumbein, a New York state party leader). All CPA officers were automatically members of the new, forty-member national committee, and most of them also served on the smaller national board (the political committee in new dress).[38]

The final act in this metamorphosis was played out at Madison Square Garden on May 23. The eighteen thousand Communists who attended that evening displayed none of the hesitations of the previous January as they cheered the assembled leaders of the new Communist Political Association. In subsequent weeks district conventions all over the country ratified the convention decisions and reconstituted themselves as state Communist Political Associations (except in the South, where they became People's Educational Associations).[39]

The whole proceeding was a triumph of showmanship, but a defeat for the principles of democratic political organization that the CPA's constitution supposedly endorsed. The Communists valued public unity as their strongest weapon in political struggle. Browder intended his pageantry to express that unity, but it had no substance; it papered over disagreements that had been given no chance to be thrashed out among the membership as a whole or even given a fair hearing among its leaders. Browder's suppression of Foster's letter was the CPA's mark of Cain. Despite the new organization's professed devotion to a nondogmatic Marxism as mediated by the "traditions of Washington, Jefferson, Paine, Jackson and Lincoln," it had inherited the worst characteristics of its predecessor. When Browder came under attack a year later, the besmirched circumstances of the CPA's birth would rob him of moral or political grounds from which he could defend his perspective, while they awarded Foster an unearned role as defender of party democracy.

In the short run none of that made much difference. The CPA and the Teheran line seemed to be great successes. The Communists' recruiting drive that spring brought in some 24,000 new recruits, with an increased proportion of the much prized category of basic industrial workers. And for the first time since the signing of the Nazi-Soviet pact, the Communist movement reached approximately the same number of members it had in 1938–1939, about 70,000 registered members with another 9,000 on leave in the armed forces.[40] Communists, outside of traditional strongholds like New York City, began to play a more visible role in their communities. Browder went to Rochester, New York, in April 1944 to give a speech, and attracted some seven hundred listeners, twice the size of any previous Communist-sponsored meeting in the city. Shortly afterward a local Communist organizer wrote to Browder that the "continued isolation of our party here was not something imposed upon us by objective factors, but our own sectarian attitudes and practices. . . . Our members now feel they belong to a movement that has to be reckoned with and that they don't have to 'defend' it—but explain it and extend its members and influence."[41]

The Continuing Strike Wave

The fact that relatively large numbers of industrial workers were joining at a time when the Communists were vigorously denouncing all strikes and edging toward the idea of extending the no-strike pledge into the postwar era suggests that the connection between shop-floor militancy and workers' political judgments is not as simple and direct as some left-wing labor historians would like to believe.[42] Wildcat strikes swept through CIO-organized factories in the auto, steel, and rubber industries in 1944, and rank-and-file union members often turned to Trotskyist militants for leadership in these struggles. But none of the various Trotskyist groups around during the war benefited very much from these strikes. Most workers, regardless of their feelings about the no-strike pledge, remained loyal to Roosevelt. The small number of workers who were seeking left-wing political affiliation found the Communists, with their support for Roosevelt, their link with the (then popular) Soviet Union, and their organizational resources (daily newspapers, paid organizers, publishing houses, party schools, and so on), a much more attractive alternative.[43]

The UAW was the most important union in which the battle over the no-strike pledge was fought out in 1944. Over half of all workers in the auto industry were involved in strikes that year. A newly organized group within the union, the Rank and File Caucus, campaigned in the months before the annual UAW convention to win enough delegate strength to force the union to withdraw its adherence to the no-strike pledge. The popular support the caucus attracted worried all the familiar factional contenders in the UAW's leadership, including Walter Reuther, who was not prepared to take a forthright stand against official CIO and government policy on the no-strike pledge.[44]

The Communists carefully monitored events in the union and on the shop floor. The UAW was the flagship of the CIO, and if it reversed direction on the no-strike pledge, it might be followed by the rest of the union movement. Browder received a memo in the summer of 1944 from a Communist organizer in the UAW who reported that the attitude that "the no-strike pledge is so much double-talk was reflected in the talks I had with lots of rank-and-filers who simply glibly accept this and tell it to you in the most casual fashion." He had recently spoken with UAW secretary-treasurer George Addes, who told him that the union's president, R. J. Thomas, was negotiating with the War Department for permission to visit the war zone in Europe. According to Addes, Thomas feared that unless he was able to go before the September UAW convention and say something like "I've just come back from the Normandy battlefronts and saw our brothers fighting and dying, saw the material of war which you, their brothers back home, are producing and they need . . ." union leaders would be unable to head off the Rank and File Caucus's demands for abandoning the no-strike pledge. Thomas's maneuver was designed to reinforce a position that the Communists themselves strongly favored, but Browder's correspondent could not refrain from adding, "By and large I felt that the cynicism and politics that go on here make the Hague and Kelly machines look like a bunch of amateurs."[45]

Thomas made his trip to Normandy, but the delegates at the September convention refused either to reaffirm or directly repeal the no-strike pledge. Instead they scheduled a membership referendum on the question, to be held after the fall's national elections were safely past. UAW Communists were pleased that Reuther's equivocal position on the no-strike question cut into the gains he had made over the previous years. Losing his position as UAW vice-president to Frankensteen, he had to settle once more for the second vice-presidency. But the idea of a membership referendum on the no-strike pledge made the Communists nervous, and they threw all their resources into the campaign for its reaffirmation. (Josephine Truslow Adams, presumably acting at Browder's suggestion, wrote to Eleanor Roosevelt in December 1944 suggesting that General Eisenhower cable the UAW leadership to express his support for reaffirmation of the pledge. She also suggested that the War Department distribute absentee ballots to the thousands of UAW members in the armed forces "as those most vitally interested" in the referendum's results.)[46] In the end, UAW members did vote to reaffirm the pledge—but continued to walk out on strike in large numbers for the remainder of the war.

In the aftermath of Lewis's successful defiance of the War Labor Board in 1943, Roosevelt sought a legislative solution to the problem of wartime strikes. In his State of the Union message in January 1944 he announced support for the Austin-Wadsworth Bill, a proposed "national service" law which would in effect allow the government to draft civilians for employment in war industries. The bill was opposed by most of the labor movement and found little favor among corporation leaders, who feared the increasing government control that would accompany such a draft. One group of union leaders was willing to support it. According to a confidential FBI report, Roy Hudson, the CP's trade-union secretary, met with National Maritime Union vice-president Blackie Myers shortly after Roosevelt's speech, instructing him "to take a specific stand as being strictly in favor of [national service] legislation. . . . Following this discussion with Myers, Hudson is reported to have prepared a release to be issued by the National Maritime Union concerning its stand on national service legislation."[47]

Longshoremen's president Harry Bridges also endorsed the bill. When Philip Murray met with Roosevelt to argue against national service, Roosevelt produced a telegram from Bridges expressing his full support for the legislation. Murray, not amused, forced Bridges and other left-wing CIO leaders to repudiate their initial support for the bill. But the Communists, unwilling to let any domestic issue come between them and Roosevelt, continued their own support down through the spring of 1945, when the bill finally died in House-Senate conference.[48]

The Campaign for Roosevelt

Browder's watchword for 1944, "For or Against Teheran," could just as accurately have read "For or Against Roosevelt." In March of that year Browder wrote, "President Roosevelt is the only political figure in our country whose election next November would constitute a guarantee that the policy of Teheran would guide our country in the ensuing four years."[49]

There was one contender for the Republican presidential nomination to whom the Communists were favorably disposed: Wendell Willkie, author of a best-selling pro-Soviet book, *One World,* and who, as attorney, had represented William Schneiderman in his successful appeal to the Supreme Court in 1943. On several occasions early in 1944 Browder suggested a national unity "dream ticket" of Roosevelt running for reelection as President with Willkie as his running mate.[50] When it became apparent that New York governor Thomas E. Dewey had outdistanced Willkie in the race for the Republican nomination, the Communists began to portray the coming election in apocalyptic terms. The founding convention of the CPA adopted a resolution declaring that the "appeasers and defeatists" of the "Hoover-Taft-Vandenberg-Dewey machine" were part of a cabal plotting to "use the elections to prolong the war, to bring about a compromise peace with Nazism-fascism and to establish a pro-fascist government within the United States."[51]

Though the Communists did not have a single candidate on the ballot, the 1944 election saw the greatest electoral effort of their history.

Although there were not many Communists in the United States, they were concentrated in areas of strategic political importance. If Roosevelt were to win in 1944 he had to carry the big industrial states, especially New York. In 1942 Dewey had soundly defeated the Democratic candidate in the New York gubernatorial election, benefiting from the inefficiency and internal division of the regular Democratic machine and the lowest voter turnout in eight years. Robert Sherwood, one of Roosevelt's speechwriters, later described the considerable alarm with which the President's advisers viewed the coming elections: "There appeared to be a considerable amount of lethargy among the voters which could result in a small registration and an even smaller turnout on election day. This had happened in the Congressional election of 1942 and had resulted in substantial Republican gains. It was obvious that if large masses of people, particularly in organized labor, were so sure the President could not lose that they would feel no need to register and vote, the President could be defeated."[52]

The Communists had upward of forty thousand members in New York, as well as pockets of strength in other important industrial states like California, Michigan, Pennsylvania, and Illinois. Securing Roosevelt's reelection became their top political priority in 1944.

The 1942 congressional elections had been a disaster for organized labor. The passage in 1943 of the Smith-Connolly Act—a rather inept piece of legislation designed to eliminate wartime strikes—symbolized the anti-labor temper of the new Congress. One of the more galling provisions of the act restricted the amount of financial support unions could contribute to political campaigns. To sidestep these restrictions, and to avoid a repetition of 1942's dismal returns in the 1944 congressional and presidential elections, CIO leaders Murray and Hillman announced the formation of the CIO Political Action Committee in midsummer 1943, with Hillman as its chairman. Since stepping down from the Office of Production Management in the spring of 1942, Hillman had been languishing far from the seat of power. Now he poured his dynamic organizing abilities into the PAC. And, as John L. Lewis had done before him in the initial CIO organizing drives, Hillman turned to the Communists to find the necessary skilled and committed organizers to staff national and regional PAC offices.[53]

Hillman found the Communists particularly valuable allies in New York. He wanted to use the American Labor Party as the local affiliate of the PAC. Though he had been one of the ALP's founders, he had not played a significant role in its leadership. ILGWU President David Dubinsky, along with Alex Rose of the Milliners union and George Counts of the American Federation of Teachers, had long dominated the ALP's state machinery, though facing an increasingly powerful challenge from Communist-influenced ALP county committees in New York City. Hillman and Dubinsky had a long history of bad personal relations, exacerbated by jurisdictional battles between their two unions after Dubinsky took the ILGWU out of the CIO. Hillman decided to wrest control of the ALP away from Dubinsky in the spring 1944 primaries, an effort requiring close cooperation with the Communists.

In February Dubinsky met with Vice-President Henry Wallace to brief him on the factional battle within the ALP. According to Wallace's notes on the meeting, "Dubinsky says the Communists are very hard workers, that they are fanatics. . . . Dubinsky says the Communists today are for the President in the war effort just as strongly as they were against the President in the war effort three years ago."[54] Dubinsky probably intended these observations as a comment on the hypocrisy of the Communists' support for the Administration, but a master politician like Roosevelt was hardly going to be disturbed by the impure motives of some of the most self-sacrificing workers in his reelection effort. Though formally repudiating the CPA's endorsement of his reelection, he remained neutral in the battle between Dubinsky and Hillman in the ALP, and made no effort to have the Communists ousted from the various PAC operations they controlled.

Hillman's challenge proved successful. In the March primaries the Hillman-Communist coalition swept all five New York City boroughs and for the first time showed strength upstate, winning more than 600 of the 750 seats on the ALP state committee. While the committee met to elect Hillman ALP chairman, Dubinsky and Rose led their followers out of the ALP and into the newly established Liberal Party. In a parting shot, the ILGWU's newspaper *Justice* proclaimed: "The primary results leave no doubt that Mr. Earl Browder has captured the American Labor Party."[55]

Even before the election campaign got into full swing, Martin Dies had attacked the PAC as a Communist front, declaring on the floor of Congress that "Sidney Hillman will soon succeed Earl Browder as head of the Communists in the United States."[56] The Republicans decided to make this the main theme of their own attempt to unseat Roosevelt. Dewey had few other effective issues. After the invasion of Normandy, little doubt remained that the war in Europe would soon be brought to a successful conclusion. Though Dewey sniped at the "muddling" of the Roosevelt Administration's domestic policies, the Republican party platform officially embraced the National Labor Relations Act, the Social Securty Act, and other Roosevelt-sponsored social legislation. Dewey's attempts to outflank Roosevelt on the left with calls for extended social security and old age and unemployment coverage met with general public skepticism: the *New York Times* commented that Dewey seemed to be "running for the Presidency on the domestic platform of the New Deal." Fears that an ailing Roosevelt would not live out his fourth term were probably the strongest factor Dewey had going for him in the election, but apart from pointed comments about the "tired old men" in Washington, it was not the kind of issue he could bring up directly. Bereft of other things to talk about, the Republicans put their main energy into accusing Roosevelt of Communist ties, playing on vague popular fears that his domestic policies were promoting "totalitarian collectivism" at home, while his foreign policies would lead to a Communist-dominated postwar Europe.[57]

The Republicans chose the highly visible role that Hillman's PAC was playing in Roosevelt's reelection campaign as the focus for their attack. The Communists were an important component in PAC, and PAC was the President's single most important supporter. Hence, the Republicans argued, the Communists controlled the Administration. The Republicans had made similar charges in 1936, but their campaign that year was a model of restraint and decorum compared to 1944. Dewey charged that Roosevelt had freed Browder in 1942 to gain the Communists' support in his campaign for a fourth term. His running mate John Bricker flatly asserted that "the great Democratic Party has become the Hillman-Browder communistic party with Franklin Roosevelt as its front." Roosevelt's alleged instruction to his aides while pondering his vice-presidential choice at the Democratic convention, "Clear it with Sidney," was reworked by the Republicans into "Clear everything with Sidney" and trumpeted from coast to coast as evidence of Roosevelt's subservience to organized labor, the Communists, and, in its seamiest version, the Jews.[58]

PAC's vulnerability to such tactics undoubtedly cost Roosevelt some votes, but in its organizing efforts PAC displayed considerable political muscle. Not the least of Martin Dies's animus to Hillman derived from the fact that PAC singled out his home district in

Texas as a special target. When thousands of CIO workers paid the poll tax and swelled the voting lists in Dies's congressional district, he decided it was time to retire, stepping down in time to avoid a humiliating defeat in the Democratic primary. Two other members of the House Un-American Activities Committee, Joseph Starnes of Alabama and John Costello of California, had lacked Dies's foresight and were defeated by PAC-supported candidates in the spring primaries.[59] PAC campaigned to overturn the poll tax, and to allow soldiers overseas to vote. With its satellite organization, the National Citizens Political Action Committee, it conducted a massive voter registration project, canvassing door to door and distributing millions of pieces of campaign literature for Roosevelt, staged mass rallies, and raised about a fifth of all the money Roosevelt spent on the campaign.[60] For thousands of American Communists, the effort to reelect Roosevelt in 1944 provided invaluable experience in the mechanics of running a national political campaign. The 1948 Progressive party campaign for Henry Wallace was staffed largely by veterans of the 1944 PAC operation.

PAC's efforts, the favorable war news, and Roosevelt's vigorous campaigning in the last weeks before Election Day (including his inspired defense of his Scottish terrier Fala against Republican slanders) turned the tide in his favor. But he won by the smallest margin of his four presidential campaigns, and it was the big industrial states like New York and Michigan that carried the day. Michigan was one of the few states in which more voters turned out in 1944 than in 1940, and New York was the only one in which Roosevelt's victory margin increased over that of the previous election. In both states PAC probably had made the difference.[61]

Of course, Roosevelt might have won without PAC, but at best by a razor-thin margin. And PAC might have functioned without the Communists, but it would have lost many of its most tireless cadres as well as much of the fervor of social mission that colored its appeal that year. The election results were not the triumph of the "Hillman-Browder Axis" that Republic propagandists had warned against, since Roosevelt was hardly a front for either man's ambitions. It did seem to the Communists nevertheless that the election had been a decisive triumph for the "spirit of Teheran," and a harbinger of political victories to come. The day after the election Browder declared that Roosevelt's victory cleared "the way for a quick victory in the war, for consolidation of the United Nations, and for a lasting and prosperous peace for our country and the world.'' He believed that his bold experiment, dissolving the Communist party and organizing the Communist Political Association, had paid off. The Communists had proven, through their contributions to Roosevelt's reelection campaign, that they were sophisticated and desirable political allies. Browder predicted the Communists would remain a "small, if important sector of the great patriotic coalition" in the years to come.[62]

As had so often happened in the recent past, events of the coming year would prove Browder a bad prophet.

10 THE PARTY RESTORED
January 1945 to February 1946

> Browder's analysis of capitalism in the United States is not
> distinguished by a judicious application of Marxism-Leninism.
> —JACQUES DUCLOS, April 1945

> All members of our Party will understand that the struggle against
> Browder and Browderism has entered a new stage. . . . It is now a
> struggle against an active opponent of the Party, against an enemy-
> class ideology and platform.
> —*Daily Worker*, February 7, 1946[1]

THE YEAR 1945 began auspiciously and ended disastrously for Browder
and his Teheran policies. As in 1939 and 1941, international events
beyond the control of American Communists forced them to reverse
political direction. Browder now paid the price for the heavy-handed
fashion with which he had reshaped the American Communist movement. And Foster, who had waited many years for this opportunity,
did his best to cast Browder and "Browderism" into disgrace and
excommunication.

Victory and Discord

In the spring of 1945 the Allied armies fought their way into Nazi
Germany from the east and the west. American and Russian troops
met at the German town of Torgau on the Elbe River on April 25 and
embraced as victorious comrades in arms. CIO leaders met in London
in February with British and Soviet trade-union leaders to organize the
World Federation of Trade Unions: Alvah Bessie's November 1942
prediction that "the international solidarity of all who toil is being
cemented" did indeed seem finally to be achieved. At home, events
also seemed to go well for Browder's Teheran policies. CIO leader
Philip Murray and AFL leader William Green met on March 28 with
Eric Johnston, president of the U.S. Chamber of Commerce, and

signed a "New Charter for Labor and Management," pledging that the labor movement would respect "the inherent right and responsibility of management" to direct the operations of business and industry in exchange for the recognition of labor's right to organize and engage in collective bargaining. "It's industrial peace for the postwar world!" the *CIO News* declared enthusiastically.[2] And the Communists moved another step toward inclusion in the "democratic coalition" when Ben Davis Jr., who had quietly registered as a Democrat earlier in the spring, received Tammany Hall's endorsement in May in his bid for reelection to the New York city council. Adam Clayton Powell told a cheering Harlem audience that "the new world we hear about as a'coming is already here when Tammany Hall nominates a Communist."[3]

Browder was pleased with the way postwar relations between the Soviet Union and its wartime allies seemed to be shaping up. In *Teheran*, he had urged American policymakers to reconcile themselves to the "people's democratic revolution" that was sweeping away "relics of feudalism" along with the Nazi armies in Eastern Europe, and that after the war would help usher in a "new democratic Europe . . . capable of buying and selling on the world market, and *paying its bills*, in a new fashion and on a scale necessary to fit, with America, into a single world order."[4]

American Communists applauded when the American and British governments shifted their support from the anti-Communist chetniks to Tito's Partisans in Yugoslavia. They applauded the Western Allies' gradual disentanglement from the Polish government-in-exile, and Churchill's and Roosevelt's reluctant recognition that the Soviet-sponsored Lublin provisional government would form the basis of the postwar Polish regime. They applauded as England and the United States extended recognition to the new pro-Soviet provisional governments in Bulgaria, Rumania, and Hungary.

They did not applaud when British tanks crushed Communist-led resistance forces in Greece in December 1944, but neither did they protest strongly. The Communists had no direct knowledge of Churchill's "percentages" deal with Stalin, in which in October 1944 the British leader casually awarded the Russians predominant influence in Rumania, Bulgaria, and Hungary in exchange for Britain's superiority in Greece. But as always they were careful readers of the Soviet press, which remained silent on the armed suppression of the Greek resistance. Browder attributed British actions in Greece to insecurity over their postwar economic position vis-à-vis their prosperous American ally. He warned against any "short-sighted and shallow agitation of distrust" against Britain, despite its "damaging mistakes" in Greece. Browder now pushed "markets" as the solution for all international problems the same way he had previously pushed incentive pay as a panacea for all problems in labor relations. To avoid future tragedies like Greece, America had to "reach agreements in economic policy for the post-war world, with both Britain and the Soviet Union, which will organize markets big enough to keep the economy of each country going at full capacity, so that no one loses out, and the whole world is improved and reconstructed."[5]

Browder was convinced that no fundamental issues divided the Soviet Union and the Western powers. After the February meeting of the Big Three in Yalta, he assured readers of *Political Affairs* (formerly *The Communist*, renamed in January 1945) that the decisions taken at Yalta "undeviatingly continued and further developed the line already indicated clearly at Moscow and Teheran."[6]

Browder had displayed a weakness for wishful thinking in the past, most notably in the months before the Nazi-Soviet pact when he categorically denied such a possibility. He now refused to admit the possibility that the Grand Alliance could unravel after the defeat of the Nazis. At the end of May 1945, with the Western Allies and the Soviet Union bitterly split over the composition of the new Polish government, Browder wrote, "The alignment apparently taking place of Britain and America against the Soviet Union expresses *a conflict of mood and opinion but not a conflict of interest*." There were only two possible alternatives to the continuation of the Grand Alliance: "An Anglo-American war against the Soviet Union, or an 'armed peace' directed against the Soviet Union, which is another name for diplomatic and economic war without drawing the military conclusions." But either course would lead to a "postwar world of chaos and disorder." The prospect of such a disaster, he maintained, would "force the re-welding of the Coalition."[7]

The Duclos Letter

Browder knew that not all Communist parties shared this assessment, and he had heard rumors in the late winter of 1945 that some French Communist leaders were particularly distressed by his post-Teheran pronouncements.[8] But he attached little importance to the rumors, seeing in them only the same kind of parochial resistance he had encountered in his approaches to British and Australian Communist leaders. Besides, he had received a letter the previous spring from André Marty, a member of the French Communist party (PCF) politburo, congratulating him on his "beautiful speech of January 1944."[9] A divided French leadership was nothing to worry about, and even if united could hardly prevail against Dimitrov's implied support of the previous year. At the end of March Browder wrote to L. L. Sharkey, the Australian Communist leader, to criticize the Australian CP's recently published program, which he felt was "insufficiently based on Teheran." Browder noted that American Communists had not held any formal international ties since their disaffiliation from the Comintern in November 1940, but added, "We have continued unimpaired our intense interest in the progress of fellow Marxists in all lands. The dissolution of international organization ties should not mean the ending of free discussion across national boundaries."[10]

About the same time Browder was writing these words, French printers were setting in type the April edition of the PCF's theoretical journal *Cahiers du Communisme*. The issue included an article entitled "On the Dissolution of the American Communist Party," written by Jacques Duclos, the PCF's second-in-command. Duclos's article was more modest in its proclaimed intention than Browder's assertion of the right to influence the programs of other Communist parties, saying only that "many readers" of *Cahiers du Communisme* had asked for "clarification" of developments within the American Communist movement. Having received "some information on this very important political event," Duclos proposed to satisfy their curiosity.

Quoting both from published sources like the *Daily Worker* and from such unpublished materials as Foster's January 1944 letter to the national committee and the minutes of the January and February meetings of the CP's leaders, Duclos outlined the "erroneous conclusions in no wise flowing from a Marxist analysis" that Browder had drawn from the meeting of the Big Three at Teheran. After a lengthy presentation of Browder's positions, Duclos listed the lessons he drew from the American events. First, he argued, "the course applied under Browder's leadership ended in practice in liquidation of the independent political party of the working class in the U.S." Second, "one is witnessing a notorious revision of Marxism on the part of Browder and his supporters, a revision which is expressed in the concept of a long-term class peace in the United States." Third, in "transforming the Teheran declaration of the Allied governments, which is a document of a diplomatic character, into a political platform of class peace in the United States in the postwar period, the American Communists are deforming in a radical way the meaning of the Teheran declaration." Finally, Duclos believed this was an issue of international importance for the Communist movement since Browder's ideas had already found critics in several countries as well as supporters in Latin America. Duclos cautioned his readers not to "lose sight for a single moment of the necessity of arraying ourselves against the men of the trusts," nor to close their eyes "to the economic and political circumstances which engendered fascism."[11]

Duclos's introduction was somewhat disingenuous. The article was intended for American rather than for French readers (French Communists had never before been known to display much interest in the affairs of the tiny American Communist movement). Nor was it customary for leaders of the member parties of the former Communist International casually to criticize one another's pronouncements in public. And, as Browder and Foster recognized as soon as they saw the article, there was only one place where Duclos could have gotten the unpublished documents he cited so freely. Maurice Thorez, the general secretary of the PCF, returned to France from wartime exile in Moscow in December 1944, and it is probable that he brought the documents with him and passed them on to Duclos.[12] The Duclos article was a message from Moscow—but what exactly did the message mean?

Years after the appearance of the Duclos article Browder decided it was meant to be "the first *public* declaration of the Cold War," an interpretation shared by some diplomatic historians. This interpretation rests largely on two passages in the article. In the first, Duclos noted that Browder believed the Teheran Declaration meant that "the greatest part of Europe, west of the Soviet Union, will probably be reconstituted on a bourgeois-democratic basis and not on a fascist-capitalist or Soviet basis." And in a second passage Duclos noted "confusion" in certain of Browder's comments on the nationalization of monopolies. Nationalization, Duclos insisted, "is simply a matter of reforms," while the "achievement of socialism [is] impossible to imagine without a preliminary conquest of power." In the late spring of 1945 State

Department analysts, already disturbed by the heavy-handed measures Stalin was using to consolidate Communist control over the new Eastern European governments, saw the Duclos article as a signal to Western Europe's Communists to prepare to emulate their comrades in the east.[13]

In retrospect, this interpretation seems questionable. Duclos did not condemn every position he attributed to Browder: for example, he noted approvingly how Browder had praised the Soviet Union as "the irreplaceable force which saved the world from fascist slavery." Duclos's text indicated neither explicit approval nor disapproval for Browder's belief in the "bourgeois-democratic" future of Western Europe; given what we know about the PCF's actions in the postwar years, it seems likely that Duclos shared this conviction with Browder. In the second passage, in which Duclos insisted that socialism could not be achieved without the conquest of state power, he was restating the orthodox Leninist position—in opposition to, and in apparent misunderstanding of, Browder's Teheran line, which did not call for a program of nationalization as a step toward socialism or even as a means of reforming capitalism. Since the French, no less than the American Communists, had postponed the struggle for socialism to the distant future, this hardly amounted to a call to the barricades. In 1944–1945 the French Communist leaders ordered their followers in the resistance to surrender their weapons to the new French government; they joined that government as junior partners; they opposed strikes and called on French workers to increase their productivity; they did not agree with the French Socialists, who were calling for nationalization of large sections of the country's economy; and they defended the French government's colonial policies in Algeria (while Browder, notorious revisionist that he might have been, at least made an argument in *Teheran* for Puerto Rican independence). If Duclos's article was indeed intended to signal a new and aggressive Communist stance in Western Europe, then French Communists, who continued to pursue Popular Front–style policies for another two years, somehow failed to get the point.[14]

Stalin must have realized that the Duclos article would be carefully scrutinized by the State Department, and may well have intended it as a reminder of the political resources with which he could make trouble in Western Europe if the Americans sought to tamper with his plans for Eastern Europe. If so, the gesture proved badly timed. Roosevelt understood Stalin's devious diplomatic gestures, even if he was occasionally exasperated by them. But Roosevelt died shortly before the article appeared in print, and his successor, Harry S. Truman, had no patience for subtle interpretations of ambiguous diplomatic maneuvers. To Truman, and to his closest advisers, Soviet recalcitrance could mean only one thing: that Stalin had already decided to march the Red Army to the English Channel and beyond as soon as possible. The appearance of the Duclos article confirmed the darkest suspicions of the State Department's Eastern European desk.[15]

If the Duclos article's message to the State Department was ambiguous, its message to American Communists seemed clear enough: Browder's policies had to be reversed. Stalin could have ordered American Communists to change course by means of shortwave broadcast, coded cable, or private messenger. Since he chose instead to employ such a public forum, Stalin obviously would not be satisfied with simply having Browder write a new book explaining that Teheran did not mean long-term class peace in the United States after all. Moreover, Duclos's article could have been written without any reference to Foster or his dissent in 1944. As written, the article led Communist readers inescapably to the conclusion that Foster had been the guardian of orthodox Marxism-Leninism in the United States.

Did Stalin want the results that the Duclos article would finally obtain—Browder's expulsion and Foster's accession to power? American Communist leaders quickly arrived at this conclusion. But the absence of any criticism of Browder in the Soviet press, and the invitation he received to visit Moscow the following year, suggest that the Soviet leaders were not entirely pleased with the way things had turned out. The last American Communist leader to be deposed from power on Soviet orders, Jay Lovestone, had never received such considerations. When Jacques Duclos was asked in 1947 by an American Communist leader if he would be willing to offer public advice on another dispute engaging the attention of the CPUSA, he quickly declined, reportedly saying something to the effect of "Look what you did with that other article of mine."[16]

If Stalin did not want Browder deposed, what else could he have wanted? Here we can only speculate, but it is possible that the Duclos article was intended to have a less drastic effect. Perhaps Stalin wanted Browder to retain his position as general secretary of a reconstituted

American Communist party, while Foster was elevated to an active second-in-command with enough independent authority to block any future tendency on Browder's part to go overboard with "Americanization." Such a compromise would have required Browder to admit his past mistakes publicly, and Foster to restrain his ambition. If this was what Stalin had in mind, he had not taken the personalities of these two old antagonists sufficiently into consideration.

First Reactions

The Duclos article, published in France in April, reached its intended audience by a circuitous route. Two French Communist leaders, Benoît Frachon and François Billoux, were among the delegates sent by the French government to the founding convention of the United Nations in San Francisco. They had gone directly to San Francisco, but sometime in early May returned to the East Coast. Frachon then stopped by Browder's New York City office and gave him a copy of the Duclos article. Browder had it translated by a member of the *Daily Worker*'s foreign desk, and discovered that he was in serious trouble. He, Foster, and Dennis immediately went to Washington, D.C., to meet with Billoux. When Browder told Billoux that if the Communists accepted Duclos's criticisms he would be "cleaned out" of the leadership, Billoux denied this was the intention of the article. The three American Communist leaders returned to New York, where for the next few weeks they sat on the article, keeping its existence a closely guarded secret.[17]

The New York *World-Telegram*, which had revealed Foster's and Darcy's objections to the Teheran policy in 1944, forced Browder's hand. The newspaper had gotten hold of the article through sources of its own, and announced its existence on May 22. The full national board met in emergency session that evening and into the next day to discuss its implications and the CPA's response.[18] Two questions had to be addressed immediately: when and how the article should be presented to CPA members and what response, if any, CPA leaders should make directly to Duclos. Browder came to the meeting armed with an introduction he had written to accompany publication of the article in the *Daily Worker*, while Foster came with the text of a telegram he wanted sent to Duclos. Foster's telegram accepted "the basic content if not all of [the] criticisms" made in the article, while affirming that "despite errors and shortcomings, the main line of our policy has been correct."[19]

Considering the tremendous advantage Foster had suddenly been awarded in his decade-long battle with Browder, the tone of his telegram and his comments at the start of the meeting were surprisingly mild. Past defeats had taught him to be cautious. He called on Browder to chair the meeting, declaring that "we should not start leaderless, even in this discussion here, and certainly not before the Association as a whole." But if Foster initially showed a willingness to compromise, Browder did not. He opposed sending Foster's telegram to Duclos, and declared himself unwilling to "offer any blanket declaration of approval" of Duclos's criticisms. Foster warned him that opposing the article's line would be "a major political mistake," but said nothing to indicate that it had yet occurred to him to challenge Browder's right to continue as leader of the Communist movement. Browder, he argued, should "grasp the sword by the handle and speak out as a Communist leader of the country should speak out in this situation."

There was no consensus among other Communist leaders on how to respond to Duclos. Dennis and Green, despite their long and close association with Browder, seemed to have a better sense than most of their colleagues about which way the wind was blowing. They both expressed regret for articles they had written and speeches they had delivered in support of the Teheran line, and Dennis warned that the CPA's leaders would have to be prepared to "remove from posts of responsibility all who resist or fight the main line of the Duclos article." Morris Childs, James Ford, and someone identified in the minutes of the meeting as "Comrade J." (union leaders were frequently identified only by their initials in such inner party documents) all expressed basic agreement with Duclos's criticisms.

John Williamson went along with his acquiescent colleagues, but was clearly irritated with what was happening. At one point he began a sentence by observing, "Since everyone of us including myself (except possibly Comrade Foster) were responsible insofar as we voted for Earl's report . . ." when Foster interjected, "Why do you say 'possibly'?" Williamson responded, "Because I don't think your position was the same as Duclos' article." Browder may already have been brought down a peg by the Duclos article, but there was as yet no stampede among Communist leaders to line up behind Foster. Williamson also complained that, in the year and a half since Browder made his Bridgeport speech, American Communists had received no "indication of other Marxists having any different opinions" until they received Duclos's "political blast . . . which includes conclusions which it is hard to interpret in any other way than the manner in which you deal with a leadership in the last stage of struggle against it."

Roy Hudson, Robert Minor, Benjamin Davis, and Elizabeth Gurley Flynn all defended the CPA and Browder against Duclos's charges, and expressed resentment over the form in which the criticisms were delivered. Flynn was particularly angered. As recorded in the minutes, she criticized Green and Williamson for having accepted Duclos's criticisms so quickly: "It seems to me," she said, "that we should be able in this Board to arrive at the conclusion we were wrong, by our own thinking and by our own effort rather than to have it suddenly catapulted at us by a Communist Party from another country, and then suddenly realize we were wrong. I confess quite frankly I don't altogether understand the mental processes by which the comrades do that."

Only one national board member who spoke that evening seemed entirely comfortable with the new direction pointed by the Duclos article. Robert Thompson, new to the Communists' top leadership, had spent half the previous decade in combat, first in Spain and then in the South Pacific. He now addressed the issue at hand with military precision: "I think it is certainly unfortunate that we have to have errors in our basic policy pointed out to us by Communists of other countries. But that certainly is not the big danger. The big danger is the one this article is going to save us from, and that is the danger of *taking our policy from the American capitalist class*." And he concluded with what was, in essence, a nominating speech for Foster: "I for one think that the essence of the points made in Comrade Duclos' article, the essence of his criticism of our policy has been consistently embodied in the position taken during this period by Comrade Foster."[20]

The meeting ended inconclusively. But when the leaders reassembled the following day, Foster had had enough time to mull over the significance of Thompson's remarks. His attitude toward Browder was far less conciliatory than it had been the previous evening. "I think everybody in the room wants Earl to continue as the head of the Party,'' Foster said, ''but if he goes to the Association with such a line as he presented last night, he is jeopardizing his leadership.''

Browder still offered no concessions. He made it clear to his subordinates that he felt he had nothing to apologize for: ''At no time in the future am I ever going to be a political zombie.'' When Dennis, who had already begun to make his peace with Duclos, asked him to define ''zombie,'' Browder replied, ''A zombie is a modern myth about a dead person who has been raised up by some magical process and walks around under the control of another will.''

Browder's resistance was stiffened by a serious misjudgment about his independent strength within the CPA and the international movement. He apparently believed that in a contest of ideas and influence he could defeat Duclos and his backers. In the coming weeks he planned to devote himself to a ''principled discussion of Marxian politics in the American situation. . . . If anyone accuses me at any time of not being a good Communist because of this, I will answer in the words of Chou En-lai when he was told Molotov had said the Communists of China are not real Communists. Chou En-lai said, 'That merely proves the Chinese Communists are doing their own job.' ''[21]

Those were brave words, well spoken, and in defense of an admirable principle. Whether Browder would have spoken them had he fully realized the consequences of his defiance is questionable, given his past record of conforming to Moscow's demands. He may have misjudged the extent to which Soviet-American relations had already deteriorated; he certainly felt great revulsion to the idea of knuckling under to Foster. Over the next few months Browder would learn that leaders of the Chinese Communist party enjoyed a certain latitude in policy and speech that he did not.

Though unable to bridge the gap between Browder and Foster, the national board agreed to print Duclos's article in the next day's *Daily Worker*, along with Browder's introduction. Foster's telegram was set aside. The board appointed a five-man subcommittee, made up of Browder, Foster, Dennis, ''Comrade J.,'' and Williamson, to draft a resolution on the Duclos article for the next national board meeting, scheduled for June 2. The board also briefly discussed the recent activities of Giuseppe Berti, one of the Italian Communist leaders who had spent the war years in the United States.

Along with his colleague Ambrogio Donini, Berti had occasionally put out a newspaper in English and Italian called *Italy Today*. The first issue of *Italy Today* to appear in five months was published on May 23, and it carried the complete text of the Duclos article. Berti presumably received a copy through his own contacts in Europe, and decided it provided a suitable occasion for declaring the independence of the Italian exiles from the control of the American Communist movement; the May 23 *Italy Today* was issued, for the first time, in the name of the "Delegation of the Italian Communist Party in North America." The PCI enjoyed great prestige among American Communists, some of whom had worked with PCI leaders during the Spanish Civil War. Browder was furious at Berti because he knew that many American Communists would interpret the publication of the article in *Italy Today* as evidence of the PCI's endorsement of Duclos's criticisms, further undermining Browder's already shaky position.

At the national board meeting Browder accused Berti of leaking the article to the New York *World-Telegram*, and implied he might have some secret factional ties with unnamed members of the board. Gil Green conceded that "frankly . . . the question is not even answered as to whether the *World-Telegram* didn't get it from a source of that kind," but added, "I don't think any member of this Board . . . is connected with Berti." Berti and Donini soon returned to Italy—where they were reprimanded by Togliatti for meddling in American Communist affairs—and the question was never resolved as to their role in tipping off the press to Browder's dilemma.[22]

The May 24 *Daily Worker* featured the article, along with Browder's introduction. Browder chose his words carefully, admitting that the Duclos criticism "reflects the general trend of opinion of European Marxists in relation to America," but minimizing its importance. "It has been clear at all times," he wrote, "that the end of the war in Europe would require a fundamental review of all problems by American Marxists. . . . The article of Duclos may conveniently provide a starting point for this fundamental review which the CPA leadership had independently begun some time ago." The CPA, Browder insisted, "will make its own decisions after its own discussions," and in the meantime American Communists would continue to work "along established lines."[23]

At first it seemed that Browder might be able to ride out the storm. The article had shocked CPA members, but the anger and resentment it stirred could go one of two ways. Some Communists like William

Auer, a veteran of thirteen years in the party, were disturbed at the revelation that Browder had suppressed Foster's letter of January 1944. Auer wrote to Browder on the day that the article appeared in the *Daily Worker*, complaining that in 1944 he had swallowed his own doubts about the wisdom of the Teheran line: "I thought your judgement better than mine, I felt that we ought to give this policy a chance to work, and judge by experience. Not knowing Foster's position I assumed that the expulsion of Darcy was correct. Now I don't know, because I don't know the facts."

But other Communists rallied to defend Browder against what they felt to be unwarranted interference from abroad. Anna Rochester, a veteran of the CP's labor defense and women's activities, wrote Browder on May 25 to express her support. Duclos, she felt, had displayed "colossal ignorance" of American political conditions and failed to "grapple with our basic problem: How can a small minority function best in building towards socialism in this country where for historical reasons even the majority of the working class has been hostile to socialism and filled with unreasoning prejudices against the Reds?"[24]

Most Communists probably fell between these two poles, expecting Browder to modify his position along the lines suggested by Duclos, and to continue as the CPA's leader. And in public utterances during the next week, Browder did bend a little. In a speech on May 25 he declared that during the first weeks of the United Nations conference, "the American government departed from the Roosevelt policy, broke the unity of the Big Three and practically put our international relations into the melting pot for complete recasting." He accused Churchill of promoting a "new pattern" of international relations, based on a "world polarized around Soviet-American antagonism."[25]

If Browder had stuck with this theme, he might have salvaged some portion of his power. But by the time the national board reassembled on June 2, he had dug in his heels. Duclos's criticisms of the decision to dissolve the CP, he insisted to the other national board members, were irresponsible: if American Communists had not taken that step in 1944 "Roosevelt would have lost." And, despite all appearances of growing Soviet-American enmity, Browder still believed it remained in the economic interest of American capitalists to uphold the Teheran accords.

Foster disagreed, arguing that without the restraining influence of the "democratic forces" in the United States, "the bourgeoisie would be at war with the Soviet Union in six months." The draft resolution written by the subcommittee appointed at the last national board meeting showed that Foster's views were clearly becoming ascendant. The resolution, entitled "The Present Situation and the Next Tasks," declared that "important groupings of American capital" who had backed the anti-fascist cause until the defeat of Nazi Germany were now seeking to curb "democratic advances in Europe," reestablish a *cordon sanitaire* around the Soviet Union, and place "the entire cost of the war and the difficulties of reconversion upon the shoulders of working people" in America. To counter this threat, American Communists needed to repudiate "erroneous conclusions" they had drawn from the Teheran meeting, including "utopian economic perspectives" and "tendencies to obscure the class nature of bourgeois democracy." The resolution acknowledged the "important contributions which Comrade Foster made in the struggle against opportunism" as well as the influence of the "sound, fraternal, Marxist opinions expressed in the recent article of Jacques Duclos."

Though the resolution repudiated many of Browder's optimistic pronouncements about the postwar world, the program it outlined differed very little from what American Communists were already doing. It listed winning the war against Japan, the sole remaining Axis partner, as the Communists' top priority, and exhorted workers to "continue uninterrupted war production and uphold [the] no-strike pledge for the duration." National unity remained the watchword for Communist activity. The resolution included several favorable references to President Truman, and called on the unions to "utilize the Labor-Management Charter" to secure jobs, union recognition, and higher wages. The resolution said nothing about changing the Communist Political Association back into a Communist party, although it did say that the "character" of the CPA should be that of an "independent, Marxist Party of the working class," regardless of its formal electoral status.

The resolution was close enough to Browder's own perspective that he told the national board he would vote for it if it was amended to include a section calling for the expansion of foreign markets for American goods. But other CPA leaders would no longer humor Browder in his fixation with markets. When the resolution came up for a vote, only Browder voted against it. (Roy Hudson initially abstained, but a day later changed his vote to support it.) All the other board members who had been undecided or opposed to the Duclos criticisms

in May had made their peace with the new order. In words more than
a little reminiscent of Browder's warning to Foster in February 1944,
Foster cautioned Browder not to challenge the tradition of presenting
an appearance of monolithic unity among the movement's leadership:
"If you vote against this resolution you commit political suicide in this
Party. Pay attention to what the Comrades here are saying; they are
not going to allow you to disorient this Party."[26]

The more pressure Foster put on Browder, the more unbending he
became. He would not make himself vulnerable to the kind of humiliation and browbeating that he himself had inflicted on Foster the
previous year. After fifteen years of adulation as the "great-hearted
pilot" of the American Communist movement, after having stood so
many times before an audience of twenty thousand people in Madison
Square Garden and listened as they sang "Browder is our leader, we
shall not be moved," he could not bring himself to take that step.

By the time the CPA's national committee assembled on June 18
for a three-day meeting to consider the board's draft resolution, Browder was unwilling even to sit through its meetings. He delivered a
lengthy speech at the first evening's session, consisting largely of quotations from his own wartime speeches and articles. In defense of his
unwillingness to accept Duclos's criticism, he quoted Stalin to the
effect that "the value of a Communist, among other things, lies in that
he is willing to defend his convictions." (Browder probably did not
select the quotation for ironic effect.) Having said that much, he then
withdrew from any further discussion.

Steve Nelson, who had been an enthusiastic backer of the Teheran
line until the publication of the article, believed that Browder contributed to his own downfall by his behavior at the national committee
meeting: "You know what he did? He went upstairs. We were meeting
on the fifth floor, the New York District office of Party headquarters,
and he went up to the ninth floor and stayed there by himself. . . .
Here's a guy who worked with us all these years and now he's being
challenged, and when the issue is being debated he doesn't even want
to listen to his co-workers."[27]

Browder could not have prevailed at that meeting against the force
of Soviet disapproval implicit in the Duclos article, but his withdrawal
turned defeat into a rout. Denunciations of his policies took on a new
dimension. Elizabeth Gurley Flynn found a sympathetic audience
when she offered an analysis that rooted Browder's revisionist tend-

encies in his character defects. "My advice to Comrade Browder," she said, "is to break down your reserves, which have been a barrier between you and your fellow-workers, and find your answers among people, not in research and study alone. You are a hard man to talk to, nobody feels he really knows you, nobody feels free to approach you." Browder's personal aloofness made him "magnify the importance of contacting influential persons rather than masses." Flynn advised him to make a pilgrimage around the country, "unhonored and unsung" to "find the key to unlock the closed mind and once again 'Free Earl Browder.' "[28]

Other national committee members tore into Browder's economic and political doctrines. Once again, only Browder refused to vote for the new draft resolution (slightly amended at the meeting to eliminate the favorable reference to the Labor-Management Charter, and changing such equivocal formulations as "important groupings of American capital" in favor of the straightforward designation "American capital"). The national committee scheduled a special convention of the CPA for the end of July to consider the resolution and the future organizational status of the Communist movement. They appointed a three-man secretariat, consisting of Foster, Dennis, and Williamson, to guide CPA activities in the interim. Browder temporarily retained the title of president, but his reign on the ninth floor had come to an end.[29]

The Rank-and-File Response

Shortly after the publication of "The Present Situation and the Next Tasks," the *Daily Worker* announced it would begin carrying a page in each issue which readers could use to comment on the issues raised by the Duclos article. What followed in the month and a half between this invitation and the special CPA convention was an unprecedented outpouring of rank-and-file criticism of party policies. Perhaps a quarter of the dozens of letters printed in the *Daily Worker* in those weeks still expressed sympathy for the Teheran line—a surprisingly high percentage considering that as early as June 4, when the draft resolution was first published, it should have been apparent that if Browder was going to survive in the leadership, it would only be at the price of repudiating his past views. Yet even after June 21, when

CPA members learned that Browder had been excluded from the new ruling triumvirate, pro-Teheran letters continued to come in.[30] Another quarter of the letters simply endorsed the criticisms of the Teheran line that Foster and Duclos had made—and these included a number of contributions from leaders offering apologies for having supported Browder's position earlier. (Robert Thompson's mea culpa, for example, referred to his acceptance first of *Victory and After*, then of *Teheran*: "I conditioned myself to swallowing an opportunist gnat and as is inevitable in such cases wound up by swallowing elephants." This was one of the more colorful moments in an otherwise dreary ritual.)[31]

Most of the letters were harder to classify as either pro- or anti-Browder. Browder's suppression of Foster's January 1944 letter, rather than the Teheran policies per se, aroused the most anger. Many of the readers proceeded to a more general attack on the movement's undemocratic internal structure and political practice. One writer complained to the *New Masses* (which also opened its pages to critical letters) about the near unanimity with which Communist leaders had once backed Browder's policies, declaring, "The error arose primarily because the mentality of *New Masses* editors, like that of our entire organization, excluded independent thinking. Democratic centralism became a farce and since this is the source of the mistake, this is the greatest threat, to *New Masses* and our movement, not the revisionist error itself."[32]

Some CPA members ridiculed the agility with which their leaders had leapt from strongly pro-Teheran positions in May to equally strong anti-Teheran positions in June. Two Communist seamen, who opposed the Teheran line, wrote to the *Daily Worker* at the end of June and sent along a quotation from the third act of *Hamlet* in which Prince Hamlet, feigning madness, torments a pliable Polonius:

> HAMLET: Do you see yonder cloud that's almost in the shape of a camel?
> POLONIUS: By the mass, and 'tis like a camel indeed.
> HAMLET: Methinks it is like a weasel.
> POLONIUS: It is backed like a weasel.
> HAMLET: Or like a whale.
> POLONIUS: Very like a whale . . .

The two writers concluded, "It ill behooves our National Committee to have played Polonius. Certainly, we, the rank and file, must never again permit ourselves to play Polonius to anyone's Hamlet."[33]

Another CPA member, who did not take a position either in favor of or in opposition to the Teheran line, complained about the ideological intimidation used in the CPA's branches to stifle dissent: "The membership must be able to know and feel that they can disagree with older Communists or leading personnel without being classed as Trotskyites, Social Democrats, Nationalist Negroes, Ivory Tower Intellectuals, Male Chauvinists or disrupters. In other words, all must be made to know the difference between Marxian self-criticism and name calling."[34]

Another writer, opposed to the Teheran line, offered a critique of the Communist movement's approach to politics for many years past: "Each period's 'line' is out of the blue; the slogans of the day are treated as though they were basic, and independent concepts. Tactics are mistaken for strategy; strategy for policy. We ride our slogans to death and they all become 'at all costs' propositions."[35]

A month into the debate, criticisms of Communist policies spilled over from the letters page to the *Daily Worker*'s own columns. Most historians have dismissed Mike Gold, author of the *Daily Worker*'s "Change the World" column, as a Stalinist hack who early on squandered whatever creative gifts he may have brought to the party. During the Nazi-Soviet pact, for example, he proved himself capable of the crudest kind of polemics. But on occasion he showed a spark of independence by articulating rank-and-file sentiment, even if it meant going against the official line. Gold wrote a few columns early in the summer of 1945 celebrating the post-Duclos discussion as a model of democracy in action. But in mid-July he abruptly changed tone. In a column entitled "The Heat Wave and Aaron Burr," he offered some whimsical observations intended to conceal—though just barely—a highly unflattering assessment of the CPA's leaders.

Gold began with some conventional comments about Aaron Burr, whose flirtation with the British in the early nineteenth century had often been pointed to by American Communists seeking a local analogy for the acts of treason allegedly revealed by the Moscow trials. Burr was "brilliant and unstable, with an ego big as hell. The Trotsky of the American Revolution." Gold took comfort in the idea that such leaders usually met their just desserts while the "great people's movement rolls inevitably onward." Thus far the column seemed to be a portrait of Burr as Trotsky as Browder. Then Gold suddenly broadened the attack. "Hot weather makes me feel irritable, however, about leaders who get too big for their breeches," he wrote. "Our leadership is now complaining about a lack of push buttons in their offices. Their idea of a perfect society is one where our leaders sit and push buttons and the people act and think in response.''

Gold suggested that the Communist movement could be strengthened if, in the future, it held all speeches down to ten minutes and if it reinstituted ''the old IWW theory of rotation in office,'' restricting leaders to a one-year term, subject to immediate recall by the members. Of course, Gold continued, it was a hot day, and he was not thinking clearly at all, but he had one more suggestion: ''How about giving the women a chance? Women are as smart as men. . . . Women are realistic, and rarely succumb to a lot of fine-spun abstract theory. . . . A male leadership often shows the most unusual talent in hindsight. They can explain brilliantly every error and crime of the past. But why do they show so little foresight?'' He went on in the same vein for several paragraphs, then concluded, ''We need a real sweeping, dusting, cleaning of the house. Women can do it. It's a hot day, ladies, gentlemen and comrades, and this is all I can think up today.''[36]

The last thing the CPA's new leaders wanted was a ''real cleaning of the house.'' They wanted a nice, manageable discussion that could be turned off at the appropriate moment, and then have things return to normal, with a new line and a few different names on the office stationery. Gold's column signaled that the debate was getting out of hand. In the next week's *Worker* Elizabeth Gurley Flynn was assigned the task of informing Gold that women were not necessarily any smarter than men. She also presented Gold with a none too discreet ultimatum: ''If I felt as you do, Mike, I'd quit writing my column.'' And in the next day's *Daily Worker* she warned against excessive self-flagellation in the party's current reevaluation: ''Our collective duty is to get our ship back on its charted course with as few fatalities as possible. The captain may jump overboard (at present he remains in his cabin and his intentions are obscure), but should we demand the crew jump overboard, too?''[37]

Two days later the *Daily Worker* printed its last discussion page, and the Communist movement's brief experiment with internal free speech came to an end.

But even earlier, as the debate raged in the pages of the *Daily Worker* and the *New Masses*, Communists across the country assembled in branch, city, and state meetings to repudiate the Teheran line and to call for a return to the name ''Communist party.'' On occasion these meetings became the scene for hysterical scenes of self-criticism and denunciations of past revisionist crimes. The pressure against any public dissent became intense.[38] Not many Communists could stand against it.

In a letter to the *Daily Worker* in mid-June, Whitey Goodfriend, a member of the Maryland CPA, describing an experience he had at a meeting of the Maryland state committee a few days earlier, wrote: "One of our old time members who has been through the 'wars' for 30 years met me. He asked 'Where do you stand in this business?' I answered, 'Well I'm still with Teheran.' He said, 'Listen, if you get up at that meeting and take Browder's position, I'll throw you out of the hall.'" Goodfriend took that as a symbol. "That was the working class saying it would reject and discard me, and the working class [would] because of its class instinct, reject us and our organization for following Teheranism." As a result of this experience, he was now a firm supporter of the new line. He offered Browder this advice: "Forget your formulations, systems of ideas and thinking. Forget your theories and listen to my feeling—listen to the working class instincts."[39]

It proved easy for the Communists, marginal to American working-class life even at the height of their influence, to turn themselves inside out in the name of remaining true to their "working class instincts." Goodfriend's blood-and-soil rhapsody all too accurately reflected the quality of the Communists' deliberations that summer.

The End of the CPA

The pull of party loyalty and the anticipation of returning to the class struggle guaranteed Foster absolute control by the time of the July convention. Who, after all, wanted to shake J. P. Morgan's hand at a time when Communists throughout Europe and Asia either held or were on the brink of grasping state power, and when Churchill's defeat in the parliamentary elections seemed to show that even in the most developed capitalist countries the thunder could be on the left? Browder's continued calls for national unity and expanded foreign markets already had a kind of musty odor.[40] Most of the Communists who had initially supported Browder had by this point fallen silent or publicly recanted, as Anna Rochester would in a letter to the *Daily Worker* in late June.[41]

When the CPA's emergency national convention assembled at the end of July, there was no longer any room for debate. Browder knew it, and though he offered some criticisms of the draft resolution, he did so, as he told the delegates, without "any expectation of changing your basic decisions." He pledged not to form a "Browder opposition" within the party, but warned the delegates that it was "a naive view that this convention of the CPA will decide and close the discussion on all these questions." His reference to the ultimate authority in Communist affairs was unmistakable. He had by this point convinced himself that he was the victim of some Byzantine conspiracy in the Kremlin carried out without Stalin's sanction, and he hoped to regain his leadership through a favorable decision on appeal in Moscow.[42]

Browder's warning did not impress the delegates. They proceeded with a minimum of discussion and no dissent to reestablish the Communist party and to elect Foster as its chairman. They also passed an amended version of the board's draft resolution. The resolution had previously noted the "important contributions" Foster had made in the struggle against revisionism, but it was now amended to praise the "sterling leadership and important contributions" of Comrade Foster. During the convention Foster condemned the "sickening adulation and hero-worship" of the Browder period, but after so many years in the wilderness he was already showing signs that he was not averse to receiving a little of that adulation for himself.[43]

The delegates elected a national board and national committee that purged some of Browder's former allies. For the time being, the CP functioned without anyone in the post of general secretary, and was led instead by a four-man secretariat consisting of Foster, Dennis, Williamson, and Thompson. Dennis and Williamson had retreated in good order from their previous support for Teheran; both were highly skilled inner-party technicians, and Foster needed their support in consolidating the new regime. Thompson was brought into the innermost circle of leaders as Foster's protégé and would soon replace Gil Green as the leader of the CP's important New York state organization. Green, who had retreated in good order, remained on the national committee and was appointed leader of the Illinois CP. But he would spend many years living down his past close association with Browder.

Thompson's promotion to the leadership of the New York organization also reflected neo-populist suspicions within the party that New York City's "petty-bourgeois" influences had prepared the way for Browder's revisionism. One CPA member wrote to the *Daily*

Worker during the pre-convention debate to suggest that Communist national headquarters be moved to Detroit, and New York district headquarters to Buffalo, since the corrupting environs of New York City could not "give our leadership a correct pulse of the basic worker."[44] Though the CP headquarters remained where they were, Louis Weinstock of the Painters Union, Irving Potash of the Fur Workers Union, and Josh Lawrence of the National Maritime Union were all promoted to the new CP national board, replacing familiar faces from the Browder era like Ford, Hudson, and Minor.[45]

In the weeks after the convention the new leaders struggled to get the organization functioning again. The prolonged dispute over the Duclos article had paralyzed most of the Communists' external political activities, and had not helped the movement's internal life. Recruiting ceased, the *Worker*'s circulation dropped precipitously, dues payments and attendance at meetings fell, and many members drifted away.[46] The Communists began a circulation drive for the *Worker* and tightened up dues-payment procedures and attendance requirements. Foster reversed Browder's emphasis on large, neighborhood-based branches. The biggest clubs were split up into smaller units, and the party reestablished its system of shop units for trade-union members.

The war ended a month after the CP's reconstitution. American workers responded to victory by launching just such a "great outburst of strike struggles" that Browder had earlier warned against and which the Communists now welcomed. Bottled-up wartime demands gave way to the greatest strike wave since 1919. The Communists were convinced that another great depression was imminent, and that a militant, well-organized labor movement would provide fertile ground for the growth of class consciousness. The mood among CP members resembled that which had followed the publication of Browder's "Open Letter" of 1933, which had made it the primary task of Communists to root the party's organization in industry—but this time the Communists could draw on a sizable trade-union base and a pool of experienced cadres unlike anything they possessed a dozen years before.

At the July convention Williamson outlined a program for recruiting heavily among industrial workers, with the goal of making them a majority in the New York, California, and eastern Pennsylvania districts, and three-quarters of the membership in Michigan, Illinois, and Ohio in 1946.[47] In December he unveiled a plan to send "six of our most experienced and leading comrades" to the small industrial heart-

land cities of Youngstown, Gary, Flint, McKeesport, Toledo, and
Kansas City, "with the task of building the party during 1946 to
500–1000 dues-paying members in each city."[48] This ambitious plan
caught the party's imagination and fueled a kind of "No fortresses
Bolsheviks cannot storm" mood within the ranks.

In his December remarks, Williamson laid particular stress on the
need to reinvolve the thousands of CP members and YCLers returning
from service in the armed forces. He frankly described the importance
of these veterans to the party's plans for broadening its influence outside of New York: "Aside from the invaluable experience and political
prestige these comrades have, they will also have something that none
of us at home have had the opportunity to acquire—the ability to mix
and get along with a cross-section of average Americans."[49]

But CP leaders also felt some apprehension about the veterans'
return. The veterans had left for the armed forces when Browder was
still the undisputed leader; they had not shared direct responsibility
for the "revisionist errors" of the war years, and thus were not likely
to be stampeded by a sense of guilt into repudiating Browderism; and
their experiences in the military had often led them to feel that the CP
needed to be doing even more to Americanize its structure and ideology
than it had done under Browder. As one former Brooklyn section
leader later described his feeling after three years in the Army Air
Corps:

> I came out convinced, first, that despite all the prejudice that this or that
> guy might have, if you scratched him you'd find a very deep-set democratic
> tradition. If you were skillful enough to reach that, you were able to go
> places with him. But to do so we had to learn a whole new vocabulary.
> Second, we had developed a deep feeling of patriotism. Before we had
> made a cardinal error in allowing ourselves to be presented as anti-Amer-
> ican and pro-Russian. The starting point for American Marxists would
> have to be that of a passionate defense of the whole concept of American
> democracy. And third, I learned you couldn't operate under false premises.
> You couldn't talk to guys about one thing and use that as leverage to get
> them into something else. These things came to me piece by piece, but
> when I got out of the army I already had a rough framework.

Such ideas, he noted, however inchoate they might have been in 1945,
made the veterans potential "political dynamite" within the party.[50]

The new party leaders organized a veterans commission and published a special pamphlet for returning veterans, carrying greetings

from Foster, his January 1944 letter opposing the Teheran line, and Duclos's article. Many former rank-and-file Communists never got around to reading the pamphlet. They took the opportunity provided by their uprooting and the GI Bill to get established in new communities, start in business, or return to school. Those departing did not usually openly break with the party; they simply failed to reestablish contact or drifted away after a few months of casual membership.[51]

But the Communists had more success in winning back those veterans who came out of the secondary leadership. They were offered the most attractive positions in the hierarchy. Many had been in the movement for ten or fifteen years, and it seemed to them that they were now coming into their own. All they had to do was to accept the new leaders, recite a few ritual phrases in condemnation of Browder's policies, and then claim their inheritance.

George Charney returned to New York in the spring of 1945 after fighting in the South Pacific. He was offered, and accepted, the position of county organizer for the Manhattan CP organization. Though he had previously sympathized with the Teheran line, he now had the responsibility of upholding the "anti-revisionist" cause. He later offered this description of the August 1945 convention that reconstituted the CP in Manhattan: "Over 1,500 delegates and visitors crowded every inch of space at Irving Plaza, and my report was greeted with tumultuous applause. I was excited and tremendously proud, and yet I could not help thinking of the Roman general in Plutarch who, after returning from a victorious campaign, addressed the multitude and, when a certain remark evoked great applause, turned to his friend and asked, 'What have I said amiss?' "[52] But it was much easier for Charney and the other returning veterans to accept the applause than to make a futile stand on as yet ill-defined differences with Foster's policies.

Besides, there still seemed to be a great deal of continuity between Browder's policies and those adopted by the newly reconstituted CP. Foster, reporting on the July convention, made it clear that the party did not expect to be leading a revolution in the immediate future. The convention had made socialism "a matter of mass education, but not . . . an issue of today's political struggle."[53] The party remained committed to the "Center-Left" coalition under Murray's leadership in the CIO, to working with Hillman in the ALP, to backing the Democratic candidate William O'Dwyer in the fall's New York City mayoral election, and to cooperating with New Deal Democrats like Henry Wallace, then Secretary of Commerce (who had received two favorable references in Duclos's article), to keep the Truman Administration loyal to the "Roosevelt legacy."

The new political directions the party took in the next year were less changes in program or strategy than changes of mood and tactic. As Gil Green had noted back in 1939, with Browder the "main emphasis" was always being placed on "the question of the Party in long term alliances with the . . . democratic front," while with Foster the emphasis was on "the individual role of the Party without . . . worrying about the relationship of the Party to this broader mass movement."[54]

What that difference in political emphasis would mean began to become apparent in Ben Davis's city council reelection campaign in the fall of 1945. Tammany Hall had withdrawn its earlier endorsement of Davis, under pressure from O'Dwyer, who did not want to share a ticket with a Communist. The ALP had its own candidate in the field for councilman from Manhattan, Eugene Connolly, who had worked closely with the Communists in the past. But Davis feared that an independent ALP candidacy would threaten his own chances for reelection. Despite Hillman's and Marcantonio's opposition to having the ALP endorse him, Davis pressured Connolly to withdraw from the race, arguing that any compromise on the issue would represent a capitulation to white chauvinism. Gil Green worked to prevent an open split over the issue, and eventually both Davis and Connolly were elected, but unnecessary bad feelings had been stirred up between the party and some of its closest political allies. Green, in a short time, would not be around to act as conciliator, and his successor, Thompson, was not known for a willingness to compromise.[55]

The Cold War Begins

As the Communists moved to the left, American foreign policy (followed by American public opinion) moved to the right. By May Truman had already begun to adopt a "get tough" stance toward the Soviet Union. When American planes dropped atomic bombs on Hiroshima and Nagasaki in August the Communists raised no objection, particularly since the Soviet Union had officially joined the war against Japan that month. But they were not oblivious to the new factor these bombs introduced in American-Soviet relations. "Some voices already have been heard," the *Daily Worker* noted on August 8, "that because the

United States is splitting the atom, the United States can afford to split the United Nations."[56] The Communists, who under Browder had campaigned for maintaining the draft in the postwar era, now came out for rapid demobilization. By late autumn the CP had called its followers into the streets to demonstrate against American military intervention on behalf of Chiang Kai-shek, while the National Maritime Union threatened a work stoppage to dramatize its call for bringing American soldiers home from Europe and Asia.[57]

The political tolerance the Communists had enjoyed during the war unraveled as swiftly as the Soviet-American alliance. Hearings before the House Military Affairs Committee in the spring of 1945, probing alleged Communist "infiltration" of the army's officer corps, were one harbinger of evil days to come. Another was the *"Amerasia* case" in the summer of 1945 when a journalistic leak to an independent leftist magazine was blown up by the Justice Department and the newspapers into a spy scandal. For the first time the issue of Communist infiltration of the State Department had been publicly raised, and a pattern of identification between communism and Soviet espionage, dormant since the days of the Nazi-Soviet pact, had been revived.[58]

The defection of *Daily Worker* editor Louis Budenz later that fall reinforced this image. Budenz announced in testimony before the House Un-American Activities Committee that "the Communist Party in the United States is a direct arm of the Soviet Foreign Department," and that every American Communist "is a potential spy against the United States."[59]

Budenz's defection came as a shock to the Communists, and the CP's leaders were quick to blame Browder's ideological laxness for permitting a former member of an "enemy organization" to rise to such a responsible position (Budenz had been a member of A. J. Muste's Workers party before joining the CP in 1935). They used the occasion of Budenz's defection to tighten further their ideological control within the party. Williamson declared in the December issue of *Political Affairs* that "the main lesson from the Budenz case is to recognize that we are not only surrounded by the class enemy, but that the enemy's agents are also at work inside our ranks." He made it clear that he was not just talking about FBI plants—of whom there were a large number in the CP, and who for the most part would go undiscovered until they chose to reveal themselves as prosecution witnesses at the Smith Act trials—but instead was concerned with genuine Communists who might, by dint of being exposed to one or another political heresy, follow Budenz's route. The CP had established a national review commission at its July convention, charged with overseeing the party's internal security. Now Williamson declared that "the Review Commission must examine the leadership from top to bottom and emphasize the need of constant vigilance against political deterioration."[60]

Even as it was seeking new recruits to fill depleted ranks, the party began a wave of expulsions against those who strayed too far to the right or the left in political outlook. Bella Dodd, the CP's New York state legislative director, fell into disfavor in 1946 for her reluctance to abandon a Browder-style coalitionist approach to non-Communists in the ALP; she lingered on in the party's periphery until finally being expelled in 1949.[61] More numerous were the expulsions on the left, of those who felt that Foster had not gone far enough in breaking with Browder's policies and associates. Among this group were Ruth McKinney and Bruce Minton of the *New Masses*, old-time party leaders like William Dunne and Max Bedacht, ex-Wobblies like Vern Smith and Harrison George, and a number of NMU leaders and rank-and-file members. Perhaps as many as several thousand Communists were expelled for one or another brand of "political deterioration" in the first years after the war. (Some of those expelled for "left deviations" formed little sect groups devoted to winning the CP back to their vision of true Marxism-Leninism. One such New York–based group, the Maritime Committee for a Communist Party, attracted the temporary adherence of Sam Darcy. In the aftermath of the Duclos affair many Communists expected Darcy to return in honor to the CP's leadership, but Foster, for obvious reasons, found Darcy's presence embarrassing. When Darcy met with the CP's new leaders in the summer of 1945 he bridled at the suggestion that he submit his writings to them to be judged for ideological purity.)[62]

Browder's Expulsion

During all the uproar in the fall of 1945, little was heard from the party's former leader, in exile in his home in Yonkers. Nominally a member of the Yonkers party club, Browder stayed away from its meetings and neither sought nor was offered any political assignments. To support himself, and to secure an outlet for his economic doctrines, he started a mimeographed publication entitled *Distributor's Guide*, subsidized by a small group of businessmen close to the party. Though he refrained from using it for any direct comment on CP policies, party leaders decided to treat the *Distributor's Guide* as Browder's first move in a factional campaign. Williamson wrote to Browder in early January, declaring that the views expressed in his newsletter were "not in accord with the policies of the Party."

In the weeks that followed, the national board publicly charged Browder with neglecting his party duties, with spreading Keynesian and "social-imperialist" ideas, and with factionalism. Browder refused to take part in tribunals held before the party's secretariat and its national board. On February 12 the Yonkers club voted for his expulsion, with the only dissenting vote cast by Browder's brother William, who would shortly be expelled from the CP. The next day the national committee unanimously upheld Browder's expulsion. Robert Thompson expressed satisfaction with the vote: "It will close the door with finality on the period in which our Party has been an arena of struggle between Browderism and Marxism."[63]

The triumph of the Foster-Thompson leadership closed the door on a lot more than was apparent to the Communists at the time.

The End of Browderism

What was this "Browderism" that Thompson so scorned? The party did not, and could not, abandon overnight the attitudes and tactics it had adopted in the years of Browder's leadership. The coalition policies to which the Communists remained formally committed up to and past the Progressive party campaign in 1948 were not so different from what Browder himself might have ordered had he remained in power. But if willing to leave the form of party activity unchanged for the moment, the new leaders were determined to change its content. For Thompson, "Browderism" meant a utopian belief in the possibility of peaceful coexistence between socialism and capitalism in international relations. Browder's successors in the CP's leadership found their authority strengthened in the years after 1945 by the fact that, after all, Browder had clearly been proven wrong on this point. The "spirit of Teheran" was a distant memory and hollow joke by 1946.

But to understand "Browderism" simply in the terms in which it was presented to party members in 1945–1946, as a set of easily disprovable economic and political doctrines, misses the most important difference between Browder's leadership and that which came after him. "Browderism" held the potential for leading to something other than itself—sheltering and lending legitimacy to the efforts of those American Communists who had the capacity for and commitment to finding what would later be described as the "American Road to Socialism"—even if in 1944 and 1945 taking any road to socialism was the last thing on Browder's mind. Foster looked to political and economic cataclysms—a new depression, the triumph of fascism in America, a third world war—as the motor for social change. It was all right for the Communists to dabble in coalition politics in the meantime, as they would with the Progressive party campaign in 1948, but that could never represent more than a tactical orientation. When it came time to launch the struggle for socialism, when events had finally produced a working class ready to respond to revolutionary leadership, the Communists would follow the classic outline derived from the Bolsheviks' experience in 1917.

By the end of the Second World War Browder no longer had much interest in revolution, but he had begun to understand a great deal more about the nature of class consciousness than Foster's catastrophic determinism allowed for. As he wrote to L. L. Sharkey in the spring of 1945, criticizing the Australian Communists' policies, the "practical task" of Communists in Australia (and, by implication, in the United States) "may be summed up in the organization and training of the working class in the solution of all the problems of the nation, to make it capable of becoming the ruling class some day. . . . We must not sentimentally idealize the working class as it now exists, but must realistically evaluate and energetically combat all those characteristics that show themselves within the working class that reduce its capacity of leadership in the nation."[64]

Browder did not intend to wait for catastrophes. He wanted the Communists to play as important a role as they could in the country's political affairs—which in 1944–1945 meant to him working closely with the mainstream leaders of the CIO and the Democratic party. His political vision was limited by his craving for respectability, his penchant for behind-the-scenes maneuvering, his attachment to the chimeras of Teheran. But something else might have been built on the foundations he provided.

In the aftermath of the 1956 crisis Browder found an unlikely admirer in the person of an old adversary, Alexander Bittelman. Bittelman had been one of Foster's most consistent allies during the 1930s in the disputes within the CP's leadership. But in a book he had privately published in 1960 (having been expelled from the CP the preceding year for expressing these and other heretical ideas), Bittelman conceded that under Browder's leadership, "the Party was beginning to find its way to the peculiar and specific approaches to the masses of American labor and its allies. . . . Browderism was an attempt to *generalize* the Party's experience of that period and to draw certain technical and political conclusions." Though retaining many disagreements with Browder's wartime policies, Bittelman now disapproved of the way the party broke with Browderism. "The Party leadership completely threw overboard the experiences and successes gained in the New Deal and World War II," he wrote, "instead of utilizing, modifying and adjusting them to the period of the 'cold war.'"[65]

Browderism was not the American Road to Socialism. But the Communists faced a more prosaic task in 1945: finding the road to a stable, ongoing, genuinely democratic socialist movement. When they stepped back from Browderism they took a fatal detour off that road.

EPILOGUE:
GENERATIONS IN CONFLICT
The 1950s and the 1960s

What is the price of Experience? do men buy it for a song?
Or wisdom for a dance in the street? No, it is bought with
  the price
Of all that a man hath, his house, his wife, his children.
Wisdom is sold in the desolate market where none come to buy,
And in the wither'd field where the farmer plows for bread in vain.
    —WILLIAM BLAKE[1]

THE YEARS THAT FOLLOWED the Second World War were, in Dalton Trumbo's apt phrase, "the time of the toad." Anti-communism became for many in the United States a state religion, and informing a kind of sacrament.[2] The earlier Red Scares of the century, following the First World War and during the Nazi-Soviet pact, had run their course in a matter of a few years, and even at their height Communists had been able to find refuge and some defenders in the ranks of labor, liberals, and civil libertarians. But this time the investigating committees, the loyalty oaths, the firings and blacklistings, the spy trials and sedition trials rolled on year after year with little sign of slackening.[3]

The American Communists held a fortress besieged by overwhelming forces in those years. Whatever judgment one makes of their beliefs and actions, the fact that so many persevered through the worst of the anti-Communist hysteria of the late 1940s and early 1950s stands as eloquent testimony to their courage and commitment. More than a hundred leaders of the Communist party, including many of those who figured prominently in the events of 1939 to 1945, were indicted and convicted under the Smith Act. Many served long terms in prison, and all expected to. Screenwriters in Hollywood, schoolteachers in New York City, and thousands of other people around the country were driven from their jobs for having joined or sympathized with the party or one of its front organizations, or simply for refusing to inform on others. Membership in the party made one not only a political pariah but a criminal. The 1950 McCarran Act declared that Communists "in effect repudiate their allegiance to the United States and in effect transfer their allegiance" to the Soviet Union. The law required all Communists to register with the Attorney General and gave the federal government authority to arrest and imprison them in the event of an "internal security emergency."[4]

During the years between Pearl Harbor and the defeat of Germany and Japan, the Communists had hoped their wartime service would entitle them to full political and legal citizenship. Instead, when the war ended they found their contribution to the victory over fascism interpreted as further evidence of their subversive intentions. Carl Marzani, who served in the economics division of the OSS during the war and was transferred with the rest of the division to the State Department at war's end, found himself indicted for having denied Communist party membership in hearings before the Civil Service Comission. According to Marzani, OSS leaders from Donovan on down knew perfectly well about his past affiliations, and encouraged him in his lack of candor as the only way to circumvent the anti-Communist provisions of the Hatch Act. Earl Latham, a historian writing on the "Communist controversy in Washington" years after the passions of that controversy supposedly had died away, noted Marzani's exemplary record of service in both the OSS and the State Department and commented: "Thus did professional skill lead to advancements which enlarged the opportunity for devious service."[5] That neither Marzani nor any other Communist veteran of the OSS was ever formally charged, let alone convicted, of acts of "devious service" did not seem to matter.

Military veterans of the war fared as badly. Robert Thompson's Distinguished Service Cross entitled him, in the eyes of Judge Harold Medina at the 1949 Smith Act trial of Communist leaders, to merely a slightly reduced prison sentence. When Thompson died in 1962, an unforgiving government tried to keep him from being buried with other veterans in Arlington National Cemetery. Saul Wellman, like Thompson a veteran of both the Lincoln Brigade and the U.S. Army, severely wounded at Bastogne, found his disability payments cut off by the Veterans Administration after his Smith Act conviction and was billed nearly $10,000 for back payments.[6]

The Communists were not the only ones to suffer. Accusations of being "soft on Communism" destroyed the careers of some liberal politicians, and led others to embrace the policies of their opponents in order to survive in the poisoned atmosphere of the Truman-Mc-Carthy Red Scare.

The aftereffects of a decade of witch hunts are still felt in American public life. The ideological intimidation of those years skewed to the right the public debate over America's domestic and—especially—foreign policies. Each successive presidential administration strove to prove it could be a tougher opponent of the international Communist conspiracy than its predecessor—a narrowing of policy choices that eventually led to the Gulf of Tonkin and the roof of the American embassy building in Saigon.

"Five Minutes to Midnight"

Within this greater madness, American Communists embraced policies of suicidal delusion. With the United States preparing for conflict with the Soviet Union, the Communists were going to be in for a bad time regardless of what they did. But, as even Foster would later concede, the actual political choices they made in the decade after the Second World War made matters much worse than they need have been.[7] With Foster and Thompson pointing the way, the Communists adopted what came to be known as the "five minutes to midnight" line, expecting in short order a new depression, the triumph of domestic fascism, and the outbreak of war between the United States and the Soviet Union.

Rather than taking full advantage of the political space still available to them to maneuver in, the Communists adopted a last-ditch-stand mentality. They squandered on Henry Wallace's doomed 1948 Progressive party campaign the political resources they had so painstakingly built up during the Popular Front and the Second World War.[8] By insisting that the party's trade-union influentials go down the line in support of Wallace and in opposition to the Marshall Plan, the Communists handed the mainstream leaders of the CIO the weapon they needed to expel the left-led unions. In a series of pointless confrontations, the Communists forced the leaders of the Transport Workers Union, District 65, and other left strongholds to choose between their allegiance to the party and their responsibility to their own union membership—a choice that almost invariably went against the party.[9]

In imitation of events in the Eastern European "People's Democracies," the Communists conducted an internal purge of their membership, driving hundreds out of the party and some into the arms of the FBI.[10] When the top party leaders were brought to trial in 1949, Foster insisted that they undertake an active defense of their theoretical and political positions, rather than concentrating on civil liberties issues. As a result, the eleven defendants and their lawyers wound up in long, fruitless exchanges with the prosecution over the true meaning of passages in the works of Marx, Lenin, and Stalin—a strategy that brought neither legal nor political benefit.[11]

When the U.S. Supreme Court rejected the appeal of the first Smith Act trial defendants in 1951, opening the way for a wave of indictments against the party's "second string" leadership, the Communists responded by setting in motion long-established plans to move to an underground organization. This decision took hundreds of the most trusted and experienced activists—precisely those who should have been representing the Communists' public face in those difficult years—and removed them from effective political activity. At a time when recruiting was out of the question, thousands of Communists were dropped from the party's membership rolls for a suspected lack of commitment, part of the preparation for illegal struggle. Four of the eleven CP leaders convicted in 1949 added years to already stiff prison sentences by becoming "unavailable" instead of surrendering to federal authorities in 1951, and if Foster had had his way, the other seven defendants would have joined them in this folly.[12]

Were any Communists of a mind to challenge Foster's leadership, he could whip them back into line with charges of "Browderism," a term of abuse which had by then acquired the same proscriptive force that had formerly been reserved for the charge of "Trotskyism."[13]

The Challenge to Orthodoxy

Yet even during these years, this "Zhdanov era" of American communism when external and internal pressures converged to enforce ideological conformity, faint stirrings of dissent could be heard. The Communists' "second string" leaders in New York and California, on trial for violation of the Smith Act, rejected the legal strategy that had served the Foley Square defendants so poorly. Foster attacked them for "legalistic illusions," but the California defense—centering on constitutional and civil libertarian arguments against the Smith Act—

served as the basis for later successful appeals.[14] Differences in legal strategy reflected differences on larger political questions. California state leaders disputed Foster's estimate of the imminence of war and fascism, and resisted pressure from the CP's national leaders to close down the party's public activities and shift to the underground existence already adopted in other states. Foster labeled them "right opportunists," but the California CP survived the worst years of the Cold War with a significantly smaller membership loss than that suffered in other parts of the country.[15]

In New York the state's underground leadership provided the core of dissent from official policies. The underground cadres were drawn largely from the generation which entered the party in the early 1930s, and for whom the Popular Front and the Second World War were formative political experiences. For many of them, their self-imposed exile in the early 1950s represented the first opportunity they had enjoyed to study and question their own past political history; by 1953–1954 they had grown very critical of Foster's leadership. When the Communists began to dissolve their underground apparatus in 1954, the former "unavailables" carried their own questions back to a wider audience within the party.[16]

The *Daily Worker*'s foreign desk represented another center of dissent, as foreign editor Joseph Starobin and his successor Joseph Clark both came to question Foster's doctrine on the imminence of war. After Starobin and Clark initially raised the issue in the early 1950s, Foster attempted to have them expelled. In 1955 Starobin refrained from formally re-registering as a party member in protest of Foster's policies; his book *Paris to Peking*, published that year by a non-Communist publisher and attacked in the Communist press for its cautious criticism of past policies, found a substantial readership within the party.[17]

Events in the Soviet Union and Eastern Europe in the years following Stalin's death fed into the ferment within the American CP. In 1949 Stalin denounced Tito, the independent-minded leader of the Yugoslav Communist movement, as an agent of western imperialism. In 1955 Khrushchev traveled to Belgrade to apologize. If Tito was not an American hireling, then the charges brought against other Eastern European Communist leaders like Laszlo Rajk and Rudolf Slansky, arrested and executed as Tito's agents, no longer made any sense. And if the Soviets could now acknowledge that the Yugoslav Communist party had the right to find its own road to socialism, might they not have been mistaken in 1945 when they engineered the demotion of Browder, so long scorned by his former comrades as the American Tito?

Few American Communists made all the connections before the spring of 1956, but once the first questions were asked, they suggested a hundred more. Starobin would later describe the mood in Communist circles in the months before the Soviet Communist party's Twentieth Congress as "a vast intellectual black market in which many of us traded, half in a daze, unable to voice everything on our minds."[18] When Eugene Dennis and John Gates returned to active roles as leaders in January 1956 after serving their Smith Act prison sentences—Dennis as general secretary and Gates as editor of the *Daily Worker*—they found many party members ready to embrace the "re-examinationist" views they had both come to hold while in jail. In 1956, Khrushchev's speech attacking Stalin would, at one and the same time, lift the American CP's reevaluation to a qualitatively higher level and undermine the whole process.

Khrushchev delivered his speech on February 24 and 25 to a closed session of the Twentieth Congress in Moscow. Rumors of its contents, and some public criticism of Stalin in the Soviet press, followed in the next few months and drew the attention of Western Communists. But American CP leaders did not receive a full report on Khrushchev's charges until the end of April, when the national committee met in an enlarged session in New York City, its first meeting in five years.

Dennis delivered the main report at the meeting, criticizing the underlying political assumptions about the imminence of war, fascism, and economic collapse that had guided party policy over the preceding decade. Although many of Dennis's listeners were prepared to go further in their criticisms than Dennis, this was still an unprecedented occasion—the first time a sitting general secretary had offered such an indictment. Out of forty delegates in attendance, only Foster voted against accepting Dennis's report; three other delegates abstained.[19]

But Dennis's presentation was overshadowed in his listeners' memories by the reading of a copy of Khrushchev's secret speech. The effect was devastating, as people who had devoted two or three decades of their lives for a cause they believed the Soviet Union embodied listened to Khrushchev's authoritative account of the tortures, frame-ups, unjust imprisonments, and executions that Stalin had ordered in the name of defending socialism. Steve Nelson, who chaired the session when the report was read, recalled: "I could see people, old Party leaders, crying in the audience. When the report was finished, I made the first comment. I said something like 'This is not the reason why I joined the Party. From now on we have to reject this; we have to make our own decisions; there are no more gods.'"[20]

Even before the national committee met, the *Daily Worker* had editorially criticized the "cult of personality"—the euphemism Khrushchev used in a public speech to the Twentieth Congress to criticize Stalin—the suppression of Yiddish culture in the Soviet Union, and the purge trial that had claimed the life of Laszlo Rajk, posthumously "rehabilitated" that spring in Hungary. As in the summer of 1945, the *Daily Worker* threw its pages open to letters from its readers. In early June, when the State Department released a full transcript of Khrushchev's secret speech, the *Daily Worker* reprinted it along with an editorial criticizing Soviet leaders for not having made it public themselves.[21]

The battle that followed was unlike any other event in the party's history. Foster had been able to cut off the 1945 debate when he felt it had gone far enough, without risking substantial membership losses. No "Browder faction" arose in 1945 to compete for power. But in the summer of 1956 the most important state organizations, New York and California, the party's major newspapers, the *Daily Worker*, the *People's World*, and *Freiheit*, and a majority of CP members supported those who challenged Foster's leadership. The issues they fought over cut far deeper than those dividing the party in 1945. At the end of the Second World War, both Browder and Foster believed they were fighting for policies approved by Moscow. By the autumn of 1956 Gates and his allies could have no illusions about Soviet attitudes.

The Russians did everything they could to squelch debate in the American CP. *Pravda* went out of its way in September to praise Foster as a "noted theoretician and Marxist historian," reviewing a book of his on black American history that had been published a year earlier in the Soviet Union. Several Soviet journals that fall and winter published attacks on the *Daily Worker* and on Joseph Clark for political deviations. Even Jacques Duclos reappeared with a warning to the February 1957 national convention of the American CP against departures from orthodoxy.[22]

This time, however, it did not matter which way the wind was blowing in Moscow. If anything, the dissenters felt that to reestablish the Communist movement as a legitimate force in American public life they would have to take a stand outside the Soviet-defined boundaries of orthodoxy. The *Daily Worker* praised Khrushchev's speech as the beginning of necessary reforms within the Soviet Union, denied that "the evils of the Stalin era are inherent in socialism," but clearly and repeatedly expressed its dissatisfaction with the attempts by Soviet leaders to place all the blame for those evils on Stalin as an individual. In late June the national committee announced that they could not accept "an analysis of such profound mistakes which attributes them solely to the capricious aberrations of a single individual, no matter how much arbitrary power he was wrongly permitted to usurp." They called on Soviet leaders to undertake "further and deeper examination of such questions as the structure and operation of socialist democracy in the Soviet Union and other socialist countries," and pledged that in the future American Communists would reserve the right "to engage in friendly criticism of the theory or practice of the Marxists of any country, whenever they feel this is necessary."[23]

For the first time in its history the American CP found itself playing a truly vanguard role within the international Communist movement, asking questions about the nature of Soviet society and past party history that went further than those considered by most other Communist parties. Italian Communists, under Togliatti's leadership, went almost as far as the American Communists, calling for a "polycentric" Communist movement which would allow "a diversity of paths of development towards socialism."[24] Togliatti carried considerable weight in the international movement, and his stand encouraged the American dissenters to continue their struggle. But in France and England party leaders quickly smothered the post–Twentieth Congress debate, at the cost of a few intellectual supporters in France and a quarter of the membership in England. When British Communist dissenters Edward Thompson and John Saville started their own journal to carry on the discussion suppressed by the official party press, two out of the three articles they included in their first issue were reprinted from the American Communist press.[25]

By the summer of 1956 the dissenters in the American CP had linked their criticism of the Soviet Union to a reappraisal of "bourgeois democratic rights" in the United States and to a call for the reorganization of the Communist movement along genuinely democratic lines. Since 1935 the CP had portrayed itself as the defender of democratic rights under capitalism, but had never spoken of a vision of socialism different from that prevailing in the Soviet Union. Now the *Daily Worker* insisted that Communists dedicate themselves to finding the "American road" to a "society of democratic socialism in which the civil and political rights of the individual and of groups will be guaranteed under the Constitution."[26]

In an article in *Political Affairs* that fall Steve Nelson quoted Rosa Luxemburg's 1918 criticisms of the Bolsheviks' suppression of their political opposition in Russia, and urged American Communists to discard once and for all the concepts of "monolithic unity" and "one-party rule."[27] In the same issue John Gates called for a "party of a new type" oriented to a "peaceful and constitutional struggle" for socialism. Old ideas of democratic centralism, he argued, had led to "maximum centralization and minimum democracy." Dissent and discussion within the party had to be permitted at all times: "We need unity and discipline but this should flow from conviction as the result of vigorous democratic debate . . . not from compulsion as it has tended to do in the past." The "great lesson" that Gates drew from the revelations of the Twentieth Congress was that "the expansion of democracy is not automatic under socialism but must be fought for."[28]

Gates proposed that the current party structure be replaced by a "political action association"—a proposal carrying a distinctly "Browderist" ring. Browder was much on every veteran Communist's mind those days. He had led the party during the Popular Front and Grand Alliance years—a time which now seemed like a golden age to many American Communists. His defeat at Foster's hands in 1945 had coincided with the beginning of the American CP's time of troubles. There were obvious parallels between Browder's efforts to Americanize the party and the current emphasis on finding the American road to socialism—though Browder undertook his own efforts in the belief he was conforming to Soviet policy, while the reformers in 1956 knew they were striking out on their own.

But few of the leaders of the 1956 uprising cited Browder's example. As one Communist who left the CP after 1956 recalled, "There was still an inhibition about talking about Browder. Too many of us had put the knife into Caesar."[29] A question of tactics was also involved. Foster was quick to label any criticism of his regime as an example of the "new Browderism," and favorable references to Browder only supplied him with more ammunition.[30] Finally, Gates and his allies did retain significant differences with Browder's position in 1944–1945. Browder had tied his own Americanization of the party to a political estimate of the meaning of the Teheran accords, which clearly had no basis in postwar realities. As Gates argued in *Political Affairs* in 1956, "Our big mistake under Browder was not the formation of the Communist Political Association but the wrong content we put into it, namely the mistaken concepts of progressive capitalism and postwar national unity."[31] Browder's policy may have been the starting point from which their own dissent later grew, but Gates and his allies did not intend to be bound by its limitations.

In the summer and early fall of 1956 the party dissenters seemed to have a clear field ahead of them. They looked forward to the February 1957 national convention for the confirmation of their triumph. They did not move decisively to consolidate organizational control, nor did they attempt to drive Foster and his remaining followers out of the CP. However consistent it was with their advocacy of a genuinely democratic organization, this would prove a serious political mistake. Though the Gates forces held a majority at the February convention, their continuing compromises with Foster's diehards vitiated the force of their criticisms and left their supporters within the party increasingly demoralized.

Part of the dissenters' problem was that they lacked effective leadership. Dennis soon retreated from the relatively critical positions he had adopted in the spring, as Moscow made it clear that the boundaries of permissible dissent had been crossed. He opposed efforts by Gates and others to have the party's national committee adopt an unconditional condemnation of Soviet military intervention in Hungary in November; the compromise resolution finally adopted satisfied no one, least of all the thousands of party members who took the Soviet action as the signal for their departure from the movement.[32] Gates, the best known of the dissenters, felt he lacked the stature to challenge both Dennis and Foster for leadership, and like many of his supporters he already had one foot outside the party.

The unity of the dissenters was more apparent than real even at the height of their strength. They shared opposition to Foster, and hopes for an autonomous American Communist movement. But they had no common program for what that movement should look like. Freed from the rigid ideological guidelines of the Foster years, they started going off in all directions—some toward the liberal wing of the Democratic party and the AFL-CIO, some toward a social-democratic or Fabian model, and some toward a democratic—but still revolutionary—Marxism. Thousands of Communists who had stuck with the party through the worst years of the Cold War left in the months immediately after the Khrushchev speech, and even more left after the Hungarian events. The party, which had about twenty thousand members in January 1956, lost at least half of them by the summer of 1957, and shrank to a mere three thousand members the following summer.[33]

Foster recognized early in the crisis that all he had to do was sit tight, make as few concessions as possible, and wait for control of the decimated organization to fall into his lap. As it became clear that Foster's strategy was working, Gates and other leaders of the re-examinationist wing of the CP began to drop out. Steve Nelson was one of the last to leave. In 1956 he believed that "we had a chance to take over the Party. We had a majority. But what are you going to do when Gates gets up and says, 'I'm walking out.' And Charney says, 'I'm walking out.' And the whole New York leadership decides to walk out. I remained there for another eight months or so, and then I said, 'What the hell am I doing here?' and I walked out."[34]

By 1956 the party had virtually no influence outside its own ranks; it had produced no first-rate leaders—no one of the stature of a Tito or Togliatti (or Debs)—who might have been able to lead it to a significant place in American political life. But it did possess one important resource: a generation of members who had gained valuable political experience in organizing the unemployed and the CIO during the Depression, in fighting in Spain and during the Second World War, in surviving the repression and isolation of the Truman-McCarthy years, in learning how to elect candidates in New York city council elections, and in running national political campaigns through the PAC in 1944 and through the Progressive party in 1948. They had paid a bitter price, had made many costly errors, but had passed through a period of testing and training similar to the experience of the generation of European Communists who after the Second World War would build their parties into mass working-class movements.

Most American Communists were in their mid-forties in 1956, in the prime of their political lives. They were lost to the left after 1956. According to Peggy Dennis, who remained in the CP for another two decades, "The core of those who left was that whole generation of younger people who had come into the party from the YCL, the Spanish vets, and the people who had been active in the mass movements. Afterwards there just weren't any real know-how people left in the party, and we weren't able to pick up the pieces."[35]

The Next Generation

The Communist party stood in hostile isolation from most of the new currents that grew up on the left in the United States during the 1960s. This "New Left," centered in the Students for a Democratic Society (SDS), began its political history by repudiating the traditions and outlook of the Communist movement. The New Leftists had no use for the Soviet Union, did not look to the industrial working class as the cutting edge of social change, and made a vaguely defined "participatory democracy" their organizational principle and political goal.

Despite the SDS's origins as the student affiliate of the resolutely anti-Communist League for Industrial Democracy, many of its earliest adherents were "Red Diaper babies"—children of former Communists or Popular Front supporters who had grown up in homes with Howard Fast novels on the bookshelf and *I. F. Stone's Weekly* on the coffee table. Yet surprisingly few political lessons seem to have been passed down from the older generation to the younger. The search for a comprehensive political strategy led many New Leftists to end the 1960s embracing variants of the American CP's earlier outlook and tactics. By the end of the decade, competing factions at SDS conventions were chanting the name of one or another Third World revolutionary leader to drown out their opponents—an exercise in "proletarian internationalism" that left observers from the Old Left shaking their heads in dismay. The veteran community organizer Saul Alinsky would complain in the late 1960s that "there was a radical continuum that went on in the Depression. Today there's a chronological cut-off for the kids. They don't believe anything happened in the past. It's a wonder these kids don't reinvent the wheel."[36]

Veterans of the Communist movement, defeated and dispersed, could provide neither practical leadership nor philosophical guidance to the New Left; in effect, SDS was called on to reinvent the wheel, with predictable results. It had taken the Communists a quarter of a century to learn that the American left could not be built on foreign models; that civil liberties and democratic institutions should be at the center of any vision of an American socialist future; and that Marxists had as much to learn from other political traditions as they had to teach about American political realities. When these lessons were finally learned, they came too late to be of use to the generation that had learned them, and too early to be of use to the generation that followed.

SOURCES

PREFACE

1. Theodore Draper, *The Roots of American Communism* (New York: Viking Press, 1957), p. 395. Other books in the "Communism in American Life" series include Daniel Aaron, *Writers on the Left* (New York: Harcourt, Brace and World, 1961); Theodore Draper, *American Communism and Soviet Russia* (New York: Viking Press, 1960); Nathan Glazer, *The Social Basis of American Communism* (New York: Harcourt, Brace and World, 1961); Robert W. Iverson, *The Communists and the Schools* (New York: Harcourt, Brace and Co., 1959); Frank S. Meyer, *The Moulding of Communists, The Training of the Communist Cadre* (New York: Harcourt, Brace and Co., 1961); Clinton Rossiter, *Marxism: The View from America* (New York: Harcourt, Brace and Co., 1960); Ralph L. Roy, *Communism and the Churches* (New York: Harcourt, Brace and World, 1960); and David Shannon, *The Decline of American Communism, A History of the Communist Party since 1945* (New York: Harcourt, Brace and World, 1959).
2. In one startling passage in their acerbic account of the history of American communism, Irving Howe and Lewis Coser wrote: "Those who joined or were influenced by the Young Communist League were never to comprise more than a very small minority of their generation—but a minority that, because of its devotion and energy, left its imprint upon many others. No matter how hostile one may be towards the politics of these young Communists, honesty requires the admission that some of them were among the best of their generation, among the most intelligent, selfless, and idealistic." Howe and Coser, *The American Communist Party, A Critical History 1919–1957* (Boston: Beacon Press, 1957), pp. 198–199.
3. Browder Papers, I-59, MS. Browder to Rossiter, November 22, 1957. All references citing the Browder Papers are in the Earl Browder Papers, Arents Research Library, Syracuse University, Syracuse, New York.
4. Recent accounts by veterans of the Communist movement include George Charney, *A Long Journey* (Chicago: Quadrangle, 1968); Al Richmond, *A Long View from the Left, Memoirs of an American Revolutionary* (New York: Delta, 1972); Peggy Dennis, *The Autobiography of an American Communist* (Westport, Conn.: Lawrence, Hill and Co., 1978); Harry Haywood, *Black Bolshevik, Autobiography of an Afro-American Communist* (Chicago: Liberator Press, 1978); Nell Painter, *The Narrative of Hosea Hudson, His Life as Negro Communist in the South* (Cambridge: Harvard University Press, 1979); Joseph Starobin, *American Communism in Crisis, 1943–1957* (Berkeley: University of California, 1972); and Max Gordon, "The Communist Party of the Nineteen-Thirties and the New Left," *Socialist Revolution*, VI (January-March 1976), pp. 11–66. For accounts by historians with roots in the New Left, see Jim O'Brien, "The Ambiguous Legacy," *Radical America*, X (July-August 1976), pp. 63–71; Roy Rosenzweig, "Organizing the Unemployed: The Early Years of the Great Depression, 1929–1935," *Radical America*, X (July-August 1976), pp. 36–60; Mark Naison, "Harlem Communists and the Politics of Black Protest,"

Marxist Perspectives, I (Fall 1978), pp. 20–50; and Paul Buhle, "Jews and American Communism: The Cultural Question," *Radical History Review*, No. 23 (Spring 1980), pp. 9–33.

5. Joseph Clark has criticized recent positive appraisals of the party's history. See Clark, "Dreams and Nightmares," *Dissent* (Summer 1978), pp. 275–281. Also see Draper, "The Romanticizing of American Communism," *New Leader*, LXI (March 13, 1978), pp. 20–22.

6. Howe and Coser, *The American Communist Party*, pp. 506, 519.

7. James Green, in his article "Working Class Militancy in the Depression," *Radical America*, VI (November-December 1972), pp. 1–35, defends the CP's trade-union policies in the early 1930s against charges of sectarianism, and sees CP policies after 1935 descending into a morass of bureaucracy and opportunism. Staughton Lynd, in his article "The United Front in America: A Note," *Radical America*, VIII (July-August 1974), pp. 29–37, describes the CP's post–Third Period but pre–Popular Front policies of 1934–1935 as a "promising beginning" in the development of a mass radical movement that all too soon gave way to "an amorphous coalition of so-called progressive forces."

8. Charney, *A Long Journey*, p. 59.

9. Hal Draper, a Socialist student leader in the 1930s, later wrote that the CP's National Student League was "one of the most successful of the Communist-led movements of the thirties; and it was also one of the most competently led. Among its top leaders were Joseph Starobin, Joseph Cohen (Joseph Clark), James Wechsler—all of New York—and, from the West Coast Serril Gerber and Celeste Strack. In general, they were more imaginative and less muscle-bound in style than the cliché-ridden hacks who presided over other Communist Party enterprises in the earlier years. In a real sense the NSL pioneered the Popular Front pattern." Draper, "The Student Movement of the Thirties," in Rita James Simon, ed., *As We Saw the Thirties* (Urbana, Ill.: University of Illinois Press, 1967), p. 153.

10. Ortega y Gasset, "The Concept of the Generation," in *The Modern Theme* (New York: Harper and Brothers, 1961), pp. 14–15. Also see the recent special issue of *Daedalus*, CVII (Fall 1978), on "Generations."

Chapter 1: PRELUDE TO WAR, AMERICAN COMMUNISTS IN THE 1930s

1. Prosper O. Lissargay, *The History of the Commune of 1871*, trans., Eleanor Marx Aveling (London: Reeves and Turner, 1886), p. ix.

2. Recent accounts of the events of World War Two sympathetic to the Communist party include Philip Bart, ed., *Highlights of a Fighting History, 60 Years of the Communist Party USA* (New York: International Publishers, 1979), pp. 179–224; and Roger Keeran, *The Communist Party and the Auto Workers Unions* (Bloomington: Indiana University Press, 1980), pp. 226–249. For an anti-Communist account, see Irving Howe and Lewis Coser, *The American Communist Party*, pp. 424–433. And for an account from a non-communist left position, see James Weinstein, *Ambiguous Legacy, The Left in American Politics* (New York: New Viewpoints, 1975), pp. 93–102.

3. Joseph Starobin, *American Communism in Crisis*, p. xii.

4. For Browder's activities in these years, see James G. Ryan, "The Making of a Native Marxist: The Early Career of Earl Browder," *The Review of Politics*, XXXIX

(June 1977), pp. 332–362. Also see Max Shachtman, "The Reminiscences of Max Shachtman," Vol. I, p. 31. Shachtman's reminiscences were taped in 1962–1963 and are deposited in the Columbia University Oral History Collection.

5. Shachtman, "Reminiscences," Vol. IV, p. 429.

6. Alexander Bittelman, "Autobiography," pp. 595–596. Bittelman's unpublished autobiography, written in 1962, is deposited in the Tamiment Institute, New York University.

7. *New Masses*, III (February 1928), pp. 18–21.

8. For a discussion of the doctrine of "American exceptionalism," emphasizing its relation to the power struggle in Moscow in the late 1920s, see Draper, *American Communism and Soviet Russia*, pp. 268–281.

9. Charney, *A Long Journey*, pp. 93–95.

10. Howe and Coser, *The American Communist Party*, p. 341; Weinstein, *Ambiguous Legacy*, p. 75.

11. Browder Papers, I-84, MS. Young to central committee, November 5, 1936.

12. The exact percentage of Jewish membership in the American Communist party in the 1930s and 1940s is hard to determine. Nathan Glazer devotes three pages of footnotes in *The Social Basis of American Communism* to a review of the fragmentary evidence on the question, then fails to offer an estimate. Glazer does point out that the New York county membership (accounting for about one-fifth of the total CP membership in 1948) was largely Jewish. Other centers of Communist strength like Los Angeles, Philadelphia, and Chicago also had high percentages of Jewish membership. See Glazer, pp. 220–222. In a more recent study Arthur Liebman concludes simply that "in the late 1940s the Communist Party rested upon a Jewish base." Liebman, "The Ties That Bind: The Jewish Support for the Left in the United States," *American Jewish Historical Quarterly*, LXVI (December 1976), p. 306.

13. George Watt, a YCL activist in New York in the 1930s, was told stories as a child about how his grandfather had led the first strike of Jewish workers in the Russian textile center of Lodz. In becoming a Communist he felt he was "following pretty closely in the traditions of my parents." In the early 1930s, he later recalled, "those of us in the youth movement were working with university groups all over the country, with a lot of liberals, non-Marxist youth, and we began to feel like we were really part of the American scene. We were looking for some kind of legitimation of our feeling about becoming even more American. Browder came along and sort of articulated this. He called it 20th Century Americanism." Interview with George Watt, January 7, 1978.

14. Richmond *A Long View from the Left*, pp. 220–249.

15. Quoted in Henry Hart, ed., *The Writer in a Changing World* (London: Lawrence and Wishart, Ltd., 1937), p. 239.

16. See Lee Lowenfish, "The American Testament of a Revolutionary," *Columbia Library Columns* (February 1978), pp. 3–13; and Joseph Freeman, *An American Testament: A Narrative of Rebels and Romantics* (New York: Farrar and Rinehart, 1936).

17. Quoted in Richmond, *A Long View from the Left*, p. 228. In Richmond's view "the People's Front proved to be an effective and viable *beginning* in the search for forms of transition or approach to revolution." Richmond, p. 231. (Emphasis in original.)

18. Bittelman, "Autobiography," p. 625.

19. Browder, "The Reminiscences of Earl Browder," Vol. IV, p. 400. Hereafter cited as Browder, "Reminiscences." These were taped in 1963 and are deposited in the Columbia University Oral History Collection.

20. For Foster's career as a labor organizer and a Communist leader, see Draper, *Roots of American Communism*, pp. 311–314, 321–322, and *American Communism and Soviet Russia*, pp. 431–432. For Foster's complaint to Browder, see "Pre-Plenum Meeting of Political Committee," TS., March 23, 1939, p. 7. In the private collection of Philip Jaffe, hereafter designated Jaffe Collection.

21. William Appleman Williams, *The Contours of American History* (Cleveland: World Publishing Co., 1961), p. 19. For a brief exchange on the CP and the concept of a "usable past," see letters from Staughton Lynd and Maurice Isserman in *Radical America*, XIV (July-August 1980), pp. 77–79.

Chapter 2: THE LAST DAYS OF PEACE

1. *History of the Communist Party of the Soviet Union (Bolsheviks), Short Course* (New York: International Publishers, 1939), p. 355, for Browder quotation, see *Daily Worker*, July 6, 1939, 1:5.

2. Archibald MacLeish, *America Was Promises* (New York: Duell, Sloan and Pearce, 1939), p. 19. As keynote speaker at the opening session of the 1937 Congress of the League of American Writers, MacLeish ridiculed those who feared being "used" by Communists: "The answer is, of course, that the man who refuses to defend his convictions for fear he may defend them in the wrong company has no convictions." Quoted in Hart, ed., *The Writer in a Changing World*, pp. 56–62.

3. For estimates of CP strength in 1939, see Howe and Coser, *The American Communist Party*, p. 386; and Nathan Glazer, *The Social Basis of American Communism*, p. 115.

4. For Communist political influence in the late 1930s, see David Saposs, *Communism in American Politics* (Washington, D.C.: Public Affairs Press, 1960), pp. 33–34, 41, 45–46; Browder, "Reminiscences," Vol. III, p. 368; Alan Schaffer, *Vito Marcantonio, Radical in Congress* (Syracuse: Syracuse University Press, 1966), pp. 52–53; Si Gerson, *Pete, The Story of Peter V. Cacchione, New York's First Communist Councilman* (New York: International Publishers, 1976), pp. 82, 85; Kenneth Waltzer, "The Party and the Polling Place: American Communism and the American Labor Party in the 1930s," *Radical History Review*, No. 23 (Spring 1980), pp. 104–129, and the response by Max Gordon in the same issue, pp. 130–135.

5. Earl Browder, *Fighting for Peace* (New York: International Publishers, 1939), p. 200.

6. Max Kampelman, using the rather vague criterion of "complete or partial control," awarded the CP 40 percent of CIO strength in 1938. Kampelman, *The Communist Party vs the CIO* (New York: Praeger, 1957), p. 18. More responsible estimates usually credit the CP with control of about 20 percent of the CIO membership on the eve of the war. See Irving Bernstein, *Turbulent Years: A History of the American Worker, 1933–1941* (Boston: Houghton Mifflin, 1971), pp. 782–783. The most detailed studies of CP strength in various CIO unions are found in Walter Galenson, *The CIO Challenge to the AFL* (Cambridge: Harvard University Press, 1960), Bert Cochran, *Labor and Communism, The Conflict That Shaped American Unions* (Princeton: Princeton University Press, 1977), and Roger Keeran, *The Communist Party and the Auto Workers Unions, passim*.

7. Barrington Moore, "The Communist Party of the USA; An Analysis of a Social Movement," *American Political Science Review*, XXXIX (February 1945), p. 37.

8. Peggy Dennis, *Autobiography*, p. 93.

9. *Party Builder* (April 1939), p. 3. Also see Dennis, *ibid.*, p. 129. The formal aban-

donment of party fractions in the unions did not mean much in practice. Max Gordon, a CP organizer in the Schenectady, New York, area in the late 1930s, recalled: "We never really resolved the problem of the Party dominating its allies in united fronts. As Party organizer I used to meet with the Party club, and while formally we would try to keep away from union business, we never did. And then I used to meet behind closed doors with the [UE] leadership. So it was manipulative, no question about it." Interview with Max Gordon, February 15, 1977.

10. Howe and Coser, *The American Communist Party*, p. 353.
11. In 1939 the AYC claimed an affiliated membership of nearly 5 million. Howe and Coser, *ibid.*, p. 359. Also see George P. Rawick, "The New Deal and Youth: The Civil Conservation Corps, the National Youth Administration and the American Youth Congress," Ph.D. diss., University of Wisconsin, 1957, pp. 295–296.
12. Naison, "Harlem Communists," pp. 34–35; Lawrence S. Wittner, "The National Negro Congress: A Reassessment," *American Quarterly*, XXII (Winter 1970), p. 887.
13. *Daily Worker*, June 7, 1939, 7:6.
14. Paul Robeson, "Ballad for Americans," Vanguard Recording, VRS-9193.
15. Joseph Lash, *Eleanor Roosevelt, A Friend's Memoir* (Garden City, N.Y.: Doubleday and Co., 1956), p. 198. For the links between Popular Front radicalism and the cultural nationalism of the later 1930s, see Alfred Kazin, *On Native Grounds* (Garden City, N.Y.: Doubleday and Co., 1956), p. 394, and Warren Susman, "The Thirties," in Stanley Coben and Lorman Ratner, eds., *The Development of an American Culture* (Englewood Cliffs, N.J.: Prentice-Hall, 1970), pp. 179–218, *passim*. For the special appeal of Popular Front culture to New York City Jews, see Kenneth A. Waltzer, "The American Labor Party: Third Party Politics in New Deal–Cold War New York, 1936–1954," Ph.D. diss., Harvard, 1978, pp. 170–176.
16. For a description of the evolution of the CP's internal structure, see Robert Jay Alperin, "Organization in the Communist Party, USA, 1931–1938," Ph.D. diss., Northwestern, 1959, *passim*. Political committee members in 1939 included Browder, Foster, Jack Stachel, James Ford, Alexander Bittelman, Charles Krumbein, Clarence Hathaway, Rose Wortis, Henry Winston, Roy Hudson, Robert Minor, Eugene Dennis, and Gil Green.
17. Browder, "Reminiscences," Vol. III, p. 354; interview with Sam Darcy, May 2, 1977. For a list of Browder's trips to Moscow, see "Investigation of Un-American Propaganda Activities in the United States," Special Committee on Un-American Activities, 76th Congress, 1st Session, Vol. VII, pp. 4500–4506.
18. Peggy Dennis, *Autobiography*, pp. 120–124; *New York Times*, March 5, 1939, 40:3.
19. Peggy Dennis offers the most detailed account available of her husband's career in her *Autobiography, passim*. Also see Starobin, *American Communism in Crisis*, pp. 12–13; Shannon, *The Decline of American Communism*, p. 12.
20. "Pre-Plenum Meeting of Political Committee," March 23, 1939, TS., pp. 2–7. Jaffe Collection.
21. *Ibid.*, pp. 8–26, *passim*.
22. *Ibid.*, p. 39.
23. *New Republic*, IC (January 20, 1937), pp. 348–349.
24. Browder, *Fighting for Peace*, p. 181.
25. *Ibid.*, p. 65.
26. *Ibid.*, pp. 206–214.
27. *National Issues*, I (January 1939), p. 3.
28. *National Issues*, I (March 1939), p. 3.

29. *National Issues*, I (March 1939), p. 9.
30. Charney, *A Long Journey*, p. 84. According to Browder, more than a thousand American Communists died in Spain. *Communist*, XVII (September 1939), p. 803. Also see Arthur Landis, *The Abraham Lincoln Brigade* (New York: Citadel Press, 1967), pp. xvii–xviii.
31. On the return of the Lincoln veterans, see Robert A. Rosenstone, *Crusade on the Left, The Lincoln Battalion in the Spanish Civil War* (New York: Pegasus, 1969), pp. 334–359. For a contemporary account that captured the bitterness the veterans felt toward the "non-intervening" democracies in 1939, see Alvah Bessie, *Men in Battle* (New York: Scribners, 1939), *passim*.
32. Joseph Stalin, *Report on the Work of the Central Committee* (Moscow: Foreign Languages Publishing House, 1939), pp. 8–17.
33. Charney, *A Long Journey*, p. 124.
34. *History of the Communist Party of the Soviet Union (Bolsheviks)*, pp. 333–334.
35. *Daily Worker*, April 1, 1939, 5:1.
36. *New York Times*, March 13, 1939, 1:6.
37. *Worker*, March 5, 1939, Sec. 2, 1:1.
38. *Nation*, CIL (July 15, 1939), p. 60; Frank A. Warren, *Liberals and Communism: The "Red Decade" Revisited* (Bloomington: Indiana University Press, 1966), p. 194.
39. Quoted in a review by Granville Hicks of a collection of Browder's writings, *The Second Imperialist War*. With obvious enjoyment, Hicks pointed out that this passage was dropped in the reprinted version of the article. *New Republic*, CII (July 15, 1940), p. 90. Also see Ralph B. Levering, *American Opinion and the Russian Alliance, 1939–1945* (Chapel Hill: University of North Carolina Press 1976), p. 19.
40. For Foster's and Bittelman's speculations about the possibility of a Nazi-Soviet agreement, see Browder "Reminiscences," Vol. IV, p. 371.
41. *Daily Worker*, July 5, 1939, 1:1; August 16, 1939, 6:1.
42. *Daily Worker*, August 20, 1939, 6:1.
43. *New Republic*, C (October 18, 1939), p. 297.

Chapter 3: WAR IN EUROPE

1. *Daily Worker*, September 13, 1939, 1:1; Joseph Stalin, *For Peaceful Coexistence* (New York: International Publishers, 1951), p. 8.
2. *New York Times*, August 21, 1939, 1:7; Melech Epstein, *The Jew and Communism, 1919–1941* (New York: Trade Union Sponsoring Committee, 1959), pp. 348–349.
3. Epstein, p. 350.
4. *Daily Worker*, August 23, 1939, 1:1.
5. *Young Communist Review*, IV (September 1939), p. 18; *Daily Worker*, August 27, 1939, 1:1; September 1, 1939, 3:2.
6. *New York Times*, August 24, 1939, 9:1; *Daily Worker*, August 24, 1939, 1:1; Epstein, *The Jew and Communism*, p. 350.
7. *New Leader*, September 2, 1939, 3:1.
8. *Daily Worker*, August 30, 1939, 1:2. Also see Richmond, *A Long View from the Left*, p. 283.
9. Charney, *A Long Journey*, p. 125; Epstein, *The Jew and Communism*, p. 351.
10. Epstein, *ibid.*, p. 364.
11. *Worker*, September 3, 1939, 6:3.
12. Granville Hicks, *Part of the Truth* (New York: Harcourt, Brace and World, 1965), pp. 182–183.

13. *New Republic*, CII (March 25, 1940), p. 403; *Daily Worker*, August 30, 1939, 6:4.
14. *Nation*, CIL (September 30, 1939), p. 344. Also see Epstein, *The Jew and Communism*, p. 365.
15. *Nation*, CIL (September 30, 1939), p. 345.
16. *New Republic*, C (August 30, 1939), pp. 88–89; (September 6, 1939), pp. 114, 118; (September 13, 1939), p. 150; CI (November 8, 1939), pp. 7–9; (November 15, 1939), pp. 104–106; (December 13, 1939), p. 225; (December 27, 1939), p. 290.
17. *New Republic*, CII (March 18, 1940), pp. 373–374; Ralph L. Roy, *Communism and the Churches* (New York: Harcourt, Brace and World, 1960), pp. 145–146.
18. League of American Writers Collection, Auden to LAW, TS., August 11, 1939. Bancroft Library, University of California at Berkeley. The letter was obviously misdated, and was probably written in mid-September.
19. Daniel Aaron, *Writers on the Left*, p. 397.
20. Michael Gold, *The Hollow Men* (New York: International Publishers, 1941), p. 125.
21. *Freiheit* editorial quoted in Epstein, *The Jew and Communism*, pp. 352–353; *New Masses*, XXXII (September 19, 1939), p. 3. On Pollitt's "two-front line" and its rapid demise, see David Childs, "The British Communist Party and the War, 1939–1941: Old Slogans Revived," *Journal of Contemporary History*, XII (April 1977), pp. 237–242.
22. *Communist*, XVIII (October 1939), pp. 923–924.
23. *Daily Worker*, August 26, 1939, 6:2; August 31, 1939, 1:5 Epstein, *The Jew and Communism*, pp. 351–352.
24. *Daily Worker*, September 13, 1939, 1:1; Epstein, *ibid.*, p. 353.
25. John Mahon, *Harry Pollitt, A Biography* (London: Lawrence and Wishart, 1976), p. 252.
26. "Discussion by CP National Committee on International Situation," TS., September 14, 1939, September 16, 1939. Jaffe Collection, *passim*. Although the minutes of this meeting are labeled "National Committee," the only speakers identified were members of the political committee. The political committee, perhaps with a few members of the national committee also in attendance, was presumably meeting and acting in the name of the larger group.
27. *Communist*, XVII (October 1939), pp. 899–904.
28. Raymond Sontag and James Beddie, eds., *Nazi-Soviet Relations, 1939–1941* (Washington, D.C.: U.S. State Department, 1948), pp. 78, 96.
29. The leaflet is in the Tamiment Institute collection, OF: CPUSA, 1939. (Emphasis in original.) Also see *Daily Worker*, September 18, 1939, 1:4. The *Freiheit* editorial was reprinted as a leaflet. See Tamiment Institute collection, OF: New York State CP, 1939.
30. *Nazi-Soviet Relations*, pp. 100, 108; *Daily Worker*, November 4, 1939, 2:1; *Molotov's Report to the Supreme Soviet* (New York: Workers Library, 1939), *passim*.
31. Quoted in Les K. Adler and Thomas G. Patterson, "Red Fascism: The Merger of Nazi Germany and Soviet Russia in the American Image of Totalitarianism, 1930's–1950's," *American Historical Review*, LXXV (April 1970), pp. 1049–1050.
32. *New Republic*, CI (November 8, 1939), p. 7.
33. Thomas R. Maddux, "Red Fascism, Brown Bolshevism: The American Image of Totalitarianism in the 1930s," *The Historian*, XL (November 1977), pp. 99–100; Corliss Lamont, ed., *The Trial of Elizabeth Gurley Flynn by the ACLU* (New York: Horizon Press, 1968), pp. 19–20. In 1974 the ACLU repealed this resolution, and in 1976 adopted a motion recognizing that "the expulsion of Ms. Flynn was not consonant with the basic principles on which the ACLU was founded and has acted for 54 years."

34. *Daily Worker*, November 23, 1939, 6:2.
35. *Communist*, XVIII (November 1939), pp. 995, 997. (Emphasis in original.)
36. On Allied plans to fight the Soviet Union, see Andre Beaufre, *1940, The Fall of France* (New York: Knopf, 1968), p. 169; Winston Churchill, *The Gathering Storm* (Boston: Houghton Mifflin, 1948), p. 573; and Douglas Clark, *Three Days to Catastrophe* (London: Hammond, Hammond, and Co., 1966), p. 8.
37. *Daily Worker*, April 10, 1940, 1:1.
38. *Communist*, XIX (May 1940), pp. 407, 411.
39. In describing these messages I have relied on Philip Jaffe's account in *The Rise and Fall of American Communism* (New York: Horizon Press, 1975), pp. 40–47.
40. *Worker*, October 22, 1939, 1:2.
41. Earl Browder, *The Second Imperialist War* (New York: International Publishers, 1940), p. 155.
42. "Un-American Propaganda," pp. 4275–4276, 4374; *New York Times*, September 6, 1939, 1:2; *Nation*, CIL (October 28, 1939), p. 45.
43. Martin Dies, *The Trojan Horse in America* (New York: Dodd, Mead and Co., 1940), p. 11.
44. Harold Ickes, *The Secret Diary of Harold L. Ickes. The Lowering Clouds, 1939–1941*, Vol. III (New York: Simon and Schuster, 1954), p. 97. For a summary of legal attacks on the CP in 1939, see the magazine of the International Labor Defense, *Equal Justice*, XIII (February 1940), pp. 7–9.
45. Browder, *The Second Imperialist War*, p. 154.
46. Quoted in *ibid.*, p. 177.
47. *New York Times*, November 8, 1939, 11:2.
48. "Memo on September 12, 1940 presidential letter to Dies," OF: 263, in the FDR Library. Also see *Nation*, CIL (December 9, 1939), p. 650.
49. Walter Goodman, *The Committee, The Extraordinary Career of the House Committee on Un-American Activities* (New York: Farrar, Straus and Giroux, 1968), pp. 74–90.
50. *Equal Justice*, XIII (February 1940), pp. 7–9; *Nation*, CIL (September 16, 1939), p. 287; CL (March 23, 1940), p. 384; *Daily Worker*, November 11, 1939, 1:3.
51. *New Republic*, CI (December 6, 1939), p. 189.
52. Peggy Dennis, *Autobiography*, pp. 138–141.
53. John Williamson, *Dangerous Scot: The Life and Work of an American "Undesirable"* (New York: International Publishers, 1969), p. 143.
54. Interview with Steve Nelson, October 13, 1977; Tim Buck, *Yours in the Struggle, Reminiscences of Tim Buck* (Toronto: NC Press, Ltd., 1977), pp. 289–299.
55. Interview with John Gates, May 17, 1977.
56. See for example Ben Gitlow, "Communist Party Now Functioning in Underground Apparatus Set Up in '40," *New Leader*, January 4, 1941, 3:2.
57. Sandor Voros, *American Commissar* (New York: Chilton Co., 1961), p. 252.
58. See for example "LaGuardia—On Wilson's Bandwagon in 1917, On Roosevelt's in 1940," *Worker*, March 3, 1940, Sec. 2, 2:7; "Two War Pilgrimages: Col. House, 1915—Sumner Welles, 1940," *Worker*, February 18, 1940, Sec. 2, 1:1.
59. Some Cold War analysts saw the ability to distort political realities to remain in the bounds of a given ideology a property peculiar to "totalitarian" systems of thought like communism. Frank Meyer described a "cadre personality" allegedly common among veteran Communists that was incapable of absorbing ideas or information from outside of a rigidly defined belief system: "If ever a trained and developed cadre Communist allows himself fully and deeply to acknowledge any reality in-

dependent of the Communist cosmos—a fact, an idea, an aspect of an order of being—the whole tense, complex structure is in imminent danger of shattering into bits." Meyer, *The Moulding of Communists*, pp. 133, 155–156. The ability of American foreign policymakers in the 1960s to convince themselves that they were defending democracy and self-determination in South Vietnam, and that, contrary to what their own intelligence analysts were telling them, the light at the end of the tunnel was in view, suggests that Communists are not the only group prone to closed systems of thought. The Munich analogy played roughly the same role for the American foreign policy establishment in the 1960s that the "First Imperialist War" analogy played for American Communists during the Nazi-Soviet pact.

60. Adam Ulam, *Espansion and Co-existence, Soviet Foreign Policy in 1917–1973* (New York: Praeger, 1974), pp. 287–291.

61. Harold Lavine and James Wechsler, *War Propaganda and the United States* (New Haven: Yale University Press, 1941), pp. 282–324.

62. *Daily Worker*, November 2, 1939, 1:1.

63. *New Masses*, XXXIV (January 2, 1941), p. 9.

64. *Daily Worker*, December 19, 1939, 1:1.

Chapter 4: THE "YANKS AREN'T COMING" CAMPAIGN

1. *New Masses*, XXXIX (May 20, 1941), p. 8.

2. Quoted in *New York Times*, May 15, 1940, 24:4.

3. Earl Browder, *Earl Browder Takes His Case to the People* (New York: Workers Library, 1940), p. 3. By Lenin's "best co-worker," Browder meant, naturally, Stalin.

4. Vivian Gornick, *The Romance of American Communism* (New York: Basic Books, 1977), p. 119.

5. *Daily Worker*, January 9, 1940, 1:5; January 13, 1940, 4:6; January 14, 1940, 3:2; January 19, 1940, 1:5; January 20, 1940, 1:5; February 7, 1940, 2:1.

6. Browder, *Browder Takes His Case to the People, passim*.

7. *New York Times*, January 23, 1940, 1:4.

8. Browder, *Browder Takes His Case to the People*, pp. 4–7; *New York Times*, January 23, 1940, 10:2; *Daily Worker*, January 23, 1940, 1:1. Gil Green still remembered this speech thirty-eight years later: "The personal vindictiveness came through, so that it made me shudder at the thought of the Party's leader speaking out loud in so subjective a fashion." Interview with Gil Green, December 31, 1977.

9. *New Masses*, XXXIV (February 20, 1940), p. 20. By way of comparison, when Morris Hillquit ran for mayor of New York City in 1917 on an anti-war platform he received 21.7 percent of the vote for the entire city, nearly a fivefold increase over the normal Socialist vote. James Weinstein, *The Decline of Socialism in America, 1912–1925* (New York: Vintage, 1969), p. 154.

10. Browder, *The People Against the Warmakers* (New York: Workers Library, 1940), p. 17.

11. Harold L. Ickes, *The Secret Diary of Harold L. Ickes. The Inside Struggle, 1936–1939*, Vol. II (New York: Simon and Schuster, 1954), p. 710; Lash, *Eleanor Roosevelt*, pp. 52–53. On preparations for the Youth Institute, see Lash, *ibid.*, pp. 6, 48–51; Rawick, "The New Deal and Youth," p. 363.

12. Lash, *ibid.*, pp. 55–56.

13. Franklin D. Roosevelt, *The Public Papers and Addresses of Franklin D. Roosevelt* (New York: Macmillan Co., 1941), Vol. IX, pp. 85–94.

14. James A. Wechsler, *Labor Baron, A Portrait of John L. Lewis* (New York: William

Morrow and Co., 1944), pp. 122–151; Melvyn Dubofsky and Warren Van Tine, *John L. Lewis, A Biography* (New York: Quadrangle, 1977), pp. 323–324; Matthew Josephson, *Sidney Hillman, Labor Statesman* (Garden City, N.Y.: Doubleday, 1952), p. 473.

15. Joseph Lash, *Eleanor and Franklin* (New York: W. W. Norton, 1971), pp. 597, 604; Rawick, "The New Deal and Youth," pp. 363–368; Eleanor Roosevelt, *This I Remember* (New York: Harper and Brothers, 1949), p. 201; Wechsler, *Labor Baron*, pp. 116–118.

16. *New Masses*, XXXIV (April 16, 1940), p. 12. For Lewis's hopes for a third party in 1940, see C. K. McFarland, "Coalition of Convenience: Lewis and Roosevelt, 1933–1940," *Labor History*, XIII (Summer 1972), p. 409.

17. Mike Quin, *The Yanks Are Not Coming* (San Francisco: Maritime Federation of the Pacific, 1939), *passim*. On the organization of Yanks Are Not Coming Committees, see Lavine and Wechsler, *War Propaganda*, p. 145.

18. *Daily Worker*, March 5, 1940, 1:6; January 8, 1941, 6:1; *Communist*, XIX (March 1940), pp. 230–231.

19. *Daily Worker*, October 3, 1940, 2:5; November 27, 1940, 6:3. Also see Earl Browder, *The Jewish People and the War* (New York: Workers Library, 1940), *passim*.

20. *Jewish Voice*, I (March-April 1941), p. 2. The party's distortion of—and thus indifference to—the nature of the threat facing European Jews in 1939–1941 underlines the inadequacy of Harold Cruse's premise in *The Crisis of the Negro Intellectual* that in the 1930s, "Jewish nationalism was winning out within the context of the Communist Party. . . . Under Jewish Communist prodding, the Communist Party took up the anti-Hitler crusade." Jewish Communists no doubt felt a special animus against Nazi anti-Semitism; this hardly made "Jewish nationalism" the determining factor of the party's international line, as the "no lesser evil" argument of the Nazi-Soviet-pact period shows. Cruse's idiosyncratic book offers some valuable insights into the necessary relation of culture and politics in a revolutionary movement, but his chapter "Jews and Negroes in the Communist Party" borders on anti-Semitic paranoia. Cruse, *Crisis of the Negro Intellectual* (New York: William Morrow and Co., 1967), pp. 147–170, *passim*.

21. *Worker*, March 17, 1940, 2:1; May 26, 1940, 4:1; Elizabeth Gurley Flynn, *I Didn't Raise My Boy to Be a Soldier—For Wall Street* (New York: Workers Library, 1940), *passim*; Earl Browder, *The People's Road to Peace* (New York: Workers Library, 1940), p. 31.

22. *New Masses*, XXXV (July 2, 1940), p. 3.

23. *Daily Worker*, September 5, 1940, 1:1.

24. On the ALPD's demise, see *New York Times*, February 2, 1940, 1:2; *New Republic*, CII (March 18, 1940), pp. 373–374; Roy, *Communism and the Churches*, pp. 146–147. On the CP's relations with the KAOWC, see Charles Chatfield, *For Peace and Justice, Pacifism in America, 1914–1941* (Knoxville: University of Tennessee Press, 1971), pp. 319–320; Justus D. Doenecke, "Non-Interventionism on the Left: The Keep America Out of the War Congress, 1938–1941," *Journal of Contemporary History*, XII (April 1977), pp. 225–226.

25. *Worker*, April 7, 1940, 1:3; September 3, 1940, 1:3; *New Masses*, XXXIX (May 6, 1941), pp. 5–7; Roy, *Communism and the Churches*, pp. 152–153.

26. *Daily Worker*, April 10, 1940, 1:5; May 11, 1940, 1:1; *People's World*, April 10, 1940, 4:1; *Worker*, May 12, 1940, Sec. 2, 5:1.

27. Browder, "Reminiscences," IV, p. 384; *Young Communist Review*, V (February 15, 1940), p. 13; interview with John Gates, May 17, 1977.

28. *New Masses*, XXXV (May 28, 1940), pp. 3–4.
29. *Daily Worker*, June 12, 1940, 6:4.
30. Earl Browder, *The Way Out* (New York: International Publishers, 1941), pp. 54–55. Also see *New York Times*, May 26, 1940, 20:1.
31. *New Republic*, CII (July 15, 1940), p. 69. Also see Lash, *Eleanor Roosevelt*, pp. 122–126; Rawick, "The New Deal and Youth," p. 372; Roy, *Communism and the Churches*, p. 148; "An Analysis of the AYC Convention at Lake Geneva, Wisconsin, July 3–7, 1940," Mimeo. OF: AYC, Tamiment Institute.
32. Adam Ulam, *Expansion and Co-existence, 1917–1973*, pp. 297–302.
33. Alexander Werth, *Russia at War* (New York: Dutton, 1964), pp. 91–92.
34. Communist Party, *Election Platform* (New York: Workers Library, 1940), p. 12.
35. Committee for Defense of Civil Rights of Communists, *The Conspiracy Against Free Elections* (Pittsburgh, 1941). The ACLU's 1940 annual report declared: "At no period in the 20 years of its existence have the Civil Liberties Union and other agencies engaged with protecting civil rights been confronted with such an array of threatened measures of repression." This was written before the major efforts to drive the CP off the ballot were launched. ACLU, *In the Shadow of War, The Story of Civil Liberty 1939–1940* (New York, 1940), p. 4.
36. *Daily Worker*, January 5, 1940, 1:6; January 26, 1940, 5:6; February 9, 1940, 1:4; February 21, 1940, 1:3; February 27, 1940, 4:1; April 11, 1940, 1:5; May 4, 1940, 1:1; *Equal Justice*, XV (Winter 1941), pp. 22–23; Fred J. Cook, *The FBI Nobody Knows* (New York: Macmillan, 1964), pp. 247–251. According to the ACLU, under Attorney General Murphy "numerous prosecutions were undertaken which struck at minority political groups. . . . While no proof existed that the prosecutions were politically motivated, they were accompanied by such violations of civil rights as excessive bail, unduly severe sentences, delays, and prejudicial treatment of defendants." ACLU, *In the Shadow of War*, pp. 16–17.
37. Michael Belknap, "The Smith Act and the Communist Party: A Study in Political Justice," Ph.D diss., University of Wisconsin, 1973, pp. 83–84; Kathleen L. Barber, "The Legal Status of the American Communist Party: 1965," *Journal of Public Law*, XV (1966), p. 96; Schaffer, *Marcantonio*, pp. 78–79.
38. *Daily Worker*, July 11, 1940, 1:1; *Equal Justice*, XV (Winter 1941), p. 37.
39. *New York Times*, April 6, 1940, 1:6; May 25, 1940, 4:2; Goodman, *The Committee*, pp. 99–100.
40. Edward L. Barrett, *The Tenney Committee, Legislative Investigation of Subversive Activities in California* (Ithaca: Cornell University Press, 1951), pp. 1–8; ACLU, *Liberty's National Emergency, The Story of Civil Liberty in the Crisis Year, 1940–1941* (New York, 1941), p. 24; Robert W. Iverson, *Communists and the Schools*, pp. 208–222; Committee for Defense of Public Education, *The Conspiracy Against the School, An Analysis of the Rapp-Coudert Committee, March 1940 to January 1941* (New York, 1941), *passim*; Marvin Gettleman, "Communists in Higher Education: CCNY and Brooklyn College on the Eve of the Rapp-Coudert Investigation, 1935–1939" (unpublished paper presented to the Organization of American Historians, April 9, 1977); interview with Morris U. Schappes, December 29, 1977.
41. "Minutes of National Committee Meeting, November 16–17, 1940," TS., p. 5. Jaffe Collection.
42. *Equal Justice*, XV (Winter 1941), pp. 16–18, 43–44; (Spring 1941), p. 8; XVI (Winter 1942), p. 6; *New Republic*, CIII (October 21, 1940), pp. 547–549.
43. *New York Times*, August 7, 1940, 20:3; September 24, 1940, 12:5; October 9, 1940, 32:4; October 18, 1940, 15:3; October 23, 1940, 17:1; October 26, 1940, 13:5; October

30, 1940, 25:3; *New Republic*, CIII (October 21, 1940), pp. 547–549; *New Masses*, XXXVIII (October 29, 1940), p. 12; Roscoe Baker, *The American Legion and Foreign Policy* (New York: Bookman Associates, 1954), pp. 95–96.

44. *New York Times*, September 23, 1940, 10:6; "Minutes, National Committee Meeting, November 16–17, 1940," TS. Jaffe Collection. The ACLU's 1940–1941 annual report stated: "In no previous election in American history were so many restrictions put upon minority parties as in the campaign of 1940." ACLU, *Liberty's National Emergency*, p. 19.

45. *Worker*, November 3, 1940, 4:1; *New York Times*, November 4, 1940, 1:6; *New Masses*, XXXVII (December 24, 1940), p. 20.

46. Browder, *The People Against the Warmakers*, p. 23.

47. Louis Budenz, *This Is My Story* (New York: McGraw-Hill, 1947), p. 100.

48. Budenz, *ibid.*, pp. 209, 220; *Daily Worker*, August 1, 1940, 1:2; "Minutes, National Committee Meeting, November 16–17, 1940," TS. Jaffe Collection.

49. Bittelman, "Autobiography," pp. 672–673.

50. *Daily Worker*, November 17, 1940, 1:2; November 25, 1940, 2:1; Browder, "Reminiscences," Vol. IV, pp. 408–409.

51. "Minutes, National Board Meeting, May 22–23, 1945," TS., pp. 1–2. Jaffe Collection.

52. Browder, *The Way Out*, pp. 112, 116.

53. Quoted in Joel Seidman, *American Labor from Defense to Reconversion* (Chicago: University of Chicago Press, 1953), p. 21.

54. *Communist*, XX (January 1941), p. 9. For the growing antagonism between Lewis and Hillman, see Josephson, *Sidney Hillman*, pp. 470–471. For Hillman's role in the NDAC, see Bruno Stein, "Labor's Role in Government Agencies During World War II," *Journal of Economic History*, XVII (1957), pp. 392–393.

55. Galenson, *CIO Challenge*, p. 296.

56. Quoted in Galenson, *ibid.*, p. 217.

57. Len DeCaux, *Labor Radical* (Boston: Beacon Press, 1970), pp. 348, 361–362; Cochran, *Labor and Communism*, p. 148.

58. Quoted in L. H. Whittemore, *The Man Who Ran the Subways, The Story of Mike Quill* (New York: Holt, Rinehart and Winston, 1968), p. 91.

59. *Communist*, XIX (May 1940), p. 409.

60. *Communist*, XX (May 1941), p. 416.

61. Vernon Jensen, *Lumber and Labor* (New York: Farrar and Rinehart, 1945), pp. 235–242; Galenson, *CIO Challenge*, pp. 399–406, 561–564; Iverson, *Communists and the Schools*, pp. 202–208; Bella Dodd, *School for Darkness* (New York: P. J. Kennedy and Sons, 1954), p. 128.

62. According to Bert Cochran, the Communists at the 1940 UAW convention "stood exposed as a very small group with a diminishing influence; not the locomotive of the Addes-Frankensteen train, but the caboose." Cochran, *Labor and Communism*, p. 153. Pro-Reuther historians like Irving Howe tend to overstate Communist influence in the UAW after 1939, to add greater glory to Reuther's struggle for power. See Howe, *The UAW and Walter Reuther* (New York: Random House, 1949), pp. 150–151.

63. Mortimer is quoted in Galenson, *CIO Challenge*, p. 177.

64. In the debate over the Roosevelt endorsement Walter Reuther recalled the "beautiful resolution" that Communist delegate Nat Ganley had introduced on behalf of a third term for Roosevelt at the 1939 UAW convention. For CP reaction to the convention, see *Daily Worker*, July 9, 1940, 1:2; July 10, 1940, 6:2. For the convention itself, see

Cochran, *Labor and Communism*, pp. 151–153; Galenson, *CIO Challenge*, pp. 177–178.

65. *Worker*, October 27, 1940, 1:1; Charles Larrowe, *Harry Bridges: The Rise and Fall of Radical Labor in the United States* (Westport, Conn.: Lawrence Hill, 1972), p. 225; Kampelman, *Communist Party vs the CIO*, p. 23; DeCaux, *Labor Radical*, p. 364; Wechsler, *Labor Baron*, p. 126. Curiously enough, four days before Lewis made his speech, the *Daily Worker* carried an advertisement from the Republican-sponsored "National Committee to Uphold Constitutional Government" opposing the third term. When the Democrats began making political capital out of this apparent collaboration between Republicans and Communists, Browder publicly denied that the CP was calling for votes for Willkie. The advertisement, he insisted, was simply a question of business policy: "Since the [*Daily Worker*] is no longer the official organ of the Communist Party, it was clearly within the province of the management to accept advertising if it saw fit." Whatever one thinks of Browder's assertions about the autonomy of the *Daily Worker*, it is true that the paper was strapped for funds, and may well have accepted the advertisement for financial reasons. Nevertheless, it is hard to imagine the paper accepting a pro-Roosevelt advertisement in 1940. The incident raises the question of whether the Communists might not have welcomed a Willkie victory in the election, a victory which at the least would have reduced the prestige of Sidney Hillman, their chief opponent in the union movement. See *Daily Worker*, October 21, 1940, 4:5; Browder, *The Way Out*, pp. 155–156.

66. DeCaux, *Labor Radical*, pp. 378–382.

67. *Daily Worker*, November 30, 1940, 6:2. For the CIO convention, see Galenson, *CIO Challenge*, pp. 61–63; Cochran, *Labor and Communism*, pp. 145–146; Josephson, *Sidney Hillman*, pp. 492–502; Bernstein, *Turbulent Years*, pp. 721–726.

68. Mortimer quoted in *Daily Worker*, November 24, 1940, 1:6. For public hostility to strikes in 1940, see Seidman, *From Defense to Reconversion*, pp. 25, 41–43. For the Vultee strike, see Wyndham Mortimer. *Organize, My Life as a Union Man* (Boston: Beacon Press, 1971), pp. 166–173; Cochran, *Labor and Communism*, pp. 158–159.

69. Browder, *The Way Out*, pp. 161–175, *passim*.

70. *Daily Worker*, December 25, 1940, 5:1.

71. *Daily Worker*, August 3, 1940, 3:2.

Chapter 5: THE LAST DAYS OF THE NAZI-SOVIET PACT

1. Almanac Singers, "Talking Union," Folkways Records, FH 5285; *Worker*, June 22, 1941, 5:1.

2. Joseph Lash, *Roosevelt and Churchill, 1939–1941: The Partnership That Saved the West* (New York: W. W. Norton and Co., 1976), pp. 260–265, 282–283.

3. Browder, *The Way Out*, pp. 201–202; *New York Times*, January 14, 1941, 1:1.

4. *New York Times*, January 4, 1941, 4:8; *Daily Worker*, January 17, 1941, 1:2; February 2, 1941, 1:1; February 9, 1941, 1:2; February 10, 1941, 1:4; February 11, 1941, 1:5; February 12, 1941, 2:1; Lash, *Eleanor Roosevelt*, p. 231.

5. *Labor Fact Book*, Vol. V (New York: International Publishers, 1941), p. 57; *Daily Worker*, November 14, 1940, 1:5; April 6, 1941, 1:4; May 17, 1941, 1:7.

6. Wayne S. Cole, *America First, The Battle Against Intervention, 1940–1941* (Madison: University of Wisconsin Press, 1953), pp. 30, 32, 72, 74.

7. *Communist*, XX (February 1941), pp. 101–102.

8. William Bilderback, "The American Communist Party and World War Two," Ph.D

diss., University of Washington, 1974, p. 74; interview with George Watt, January 7, 1978.

9. Draper, *Roots of American Communism*, pp. 122–126.

10. Dennis, *Autobiography*, p. 145.

11. *Daily Worker*, March 25, 1941, 1:2; March 26, 1941, 1:1; March 28, 1941, 1:4.

12. The Earl Browder Papers, Series I-46, contain what appears to be the complete correspondence between Minor and Browder while Browder was in Atlanta. In a letter to Browder's wife in August 1941, Minor described the "Aesop" language that he and Browder were using to discuss the question of whether party lawyers should attempt to win release for Browder on parole, and also how Browder inserted his own words into a "quotation" from Plutarch, to make a political point. Minor to Raissa Browder, August 15, 1941.

13. Interview with Gil Green, December 31, 1977.

14. *New York Times*, June 18, 1941, 14:4.

15. Seidman, *From Defense to Reconversion*, p. 29; Josephson, *Sidney Hillman*, pp. 529–530; Stein, "Labor's Role," p. 398; *CIO News*, III (December 30, 1940), 3:3.

16. *Young Communist Review*, IV (February 3, 1941), p. 13; *Communist*, XX (February 1941), p. 108.

17. Seidman, *From Defense to Reconversion*, pp. 41, 52; Cochran, *Labor and Communism*, p. 160; Nelson Lichtenstein, "Industrial Unionism Under the No-Strike Pledge: A Study of the CIO During the Second World War," Ph.D diss., University of California at Berkeley, 1974, p. 95.

18. Bennett is quoted in Seidman, *ibid.*, p. 47. Also see Bernstein, *Turbulent Years*, pp. 728, 742–746.

19. *American Mercury*, LII (February 1941), pp. 202–203. Also see the article by Jan Valtin, "ABC of Sabotage," in *American Mercury*, LII (April 1941), pp. 417–425.

20. "Morgenthau Diaries," Vol. 264, TS., p. 281. FDR Library. Also see Ickes, *The Lowering Clouds*, p. 190.

21. OF: 263. FDR to Stimson and Knox, June 4, 1941. TS. FDR Library.

22. Ickes, *The Lowering Clouds*, p. 461.

23. Seidman, *From Defense to Reconversion*, pp. 55–56.

24. For a portrait of Christoffel, see Cochran, *Labor and Communism*, pp. 166–172.

25. Cochran, *ibid.*, pp. 166–176; Josephson, *Sidney Hillman*, pp. 538–544; Lichtenstein, "Industrial Unionism," pp. 103–105.

26. *Time*, XXXVII (April 14, 1941), p. 20. Some historians have shared this judgment. Max Kampelman wrote: "To carry out their 'isolationist' political objectives during the period from the Nazi-Soviet Pact in 1939 until the invasion of Russia in June 1941, Communist-led trade unions began a series of strikes designed to hamper and embarrass America's defense efforts. . . . The most serious Communist-inspired defense strike was the 76-day affair at Allis-Chalmers." Kampelman, *Communist Party vs the CIO*, pp. 25–26.

27. *CIO News*, IV (February 17, 1941), 1:1.

28. Seidman, *From Defense to Reconversion*, p. 44.

29. *Worker*, January 26, 1941, Sec. 2, 5:1. Also see Mortimer, *Organize*, pp. 168, 172.

30. *New York Times*, June 10, 1941, 22:1.

31. *CIO News*, III (December 2, 1940), 2:1.

32. Lichtenstein, "Industrial Unionism," pp. 121–124.

33. *CIO News*, IV (March 17, 1941), 7:1; (March 31, 1941), 3:2; Galenson, *CIO Challenge*, p. 189; Josephson, *Sidney Hillman*, p. 540.

34. Whittemore, in his biography of Mike Quill, offered this analysis of the 1941 bus

strike: "In theory, the Communists planned to use strikes to capture basic American industries in order to interfere with the normal economic life of the country if this were necessary to carry out the foreign policy of Russia. . . . The Party line was geared to slowing down the American efforts to prepare for war. As a Soviet agent [TWU Secretary-Treasurer] John Santo was in a perfect position to put all this theory into motion. . . . Santo wanted no victory without a strike." Whittemore, *Mike Quill*, pp. 97–98. Whittemore does not make clear just how the bus strike interfered with American defense efforts. In his discussion of the far more extensive transit strike in New York City in 1966 he does not argue that that conflict had any effect on American ability to wage war in Vietnam.

35. *American Mercury*, LII (February 1941), pp. 202–210.
36. Galenson, in his anti-Communist but sober history of the CIO, took issue with Max Kampelman's assertion that "UE set in motion a general strike campaign throughout the industry in October 1940." Galenson noted: "No major strikes were called, indicating either that the communist leaders were uncertain of their hold on the rank and file or that they were unwilling to risk hard-earned collective agreements in political adventures. Perhaps obligations to the Communist Party were considered fulfilled merely by cheering the aircraft workers who were engaged in serious defense strikes." Galenson, *CIO Challenge*, p. 260.
37. Cochran calculated that Communist-led strikes accounted for only about 13 percent of the total number of strikes certified by the NDMB between March and November 1941, while the number of strikes in defense industries actually increased by 20 percent *after* June 1941 when the Communists began opposing strikes. Cochran, *Labor and Communism*, pp. 164–165. Also see Lichtenstein, "Industrial Unionism," p. 102.
38. *Communist*, XX (January 1941), p. 93.
39. *Daily Worker*, April 5, 1941, 6:3.
40. *Daily Worker*, May 9, 1941, 6:1.
41. *Newsweek*, XVII (June 2, 1941), p. 17.
42. For the growing power of the NDMB, see Seidman, *From Defense to Reconversion*, pp. 48–49. Also see Galenson, *CIO Challenge*, pp. 403–404; Cochran, *Labor and Communism*, pp. 181–182.
43. Franklin D. Roosevelt, *Public Papers and Addresses, 1941*, Vol. X (New York: Harper and Brothers, 1950), pp. 191–192.
44. Mortimer, *Organize*, pp. 174–179; Cochran, *Labor and Communism*, p. 177.
45. Mortimer, *ibid.*, pp. 179–185; Cochran, *ibid.*, pp. 176–182; Lichtenstein, "Industrial Unionism," pp. 133–134, 183.
46. *Daily Worker*, June 10, 1941, 1:1.
47. *Life*, X (June 23, 1941), pp. 32–34.
48. *Newsweek*, XVII (June 16, 1941), p. 35.
49. *CIO News*, IV (June 16, 1941), 2:4.
50. DeCaux, *Labor Radical*, pp. 400–401.
51. Cochran concluded his account of the North American strike by observing: "The Communist leadership was wiped out at North American. The officers suspended by the army were never reinstated, the organizers fired by Frankensteen were never returned to the payroll, Communist influence in aircraft was never revived. The adventure cost the Party dearly." Cochran, *Labor and Communism*, p. 182.
52. Ulam, *Expansion and Co-existence*, pp. 299–305; *Nazi-Soviet Relations*, pp. 217–264.
53. Ulam, *ibid.*, pp. 305–306; Werth, *Russia at War*, pp. 116–118.

54. *New Masses*, XXXIX (April 15, 1941), pp. 5–6; John Gates, *The Story of an American Communist* (New York: Thomas Nelson and Sons, 1958), p. 80; interview with John Gates, May 17, 1977; *Communist*, XX (May 1941), p. 424; Bilderback, "The American Communist Party and World War Two," pp. 76–78.

55. *Daily Worker*, May 14, 1941, 1:2; May 25, 1941, 1:4; *New York Times*, July 27, 1941, 16:1.

56. Ulam, *Expansion and Co-existence*, pp. 305–306.

57. *Daily Worker*, June 20, 1941, 6:1; June 21, 1941, 6:2; *Worker*, June 22, 1941, Sec. 2, 1:6.

Chapter 6: THE RETURN TO ANTI-FASCISM

1. *New Masses*, XL (July 8, 1941), p. 3.

2. *Daily Worker*, June 25, 1941, 6:4.

3. Quoted in Aaron, *Writers on the Left*, p. 237.

4. Richmond, *A Long View from the Left*, p. 285.

5. Interview with George Watt, January 7, 1978.

6. Winston Churchill, *The Grand Alliance* (Boston: Houghton Mifflin, 1950), pp. 371–373.

7. *Daily Worker*, June 23, 1941, 1:1.

8. Raymond H. Dawson, *The Decision to Aid Russia, 1941* (Chapel Hill: University of North Carolina Press, 1959), pp. 108, 113–119.

9. *Ibid.*, pp. 224–226, 282–284.

10. *Daily Worker*, June 26, 1941, 1:1; 2:1; 5:3.

11. *Daily Worker*, June 26, 1941, 6:3.

12. Browder Papers, I-46, Minor to Browder, June 27, 1941. TS.

13. *Communist*, XX (August 1941), pp. 707–708.

14. William Z. Foster and Robert Minor, *The Fight Against Hitlerism* (New York: Workers Library, 1941), p. 21.

15. *Daily Worker*, June 30, 1941, 2:2.

16. *Daily Worker*, July 7, 1941, 6:6.

17. *New Masses*, XL (July 22, 1941), p. 3.

18. *Weekly Review*, VI (December 9, 1941), p. 14.

19. The CP has never admitted that there was anything questionable about the policies it followed during the Nazi-Soviet pact. In his 1952 history of the CP, Foster acknowledged that the war had a "deep people's content" from the outset but had no criticism of the "Yanks Are Not Coming" line. William Z. Foster, *History of the Communist Party of the United States* (New York: International Publishers, 1952), p. 383. The CP recently published a documentary collection, *Highlights of a Fighting History*, which reprints a portion of Foster's book as its sole entry dealing with the party's international line from 1939 to 1941. *Highlights*, pp. 185–186.

20. *New Masses*, XL (July 8, 1941), p. 3.

21. Browder Papers, I-46, Earl Browder to Raissa Browder, June 23, 1941; July 6, 1941, TS.

22. *Weekly Review*, VI (July 7, 1941), p. 2.

23. *Weekly Review*, VI (July 21, 1941), pp. 4–5; *New York Times*, July 6, 1941, 22:3; *Daily Worker*, July 7, 1941, 1:5.

24. *New York Times*, July 24, 1941, 5:1; July 27, 1941, 16:1; *Daily Worker*, August 1, 1941, 5:7.

25. *New Republic*, CIV (June 30, 1941), p. 877.

26. *Communist*, XX (August 1941), p. 710.

27. Foster, *History of the Communist Party*, p. 420.

28. *New York Times*, August 20, 1941, 5:1; August 21, 1941, 16:1; September 25, 1941, 2:3.

29. *New York Times*, July 20, 1942, 5:1; "Report on the American Slav Congress," Committee on Un-American Activities, House Report No. 51, 81st Congress, 2nd Session, pp. 12–15.

30. Ralph B. Levering, *American Opinion and the Russian Alliance, 1939–1945* (Chapel Hill: University of North Carolina Press, 1976), pp. 100–103; Congress of American-Soviet Friendship, *Salute to Our Russian Ally* (New York, 1942), *passim*.

31. *Communist*, XX (August 1941), pp. 685–689.

32. *Daily Worker*, June 25, 1941, 1:1.

33. *Worker*, July 20, 1941, 1:1; Wechsler, *Labor Baron*, p. 148.

34. Quoted in Wechsler, *ibid.*, p. 147.

35. There is some dispute on this point. Wechsler, in his 1944 biography of Lewis, suggested that "Pressman, Bridges and others endeavoured to persuade him to haul down his isolationist flag." Wechsler, *ibid.*, p. 147. But a "prominent" left-wing CIO official told Saul Alinsky in the late 1940s that no efforts had been made to win over Lewis. Alinsky, *John L. Lewis*, p. 231. DeCaux, who described the "cold shock" he felt when Lewis signed the August 5 statement, did not mention any attempt on his part or by other CIO left-wingers to convince Lewis to change his stand. DeCaux, *Labor Radical*, p. 384.

36. *Communist*, XX (September 1941), p. 768; *Daily Worker*, September 16, 1941, 1:1; DeCaux, *ibid.*, p. 384.

37. Quoted in Galenson, *CIO Challenge*, p. 186.

38. Galenson, citing *New York Times* labor analyst Louis Stark, argued that Haywood attended the UAW convention as Lewis's representative. He saw Haywood's efforts on behalf of Addes as part of Lewis's effort to "undermine" Murray's authority in the CIO. Actually, Haywood would soon give formal notice of his shift in allegiance to Murray by resigning his office in the UMW. The point is important, because it shows that Murray had already decided on a policy of working with the Communists in the CIO. If he had wanted to drive them entirely out of the UAW all he had to do was let the Reuther-Frankensteen alliance continue undisturbed. Galenson, *ibid.*, p. 190; Dubofsky, *John L. Lewis*, p. 411. For the UAW convention, see Cochran, *Labor and Communism*, pp. 184–195, Galenson, *ibid.*, pp. 186–191.

39. *Daily Worker*, August 31, 1941, 1:3.

40. Galenson, *CIO Challenge*, pp. 404–406, 563–564.

41. Julius Emspak, "The Reminiscences of Julius Emspak," p. 272. In the Columbia University Oral History Collection. Also see James Prickett, "Communists and the Communist Issue in the American Labor Movement, 1920–1950," Ph.D diss., University of California at Los Angeles, 1975, p. 338.

42. Quoted in Galenson, *CIO Challenge*, p. 263.

43. *Ibid.*, pp. 260–261. According to Herbert Northrup, Carey was "neither a good administrator nor an effective bargainer. . . . He started too late to concern himself with intra-union affairs, and he had against him not only the Communists, but a number of anti-communists who resented his cavalier handling of people, and his lack of attention to his union job." Northrup, *Boulwarism* (Ann Arbor: University of Michigan Press, 1964), pp. 41–43.

44. For descriptions of the growth of Communist influence in the UE, see Cochran,

Labor and Communism, pp. 285–287; and Ronald L. Filippeli, "The United Electrical, Radio and Machine Workers of America, 1933–1949: The Struggle for Control," Ph.D diss., Pennsylvania State University, 1970, *passim*.

45. Cochran, *ibid.*, p. 209.

46. *Daily Worker*, November 15, 1941, 1:2.

47. See for example Mark Naison, "Harlem Communists and the Politics of Black Protest," pp. 20–50; Charles H. Martin, "Communists and Blacks: The ILD and the Angelo Herndon Case," *Journal of Negro History*, LXIV (Spring 1979), pp. 131–141; and Hosea Hudson's description of the early years of Communist organizing in Birmingham in Painter, *The Narrative of Hosea Hudson*.

48. *Communist*, XIX (June 1940), pp. 548–549. Also see Wittner, "The National Negro Congress," pp. 898–901.

49. Richard M. Dalfiume, "The 'Forgotten Years' of the Negro Revolution," in Bernard Sternsher, ed., *The Negro in Depression and War* (Chicago: Quadrangle, 1969), pp. 302–306.

50. *Communist*, XX (August 1941), pp. 699–704.

51. *Communist*, XX (October 1941), pp. 894–895. On the CP's shifting attitude toward the March on Washington Movement, also see Herbert Garfinkel, *When Negroes March* (Glencoe, Ill.: Free Press, 1959), pp. 42–53.

52. During the war the black sociologist Horace Cayton charged that "the record shows that where and when the Communists seemed to be fighting for Negro rights, their objective was simply to strengthen the hand of Russia. When this was accomplished, they abandoned the fight and turned to something else." Cited in Wilson Record, *The Negro and the Communist Party* (Chapel Hill: University of North Carolina Press, 1951), pp. 222–223. Bayard Rustin, a member of the Young Communist League in the spring of 1941, was one of a few black Communists who did break with the party over the change in line that year. See Milton Viorst, *Fire in the Streets* (New York: Simon and Schuster, 1979), pp. 201–202.

53. Kenneth Waltzer, "The American Labor Party," pp. 226–246.

54. *Daily Worker*, August 3, 1941, 1:1.

55. *Daily Worker*, October 11, 1941, 1:2; October 26, 1941, 4:5.

56. Under the proportional representation (PR) system, instead of voting for a single candidate, a voter marked his or her order of preference among the candidates listed for any given office. Because votes were switched to other candidates if the voter's first choice was eliminated, the PR system enabled the Communists to overcome the traditional roadblock faced by third parties in American politics, the "lesser evil" syndrome, in which voters with radical sympathies cast their ballots for moderate candidates in order to keep conservatives out of office. Under PR, a voter could make the radical candidate his or her first choice and the moderate candidate his or her second choice, without the fear of "throwing away a vote." If the radical was eliminated from the counting, the vote would go to the moderate and still keep the "greater evil" out of office. In New York city council elections, each borough of the city elected a number of council members on a borough-wide basis. This meant that the Communists did not need to win a majority of votes in any given district within the borough to be represented in the city council. With X number of positions open for a given borough, they had to win only 1 out of X votes from across the borough to gain representation, as long as they ran only one candidate for each borough. New York voters repealed proportional representation in 1947, with the anti-PR campaign based largely on an appeal to anti-Communist sentiments.

See Gerson, *Pete*, pp. 61–62; Belle Zeller and Hugh A. Bone, "The Repeal of P.R. in New York City," *American Political Science Review*, XLII (December 1948), pp. 1127–1148.

57. Interview with a former Brooklyn Communist (hereafter designated B.C.), January 8, 1978. B.C. was a member of the Communist party from 1932 to 1956. He was an Unemployed Council organizer in the early 1930s, and later a section leader in Brownsville and a member of the CP county committee in Brooklyn. He asked to remain anonymous.

58. *Communist*, XX (December 1941), pp. 1065–1066. Communist candidates received 71,399 first-choice votes throughout the city in 1941, a decline of 3 percent from 1937.

59. Interview with B.C., January 8, 1978.

60. *Communist*, XIX (June 1940), p. 551; *Daily Worker*, November 13, 1941, 6:3.

61. *Time*, November 17, 1941, p. 17.

62. Browder Papers, I-46, Minor to Raissa Browder, August 15, 1941, TS.

63. Elizabeth Gurley Flynn, *Earl Browder, The Man from Kansas* (New York: Workers Library, 1941), p. 9; *Daily Worker*, August 18, 1941, 1:1; September 30, 1941, 1:4.

64. *Free Earl Browder* (New York: Citizens Committee, 1942), *passim; Daily Worker*, November 29, 1941, 1:1.

65. *Daily Worker*, December 19, 1941, 1:2. Two hundred thousand signatures was not a very impressive total for a national campaign. Four days later the *Daily Worker* slurred over the difference between the 200,000 individual signatures and the million and a half supposedly represented by group resolutions, claiming that the Citizens Committee "last week presented petitions signed by 1,700,000 persons" to Biddle. *Daily Worker*, December 23, 1941, 1:2.

66. Flynn, *Earl Browder*, p. 30.

67. OF: 263, Molly Dewson to Eleanor Roosevelt, November 21, 1941, MS. FDR Library.

68. *Communist*, XX (June 1941), p. 498.

69. *Daily Worker*, July 12, 1941, 6:1. For the Socialist Workers party's actual attitude toward the war, see James Cannon, *The Socialist Workers Party in World War II* (New York: Pathfinder Press, 1975), pp. 207–210.

70. For accounts of the Minneapolis Smith Act trial, see Thomas L. Pahl, "The G-String Conspiracy, Political Reprisal or Armed Revolt?" *Labor History*, VIII (Winter 1967), pp. 30–52, *passim*; and Constance Myers, *The Prophet's Army* (Westport, Conn.: Greenwood Press, 1977), pp. 179–186.

71. *Daily Worker*, August 16, 1941, 5:2.

72. "National Committee Meeting," April 4, 1942, TS., p. 29. Jaffe Collection.

73. *New Masses*, XL (July 1, 1941), p. 2.

74. *Clarity*, II (Summer 1941), p. 67. *Clarity* was the YCL's theoretical journal.

75. *Daily Worker*, July 30, 1941, 3:4. The *Young Communist Review* for June 23 had labeled proposals to draft women a "plan to make prostitutes out of hundreds of thousands of young women . . . outdoing even the worst of the Hitler methods." Three months later Claudia Jones wrote that the conscription of women "would mobilize the tremendous strength and skill and talent of millions of young women for the defense of the United States. The young women of America will be at the side of the men in the armed forces in the great crusade for the destruction of Hitler." *Young Communist Review*, VI (June 23, 1941), p. 16; (October 7, 1941), p. 24.

76. *Daily Worker*, July 13, 1941, Sec. 2, 5:1; July 27, 1941, 1:6.

77. Werth, *Russia at War*, pp. 228, 240–260.
78. *Daily Worker*, October 9, 1941, 1:1; October 12, 1941 1:1; October 16, 1941, 1:1; October 19, 1941, 5:1.
79. *Daily Worker*, October 30, 1941, 6:3.
80. *Daily Worker*, November 1, 1941, 6:1.
81. *Daily Worker*, September 29, 1941, 1:2.
82. *Communist*, XX (December 1941), p. 1045.
83. Browder Papers, I-46, Browder to Minor, December 7, 1941, TS.
84. Charney, *A Long Journey*, p. 126.

Chapter 7: THE GRAND ALLIANCE

1. "Pete Seeger Sings Woody Guthrie," Folkways Records, FTS 31002; Earl Browder, *Victory and After* (New York: International Publishers, 1942), p. 102.
2. *CIO News*, V (July 6, 1942), 8:3; *Chicago Tribune*, June 5, 1942.
3. Joseph E. Davies, *Mission to Moscow* (New York: Simon and Schuster, 1941), p. 20.
4. *New Masses*, LXII (January 13, 1942), p. 20. For Davies's role in influencing American opinion about the Soviet Union, see Levering, *American Opinion and the Russian Alliance*, p. 58, and Elizabeth Kimball MacLean, "Joseph E. Davies and Soviet-American Relations, 1941–1943," *Diplomatic History*, IV (Winter 1980), pp. 73–94.
5. "Russian Ambassador Litvinoff has made a highly favorable impression on Congressmen who have talked with him, even on those who hold marked prejudices against the Soviet." *Newsweek*, August 17, 1942, p. 13.
6. *Newsweek*, September 7, 1942, p. 53; *Time*, September 28, 1942, p. 60.
7. Levering, *American Opinion and the Russian Alliance*, p. 126; *Reader's Digest*, May 1942, pp. 122–124. The *Reader's Digest* also reprinted an abridged version of *Mission to Moscow* in 1942.
8. Sumner Welles, *The Time for Decision* (New York: Harper and Brothers, 1944), pp. 313–315.
9. *New Republic*, CVI (June 22, 1942), p. 859; J. Samuel Walker, *Henry A. Wallace and American Foreign Policy* (Westport, Conn.: Greenwood Press, 1976), p. 89.
10. OF: 263, Byrnes to Roosevelt, memo filed February 20, 1942, and Roosevelt to Colonel McIntyre, memo filed January 13, 1942. TS. FDR Library; *New York Times*, January 29, 1942, 15:2.
11. "National Committee Meeting Minutes," April 4, 1942, TS., pp. 584–585. Jaffe Collection.
12. Adams to Roosevelt, April 15, 1942, and Roosevelt to Adams, April 27, 1942, TS. Series 10, Box 1629, FDR Library.
13. OF: 3997, Thomas to Roosevelt, February 9, 1942, TS. FDR Library.
14. *Worker*, May 17, 1942, 1:1; Earl Latham, *The Communist Controversy in Washington: From the New Deal to McCarthy* (Cambridge: Harvard University Press, 1966), p. 139.
15. *New York Times*, May 18, 1942, 1:1, 31:1; May 18, 1942, 17:1; OF: 3997, Biddle to Roosevelt, May 16, 1942, TS. FDR Library; Levering, *American Opinion and the Russian Alliance*, pp. 76–77.
16. *Daily Worker*, December 10, 1942, 4:6.
17. Record, *Negro and the Communist Party*, p. 215.

18. Robert Sherwood, *Roosevelt and Hopkins: An Intimate History* (New York: Harper and Brothers, 1948), p. 24; Peggy Dennis, *Autobiography*, p. 154.

19. *Weekly Review*, VIII (February 9, 1943), p. 3.

20. *Daily Worker*, April 9, 1942, 1:1.

21. *Daily Worker*, July 23, 1942. 1:1; *CIO News*, V (July 27, 1942), pp. 2, 5.

22. George Herring, *Aid to Russia, 1941–1946* (New York: Columbia University Press, 1975), p. 6; John L. Gaddis, *The United States and the Cold War, 1941–1947* (New York: Columbia University Press, 1972), pp. 16–17.

23. Levering, *American Opinion and the Russian Alliance*, pp. 88–89.

24. Werth, *Russia at War*, pp. 401–409.

25. *Daily Worker*, August 26, 1942, 6:1. Also see Earl Browder *et al.*, *Speed the Second Front* (New York: Workers Library, 1942), pp. 4–6.

26. *Daily Worker*, December 16, 1942, 5:6; Bilderback, "American Communist Party in World War Two," p. 188.

27. *Daily Worker*, December 16, 1942, 5:6.

28. David Montgomery, *Workers' Control in America* (Cambridge: Cambridge University Press, 1979), pp. 95–97.

29. Seidman, *From Defense to Reconversion*, pp. 64–67; Dubofsky, *John L. Lewis*, pp. 397–404.

30. Seidman, *ibid.*, pp. 80–82.

31. *Ibid.*, pp. 114–130; Lichtenstein, "Industrial Unionism," pp. 188–192.

32. *Daily Worker*, October 11, 1941, 5:1.

33. *Daily Worker*, November 14, 1941, 6:3.

34. Lichtenstein, "Industrial Unionism," pp. 214–217.

35. Browder, *Victory and After*, p. 240.

36. Filippelli, "The United Electrical, Radio and Machine Workers of America," pp. 124–126; Ronald Schatz, "The End of Corporate Liberalism: Class Struggle in the Electrical Manufacturing Industry, 1933–1950," *Radical America*, IX (July-August 1975), pp. 194–195.

37. See for example articles by James Green, Nelson Lichtenstein, Ed Jennings, Martin Glaberman, and Stan Weir in *Radical America*'s special issue devoted to "American Labor in the 1940s," IX (July-August 1975), *passim*; and Lichtenstein, "Ambiguous Legacy: The Union Security Problem During World War II," *Labor History*, XVIII (1977), pp. 214–238.

38. For a similar argument, see Joshua Freeman, "Delivering the Goods: Industrial Unionism During World War II," *Labor History*, XIX (Fall 1978), pp. 570–593.

39. See Emspak's article in *Science and Society*, VII (Winter 1943), p. 95. Nelson is quoted in *Labor Fact Book* (New York: International Publishers, 1943), p. 86. For official CIO reaction, see *CIO News*, V (March 16, 1942), 5:3.

40. Seidman, *From Defense to Reconversion*, pp. 178–179; Stein, "Labor's Role," pp. 401–402.

41. *More and Faster Production for Victory* (New York: New Union Press, 1942), p. 6.

42. Interview with Max Gordon, February 15, 1977. Also see Larrowe, *Harry Bridges*, p. 256.

43. *Daily Worker*, March 3, 1942, 1:1.

44. *Worker*, January 11, 1942, 4:1; Schatz, "The End of Corporate Liberalism," p. 195; James Matles, *Them and Us, Struggles of a Rank and File Union* (Englewood Cliffs, N.J.: Prentice-Hall, 1974), p. 183; Elizabeth Gurley Flynn, *Women in the War* (New

York: Workers Library 1942), pp. 6, 10; Elsa Jane Dixler, "The Woman Question: Women and the American Communist Party, 1929–1941," Ph.D diss., Yale University, 1974, pp. 168–169.

45. Browder Papers, III-357, Flynn to Browder, undated, MS.

46. *Daily Worker*, August 21, 1942, 7:6.

47. Interview with Peggy Dennis, September 11, 1978.

48. Howe and Coser, *The American Communist Party*, p. 416. For similar judgments, see Record, *Negro and the Communist Party*, p. 226, and Weinstein, *Ambiguous Legacy*, p. 94.

49. Sumner Rosen, "The CIO Era," in *The Negro and the American Labor Movement* (Garden City, N.Y.: Anchor, 1968), p. 197.

50. *Communist*, XXI (January 1942), p. 52.

51. *Worker*, January 4, 1942, 1:3.

52. Richard Boyer, *The Dark Ship* (Boston: Little, Brown, 1947), pp. 268–275; John Hope Franklin, *From Slavery to Freedom*, 3rd ed. (New York: Vintage, 1969), pp. 588–599; Philip S. Foner, *Organized Labor and the Black Worker*, 1619–1973 (New York: International Publishers, 1976), p. 260.

53. William S. Swift. "The Negro in the Offshore Maritime Industry," in Swift *et al.*, *Negro Employment in the Maritime Industries* (Philadelphia: University of Pennsylvania Press, 1974), pp. 80–82. Stan Weir, a former member of the Seafarers International Union and a sharp critic of the CP's wartime labor policies, contributed an article to *Radical America* in which he contrasted the SIU's militance with the NMU's all-out support for the war. "The presence of Afro-Americans in the Communist-led unions," he wrote, "was the Party's one cover for its ultra-conservatism." Weir, "American Labor on the Defensive: A 1940s Odyssey," *Radical America*, IX (July-August 1975), p. 175. Nowhere in the article does he mention the SIU's rigid Jim Crow policies. A black sailor looking for a job in 1942 might have had a different perspective on the relative militance and conservatism of the two unions.

54. Theodore V. Purcell and Daniel P. Mulvey, *The Negro in the Electrical Manufacturing Industry* (Philadelphia: University of Pennsylvania Press, 1971), pp. 34–35; Foner, *Black Worker*, p. 265. Also see Donald T. Critchlow, "Communist Unions and Racism: A Comparative Study of the Response of the United Electrical Workers and the National Maritime Union to the Black Question During World War Two," *Labor History*, XVII (1976), pp. 237–244.

55. See Geoffrey Perrett for a critical view of Roosevelt's wartime civil liberties record in *Days of Sadness, Years of Triumph* (New York: Coward, McCann and Geoghegan, 1973), pp. 357–367.

56. *Daily Worker*, January 8, 1942, 7:1.

57. *New Masses*, LII (August 8, 1944), p. 10; (August 22, 1944), p. 16.

58. *CIO News*, V (May 4, 1942), 2:3; Karl Yoneda, *A Brief History of U.S. Asian Labor* (New York: Political Affairs Reprint, 1976), pp. 11–15; Yoneda, "Japanese Labor History in the United States," mimeo, in Bancroft Library, University of California at Berkeley.

59. Yoneda served with Merrill's marauders in the fighting in Burma. He was the first Nisei veteran to become a member of the Veterans of Foreign Wars. He remained an active Communist, and was instrumental in getting the CP to adopt resolutions in 1959 and in 1972 repudiating its wartime line on the incarceration of Japanese-Americans. *CIO News*, VIII (May 21, 1945), 6:1; Yoneda, *A Brief History*, p. 15.

60. Browder, *Victory and After*, pp. 87–88.

61. *Ibid.*, p. 113.
62. Interview with Gil Green, December 31, 1977.
63. "National Committee Meeting Minutes," April 4, 1942, TS., p. 642.
64. Browder, *Victory and After*, p. 253.
65. *Ibid.*, p. 132.
66. In 1957 Adams told a Senate investigating committee that she had met with Roosevelt "approximately 38 or 40 times" during the war at the White House and Hyde Park. Senate Internal Security Subcommittee, "Scope of Soviet Activity in the U.S.," 85th Congress, 1st session, February 25 and 26, 1957, pp. 3590–3599. Joseph Lash described Adams as a "middle-aged lady in tennis shoes . . . with flashes of imaginative brilliance that sometimes shaded into hallucination." Lash, *Eleanor and Franklin*, p. 702. Also see Ann Rivington, "Josephine Truslow Adams Carries On the Torch," *Worker*, July 12, 1942, 6:3.
67. *Worker*, October 4, 1942, 1:2. Also see memo in Browder Papers, II-129, on his visit with Welles.
68. *Daily Worker*, October 16, 1942, 1:3.
69. For the Browder-Welles correspondence, see Browder Papers, I-81; *Communist*, XXII (March 1943), pp. 205–206.
70. *Communist*, XXI (September 1942), p. 694.
71. *Communist*, XXI (October 1942), pp. 832–833.
72. *Weekly Review*, VII (June 16, 1942), 2:1; interview with Steve Nelson, October 13, 1977. Nelson took over the leadership of the Oakland party organization after its previous chairman left for military service. On percentage of women in the CP and YCL in the 1930s, see Alperin, "Organization of the Communist Party," p. 65. For the war years, see *Communist*, XXII (April 1943), p. 331.
73. *Party Builder*, May 1942, p. 1. (This was an internal bulletin, issued by the New York state committee of the CP.) Also see Angela Calomiris, *Red Masquerade* (New York: J. B. Lippincott, 1950), *passim*, and David Caute, *The Great Fear, The Anti-Communist Purge Under Truman and Eisenhower* (New York: Simon and Schuster, 1978), pp. 111–138, 547–550.
74. *Communist*, XXI (May 1942), p. 324–325; *Daily Worker*, December 20, 1942, 5:1; "National Committee Meeting Minutes," April 4, 1942, TS., pp. 396, 513. Jaffe Collection.
75. *Daily Worker*, December 20, 1942, 5:1.
76. *Communist*, XXII (January 1943), p. 36.
77. *Worker*, December 6, 1942, magazine sec., p. 15; January 3, 1943, magazine sec., p. 3; January 17, 1943, magazine sec., p. 14.
78. In a wartime memorandum to Browder, Flynn commented: "We need . . . to review our language to be sure it is simple and intelligible to the average reader and listener, not marked by clichés or obscure uses of words. Why do we always 'raise a question,' instead of asking one or discussing one? Why refer to the organizational secretary as a mysterious 'Org-Sec'? . . . Does the average party member really know what 'politically developed' means? . . . Why can't we have committees instead of bureaus?" Browder Papers, III-357, "Impressions of Recruiting Drive."
79. For a discussion of the tension between the "centripetal pull" of Leninist organization and the "centrifugal looseness" encouraged by coalition politics, see Howe and Coser, *The American Communist Party*, pp. 420–422.
80. Browder, *Victory and After*, pp. 103–113, 132–133.
81. Charney, *A Long Journey*, pp. 129, 132.
82. Browder Papers, II-157, TS., undated.

83. Meyer gave an account of his CP career, and the circumstances behind his letter to Browder, in testimony to the Senate Internal Security Committee in 1957. See U.S. Senate, "Scope of Soviet Activity in the U.S.," pp. 3577–3587. Meyer left the CP shortly after the war and in subsequent years moved sharply to the right, joining the editorial staff of the *National Review*, writing *The Moulding of Communists*, and making frequent appearances before congressional committees to inform on his former comrades.
84. M. Ercoli, *The Spanish Revolution* (New York: Workers Library, 1936), *passim*.
85. Browder Papers, II-157, Meyer to Browder, November 29, 1943, TS.

Chapter 8: HOLD THE HOME FRONT

1. *Worker*, September 10, 1944, magazine sec., p. 2; *Communist*, XXIII (January 1944), p. 8.
2. *Communist*, XXII (July 1943), p. 580.
3. *New Republic*, CVII (February 15, 1943), p. 195; Werth, *Russia at War*, p. 484.
4. Paul Willen, "Who 'Collaborated' with Russia?" *Antioch Review*, XIV (September 1954), pp. 263–266.
5. *New Masses*, XLV (November 17, 1942), pp. 12–14; also see Congress of American-Soviet Friendship, *Salute to Our Russian Ally*, *passim*.
6. *The Living Record of Two Leaders of Labor* (New York: Erlich-Alter Memorial Conference, 1943), *passim*; Lucy Dawidowicz, "Two of Stalin's Victims," *Commentary*, CII (December 1951), pp. 614–616; Ulam, *Expansion and Co-existence*, pp. 321–322; Robert Conquest, *The Great Terror* (New York: Collier, 1973), pp. 644–645.
7. *New Republic*, CVIII (March 15, 1943), p. 336. Also see *PM*, March 18, 1943, and *Nation*, CLVI (March 13, 1943), p. 11.
8. Lichtenstein, "Industrial Unionism," pp. 537–540.
9. *Daily Worker*, March 22, 1943, 2:1. James Wechsler described his own and Starobin's doubts about the Moscow trials in 1936 in his memoir, *The Age of Suspicion* (New York: Random House, 1953), pp. 103–106.
10. *New Republic*, CVIII (April 12, 1943), p. 460.
11. *Monthly Labor Review*, LVI (May 1943), p. 959; LVIII (May 1944), pp. 927, 935.
12. Lichtenstein, "Defending the No-Strike Pledge," pp. 49–76, and Freeman, "Delivering the Goods," pp. 570–593, present well-reasoned and diametrically opposed positions on this question.
13. *Communist*, XXII (January 1943), pp. 19–23.
14. Earl Browder, *Wage Policy in War Production* (New York: Workers Library, 1943), p. 7. (Emphasis in original.)
15. Lichtenstein, "Industrial Unionism," pp. 394, 408; Browder, *ibid.*, p. 18.
16. Browder, *ibid.*, p. 8.
17. On American workers' long-standing opposition to incentive-pay schemes, see Montgomery, *Workers Control*, pp. 122–127.
18. Lichtenstein, "Industrial Unionism," p. 586; Browder, *Wage Policy*, pp. 22–23. Tappes's relationship to the CP is described in August Meier and Elliott Rudwick, *Black Detroit and the Rise of the UAW* (New York: Oxford University Press, 1979), p. 115 fn.
19. In the immediate aftermath of Reuther's 1947 victory, Stewart Alsop wrote prophetically: "It is difficult to overestimate the meaning of Walter Reuther's overwhelm-

ing victory at the United Automobile Workers' convention. . . . The Communists have lost their last chance to dominate or deeply influence an important segment of the American labor movement. . . . The whole internal balance of power in the CIO has been overturned and will be overturned still further." Quoted in Starobin, *American Communism in Crisis*, p. 291n.

20. Cochran, *Labor and Communism*, pp. 214–225; Clayton Fountain, *Union Guy* (New York: Viking Press, 1949), pp. 158–165.

21. Alinsky, *John L. Lewis*, p. 243; Lichtenstein, "Industrial Unionism," p. 437.

22. *Daily Worker*, April 28, 1943, 8:2.

23. *Daily Worker*, April 29, 1943, 1:1; *Communist*, XXII (June 1943), pp. 483–494, 530–536.

24. Theodore Draper, "Communists and Miners, 1928–1933," *Dissent*, XIX (Spring 1972), pp. 371–392; Glazer, *Social Basis of American Communism*, p. 115. Steve Nelson, a CP organizer in western Pennsylvania in the early 1930s and again after the war, recalled talking to Communists who had been in the coalfields in the 1943 strike: "These guys were the only ones who went back to work. It was the end of their career, it was a disaster for the Party." Interview with Steve Nelson, October 13, 1977.

25. *Communist*, XXII (June 1943), pp. 548–549.

26. *Communist*, XXII (June 1943), pp. 540–541.

27. On gains in the CP's black membership during the war, see *Communist*, XXII (October 1943), p. 923; *Daily Worker*, March 13, 1944, 3:2; April 25, 1944, 8:3; May 8, 1944, 4:1; Starobin, *American Communism in Crisis*, p. 228; Roy, *Communism and the Churches*, pp. 170–172. On the decline of the MOWM, see Garfinkel, *When Negroes March*, p. 143. On the Negro Labor Victory Committee, see *Daily Worker*, June 8, 1943, 1:2; June 27, 1944, 2:5.

28. *Daily Worker*, November 9, 1943, 1:3; November 10, 1943, 1:2; Benjamin Davis, *Communist Councilman from Harlem* (New York: International Publishers, 1969), pp. 103–114; Gerson, *Pete*, pp. 156–157.

29. Quoted in Edwin R. Lewinson, *Black Politics in New York City* (New York: Twayne Publishers, 1974), p. 78.

30. Quoted in Robert Shogan and Tom Craig, *The Detroit Race Riot, A Study in Violence* (New York: Chilton Books, 1964), p. 9. Also see Harvard Sitkoff, "Racial Militancy and Interracial Violence in the Second World War," *Journal of American History*, LVIII (December 1971), pp. 674–675.

31. *Daily Worker*, June 23, 1943, 1:1.

32. *Daily Worker*, July 8, 1943, 3:7.

33. *Daily Worker*, August 11, 1943, 3:1; Shogan and Craig, *Detroit Race Riot*, p. 92.

34. *Daily Worker*, August 3, 1943, 1:3. The 1943 Harlem riot provides an interesting example of how the Communist party itself, in its reluctance to say anything good about the period of Browder's leadership, has contributed to the myth that the CP abandoned the black struggle during the war. In *Organized Labor and the Black Worker* Philip Foner, an historian generally sympathetic to the Party, writes that it did not help "Communist prestige when [the *Daily Worker*] attacked the blacks involved in the Harlem riot of August 1943 as 'fifth columnists and pro-fascists' who were not representative of the 'good people' of Harlem. . . . Frustrated blacks often failed to see how the Communists' approach was preferable to that of traditionally anti-Negro white forces." Foner, p. 279. As reference for this passage Foner cites, not the *Daily Worker*, but an anti-Communist article by Harold Orlansky. The original editorial made clear that the legitimate social grievances of blacks had led to the

riot. The harshest term the editorial applied to the blacks in Harlem who actually took part in looting was "irresponsible elements." The reference to "pro-fascists and fifth columnists" was not made to blacks at all, but rather to those whites who might be tempted to use the riots as an excuse to attack blacks, as had been done in Detroit. White community leaders, the editorial concluded, had a special responsibility to "expose and balk any attempts by pro-fascist elements in their communities to organize attacks against Negro people or incite race hatred. They should make clear to their people the conditions that made the outbreak possible, and the necessity for eliminating these conditions." Even the most frustrated Harlemite in 1943 would have had no difficulty in distinguishing this viewpoint from that of "traditionally anti-Negro white forces."

35. *Daily Worker*, August 3, 1943, 1:3; August 7, 1943, 4:4.
36. Howe and Coser, for example, cite Wilkerson's comment as *prima facie* proof of the CP's "abandonment" of the struggle for black rights. Howe and Coser, *The American Communist Party*, p. 416.
37. *Daily Worker*, August 4, 1943, 2:1; September 10, 1943, 1:1; October 20, 1943, 1:6; December 6, 1943, 3:5; December 11, 1943, 2:3.
38. Louis Adamic *et al., Marshal Tito and His Gallant Bands* (New York: United Committee of South-Slavic Americans, 1944), *passim*.
39. Martin Esslin, *Brecht, A Choice of Evils* (London: Eyre and Spottiswoode, 1959), pp. 62–67.
40. Quoted in Goodman, *The Committee*, p. 193. Also see Budenz, *This Is My Story*, pp. 240–241.
41. Richmond, *A Long View from the Left*, pp. 260–261.
42. "Gerhardt Eisler," FBI document, NY 100-12376, dated June 14, 1951, pp. 6–17, 42. Released to Abraham Isserman under the Freedom of Information Act, October 1977.
43. "Gerhardt Eisler," p. 1.
44. Interview with Max Gordon, February 15, 1977.
45. Goodman, *The Committee*, pp. 193–195.
46. Browder Papers, II-3. "Report on National Groups." Mimeo. May 1938, p. 2.
47. Paolo Spriano, *Storia del Partito Communista Italiano*, Vol. III (Turin: Einaudi, 1970), p. 299.
48. *Ibid.*, p. 337; Vol. IV (1973), p. 119; Giorgio Bocca, *Palmiro Togliatti* (Rome: Editori Laterza, 1973), pp. 343–344.
49. Browder Papers, II-16, "Interview of Berti and Donini with Mr. Travers," TS., December 9, 1943.
50. Browder Papers, II-10, TS., undated. On Berti and Donini and other foreign Communists in the U.S. during the war, also see Starobin, *American Communism in Crisis*, pp. 260n, 270n.
51. *New York Times*, July 9, 1943, 5:1; *Daily Worker*, July 9, 1943, 1:5. Membership in the Jewish Anti-Fascist Committee proved a death warrant for its most prominent members, including Erlich, Alter, Mikhoels, and Feffer. See Yohoshua A. Gilboa, *The Black Years of Soviet Jewry, 1939–1953* (Boston: Little, Brown, 1971), pp. 81–84, 191.
52. *Daily Worker*, September 10, 1942, 2:2; October 27, 1942, 3:6; Alexander Bittelman, *Jewish Unity for Victory* (New York: Workers Library, 1943), *passim*.
53. *Daily Worker*, August 31, 1943, 3:2; *The American Jewish Conference Proceedings* (New York, 1944), pp. 264–267; *The American Jewish Conference, Proceedings of the Second Session* (New York, 1945), pp. 281–304.

54. *New York Times*, June 22, 1943, 1:2; *Daily Worker*, June 22, 1943, 1:1; *Digest of the Public Record of Communism in the United States* (New York: Fund for the Republic, 1955), pp. 171–173.

55. *New York Times*, April 26, 1943, 18:2. Also see George Counts and John L. Child, *America, Russia and the Communist Party in the Post-War World* (New York: John Day Co., 1943), pp. 63–64.

56. *Communist*, XXII (July, 1943), pp. 668–672. Also see Fernando Claudin, *The Communist Movement, From Comintern to Cominform*, Vol. I (New York: Monthly Review, 1975), pp. 15–45.

57. *New York Times*, May 23, 1943, 1:6; 30:1; IV, 3:7; May 24, 1943, 14:1.

58. *New York Times*, May 29, 1943, 12:2; 12:6.

59. *New York Times*, June 5, 1943, 14:3; 14:6; *Communist*, XXII (July 13, 1943), p. 593.

60. *New Masses*, XLVIII (July 13, 1943), pp. 3:11; LXIX (October 19, 1943), pp. 16–17.

61. *New Republic*, CVIII (May 10, 1943), p. 633.

62. *Communist*, XXII (July 1943), p. 631.

63. Interview with Gil Green, December 31, 1977.

64. *Communist*, XXII (July 1943), pp. 628–629; (October 1943), p. 929.

65. *Communist*, XXII (October 1943), p. 927. Also see Starobin, *American Communism in Crisis*, pp. 38–42; Glazer, *The Social Basis of American Communism*, pp. 124–126, 219n.

66. *Communist*, XXII (April 1943), p. 331.

67. *New York Times*, May 9, 1943, 1:2.

68. *New York Times*, October 16, 1943, 7:7; October 16, 1943, 52:1; October 18, 1943, 17:2; October 21, 1943 29:4.

69. *Daily Worker*, September 28, 1943; Gaddis, *The United States and the Origins of the Cold War*, pp. 66–72.

70. Browder Papers, Pollitt to Browder, undated MS., I-52.

71. *Communist*, XXII (July 1943), p. 632; Rosenstone, *Crusade on the Left*, p. 346; War Department Records, letter from J. H. Ulio, Adjutant General, to Commanding Generals, November 9, 1942. These records were released to the author under the Freedom of Information Act, October 1977.

72. Browder Papers, I-7, letter from Jerry Cook to Catherine Bruggeman, TS., February 14, 1943; Rosenstone, *ibid.*, p. 347; interview with George Watt, January 7, 1978. Ironically, many Communists—even as they were being kept under surveillance by military intelligence—were being assigned by their commanding officers to explain the meaning of the war to their fellow soldiers. John Gates, Joseph Clark, and other well-known Communists were appointed information and education cadre for their units. They were natural choices for the job since they were experienced public speakers and writers, and were more familiar than most soldiers with the war's background. Even restricting themselves to interpretations and information supplied by the Army's official publications, they found this a gratifying assignment. Interview with Joseph Clark, April 20, 1977; interview with John Gates, May 17, 1977.

73. *Daily Worker*, January 12, 1943, 1:1; Rosenstone, p. 349; interview with John Gates, May 17, 1977.

74. *New York Times*, February 20, 1945, 7:1; *Daily Worker*, February 22, 1945, 2:3.

75. Interview with George Watt, January 7, 1978; interview with John Gates, May 17, 1977; Rosenstone, *Crusade on the Left*, p. 350; *Worker*, December 10, 1944, magazine sec., p. 6; *Daily World*, November 3, 1979, p. 10.

76. Interview with Gil Green, December 31, 1977; interview with Peggy Dennis, September 11, 1978.

77. Interview with Carl Marzani, June 7, 1977.
78. Quoted in R. Harris Smith, *OSS* (New York: Delta, 1973), p. 11. According to Smith, "Donovan found that political leftists were often the most valiant field officers in his espionage and sabotage branches." See Smith, pp. 10–14. For FBI harassment of left-wing OSS recruits, see Browder Papers, II-139, TS., undated.
79. Interview with Vincent Lossowski, June 19, 1978; Rosenstone, *Crusade on the Left*, p. 350; Smith, *ibid.*, pp. 86, 99; *People's World*, November 16, 1945, 3:1; Stewart Alsop and Thomas Braden, *Sub Rosa, The OSS and American Espionage* (New York: Reynal and Hitchcock, 1948), pp. 25–26.
80. *New York Times*, March 14, 1945, 4:3.
81. *Communist*, XXIII (January 1944), pp. 3, 5–6, 92. For the Teheran Conference, see Gaddis, *The United States and the Origins of the Cold War*, pp. 66–72.
82. Simon, *As We Saw the Thirties*, p. 246.
83. *Worker*, October 24, 1943, 6:1.
84. *Communist*, XXIII (January 1944), pp. 3–8.

Chapter 9: REDESIGNING THE COMMUNIST MOVEMENT

1. *The Path to Peace, Progress and Prosperity, Proceedings at the Constitutional Convention of the Communist Political Association* (New York: Communist Political Association, 1944), p. 10.
2. Earl Browder, *Teheran and America, Perspectives and Tasks* (New York: Workers Library, 1944), p. 24. David Shannon noted one other, somewhat macabre problem with Browder's imagery: J. P. Morgan had been dead for nine months in December 1943. Shannon, *The Decline of American Communism*, p. 5.
3. Browder, *ibid.*, pp. 5–41, *passim*.
4. *Communist*, XXIII (February 1944), pp. 128, 134–135, 146, 148–152.
5. *Communist*, XXIII (February 1944), pp. 102–105.
6. *Daily Worker*, January 10, 1944, 1:1.
7. *Daily Worker*, January 11, 1944, 1:1; *New York Times*, January 11, 1944, 3:2.
8. *Daily Worker*, January 10, 1944, 2:2; interview with David Goldway, June 8, 1977.
9. "Plenum Meeting, National Committee, January 8, 1944," TS., p. 66. Jaffe Collection. In 1945 Foster told how he voted against Browder's proposal when it was first brought up before the political committee. *Political Affairs*, XXIV (July 1945), p. 640.
10. Interview with Sam Darcy, May 2, 1977. For Foster's letter, see *Political Affairs*, XXIV (July 1945), pp. 640–654.
11. Steve Nelson, a member of the CP's national committee in 1944, said that he and most other national committee members did not learn of Foster's letter until the publication of the Duclos article. Interview with Steve Nelson, October 13, 1977. Also see Budenz, *This Is My Story*, p. 288.
12. Darcy believes that Browder invited those trade unionists (Ben Gold, Lewis Merrill, Abram Flaxer, and Mike Quill) that he hoped would be most sympathetic to his case and who would thus offset the "working class credentials" that Foster and Darcy could present. Interview with Sam Darcy, May 2, 1977. For a list of those attending, see Jaffe, *The Rise and Fall of American Communism*, pp. 59–60.
13. However, in his 1963 interview with Browder for the Columbia Oral History program, Starobin asked Browder how his conception of Communist organization changed in 1944. "Question: 'Were you thinking of a party in the sense of a very tightly knit

organization with a semi-military character?' Browder: 'No, no, that whole concept was discarded with the change to association.'" Browder, "Reminscences," p. 416.

14. "National Board Minutes," February 8, 1944, TS., *passim*. Jaffe Collection.

15. New York *World-Telegram*, March 9, 1944, 1:1; *Daily Worker*, March 10, 1944, 1:5. For the FBI's bugging of CP headquarters, see *U.S. News and World Report*, April 16, 1954, pp. 112–116. For a confidential FBI report to Roosevelt on the split in the CP's leadership, see "General Intelligence Survey in the United States," August 1944, p. 73, OF: 10b, FDR Library.

16. Browder Papers, I-21, "Motions adopted by the Enlarged Buro meeting at Philadelphia," February 18, 1944, TS; interview with Sam Darcy, May 2, 1977.

17. *Daily Worker*, April 1, 1944, 3:4.

18. Foster, *History of the Communist Party of the United States*, pp. 428–434.

19. Jaffe, *The Rise and Fall of American Communism*, pp. 62–63.

20. Browder Papers, I-23, letter from Laurenz Harris to Foster, March 10, 1943, MS, and I-23, undated letter from "A soldier on furlough" to Foster, TS.

21. *Daily Worker*, January 14, 1944, 8:6. Gold's near-heresy did not go unnoticed. Robert Minor publicly slapped his wrist a month later in the *Daily Worker*, writing that Gold was "not the most objective among Marxists." *Daily Worker*, February 16, 1944, 8:3.

22. *Daily Worker*, May 4, 1944, 6:2.

23. Interview with Steve Nelson, October 13, 1977.

24. Interview with George Watt, January 7, 1978.

25. Browder Papers, I-27, Steve Nelson to Elizabeth Gurley Flynn, October 27, 1944, MS.

26. Browder Papers, I-46, Earl Browder to Raissa Browder, July 6, 1941, MS. In a 1954 interview Browder said he had been given responsibility at the 1935 Comintern Congress to supervise Latin-American CPs in or bordering on the Caribbean. See Robert Alexander, *The Communist Party of Venezuela* (Stanford: Hoover Institute Press, 1969), p. 207, and Draper, *Soviet Russia and American Communism*, pp. 170, 178.

27. Earl Browder, *Teheran, Our Path in War and Peace* (New York: International Publishers, 1944), pp. 56–63, *passim*.

28. Roca's letter was reprinted in *Political Affairs*, XXIV (March 1945), pp. 268–285. On the role of the Cuban CP in propagating "browderismo" in Latin America, see Salvador De La Plaza, *Antecedentes Del Revisionismo En Venezuela* (Caracas: Fondo Editorial Salvador de la Plaza, 1973), p. 30.

29. Buck, *Yours in the Struggle*, p. 344. On Browder's efforts to convert Tim Buck, see the letter from Josephine Truslow Adams to Eleanor Roosevelt, November 23, 1944, Series 100, Box 1741, FDR Library.

30. Sharkey's article can be found in the Browder Papers, II-75.

31. Adams to Eleanor Roosevelt, November 23, 1944, Series 100, Box 1741, FDR Library.

32. Interview with Al Richmond, September 8, 1978; Joseph North, *No Men Are Strangers* (New York: International Publishers, 1958), pp. 218–235.

33. *New York Times*, January 11, 1944, 18:2.

34. Max Lerner, *Public Journal, Marginal Notes on Wartime America* (New York: Viking Press, 1943), p. 360.

35. *New Republic*, CXI (July 17, 1944).

36. A copy of this interview can be found in the Browder Papers, III-153. Had Kihss been sufficiently prepared, he could have countered with a quotation from one of

Browder's own books: "The Communists . . . give these immediate struggles a higher goal than the mere winning of the demands of the moment. We fight to win these demands, but we fight even better and more uncompromisingly, because at the same time we show the workers how, by building ever stronger class organizations for this fight, we are preparing for bigger struggles that can end only by the final defeat of the capitalists and the establishing of the workers in full power in the state." Browder, *What Is Communism?* (New York: Vanguard Press, 1936), p. 212.

37. In an interview in the early 1960s, Browder displayed obvious pride in describing how he had designed the Garden meetings to achieve maximum emotional impact. Among other details, "Browder claimed that the Party was the first group to get mass audiences actually to sing the national anthem. This was achieved by placing left-wing choruses strategically throughout the Garden. Their singing swept the thousands into rousing mass singing." Robert Leroy Cleath, "Earl Russell Browder, American Spokesman for Communism, 1930–1945: An Analysis of Adaptation of Communist Ideas and Goals to a Capitalist Society," Ph.D diss., University of Washington, 1963, pp. 263–265.

38. The full list of vice-presidents included Foster, Morris Childs, Ben Davis, Eugene Dennis, Elizabeth Gurley Flynn, James Ford, Gil Green, Roy Hudson, Robert Minor, William Schneiderman, and Robert Thompson.

39. For the convention proceedings, see *Worker*, May 21, 1944, 1:1; *Daily Worker*, May 22, 1944, 2:1; May 23, 1944, 2:1; May 24, 1944, 2:4; *New York Times*, May 21, 1944, 1:2; May 22, 1944, 21:1; May 23, 1944, 38:2; May 24, 1944, 13:4. Also see *The Path to Peace, Progress and Prosperity, Proceedings of the Constitutional Convention of the Communist Political Association, passim.* Some of the reports and resolutions from the convention were reprinted in the June and July 1944 issues of *The Communist.*

40. *Worker*, July 16, 1944, 7:1.

41. Browder Papers, I-43, Donald M. Lester to Browder, April 20, 1944, TS.

42. Martin Glaberman, for example, suggested that the widespread violation of the no-strike pledge by industrial workers during the war showed that class "consciousness is as much activity as formal verbalized expression." The workers' ostensible support for the war did not mean very much, since "when patriotism and class interests conflict to a serious degree . . . the worker places his class interest above what he feels to be the needs of the nation." For Glaberman, workers' actions speak louder than their words, revealing a much more militant (potentially revolutionary) working class than the one that shows up in most accounts of labor during the war. Glaberman, "Epilogue," *Radical America*, IX (July-August 1975), pp. 106–107.

43. According to figures Williamson offered at the May convention, 58 percent of the new Communist recruits that spring were industrial workers, compared to 42 percent of CP membership in January 1944. *CPA Proceedings*, p. 52.

44. Lichtenstein, "Industrial Unionism," pp. 661–663; *Monthly Labor Review*, LX (May 1945), p. 961.

45. Browder Papers, II-155, undated, unsigned letter to Browder.

46. Lichtenstein, "Industrial Unionism," pp. 663–667, 670–672; Cochran, *Labor and Communism*, pp. 250–251; Adams to Eleanor Roosevelt, December 26, 1944, Series 100, Box 1753, FDR Library.

47. J. Edgar Hoover to Harry Hopkins, January 26, 1944, OF:10b-39, Roosevelt Papers, FDR Library.

48. Lichtenstein, "Industrial Unionism," pp. 597–598; Roland Young, *Congressional*

Politics in the Second World War (New York: Columbia University Press, 1956), pp. 76–82.

49. *Communist*, XXIII (March 1944), p. 199.
50. See Browder's highly favorable review of *One World* in the *Worker*, April 19, 1943, Magazine sec., p. 7.
51. *Communist*, XXIII (May 1944), pp. 502–503.
52. Sherwood, *Roosevelt and Hopkins*, p. 453. Also see James MacGregor Burns, *Roosevelt: The Soldier of Freedom* (New York: Harcourt Brace Jovanovich, 1970), p. 525.
53. Cochran, *Labor and Communism* pp. 231–233; Josephson, *Sidney Hillman*, pp. 593–600; Joseph Gaer, *The First Round, the Story of the CIO Political Action Committee* (New York: Duell, Sloan, and Pearce, 1944), p. 60.
54. Henry Wallace Papers, Vol. XVII, p. 3110, memo dated February 24, 1944, Columbia University collection.
55. Waltzer, "American Labor Party," pp. 297–298; *New York Times*, March 30, 1944, 1:2.
56. Goodman, *The Committee*, p. 167.
57. Gaddis, *The United States and the Origins of the Cold War*, pp. 58–59; Sherwood, *Roosevelt and Hopkins*, p. 459; Leon Friedman, "Election of 1944," in Arthur M. Schlesinger, Jr., ed., *History of American Presidential Elections*, Vol. IV (New York: McGraw-Hill, 1971), pp. 3030, 3085.
58. Dewey quoted in Friedman, "Election of 1944," p. 3033; Bricker quoted in Gaddis, *ibid.*, p. 59.
59. Josephson, *Sidney Hillman*, p. 611.
60. James Caldwell Foster, *The Union Politic, The CIO Political Action Committee* (Columbia: University of Missouri, 1975), p. 226; Friedman, "Election of 1944," p. 3034; Lichtenstein, "Industrial Unionism," p. 566; Josephson, *ibid.*, pp. 628–630.
61. Waltzer, "The American Labor Party," p. 304; Friedman, *ibid.*, p. 3034. Nearly half a million New York voters chose to vote for Roosevelt on the ALP line.
62. *Daily Worker*, November 9, 1944, 2:1.

Chapter 10: THE PARTY RESTORED

1. *Daily Worker*, May 24, 1945, 7:1; February 7, 1946, 2:4.
2. *CIO News*, VIII (April 2, 1945), 5:1.
3. Powell told the crowd that in the negotiations that brought the endorsement, "We told Tammany that if it wanted the Negro people, it would have to take Ben Davis with them." *Daily Worker*, May 7, 1945, 3:1.
4. Browder, *Teheran, Our Path in War and Peace*, p. 44. (Emphasis in original.)
5. *Worker*, January 7, 1945 (Overseas Supplement), 4:1. For Churchill's percentages deal with Stalin, see Ulam, *Expansion and Co-existence*, pp. 364–365; and Elisabeth Barber, "British Policy Towards Rumania, Bulgaria, and Hungary, 1944–1946," in Martin McCauley, ed., *Communist Power in Europe, 1944–1949* (New York: Harper and Row, 1977), pp. 201–217.
6. *Political Affairs*, XXIV (March 1945), p. 203.
7. *Political Affairs*, XXIV (June 1945), pp. 485–486. (Emphasis in original.)
8. Starobin, *American Communism in Crisis*, p. 269n.
9. Browder Papers, I-43, André Marty to Browder, April 2, 1944, TS.

10. Browder Papers, II-78, Browder to L. L. Sharkey, March 31, 1945, TS.

11. The Duclos article can be found in English translation in *Political Affairs*, XXIV (July 1945), pp. 656–672.

12. However, Philip Jaffe suggests that the article was written in Moscow by, or under the direction of, Andrei Zhdanov. Jaffe, *The Rise and Fall of American Communism*, p. 78. Since the article refers to the Yalta agreements, if Jaffe's hypothesis is correct, the article would have been brought to France from Moscow in late February or early March 1945.

13. Gaddis, *The United States and the Origin of the Cold War*, p. 297; Browder, "How Stalin Ruined the American Communist Party," *Harper's Magazine*, CCXX (March 1960), p. 45.

14. Edward Mortimer, "France," in McCauley, ed., *Communist Power in Europe, 1944–1947*, pp. 159–160.

15. Conventional diplomatic history has also taken the Duclos article as proof of the aggressive intentions of the Soviet Union in 1945. See Arthur Schlesinger, "Origins of the Cold War," *Foreign Affairs*, XLVI (October 1967), p. 43. For a very different interpretation, see Gabriel Kolko, *The Politics of War, The World and United States Foreign Policy, 1943–1945* (New York: Random House, 1978), p. 441.

16. Jaffe, *The Rise and Fall of American Communism*, p. 90; Starobin, *American Communism in Crisis*, pp. 271n, 287–288.

17. Browder, "Reminiscences," pp. 437–438, 443–444; Starobin, *ibid.*, pp. 269–270n., 271–272n. Flynn complained to the national committee meeting in mid-June that she and Roy Hudson had been left unaware of the looming crisis for some time after the arrival of the Duclos article. *Political Affairs*, XXXIV (July 1945), p. 614.

18. Starobin was mistaken when he wrote that the CPA national board first met on May 16 to discuss the Duclos article. The discussion he described in his account of this meeting actually took place on May 22. Starobin, *ibid.*, pp. 83–84; "Minutes of National Board Meeting, May 22–23, 1945," TS., *passim.* Jaffe Collection. The CPA leaders were tipped off that the *World-Telegram* intended to publish an article about Duclos's criticisms when a reporter called Darcy for a comment on the story. Darcy then called Foster to warn him. Interview with Sam Darcy, May 2, 1977; New York *World-Telegram*, May 22, 1945, 1:3.

19. A copy of Foster's proposed telegram can be found in the Browder Papers, I-20.

20. Charney offered this portrait of Thompson: "His military experience fitted in with his Bolshevik training. He was both commissar and general. . . . He was a man of indomitable courage and single-minded purpose. This was his strength, but it also proved his undoing, and ours. It was an inflexible Stalinist strength that could be ruthless, that relied on sheer power more than argument and persuasion." Charney, *A Long Journey*, pp. 136–137. Also see Shannon, *The Decline of American Communism*, p. 12.

21. "Minutes of the National Board Meeting, May 22–23, 1945," TS., *passim.* Jaffe Collection.

22. Starobin, *American Communism in Crisis*, p. 270n. A memo in Browder's papers, from an unidentified Communist involved in the CPA's Italian Commission, noted the sudden appearance of *Italy Today* at this critical juncture and commented, "The coincidence is striking, as striking as the fact that a few days before Berti—who for five months did not get in touch with the comrades of *L'Unita del Popolo* [the official CPA Italian-language publication]—gave them to understand that something of tremendous importance was in the wind." Browder Papers, undated MS. (May 1945), II-16.

23. *Daily Worker*, May 24, 1945, 7:1.
24. Browder Papers, I-1, William Auer to Browder, May 24, 1945, MS.; I-57, Anna Rochester to Browder, May 25, 1945, MS.
25. *New York Times*, May 26, 1945, 2:1.
26. For the initial version of the "Present Situation and the Next Tasks," see *Daily Worker*, June 4, 1945, 4:1. For the national board meeting, see Starobin, *American Communism in Crisis*, pp. 86–92; *New York Times*, June 5, 1945, 21:1; *Daily Worker*, June 4, 1945, 4:4; Browder Papers, II-89, "Soviet-American Relations—Is It War or Peace?" in *The Speeches and Writings of Earl Browder, May 24, 1945 to July 26, 1945*. Mimeo, pp. 3–15.
27. Interview with Steve Nelson, October 13, 1977.
28. *Political Affairs*, XXIV (July 1945), pp. 612–618.
29. Browder Papers, II-59, "Minutes of Meeting of the National Committee of the CPA, June 18-19-20, 1945," TS., pp. 1–19, *passim*; II-89, "Tasks of the American Working Class After V-E Day," in *The Speeches and Writings of Earl Browder*, pp. 16–56, *passim*. Also see *Daily Worker*, June 22, 1945, 2:1; *New York Times*, June 23, 1945, 28:2; Starobin, *American Communism in Crisis*, pp. 92–103. The revised draft of the "Present Situation and the Next Tasks" was printed in *Political Affairs*, XXIV (July 1945), pp. 579–590.
30. At the June 20 meeting Irving Potash and a few other national committee members expressed reservations about the exclusion of Browder from the new secretariat, arguing that the rank and file would "interpret this action to mean that everything is closed, that everything is already decided." Thompson made it clear that this was precisely the intention of the move. To include Browder in the secretariat, Thompson warned, might lead the rank and file to conclude that the "National Committee doesn't have the moral fortitude to draw the organizational conclusions as a result of the stand taken at the meeting here." Browder Papers, II-59, "Minutes of the Meeting of the National Committee," pp. 6, 13.
31. *Daily Worker*, June 16, 1945, 7:1.
32. *New Masses*, LVI (August 7, 1945), p. 22.
33. *Daily Worker*, June 30, 1945, 7:1.
34. *Daily Worker*, June 21, 1945, 7:2.
35. *Daily Worker*, June 14, 1945, 7:1.
36. *Daily Worker*, July 13, 1945, 4:4.
37. *Worker*, July 22, 1945, magazine sec., p. 11; *Daily Worker*, July 23, 1945, 7:1.
38. *Daily Worker*, July 27, 1945, 7:1; interview with Gil Green, December 31, 1977.
39. *Daily Worker*, June 19, 1945, 7:1.
40. For Browder's published writings that summer, see *Worker*, June 10, 1945, magazine sec., p. 7; *Daily Worker*, July 20, 1945. sec. 2, 1:1; July 24, 1945, sec. 2, 1:1.
41. *Daily Worker*, June 27, 1945, 7:5.
42. Browder, "Reminiscences," p. 450. For Browder's speech at the convention, see Browder Papers, II-89, "Speech of Earl Browder at the National Convention of the CPA, July 26, 1945," in *The Speeches and Writings of Earl Browder*, pp. 57–67, *passim*.
43. The final version of the resolution was printed in *Political Affairs*, XXV (September 1945), pp. 816–832.
44. *Daily Worker*, July 14, 1945, 7:1.
45. The complete national board was composed of Foster, Dennis, Williamson, Thompson, Davis, Flynn, Stachel, Weinstock, Potash, Lawrence, and Steve Nelson. Hud-

son remained a member of the national committee, and Ford was appointed to the new national review commission set up at the July convention and charged with overseeing the party's internal security. But Minor was stripped of all offices. He had served Browder too long and faithfully as an ideological hatchet man, and his abrupt repudiation of Browder reminded some of his similar performance in breaking with Lovestone in 1929. Minor became the scapegoat for the other Communist leaders' embarrassment about the change in line they were now making. After listening to Minor attack Browder at the June national committee meeting, Elizabeth Gurley Flynn recalled aloud how Minor had previously been "fastened to Comrade Browder's mental apron strings, even to the extent of making Browder uncomfortable at times." She did not now think, she commented sarcastically, that "Comrade Minor can convince me or anyone that he waged a continual struggle with Comrade Browder." *Political Affairs*, XXIV (July 1945), pp. 611–612. For accounts of the national CPA convention, see *New York Times*, July 26, 1945, 11:5; July 28, 1945, 1:2; July 30, 1945, 1:2; *Daily Worker*, July 25, 1945, 7:3; July 27, 1945, 3:1; July 28, 1945, 2:1; July 29, 1945, 2:1; July 30, 1945, 2:1; August 2, 1945, 7:1; *New Masses*, LVI (August 14, 1945), p. 3.

46. In December Williamson called on party members to carry out the "successful completion of the *Worker* campaign for 40,000 readers," which, he noted, "will merely return the *Worker* to its circulation of January 1945." He also expressed hope that the CP would be able to hold its loss to between 10 and 20 percent of the 63,000 members who had registered as members of the CPA the previous January. *Political Affairs*, XXIV (December 1945), pp. 1123, 1125. As it turned out, losses were on the high side, with only 50,000 Communists re-registering in January 1946.
47. *Political Affairs*, XXIV (September 1945), pp. 814–815.
48. *Political Affairs*, XXIV (December 1945), p. 1119.
49. *Political Affairs*, XXIV (December 1945), p. 1125. Williamson estimated that a total of 15,500 Communists and YCLers had gone into the armed forces during the war.
50. Interview with B.C., January 8, 1978.
51. Shannon, *Decline of American Communism*, pp. 106–110.
52. Charney, *A Long Journey*, p. 147.
53. *Worker*, August 5, 1945, 1:1.
54. "Pre-Plenum meeting of the Political Committee," March 23, 1939, TS., p. 25. Jaffe Collection.
55. Charney, *A Long Journey*, pp. 150–151; Waltzer, "American Labor Party," p. 317.
56. *Daily Worker*, August 8, 1945, 6:1.
57. *Daily Worker*, September 4, 1945, 4:1; November 10, 1945, 3:1; December 2, 1945, 1:1.
58. The Army had little patience with Red-baiting attacks on its promotion policies. When the *Chicago Tribune* printed a story questioning the loyalty of a number of American officers, including Lincoln Brigade veterans Irving Goff, Milton Wolff, and eight others, Major General Clayton Bissell, head of Army G-2, declared that "these officers have shown by their deeds that they are upholding the United States by force and violence." Nine of the ten named in the article had seen combat during the war, and three had been wounded. *Daily Worker*, March 14, 1945, 2:1. In the *Amerasia* case Philip Jaffe, the journal's editor, and five others were charged with conspiracy to violate the Espionage Act. Charges were later dropped for four of the defendants and reduced to unlawful possession of government documents for the other two. Latham, *Communist Controversy*, pp. 203–216; Caute, *The Great Fear*, pp. 55–56.

59. *New York Times*, April 4, 1946, 19:6; October 18, 1946, 1:6; November 23, 1946, 1:6.
60. *Political Affairs*, XXIV (December 1945), p. 1127.
61. Dodd, *School for Darkness*, pp. 191–220; Charney, *A Long Journey*, pp. 151–153; Starobin, *American Communism in Crisis*, p. 274n.
62. Shannon, *The Decline of American Communism*, pp. 20–23; interview with Sam Darcy, May 2, 1977.
63. For Browder's expulsion, see *Daily Worker*, February 7, 1946, 2:4; February 14, 1946, 2:1; 2:2; February 24, 1946, Sec. 3, 4:1. Also see Browder's correspondence with Williamson in Browder Papers, I-84, and "Appeal of Earl Browder to the Members of the CPUSA" (privately printed circular), in Browder Papers, II-14. William Browder's typewritten memorandum on the Westchester County and Yonkers club meetings debating Browder's expulsion can be found in the Browder Papers, II-38 and II-74.
64. Browder Papers, II-75, Browder to L. L. Sharkey, March 31, 1945.
65. Alexander Bittelman, *A Communist Views America's Future* (privately published, 1960), p. 180.

EPILOGUE: GENERATIONS IN CONFLICT

1. From "The Four Zoas," in Northrop Frye, ed., *Selected Poetry and Prose of William Blake* (New York: Modern Library, 1953), p. 201.
2. See Whittaker Chambers's celebration of the informer's role in the "war of faith" against communism. Chambers, *Witness* (New York: Random House, 1952), pp. 5–12. Also see Victor S. Navasky, *Naming Names* (New York: Viking Press, 1980), *passim*.
3. Among other useful accounts of the Cold War published in recent years, see Athan Theoharis, *Seeds of Repression, Harry S. Truman and the Origins of McCarthyism* (New York: Quadrangle Books, 1977); Mary McAuliffe, *Crisis on the Left* (Amherst: University of Massachusetts Press, 1978); and Caute, *The Great Fear, passim*.
4. The text of the McCarran Act and other anti-Communist legislation enacted in the United States up to 1955 can be found in the *Digest of the Public Record of Communism in the United States*. Steve Nelson, one of the Communist leaders whose name has appeared frequently in this book, received a twenty-year prison sentence for violation of Pennsylvania's state sedition law in addition to the five-year sentence he received for violation of the Smith Act. See Nelson, *The Thirteenth Juror* (New York: Masses and Mainstream, 1955), *passim*. For estimates of the number of political firings in this period, see Caute, *The Great Fear*, pp. 275, 345, 364.
5. Latham, *Communist Controversy*, p. 94; Interview with Carl Marzani, June 7, 1977.
6. For the fate of Thompson, Wellman, and other Communist military veterans, see Caute, *The Great Fear*, pp. 182–183.
7. In 1956 Foster admitted that the CP's leadership had made "serious 'Left' errors" in preceding years, with their "three worst mistakes" being the decision to launch the Progressive party campaign in 1948, their failure at the 1949 Smith Act trial to "put forward definitely the possibility for a parliamentary advance to Socialism in the United States," and "the approach taken to security measures." *Political Affairs*, XXXV (October 1956), pp. 15–45, *passim*.
8. Starobin, *American Communism in Crisis*, pp. 155–194, *passim*.
9. George Watt, who directed the CP's organizing efforts among longshoremen, railroad workers, and teamsters in New York after the war, recalled that "what Thompson

was doing, as Foster's front man in New York, was going after each union almost as if deliberately trying to isolate the Communists and force a confrontation." Interview with George Watt, January 7, 1978. Also see Charney, *A Long Journey*, pp. 170–171, and Starobin, *ibid.*, pp. 175–176.

10. The most dramatic and frequently cited example of these purges was the case of John Lautner, a leader for many years of the CP's Hungarian-American work, who served with the OSS during the war broadcasting anti-Axis propaganda to Hungary. During the frame-up trial of the former Hungarian Communist leader Laszlo Rajk in Budapest in late 1949, Lautner was "implicated" as an agent of Tito and American intelligence. Learning of the charges, American CP leaders had Lautner lured to an isolated location and subjected to a fruitless interrogation. Lautner was expelled as an "enemy of the working class." His wife, a loyal Communist, divorced him. After two decades of service to the Communist movement Lautner was understandably disenchanted by the experience. He put his anger at the service of government prosecutors in the Smith Act trials of the early 1950s. See Starobin, *American Communism in Crisis*, pp. 218–219; Shannon, *The Decline of American Communism*, pp. 235–239; Charney, *A Long Journey*, pp. 218–222.

11. Starobin, *ibid.*, pp. 206–207.

12. Shannon, *Decline of American Communism*, p. 229; Charney, *A Long Journey*, pp. 208–210; Starobin, *American Communism in Crisis*, pp. 220–221, 306n.

13. Dennis, *Autobiography*, p. 174. Browder cherished the illusion for several years after his expulsion that he could one day return to power in triumph. Traveling to Moscow in 1946 to plead his case, he was rewarded with a sinecure as American representative for Soviet science publishers. He met regularly with Soviet consular employees in New York to offer his opinion on American political developments. He also wrote and privately published a series of pamphlets critical of CP policies. In 1948 he reapplied for membership in the party, rather opportunistically citing the Tito-Stalin quarrel as evidence of the need to close ranks in the Communist movement. See Starobin, *ibid.*, pp. 278–279n; Jaffe, *The Rise and Fall of American Communism*, pp. 140–154. The campaign against "Browderism" in the CP found its most scurrilous expression in a 1951 pamphlet written by John Gates. Gates, who had been particularly supportive of Browder's position during the war, was now required to become the hardest fighter against it. In the pamphlet Gates declared: "In his recent writings, which pour out of Browder like pus from gangrene, Browder adds his voice to the lying testimony of the stool pigeon Budenz. . . . The only difference is that Browder has not yet reached the stage of doing his provocative work in the courtroom." Gates cited testimony at the Rajk purge trial alleging that the OSS had smuggled Browder's Teheran pamphlet into Hungary during the war to disorient Hungarian Communists. See Gates, *On Guard Against Browderism, Titoism, Trotskyism* (New York: New Century Publishers, 1951), pp. 10–11.

14. On differences in trial strategy between the Foley Square trial and subsequent trials in New York and California, see Charney, *A Long Journey*, pp. 215, 224–227, and Richmond, *A Long View from the Left*, pp. 312–314.

15. Richmond, *ibid.*, p. 367; "Draft State Report," mimeo, undated (1957), in Oleta O'Connor Yates Papers, Bancroft Library, University of California at Berkeley.

16. Starobin, *American Communism in Crisis*, p. 223; Charney, *A Long Journey*, p. 236.

17. Joseph Starobin, *Paris to Peking* (New York: Cameron Associates, Inc., 1955), pp. 18, 25, 267–277. Foster later accused Starobin and Clark of introducing "the first serious element of political confusion in the Party" and of resurrecting "some of Browder's revisionist conceptions." *Political Affairs* XXXV (October 1956), p. 16.

For Foster's attempt to expel Starobin and Clark, see Starobin, *American Communism in Crisis*, pp. 242n., 307n.; and Charney, *ibid.*, pp. 234–235.

18. Joseph Starobin, "1956, A Memoir," *Problems of Communism*, XV (November-December 1966), p. 65.

19. Shannon, *The Decline of American Communism*, p. 289.

20. Interview with Steve Nelson, October 13, 1977. Khrushchev's speech was reprinted in the Columbia University Russian Institute's collection *The Anti-Stalin Campaign and International Communism* (New York: Columbia University Press, 1956), pp. 1–88.

21. *Daily Worker*, June 6, 1951, 1:1.

22. Starobin, *American Communism in Crisis*, pp. 309–310n, 311n. Duclos's gesture showed a certain lack of tact. Even Dennis, wavering in his criticisms by that point, was moved to respond that the convention would base all its decisions on "our Marxist understanding of American reality." Quoted in Shannon, *The Decline of American Communism*, p. 325.

23. *Daily Worker*, June 6, 1956, 1:1; June 20, 1956, 5:2; June 25, 1956, 1:1.

24. See Togliatti, "9 Domandi sullo Stalinismo," and "Report to the Central Committee of the Italian Communist Party, June 24, 1956," in *The Anti-Stalin Campaign*, pp. 98–139, 193–267, *passim*.

25. These included a letter from Steve Nelson to John Gates congratulating him for a *Daily Worker* editorial on the Rajk case, and an editorial from the party publication *Jewish Life* denouncing the suppression of Yiddish culture in the Soviet Union. See John Saville, "The Twentieth Congress and the British Communist Party," in Ralph Milliband and John Saville, eds., *The Socialist Register, 1976* (London: Merlin Press, 1976), p. 6.

26. *Daily Worker*, June 6, 1956, 1:1.

27. *Political Affairs*, XXXV (November 1956), pp. 57–59.

28. *Political Affairs*, XXXV (November 1956), pp. 43–56, *passim*.

29. Interview with B.C., January 8, 1978.

30. For Foster's attack on the "new Browderism," see *Political Affairs*, XXXV (October 1956), p. 27.

31. *Political Affairs*, XXXV (November 1956), p. 35. Also see Shannon, *The Decline of American Communism*, pp. 291–292, and Starobin, *American Communism in Crisis*, p. 309n.

32. For the impact of the Hungarian events, see Shannon, *ibid.*, pp. 309–310. Also see Clancy Sigal's novel *Going Away* (Boston: Houghton Mifflin, 1961).

33. Shannon, *ibid.*, p. 360.

34. Interview with Steve Nelson, October 13, 1977.

35. Interview with Peggy Dennis, September 11, 1978.

36. Quoted in Studs Terkel, *Hard Times* (New York: Avon, 1972), p. 358. For the CP in the 1960s, see Jon Wiener's interview with Dorothy Healey in *Radical America*, XI (May-June 1977), pp. 25–45.

INDEX

About The Author

MAURICE ISSERMAN is a graduate of Reed College and the University of Rochester, where he received a PhD in American history in 1979. Since then he has published extensively in academic and political journals, and has taught labor history at Oberlin College and elsewhere. He lives in Boston, where he is employed as a word processor operator, and is a member of District 65, United Auto Workers.